Saint-Emilion

BERNARD GINESTET'S GUIDE
TO THE VINEYARDS OF FRANCE

SAINT-ESTEPHE

PAUILLAC

HAUT-MEDOC

SAINT-JULIEN

COTES DE BOURG

MOULIS
LISTRAC

POMERO

MARGAUX

HAUT-MEDOC

GRAVES

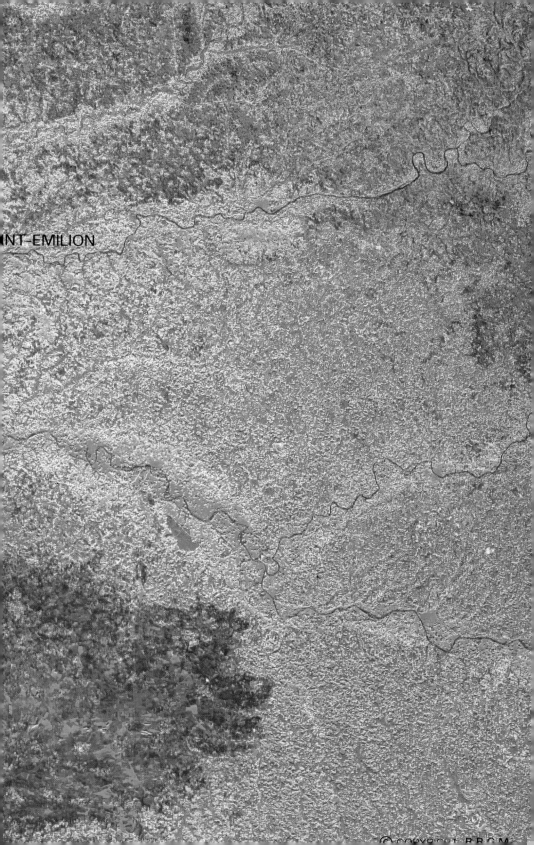

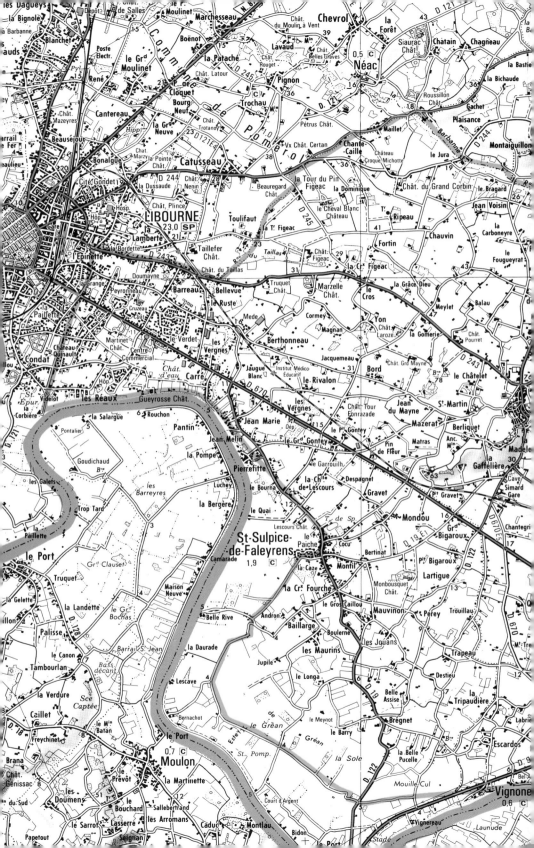

Saint-Emilion Appellation

Boundary of the Saint-Emilion AOC.
Within this area are districts not having the right to the appellation

Scale 1:50,000
Based on the IGN 1:50,000 map

© J. LEGRAND

Bernard Ginestet

Foreword by Nicholas Faith

Saint-Emilion

Translated by John Meredith

BERNARD GINESTET'S GUIDE
TO THE VINEYARDS OF FRANCE

Jacques Legrand

Originated and produced by:

Jacques Legrand SA

English version edited by:

Editor:	Nicholas Faith
Assistant editor:	Tamara Thorgevsky
Translator:	John L. Meredith
Proofreader:	Miles Smith-Morris
Editorial secretary:	Christine Fourton

Art director:	Henri Marganne
Layout:	Claire Forgeot

ISBN 0-582-07545-9 for Longman UK distribution
ISBN 2-905969-37-7 for the rest of the world

Printed in Belgium by Brepols, Turnhout

Foreword

Saint-Emilion is one of the more special of Bernard Ginestet's many old stamping-grounds in the Gironde. His grandfather owned Clos Fourtet for a time and, as a result, Bernard not only knows many of the characters involved in making wine in this, the largest and most complex of all the Gironde's many appellations, but their fathers and their grandfathers as well. (To take but one delightful example among many, look at the entry for Château La Clotte for his fond memories of the 20-stone Georges Chailleau.)

Some of the commune's inheritance – like the complete Roman palace found at La Gaffelière – are of more than local importance. And sometimes even the parochial stories are touching and hilarious – witness the long and painful path taken by the owner of La Gaffelière, Léo de Malet Roquefort, descendant of Erik the Viking, to reclaim his family's former fief, Château Tertre-Daugay.

But fondness does not imply infatuation. The cold eye and clear palate of Bernard the taster makes a clear distinction between the three, very separate, vine-growing areas which make up Saint-Emilion: the heartland, 2,000 hectares in and on the slopes immediately surrounding this delightful Italianate hill-town; the equally fine gravelly banks beneath Cheval Blanc and Figeac, banks which merge imperceptibly into the clay of their near neighbours in Pomerol; and the seemingly endless "suburban" vineyards on the flood-plain of the Dordogne, vineyards still entitled to the appellation – or to its ever-burgeoning 'satellite' subdivisions. As Bernard says, "Figeac alone could be its own appellation... it is impossible to ascribe any uniformity to the wines of Saint-Emilion... the whole of the Médoc is more uniform agrologically than the "hill of a thousand crus". Thankfully Bernard's eye for detail has not obscured his overall vision, unlike the late lamented Professor Henri Enjalbert, who "got lost in the geological maze" of Saint-Emilion.

Bernard also tackles head-on the controversy over the reclassification of Saint-Emilion's wines in 1984, which, most obviously, downgraded Beau-Séjour Bécot from its previous position as a premier cru. *After listening to well-placed locals who sincerely believe that M. Bécot has diluted the quality of his wine through extending his estate unwisely, I personally believe that the judgement, if harsh, was just.*

Bernard shows clearly that the form of the judgement was, if not illegal, at least highly irregular. But he has also dug out a far more clear-cut case, that of Jean Faure, whose cherished Château Gravet was also declassified, despite enormous efforts for more than a decade to restore the vineyard. Bernard believes he was punished for making a Médoc-style wine, astringent when young, rather than a more typical Saint-Emilion, and Bernard, as usual, is forthright in expressing his views based on that rare combination, passion and knowledge.

Nicolas Faith

I repeat that gently rising slopes, exposed to light breezes and good air temperature, which take the sun's rays at a slant and not straight down, produce a firm, rich and lasting wine, and that it will be preferable to all others.

Traité sur la nature et sur la culture de la vigne
M. Bidet (1759)

Contents

Ausonius, Emilion the Saint, John Lackland, Enjalbert and the others

For J.-P. M.,
with filial affection

In the beginning, Man loved God and the wine from the hillsides. And God created Saint-Emilion.

We do not exactly know when was the beginning. Local tradition attributes the first plantations of *vitis vinifera* to the legions of the Emperor Marcus Aurelius Probus. In France, as soon as any vineyard prides itself on its antiquity, Probus is called to the bar of history. The straight parallel furrows which were dug once upon a time in the chalky rock serve as preliminary evidence. In Saint-Emilion, just as in Vosne-Romanée or in Chablis, the vigneron suffers from chronic Gallo-Romania. This disease is benign. Fortunately, it does not prevent him from cultivating his vines according to modern methods. The perforation of the rock in order to establish plantations – technically called *"en pots de fleurs"* – proves the long-standing history of a vineyard without giving its date. It was still in practice during the eighteenth century.

But it should be recognized that certain traces of dwellings give rise to more than presumption. Indeed, there were vines in Saint-Emilion as early as the fourth century. And the likelihood that there was one of the "villas" of Ausonius becomes increasingly strong as the archeological dig at le Palat (from the Latin *palatium*: palace) progresses, at the side of Château La Gaffelière and below the present Château Ausone. Not only do the mosaics and the layout of the rooms exactly correspond to the time of the poet but the layout of this "palace" is also reminiscent of that of the houses of Trèves on the banks of the Moselle in the Palatinat, where Ausonius lived for several years before returning to the nest to enjoy a well-feathered retirement. The age was decadent and the poet minor. The require-

---

◄ *A view of part of the village of Saint-Emilion. Top-centre, the King's Tower.* 13

ment for good wine was all the more imperative. Julius Caesar and Napoléon had trenches dug for the needs of their wars, including the need to bury their dead soldiers, but not to plant vineyards. But the portly and debonair Ausonius could not imagine that a hole in the earth could have any purpose other than that of serving the glory of his table and the fame of his *cru*. The growers of Saint-Emilion claim this spiritual heritage. So be it.

In this connection, we should also speak of the saint known as Emilion. This person has usurped Ausonius in the sponsorship of local production to the extent of giving it his name. How did this come about? For today the wines of Saint-Emilion could as well be called Ausonius and Château Ausone could be called Cantenat, like its proprietor at the time of the Revolution. Did Emilion, the saint, exist? It seems to be an established fact that Saint Emilion lived in the eighth century. Legend has it that he came from Vannes in Brittany and arrived in the forest of Combes (see Saint-Laurent-des-Combes) a short time after Abd-al-Rahman and his plundering army of Saracens had passed by in 732 (the district of "Villemaurine" owes its name to them). At the turn of the last century, two local historians feverishly crossed pens. The storm broke with a thunderous memorandum published by Emilien Piganeau in the review of the Archeological Society of Bordeaux, wherein he relegated Saint-Emilion to popular fable. The *abbé* Hippolyte Caudéran came back as quick as lightning in the *Revue catholique de Bordeaux,* listing all the proofs of the saint's existence. I admit that the arguments put forward by the two protagonists appear to me to be equally admissible. But I restrain myself from drawing conclusions and limit myself to admitting that it was probable that there was a hermit called Emilian, also written as Milion or Melyon, in the well-known grotto towards the beginning of the eighth century; that is, just before the monolithic church was constructed.

However, Piganeau's researches include a hypothesis which is not without charm. He suggests that the name "Sentmelion", which is found written several times as "Semilione" in the twelfth and thirteenth centuries, might come from the Greek *Semelê ionê* which means "spring or fountain of Semelê". Semelê, the daughter of Cadmos and Harmonia, was loved by Zeus and gave birth to Dionysos, the equivalent of the Roman Bacchus. Our grape variety "Sémillon" (formerly *Semelion*) might reflect this etymology and Saint-Emilion could mean "Fountain in the middle of the vines". Piganeau also reminds us that an aunt of Ausonius was called Aemilia Aeonia.

Among the legends attached to Emilion the saint, the least credible but the most fantastic is that told by Léo Jaubert. The Breton monk Emilian, when on pilgrimage in the Holy Land, spent the night in a cowshed in Cana. In it he found an abandoned gourd and, after filling it with water, he slung it across his shoulder and continued his journey. He then was surprised to find that the water had changed into wine of the very best quality. He came back to France, dispensing the divine brew along his way to the sick and indigenous, who were cured or restored by it. He stopped one evening in a grotto near the river Dordogne on a high site where there was a spring of pure water and decided to settle there, rather than return to his na-

▲ *A superb example of the mosaics uncovered by the archeological excavations at "le Palat" near Château La Gaffelière. Here we see a libation bowl decorated with stylized vine-branches, and we can imagine Ausonius walking barefoot...*

◄ *The furrows dug out in the rock are called "Gallo-Roman" by the growers. In point of fact, this viticultural technique was in use here right up to the eighteenth century.* 15

tive Brittany. The news of the miraculous gourd spread around the countryside and many were those blessed by the hermit. After his death, a certain man stole the gourd and drank from it to such an extent that he began to reel and stagger. The precious receptacle fell and broke. From its scattered pieces there flowed a torrent of wine, which spread further, and further, and further... flooding the countryside as far as Saint-Christophe, the hillsides of Saint-Georges and even the plain of Pomerol. And afterwards, all the bushes turned into vines. This was the last miracle of Saint Emilion and his gourd. But the supernatural virtues of the hermit still exist today (see Château Laniote in the catalogue).

As from the ninth century, religious life at Saint-Emilion took shape and developed on the foundations established by the Bene-

▲ *Saint-Emilion's church tower dominates all the surrounding vineyards.*

dictine monks at the beginning of the seventh century. The famous and imposing monolithic church, doubtless the largest of its type, was hollowed out over some two hundred years. At the same time, a fortified village was constructed. From that moment, spiritual and temporal powers had to live together. The first written trace of these statutory dispositions goes back to 1199, when John Lackland, the fifth son of Henry II and Eleanor of Aquitaine, and recently proclaimed King of England, created a charter in which he specified: "We have granted and hereby confirm to our dear and trusty subjects of Saint-Emilion the right to have a commune with all privileges and liberal customs which attach to the commune." This document constitutes the birth certificate of the Jurade of Saint Emilion, whose jurisdiction extended over nine parishes. A king commonly known as John Lackland could not be called upon to be a geologist! The current boundaries of the land having the Saint-Emilion appellation spring, however, directly from the goodwill of the sovereign of England, the Duke of Aquitaine. I shall have occasion to come back to this subject a little further on. It should, however, be mentioned that at the beginning of the thirteenth century, when viticulture in the Médoc was reduced to a few sparse acres of straggly vines, the hillsides of Saint-Emilion were covered with healthy plants, whose wine was already well-known across the Channel, and the plains and plateaux were producing cereals for bread. For at least two centuries, the Bordeaux countryside attained a splendid economic zenith, and the wines held pride of place. Those of Libourne were particularly outstanding, Saint-Emilion being then the king of wines.

After John Lackland, his son Henry III was obliged to look to the protection of cargoes destined for London, deploring the attempts of the people living downstream to stop the boats getting through, as attested by an act dating from the year 1230.

We also find in 1289 the prior of the preaching Friars of Saint-Emilion, Pierre-Raymond Bernard, as the executor of the will of Pierre de Narbonne and being reprimanded by Eléonore de Castille and Edward I of England. Four years later, Guillelmus de Sancto Emiliano, the first magistrate of the town, swore fidelity to Philippe le Bel. This was for political reasons, business remaining firmly on the side of the English. The English have always shown themselves ambidextrous, their right hand not knowing what their left is doing. In 1302, Edward I drew up an agreement with the exporters of the wine of Aquitaine. This merchants' charter was doubtless the first commercial treaty in the history of the wines of Bordeaux. It concerned about 100,000 tonneaux of wine coming from this province. Libourne, that is essentially Saint-Emilion and Fronsac, represented more than ten per cent of this figure: a considerable production at that time from a limited area. One last glance at this prosperous period. In 1312, Edward II of England conferred on the jurats and the hundred leading citizens of the town of Saint-Emilion the right to elect their own mayor. He knew what he was doing, for his personal consumption was thus assured to the end of his days. The people of Saint-Emilion knew how to thank their sovereign, and in order that it should not go unnoticed, they even vaunted it: "Let all who read these present letters patent know that we, the jurats and hundred leading citizens and all the people of the town of Saint-Emilion acknowledge our gratitude and declare that, for certain legitimate reasons, we owe to his Highness and our Lord and King Edward, by the grace of God, King of England and Sovereign of Ireland and most illustrious Duke of Aquitaine, fifty tonneaux of clear, pure wine,

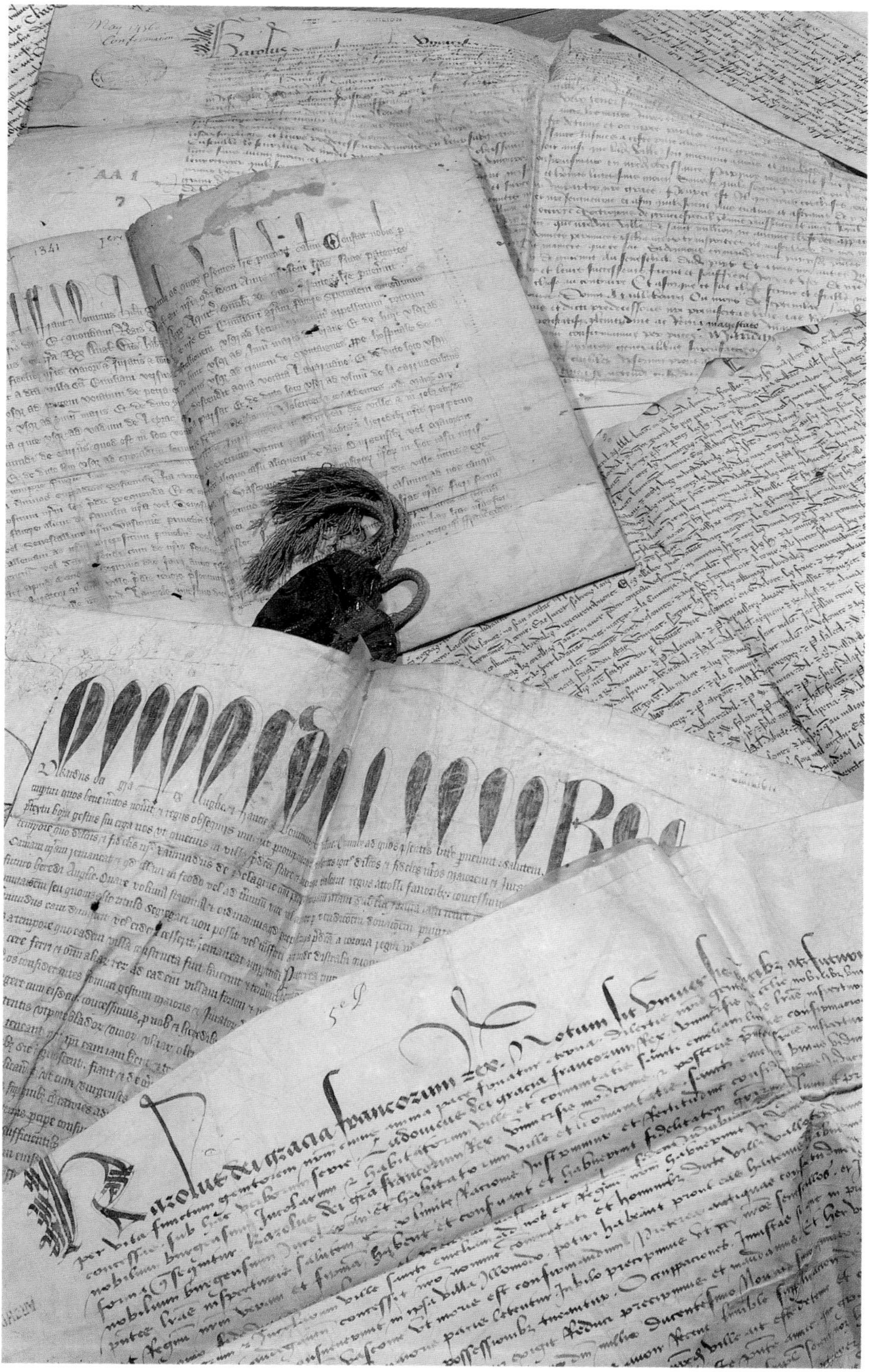

legally filled, transported and taken at our proper cost to England to
the port of the City of London, before the next Easter holiday. For
the fifty tonneaux in question (...) we, the people of the town of Saint-
Emilion, pledge our person, and our goods and chattels. In witness
whereof, we request that the Great Seal of the Town be appended
hereto. Dated at Saint Emilion this 24th day of the month of October in the year of Our Lord 1312." When it came to greasing the
palm, the town officials of Saint-Emilion did not ration the butter!

At that period, the wines of Saint-Emilion were both red and white. There was even perhaps more white produced than red. And there was also a certain mixing of colours, for a proportion of white grapes in a vat of red helps give a good start to the fermentation process. I share the opinion of those who suppose that the term "vin clairet", corresponding to *claret* in English, had no other origin than this different combination of different grapes. In any event, as from the beginning of the thirteenth century, the wines of "Saint-Milion" or "Saint-Mélion" were named among the most famous of France. They are to be found in the repertory of the troubadour Henri d'Andeli when, at the request of Philippe Auguste, he composed the *Bataille des Vins* (Battle of the Wines) in which we find an English monk comparing the best *crus*. Already the Anglo-Saxons were defending the reputation of their taste-buds, just as Michael Broadbent, Nicholas Faith, Hugh Johnson, Edmund Penning-Rowsell, Cyril Ray and others have done today. And this is without taking into account those from the other side of the Atlantic – all prelates *manqués* but evangelists of good taste whose contemporary archetype was the late High Pontiff of Wine, Alexis Lichine.

From the Middle Ages, the vineyards of Saint-Emilion were split up among the bourgeois and the clergy. From the ninth century, religious communities were numerous. We know that they were large consumers of wine and that they drew a considerable part of their revenue from the sale of their "surplus" production. The hill of Saint-Emilion, with its steep slopes, offered sites propitious both for monasteries and for viticulture. Libation and meditation together made for mystic contemplation. Of this pious past, there remains a great number of monuments, scarred to a greater or lesser extent by the ravages of time, of which the majority have been reclothed in bacchic dignity. Over several generations, cloisters or crypts, chapels or collegiate churches have undergone a praiseworthy and rewarding conversion. Antique and second-hand dealers have provided the "original furniture" so that none should doubt the testimony of history. But of course, all the growers of Saint-Emilion cannot claim to be housed under the roof of the former Father Prior of the Jacobins or the one-time porter of the Oratory. To make up for the lack of holy places, which are none the less numerous and yet insufficient to meet the new demand, it is through the label that the vine-growing disciples of Saint-Emilion declare their faith. The col-

---

◄ *The chapel of the cloisters of the Cordeliers.*

Formerly a fortified town, Saint-Emilion preserves traces of its ramparts.   ►

lector of these labels would be able to slip a pious picture in his grandmother's prayer book between each page of the rites of holy communion. Apart from the direct patronage of a considerable delegation of the saints of paradise (including paradise itself) we find a surprising anthology of more or less catholic terms. I cite from memory: L'Angélus, La Grâce-Dieu and its associated derivations, Magdelaine and its declensions such as La Chapelle-Madelaine or Curé-Bon-La-Madelaine, Le Prieuré, La Croix, Les Couvents and Palais Cardinal, etc.

The attractive region of Saint-Emilion has been baptized "the hill of a thousand *crus*". This poetic vision is a mental image deriving more from the mirage than the miracle. For in fact, the 5,200 hectares of the appellation are not all perched on the summit of the slopes nor on that of the quality of wine. The AOC area of Saint-Emilion breaks down into three principal sectors. The most classical, the one that can be called the real Saint-Emilion, covers about 2,000 hectares. It consists of the chalky plateau, rising to some three hundred feet at its highest point, and its falling slopes with their varying exposures. It is principally the land belonging to the parish, the "finage" as it is called in Chablis. Between the town of Saint-Emilion and the Pomerol appellation is a plateau of sandy gravel on a subsoil of clay. The technical boundary of this terrain is uncertain (it contains some 1,000 hectares). The boundary between Pomerol and Saint-Emilion was created more on an administrative than a geological basis. The best land for growing vines is that which is made up of deep gravel (about 20 feet in thickness) out of which the two châteaux Figeac and Cheval Blanc take the lion's share. All the *crus classés* which are not on the high chalky plateau and the slopes are to be found in this neighbourhood. The remaining 2,000 hectares are spread out over the plain of the Dordogne. The AOC stretches right down as far as Libourne now that the "Sables Saint-Emilion" has surprisingly and unjustifiably been included in the Saint-Emilion appellation. Towards the east, the low vineyards join up with the limits of the commune of Castille-la-Bataille, whose wines from the hillsides are thought very highly of and are even sometimes superior to the wines from the lower areas of Saint-Emilion. It is impossible to ascribe any uniformity to the wines of Saint-Emilion. The one thing which binds the appellation together is completely artificial and links together terrains which have nothing in common other than the different varieties of grapes which grow there. That is why any allusion to the "borough of Saint-Emilion" as a reference for a viticultural boundary is erroneous. In other words, of all the Bordeaux appellations whose names restrict them to a single commune, Saint-Emilion is undeniably the most heterogeneous. The whole of the Médoc, in the geographical sense, and all the lands of the communes in it (Margaux, Saint-Julien, Pauillac, Saint-Estèphe, Moulis, Listrac) are much more uniform agrologically than the so-called "hill of a thousand *crus*".

Professor Henri Enjalbert, who a short time before his death published a monumental treatise on the wines of the Libourne region, himself got lost in the geological maze of the Saint-Emilion wine region. The lack of an objective overview is regrettable. At my request, Pierre Laville, a geologist with the BRGM (Bureau de Recherches Géologiques et Minières) came to survey the terrain. He agreed to collect together the studies previously carried out and to guarantee a scientific presentation of the appellation. While acknowledging the impressive work of Enjalbert, I am happy that this book can ensure a deeper knowledge of the geological conditions underlying vine-growing in the area, in particular with the original publication of the first geological map of Saint-Emilion along with the relevant comments of Pierre Laville.

A Simplified Description of the Terrain of Saint-Emilion

The Saint-Emilion vineyards are an extension in a south-easterly direction of those of Pomerol. Distributed over a ridge of sub-horizontally bedded Tertiary sediments, the area is dissected by three rivers, the Isle, the Dordogne and the Barbanne. In addition to recent valley deposits, river alluvium covers the lower western and southern slopes of the promontory. Towards the east, the latter is truncated by the erosion of the limestone plateau, level with the road from Saint-Genès-de-Castillon to Sainte-Colombe.

The Saint-Emilion plateau is covered by a bed of limestone and is aligned from north-north-west to south-south-east ending at the three-hundred foot contour on the butte of Mondot. At the base of the limestone towards the west and the south, faintly marked by the level of the alluvial terraces, a regular gentle glacis is followed by a steeper slope. Towards the north and the east, the plateau falls steeply to the valley bottom. Along the river Dordogne, the glacis fingers into a broad alluvial plain.

Such a geomorphological arrangement favours a variety of exposures which is one of the characteristics of the terrain. Another factor leading to diversity is the lithology of the sediments and the superficial deposits which partly cover them. These different terrains must be reviewed in detail to understand the variety of combinations of terrain and exposure embraced by one homogeneous and typical microclimate. Among the sedimentary formations from the glacis of Saint-Sulpice-de-Faleyrens to the top of the butte of Mon-

dot, four different elements can be identified. They include several aspects which change laterally.

1.   The oldest and lowest element in the landscape is a bed of chalky molasse which causes a slight rise in the glacis near Belle Assise above the Palus de la Sole. Lower Oligocene, this bed consists partly of an

▲ *The different soils of the Saint-Emilion appellation are extremely varied. Here we see the gravelly slopes of Figeac, which strongly resemble the ridges of the Médoc.*

assemblage of marine and continental deposits. Going from north to south, these deposits become increasingly marine and, attaining a depth of some 120 feet, also contain coarse detrital material (sand, pebbles) more prevalent in the north. On the other hand, towards the south, clayey deposits predominate and give, with the carbonates, a whole succession of clayey limestone, marl or nodular clay. Towards the top, the amount of carbonates increases constituting the base of the slopes between the 75 and 150 foot contours. In the Quaternary period, these alternating degrees of resistance determined in part the levels of erosion and the formation of the alluvial deposits of the rivers Isle and Dordogne.

2.   The subjacent element is made up of thick limestones laid down in massive beds. These are marine asteroidian limestones forming the slopes and the plateau of Saint-Emilion. At their base, on the 150 foot contour, a bed of clay rich in oysters marks the limit with the detrital formation. This level is also a spring line, giving rise to small springs. Mid-Oligocene, this limestone is made up of two parts separated by a bed of clay to the east of the stream of Fontgaband. Ninety to one hundred and twenty feet thick, this limestone plateau, porous and extensively fractured, is the main feature of the Saint-Emilion area. Extremely broken up by erosion and karstified, its irregular surface presents varied exposures even for neighbouring plots of land, and there are small isolated outcrops of superficial deposits. The upper sedimentary units are confined to the buttes of Mondot, Grand Jacques and Destieu.

3.   The lower detrital element is a similar facies to that of the Castillon formation. Not very thick, it appears only as a product of weathering around the buttes. Related to the Upper Oligocene, it constitutes a formation relatively common to the east of the plateau.

4.   The upper element which ends the marine deposits corresponds to the Aquitanian limestone decalcified at the end of the Tertiary. Very shallow (about 15 feet), these silicified relics bear witness to the scale of the Quaternary erosion along the Dordogne valley. The main superficial formations masking the tract of Tertiary sediments are Quaternary deposits. Keeping to the subdivisions observed in the Graves and Médoc regions, four terraces can be made out along the rivers Isle and Dordogne. As with the sedimentary terrains, these alluvial deposits are presented from the oldest to the most recent.

The oldest known terrace on the territory of the appellation of Saint-Emilion forms a discrete butte on which flourish the vines of Cheval Blanc and Figeac. It is an extension in a southerly direction of the vineyards of Pomerol and corresponds stratigraphically to the middle terrace of the Graves, where most of the *grands crus* are to be found. Consisting essentially of gravels in a sandy matrix, deficient

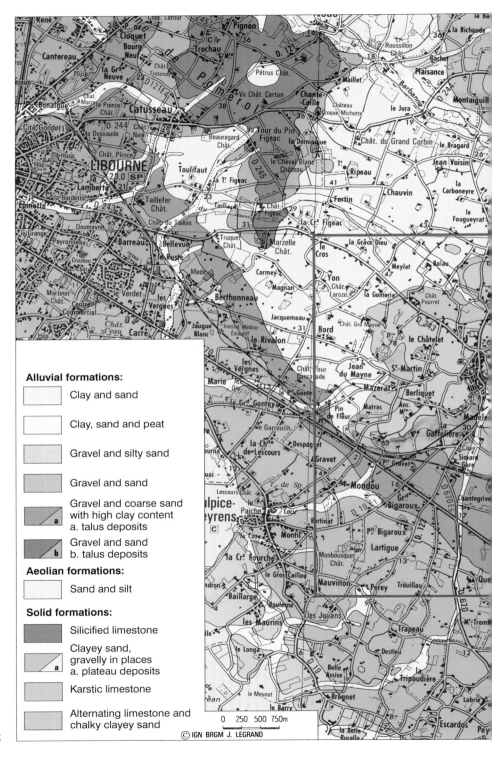

Alluvial formations:

Clay and sand

Clay, sand and peat

Gravel and silty sand

Gravel and sand

Gravel and coarse sand
with high clay content
a. talus deposits

Gravel and sand
b. talus deposits

Aeolian formations:

Sand and silt

Solid formations:

Silicified limestone

Clayey sand,
gravelly in places
a. plateau deposits

Karstic limestone

Alternating limestone and
chalky clayey sand

0 250 500 750m

© IGN BRGM J. LEGRAND

28

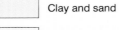

NORTH

4km

2km

Alluvial formations:

Clay and sand

Clay, sand and peat

Sand and gravel

Gravel and coarse sand
with high clay content

© IGN BRGM J. LEGRAND

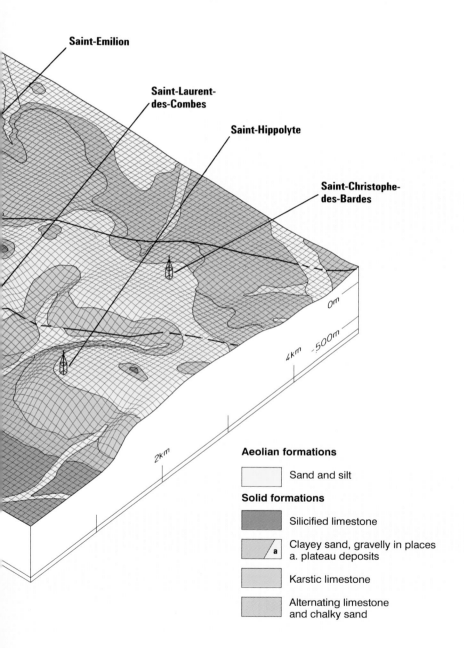

Saint-Emilion

Saint-Laurent-
des-Combes

Saint-Hippolyte

Saint-Christophe-
des-Bardes

0m

4km -500m

2km

Aeolian formations

Sand and silt

Solid formations

Silicified limestone

Clayey sand, gravelly in places
a. plateau deposits

Karstic limestone

Alternating limestone
and chalky sand

in clay and well-drained, these alluvial deposits favour deep rooting. The next terrace is clearly marked in the area of the Saint-Emilion appellation, where it covers the upper part of the glacis to the south of Saint-Emilion as well as the western slope of the butte of Figeac. Made up of sand and coarse gravel, these alluvial deposits differ from those previously mentioned because of their abundant clay and constant, though moderate, moisture content. They make up a lower terrace between the 45 and 60 foot contours.

The most common alluvial deposits correspond to the lowest terrace which, above the sands and molasse of Castillon, form the lower glacis in the south of the area covered by the appellation between the 15 and 45 foot contours. Very gravelly, these deposits have a sandy matrix, deficient in clay. They form an aquifer which restricts the penetration of the vine roots to the level of the sub-soil. The lowest and most recent alluvial gravels are overlain by sandy, clayey, even peaty, modern alluvial deposits which cover the present-day Dordogne valley and all the other valley bottoms. However, below the 15 foot level from Andron to Mouille-Cul, a succession of sandy silts barely emerges like little islands above the plain.

These different terraces are arranged in tiers and linked one to another by talus slopes of reworked material. Particularly difficult to distinguish from their parent alluvium, these formations subdue the slopes of the terraces and the substrata. Talus deposits can be most clearly identified around the butte of Figeac.

The slope formations which emerge from the hillside are difficult to distinguish from the rocks beneath them. However, there is no doubt that they occlude contact between the lower terrace and its underlying bedrock on the more elevated slopes.

To the west of the Saint-Emilion plateau, aeolian sandy formations form a continuous veil over the low terrace or its underlying deposits. The results of a dry period between the Mindel (lower terrace) and the Riss (lowest terrace) periods, they are exclusively confined to the oldest lower and middle terraces.

The soils which subsequently develop in the superficial formations and in the alluvial rocks, whether sedimentary or aeolian, will therefore be extremely varied and apart from the alluvial plains and the bottoms of the clayey valleys, few are unsuitable for the vine. Nevertheless, a hierarchy can be established as far as the quality of the wines is concerned and it is disconcerting to note that the wines from the middle terrace, from the high glacis and especially from the slopes and the plateau, that is to say from the areas where the water is kept in balance or controlled by the mineralogy of the subsoil, are of a definite type and of a quality superior to those from the vines grown on the low glacis where there is an excess of available water.

So it is the relief of the landscape and the circulation of water determined by lithology which seem to a large extent to govern how the viticultural potential of the Saint-Emilion appellation is distributed. The quality of the soil and the climatic variations which also stem from the lithology and the relief seem to be secondary considerations. To deny this influential rôle of the terrain would amount to denying the character of the wines of Saint-Emilion and to asserting that the different wines of the Bordeaux region are to be distinguished only by differing agronomic and oenological techniques, so sweeping aside all reference to their different places of origin. In 1934, in their study of the area in which the wines of Saint-Emilion are produced, this pre-eminent rôle of the soil did not escape Robert and André Villepigue who, after reviewing the different varieties and methods of vinification, declared: "It seems, therefore, that to determine the area of production of the wines of Saint-Emilion, the expert agronomist must confine himself only to orographical and geological considerations about the soil and subsoil." And they added: "Geological documents of the Saint-Emilion area are not exactly numerous, at least those of any technical value."

This observation still holds good for there is still a lack of reliable, detailed geological maps available to the public. The set of Henri Enjalbert's maps brought together by the BRGM and presented here is a first step to remedying this deficiency, but detailed cartography of the Libourne area should be undertaken rapidly to help the growers to get the best out of their land... *(and the experts to reach the best conclusions! Editor's note)*

Wherein Saint-Emilion strives to establish its identity

Pierre Laville was devilishly right to refer to Robert Villepigue. More than half a century ago, this man had perceived with astonishing scientific clarity the possible solutions to a reasoned classification of the different terrains of Saint-Emilion. His work remains valid today. The soils have not changed. It is only techniques which have developed. When Henri Enjalbert undertook his wide survey, his idea was to write a geographical and historical thesis on the vineyards of the area of Libourne. Perhaps out of modesty or diffidence, or perhaps because it was not directly his problem, he refrained from passing decisive judgement on the *crus*. And yet his work was a direct continuation of Villepigue's thesis. Despite the admiration and respect which I owe to the lamented professor, I will say in crystal clear terms that if Villepigue graded the pebbles of Saint-Emilion, Enjalbert broke them down into little pieces. That is why I think it is useful to publish a sizeable part of Robert Villepigue's conclusions (see page 36).

Once these have been put together, it is quite easy and at the same time very interesting to rediscover each of his groups in the area.

To have done so is to have effected the classification of the *crus* of Saint-Emilion.

Class One. The groups 1, 2, 3 will give the finest *crus*; they will include the hillside of la Madeleine, le Tertre-Daugay, the slopes of Pourret, of la Carte, Mazerat, Pavie, and of Villemaurine and le Cadet. Along with others we shall pick out from further groups, these first three groups will make up the body of class one of Saint-Emilion.

Class Two. Class two begins with groups 4, 5, 6, 7, 8, 9. Group 4 includes the pocket deposits of sand whose land is rather more fertile than the first three and which are formed from the sub-soil of the first three groups. It is the long sandy pocket in line with the road from Les Grandes Murailles to Libourne. It peters out into the Tertiary sands. It contains the pocket of Mazerat, the pocket of

the former gardens of Saint-Emilion, that of the hill which leads
down from Saint-Emilion towards the station. In short, groups 5, 6,
7, 8, 9 include all the limestone slopes in the communes of Saint-
Christophe-des-Bardes, Saint-Etienne-de-Lisse, Saint-Hippolyte, and
Saint-Laurent-des-Combes, and we note once more that the sands
of red clay do not begin just at the boundary of Saint-Emilion, any
more than does the Castillon limestone (Sannoisian).

▲ *A travel poster dating from the turn of the century praising the picturesque view and
the wines of Saint-Emilion.*

A. Fine or good-quality subsoil	I. Limestone with fossils or oysters on a bed of Sannoisian clay	Clayey and chalky	1
		Siliceous and chalky	2
		Clayey silex	3
		Combes silex	4
	II. Limestone with fossils on a bed of Sannoisian limestone	Clayey and chalky	5
		Siliceous and chalky	6
		Clayey and siliceous	7
		Siliceous pocket deposits	8
		Ferruginous pigments	9
	III. Alluvial gravel from the Isle with iron-pan	Gravels	10
		Sands	11
B. Common subsoil	I. Tertiary sands and clays, sometimes with iron-pan	Clayey and siliceous	12
		Siliceous	13
	II. Quaternary sandy alluvium	Sandy and clayey	14
		Sands	15
		Gravels	16
	III. Quaternary clayey alluvium	Sound land said to be of the alluvial plain	17

Group 10, as we have already seen, includes that part of the commune of Saint-Emilion which, geologically speaking, belongs rather to the land of Pomerol. To be precise, it contains only two *crus*. Its wines have always deserved to be classed along with the very best of the Saint-Emilions and, in our opinion, group 10, together with groups 1, 2, 3, make up the whole of the *Premiers Crus* of Saint-Emilion.

Group 11, a sandy soil on a subsoil of glacial gravel, would include only those of the neighbouring *crus* of group 10 which by their subsoil are related to Pomerol, but whose soil is however of lesser quality. It is through a misuse of the term "Graves" that Féret has gradually introduced them into the preceding group. Although dubbed with the title of "Saint-Emilion Graves", they are really only very good "Saint-Emilion Tertiary sands", and accordingly in class two.

Groups 12, 13 include a large part of the vineyards currently branded Saint-Emilion. We have said that the sands of which they are composed are generally débris of rocky slopes or weathering products of the underlying molasse (three types on the north-south section of Saint-Emilion) and dating from the late Sannoisian period. Most frequently they are coarse, micaceous, sometimes siliceous-chalky sands. An interesting horizon for agriculture because its composition is very varied. It would be tedious to make a list of the *crus* which make up these two classes. It would merely be a copy of fifteen or twenty pages of the last edition of Féret.

To recapitulate, class two or the second *crus* of Saint-Emilion would be made up of two wines which are rather different in their geological origin, but are of equal worth commercially. The first are the wines of the limestone slope of groups 4, 5, 6, 7, 8, 9. And after, there are the wines of the sands of groups 12, 13.

Class three would form the third *crus* of Saint-Emilion and would include, for the most part, the vineyards which ought not to have equal citizenship with "the best wines from the hillsides", but because their specifications entitle them to this right and because of ineluctable legal decrees, we are obliged to give them a place in our description. To list them all is Féret's job, not ours. So we could state that class three of Saint-Emilion is made up of groups 14, 15, 16, provided that their orographical situation is over a height of 30 feet, and reject group 17 and those belonging to groups 14 and 15 whose height is below 30 feet. We have seen in the preceding chapter that this sandy strip situated between the "Palus of Saint-Emilion" and the Tertiary débris above the 30 foot level are now the sites of the greatest number of *crus* in Saint-Emilion and that they are increasing daily...

General conclusion. In this way, I hope to have classified the *crus* of Saint-Emilion objectively and in accordance with a rigidly scientific method. (...) Shuffling groups of human beings about when each group considers itself in first place – reconstructing an army, as it were, revising all the ranks – is clearly an undertaking which can attract only hostility.

During the course of the last hundred years, the area of vineyards under production in Saint-Emilion has grown from 3,500 to 5,200 hectares. To give an idea of this size, we can say that it represents the whole of the vine-producing area of Burgundy in the department of Côte d'Or. The commune of Saint-Emilion has absorbed the seven "parishes" of the old borough together with the east sector of Libourne. I stress this point in order to make it clear that the appellation can in no way be qualified as one of a commune. Its name

On the hillsides, there is hardly any harvesting done by machine. Here, the team of Château Magdelaine. ▶

In Saint-Emilion, the vine supports are slightly higher than in the Médoc or in the Graves region.... but the pickers have to stoop none the less. ▶▶

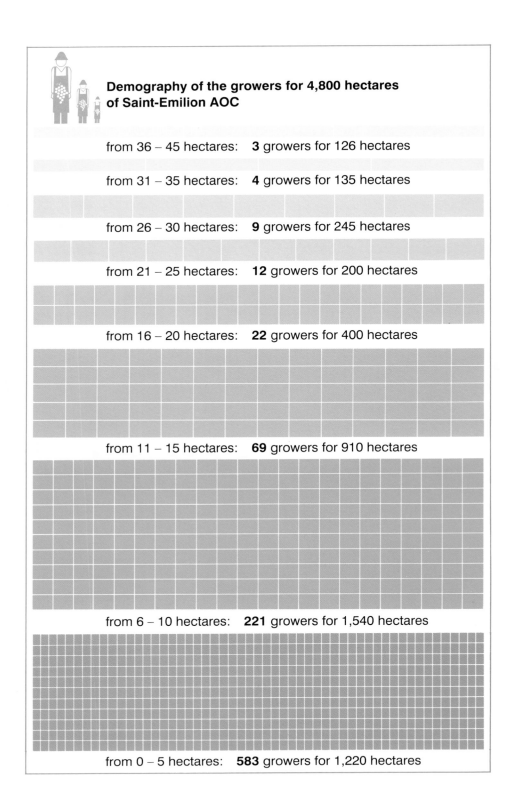

Demography of the growers for 4,800 hectares of Saint-Emilion AOC

from 36 – 45 hectares: **3** growers for 126 hectares

from 31 – 35 hectares: **4** growers for 135 hectares

from 26 – 30 hectares: **9** growers for 245 hectares

from 21 – 25 hectares: **12** growers for 200 hectares

from 16 – 20 hectares: **22** growers for 400 hectares

from 11 – 15 hectares: **69** growers for 910 hectares

from 6 – 10 hectares: **221** growers for 1,540 hectares

from 0 – 5 hectares: **583** growers for 1,220 hectares

Commune	Size under vines (hectares)	Independent growers	Co-operative members	Declared volume	Average yields (hectolitres per hectare)
St-Emilion	2,261	311	65	16,510	56.4
St-Christophe-des-Bardes	536	64	17	26,615	55.9
St-Hippolyte	272	17	23	8,958	59.7
St-Etienne-de-Lisse	515	54	29	18,859	54.6
St-Laurent-des-Combes	226	32	15	9,963	57.9
St-Pey-d'Armens	290	25	35	9,720	61.1
St-Sulpice-de-Faleyrens	592	80	57	24,311	61
Vignonet	274	38	35	10,043	59.4
Libourne	220	79	1	11,153	55.7
Total	5,188	700	277	280,563	58.11

Source: Syndicat de Saint-Emilion, harvest of 1982

continues to spread out beyond its limits. These are the "satellite" appellations: Lussac Saint-Emilion, Montagne Saint-Emilion, Saint-Georges Saint-Emilion, Parsac Saint-Emilion (this latter is gradually disappearing), comparable to Lalande-de-Pomerol in relationship to Pomerol itself. Good *crus* can be found here whose identity must not be confused with those of the Saint-Emilions, although many restau-rateurs do not burden themselves with the job of making the correct and official distinctions. It is curious to note that this phenomenon of satellite appellations is also to be found within the *crus* themselves. Figeac is the best example. Nearly fifteen *crus* claim to be members of its family; but there is also Gaffelière, Grâce-Dieu, etc. Statis-tics referring to the vineyards and the growers are given in the table above.

There is no relation between the volumes declared in each com-mune and the average yield per hectare because the growers declare in only one town hall, even if their property is split up over several communes. On the other hand, the production of the members of the co-operative group is recorded at Saint-Emilion. It represents more than 50,000 hectolitres.

The vineyards are broken up into extremely small parcels and the average size works out at about five hectares. But this figure does not give a precise picture of the breakdown of the production. In fact there are:

– 216 growers with one hectare or less
– 263 growers with from one to three hectares
– 154 growers with from four to five hectares
The viable economic threshold for a vigneron family starts at this last level. Obviously more than half of the growers in the Saint-Emilion AOC have other resources than the fruit of their vines. Certain have jobs in larger undertakings or else they have work completely unrelated to growing. The *cave coopérative* of the *Union de Producteurs* fortunately groups together many of these micro-productions. Of its some three hundred members, only seven work more than ten hectares. But this fact also explains the profusion of individual labels baptizing small units of production, which find their way more or less confidentially into elusive "commercial networks". The hill of a thousand *crus* is also the bottle of ink. Apart from the *cave coopérative*, the production of Saint-Emilion gains in status once a vineyard exceeds five hectares. However, the property remains restricted and gives the Bordeaux vineyards a rather Burgundy-like appearance. The table on page 40 illustrates this. (Statistics provided by the Syndicat de Saint-Emilion.)

The basic yield per hectare of vines in production is legally fixed at 42 hectolitres. The maximum authorized yield is 66 hectolitres per hectare. In practice, the average yield of the appellation is halfway between these two figures (58 hectolitres for the 1982 harvest), and the members of the cooperative group more often than not exceed 60 hectolitres. The overall production of Saint-Emilion represents about 290,000 hectolitres, i.e. 8.25% of the whole of AOC red wine in the department of Gironde. But it should be stated that Saint-Emilion is divided up in quite an individual way in relation to the other Bordeaux appellations into four denominations which conform to strictly controlled rulings:

– The *Saint-Emilion* appellation is applied principally to the vineyards of the plain. Theoretically, the minimum degree of alcohol is 11 degrees. Château bottling is not obligatory. A quality control takes place about six months after harvesting.
– *The Saint-Emilion Grand Cru* appellation conforms to stricter rules. The theoretical degree of alcohol is 11.5 degrees. Château bottling is obligatory after an ageing period of eighteen months and a control of quality must be carried out by a tasting commission under the authority of the INAO (Institut National des Appellations d'Origine).

The grapes are emptied into a hopper for the removal of the stalks.   ▶

A grower can request the right to the "Grand Cru" appellation for all or for a part of his harvest. This permits him to sell in bulk the vats which he considers less successful and to keep for his own "name of the château", that is his *cru*'s label, the proportion of his harvest which he reserves directly for his clientele. This is common practice. In our catalogue, we have made this distinction by indicating, where necessary, the production of a *cru* in numbers of tonneaux, together with the average number of bottles which are "château bottled". Of

course, these figures vary according to the quality of the vintage, the condition of stocks and the market situation.

The distinctions, which suppose quality, of Saint-Emilion *Grand Cru classé* and Saint-Emilion *Premier Grand Cru classé* are today separated from the notion of *appellation contrôlée*. It remains none the less the INAO which governs them. The national wine technocrats lap up the different nuances which spring from it while the consumer doesn't give a damn. In reality, a well kept confusion exists between the notion of *cru classé* and that of *appellation d'origine contrôlée*. In Saint-Emilion, no *cru classé* (endorsed by the INAO) has been subjected to a preliminary delimitation of its viticultural land. The first classification took place in 1954, to be endorsed the following

years. Two essential differences distinguish it from the classification of the *Grands Crus* of the Médoc, drawn up by the Bordeaux Chamber of Commerce in 1855 and still in force today. Firstly, at Saint-Emilion, the title of *cru classé* is "jointly managed" by the Syndicat d'appellation and the INAO. It is practically indistinguishable from the AOC, despite the ambiguous judicial distinction evoked above. Secondly, the classification of the *crus* of Saint-Emilion should be revised every ten years.

▲ *Following the pressing, the mass of grape skins, the "marc", forms huge compact cakes. Distillation in the* crus *is no longer carried out.*

Accordingly, at the request of the Federation for the Protection of the Saint-Emilion Appellation, the INAO brought the classification up to date in 1969. The *Premiers Grands Crus classés* stayed the same, twelve in number. The *Grands Crus classés* increased from sixty-three to seventy-one. A third revision should have taken place at the end of the following ten year period. Several natural obstacles delayed this formality. The first publication of the INAO's propositions was in February 1985. It set sparks flying in all directions. This is how the reporter Jean-Pierre Deroudille summed up the situation in the newspaper *Sud-Ouest* at that time: "The Commission for the classification of the *Grands Crus* appellation of Saint-Emilion has hit hard. In this age of stringency, this is perhaps normal; none the less, there are many disappointments within the walls of the mediaeval city." Take a closer look: Château Beau-Séjour Bécot, *Premier Grand Cru classé*, was downgraded to the ranks of the *Grands Crus classés*; Châteaux Cadet-Bon, Côte-Baleau, Coutet, Grandes-Murailles, Jean Faure and La Couspaude were purely and simply thrown out of the *Grands Crus classés* club. Only one château was promoted, Château Berliquet, a *Grand Cru classé* after a notorious eclipse for more than a generation. For the victims, it was a hard blow. Without going into the matter in depth, I will say that the publication of this revision by the INAO and the Federation for the Protection of the Saint-Emilion Appellation, before the ministerial decree, was at the least ill-timed, if not out of order. In itself it constitutes a procedural error capable of justifying the complainants who are asking for the new classification to be annulled. A sort of ministers' excuse-me waltz followed and the decree was signed only in the month of May 1986. I have written a few notes on the root of the trouble regarding Château Beau-Séjour Bécot in the article devoted to that château in the catalogue of the *crus*. I certainly would not have the presumption to judge the judges. The dossier has been dealt with firstly at Administrative Court level and has now been handed on to the Conseil d'Etat. My personal conviction is that this revision was not protected by all the necessary and statutory precautions which the law has envisaged. The dragging out of the procedure, far from being a guarantee that it was a serious affair, is positive evidence of a number of uncertainties. And finally, instead of adding credibility to Saint-Emilion's image, the claimed severity of those responsible for the revision throws moral doubt on all the great family of growers of the area. This is why, with my hand on my heart, I solemnly and sincerely think that the reader is better informed with the publication of the 1969 classification of the *grands crus* of Saint-Emilion, as this vintage seems to me to be better and more reliable than the 1986, whose "fermentation" was unnecessarily effervescent, with acidity, tartness

1st Grands Crus classés

A
Ausone
Cheval Blanc

B
Beauséjour
Beau-Séjour Bécot[1]
Bélair
Canon
Figeac
Fourtet
La Gaffelière
Magdelaine
Pavie
Trotte Vieille

Grands Crus classés

Balestard la Tonnelle
Bellevue
Bergat
Berliquet[2]
Cadet-Bon
Cadet-Piola
Canon-la-Gaffelière
Cap de Mourlin
Chauvin
Clos des Jacobins
Corbin
Corbin-Michotte
Côte Baleau[1]
Coutet[1]
Couvent des Jacobins
Croque Michotte
Curé Bon La Madeleine
Dassault
Faurie de Souchard
Fonplégade
Fonroque
Franc-Mayne
Grand Barrail Lamarzelle Figeac
Grand Corbin
Grand Corbin-Despagne
Grandes Murailles
Grand Mayne
Grand-Pontet
Guadet-Saint-Julien

Haut Corbin
Haut-Sarpe
Jean Faure[1]
La Carte de Beau-Séjour
La Chapelle Madeleine
La Clotte
La Clusière
La Couspaude[1]
La Dominique
La Madeleine
La Marzelle
L'Angélus
Laniote
Larcis Ducasse
Larmande
Laroze
L'Arrosée
La Serre
La Tour du Pin Figeac
La Tour du Pin Figeac (Moueix)
La Tour Figeac
Le Châtelet
Le Couvent[4]
Le Prieuré
L'Oratoire
Matras
Mauvezin
Moulin du Cadet
Pavie Decesse
Pavie Macquin
Pavillon Cadet
Petit-Faurie-de-Soutard
Ripeau
Saint-Georges Côtes Pavie
Saint Martin
Sansonnet
Soutard
Tertre Daugay
Trimoulet
Trois Moulins
Troplong Mondot
Villemaurine
Yon Figeac

1. These *crus* were declassified in 1986
2. This *cru* was re-classified in 1986
3. This *cru* has been absorbed by Ausone
4. As from 1982, this *cru* can no longer claim the *Grand Cru classé* AOC

and thick muddy lees. In the Bordeaux region, the growers are apt to say of an uneven year that it is "jealous". Was there in the 1986 Saint-Emilion classification a hint of jealousy too? None the less, I have included Château Berliquet among the *Grands Crus classés* for it is right that its merit should be recognized. As to my classification, as it is proposed in the catalogue and translated by a number of full glasses, I stress that this is the result of a personal judgement which commits only myself, being drawn up from both objective (situation, 47 varieties of grapes, agricultural and oenological methods, reputation, etc.) and subjective (tastings) criteria. Like any human endeavour, it is imperfect. Its principal merit is that it exists. But the lover of terrains with a history could profitably consult the list of winners in the 1867 Universal Exhibition in Paris which names 37 *crus* as the most illustrious of the Saint-Emilions (see page 309). The *Premiers Grands Crus classés* are divided into two groups. Group A, which includes Château Ausone and Cheval Blanc, is to all intents and purposes on a par with the *premiers crus* of the Médoc, with whose sale price they tend to be in line. Group B can be compared to the great second *crus classés* of the Médoc but the volume put out on the market is considerably less because of the relatively restricted size of the vineyards. The *Grands Crus classés* represent a level of quality which in the Médoc would group the best *crus bourgeois supérieurs* and the intermediary *crus classés*. All the Firsts of Saint-Emilion come from within the boundaries of the parent commune. The same is true for the other *crus classés* with two exceptions: Haut-Sarpe, which belongs to Saint-Christophe-des-Bardes, and Larcis-Ducasse, situated at Saint-Laurent-des-Combes.

The figure below shows how the volumes and values of the four appellations are split up.

As in the other Bordeaux AOC areas, bottling at the château or at the property tends to increase every year, swelling principally the Saint-Emilion *Grand Cru* appellation, which constitutes a worthwhile means of increasing the value of the product. It involves investing in buildings, material and stock but the resulting appreciation is considerable. It also brings about the creation or development of new commercial outlets, such as direct sales. The growers who cannot or do not wish to ensure this evolution themselves have the possi-

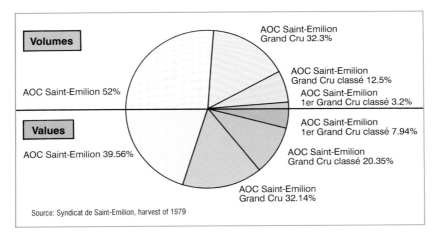

Volumes

AOC Saint-Emilion 52%

AOC Saint-Emilion Grand Cru 32.3%

AOC Saint-Emilion Grand Cru classé 12.5%

AOC Saint-Emilion 1er Grand Cru classé 3.2%

Values

AOC Saint-Emilion 39.56%

AOC Saint-Emilion 1er Grand Cru classé 7.94%

AOC Saint-Emilion Grand Cru classé 20.35%

AOC Saint-Emilion Grand Cru 32.14%

Source: Syndicat de Saint-Emilion, harvest of 1979

bility of going to the *cave coopérative* – the "Union de Producteurs de Saint-Emilion", which is remarkably well run, displays admirable dynamism and is highly quality-conscious. The counterpart to this policy is the levelling out at the bottom of the simple Saint-Emilion appellation. However, it appears best to maintain a selective approach. *A priori* the victim of an excessively wide, even lax delimitation, Saint-Emilion has created for itself an internal set of rules enabling a scale of values to be established. In this respect, the decree of October 7, 1954, defining the four appellations, represents a great step forward and its effects can be felt very positively today. I think that, ideally, the Saint-Emilion *Grand Cru* appellation should not simply depend on sensory controls (tasting) and château bottling, but on the selection of the land. For, at the end of the day, and despite the modernists at the INAO, our AOC wines are essentially wines from different soils and not technological wines. The best agronomist and the best oenologist in the world could never make a "Graves" style wine from a sandhill nor a wine from the hillside at an altitude of eighteen feet!

As we have seen, the declaration of a Saint-Emilion *Grand Cru* wine is at the choice of the proprietor. Most of the time the grower who makes the request is accepted, for he knows and respects the rules of the game. But this explains a certain fluidity in the list of the *Grands Crus*. We are publishing it because it will serve the reader as a guide without being a fixed entity once and for all. Current rules are tending to become more and more severe today, though without going so far as to be exemplary. In order to claim the title "Grand Cru classé", a proprietor must ensure that his wine is vinified and aged in a separate cellar. But what constitutes the separation? The law says that a simple curtain is sufficient. So then the question is, "What goes on behind the scenes?" Similarly, the production of a vineyard planted closest to the river Dordogne can easily be called "Grand Cru" from the moment it satisfies a minimal level of quality and its wine must be bottled on the site of production. To conclude then, the Saint-Emilion *Grand Cru* appellation would appear still to be trying to find its correct identity. Halfway between the idea of "vin supérieur" and that of "cru classé", it is a true guarantee of the origin and the authenticity of the *cru* without trying to define a type of wine characterized by the terrain.

AOC Saint Emilion Grand Cru

Badette
Saint-Christophe-des-Bardes
Bagnols
Saint-Etienne-de-Lisse
Barbeyron
Saint-Magne-de-Castillon
Barde-Haut
Saint-Christophe-des-Bardes
Bardoulet
Saint-Etienne-de-Lisse
Barry
Saint-Sulpice-de-Faleyrens
Béard
Saint-Laurent-des-Combes
Beau-Mayne
Saint-Emilion
Bellefont-Belcier
Saint-Laurent-des-Combes
Bellefont-Belcier-Guillier
Saint-Laurent-des-Combes
Bellegrave
Vignonet
Bellile-Mondotte
Saint-Laurent-des-Combes
Bigaroux
Saint-Sulpice-de-Faleyrens
Bonnet
Saint-Pey-d'Armens
Bouquey
Saint-Hippolyte
Brun
Saint-Christophe-des-Bardes
Cadet-Peychez
Saint-Emilion
Cadet-Pontet
Saint-Emilion
Calvaire
Saint-Etienne-de-Lisse
Cantenac
Saint-Emilion
Canterane
Saint-Etienne-de-Lisse
Capet-Guillier
Saint-Hippolyte
Carboneyre
Vignonet
Cardinal-Villemaurine
Saint-Emilion
Carteau Côtes Daugay
Saint-Emilion
Carteau-Matras
Saint-Emilion
Cauze
Saint-Christophe-des-Bardes
Champion
Saint-Christophe-des-Bardes
Chante-Alouette
Saint-Emilion

Chante-Alouette
Saint-Magne-de-Castillon
Chantecaille
Saint-Emilion
Cheval Noir
Saint-Emilion
Cormeil-Figeac
Saint-Emilion
Côte de la Mouleyre
Saint-Etienne-de-Lisse
Côtes Bernateau
Saint-Etienne-de-Lisse
Côtes Puyblanquet
Saint-Etienne-de-Lisse
Coudert-Pelletan
Saint-Christophe-des-Bardes
Couvent des Jacobins
Saint-Emilion
Couvent des Templiers
Saint-Emilion
Croix de Bertinat
Saint-Sulpice-de-Faleyrens
Cros-Figeac
Saint-Emilion
Faleyrens
Saint-Sulpice-de-Faleyrens
Ferrand
Saint-Hippolyte
Fleur de Lisse
Saint-Etienne-de-Lisse
Flouquet
Saint-Sulpice-de-Faleyrens
Fombrauge
Saint-Christophe-des-Bardes
Fonrazade
Saint-Emilion
Fougueyrat
Saint-Emilion
Fourney
Saint-Pey-d'Armens
Franc Bigaroux
Saint-Sulpice-de-Faleyrens
Franc Grâce Dieu
Saint-Emilion
Franc Patarabet
Saint-Emilion
Franc Pipeau
Saint-Hippolyte
Franc-Pourret
Saint-Emilion
Gaillard
Saint-Hippolyte
Gaubert
Saint-Christophe-des-Bardes
Grand Bert
Saint-Philippe-d'Aiguilbe
Grand Faurie
Saint-Emilion

Grand Mirande
Saint-Emilion
Grands Champs
Saint-Magne-de-Castillon
Gravet
Saint-Sulpice-de-Faleyrens
Gueyrot
Saint-Emilion
Guillemin la Gaffelière
Saint-Emilion
Guinot
Saint-Etienne-de-Lisse
Haut-Brisson
Vignonet
Haut Lavallade
Saint-Christophe-des-Bardes
Haut-Peyroutas
Vignonet
Haut-Plantet
Saint-Emilion
Haut-Pontet
Saint-Emilion
Haut Renaissance
Saint-Sulpice-de-Faleyrens
Haut-Rocher
Saint-Etienne-de-Lisse
Haut-Segottes
Saint-Emilion
Jacques Blanc
Saint-Etienne-de-Lisse
Jean Voisin
Saint-Emilion
Labarde (Clos)
Saint-Laurent-des-Combes
La Barde
Saint-Laurent-des-Combes
La Bouygue
Saint-Emilion
La Chapelle-Lescours
Saint-Sulpice-de-Faleyrens
La Commanderie
Saint-Emilion
La Croix Chantecaille
Saint-Emilion
La Fagnouse
Saint-Etienne-de-Lisse
La Fleur
Saint-Emilion
La Fleur Cravignac
Saint-Emilion
La Fleur Pipeau
Saint-Laurent-des-Combes
La Fleur Pourret
Saint-Emilion
La Gomerie
Saint-Emilion
La Grâce Dieu
Saint-Emilion

La Grâce Dieu des Prieurs
Saint-Emilion
La Grâce Dieu les Menuts
Saint-Emilion
Lagrange de Lescure
Saint-Sulpice-de-Faleyrens
La Grave Figeac
Saint-Emilion
La Mélissière
Saint-Hippolyte
La Mondotte
Saint-Laurent-des-Combes
Lapelletrie
Saint-Christophe-des-Bardes
Lapeyre
Saint-Etienne-de-Lisse
Laplagnotte Bellevue
Saint-Christophe-des-Bardes
La Pointe Bouquey
Saint-Pey-d'Armens
Laroque
Saint-Christophe-des-Bardes
La rose Côte Rol
Saint-Emilion
La Rose-Pourret
Saint-Emilion
La Rose-Trimoulet
Saint-Emilion
La Sablière
Saint-Emilion
Lassègue
Saint-Hippolyte
Lavallade
Saint-Christophe-des-Bardes
Le Jura
Saint-Emilion
Lescours
Saint-Sulpice-de-Faleyrens
Lespinasse
Saint-Pey-d'Armens
L'Hermitage
Saint-Emilion
Magnan la Gaffelière
Saint-Emilion
Malineau
Saint-Emilion
Marquis de Mons
Saint-Hippolyte
Mayne-Figeac
Saint-Emilion
Mazerat
Saint-Emilion
Menuts (Clos des)
Saint-Emilion
Millaud-Montlabert
Saint-Emilion
Milon
Saint-Christophe-des-Bardes

Monbousquet
Saint-Sulpice-de-Faleyrens
Mondotte-Bellisle
Saint-Laurent-des-Combes
Montlabert
Saint-Emilion
Moulin Bellegrave
Vignonet
Moulin du Jura
Montagne
Moulin Saint-Georges
Saint-Emilion
Naude la Croix Fourney
Branne
Palais-Cardinal-la-Fuie
Saint-Sulpice-de-Faleyrens
Panet
Saint-Christophe-des-Bardes
Pasquette
Saint-Emilion
Patris
Saint-Emilion
Petit-Gravet
Saint-Emilion
Petit-Mangot
Saint-Etienne-de-Lisse
Peyreau
Saint-Emilion
Peyrelongue
Saint-Emilion
Pindefleurs
Saint-Emilion
Pipeau
Saint-Laurent-des-Combes
Pontet-Clauzure
Saint-Emilion
Pressac
Saint-Etienne-de-Lisse
Puyblanquet
Saint-Etienne-de-Lisse
Puy-Blanquet
Saint-Etienne-de-Lisse
Puy-Razac
Saint-Emilion
Quentin
Saint-Christophe-des-Bardes
Reynaud
Saint-Pey-d'Armens
Rochebelle
Saint-Laurent-des-Combes
Rocher
Saint-Etienne-de-Lisse
Rol
Saint-Emilion
Rol de Fombrauge
Saint-Christophe-des-Bardes
Roquefort
Saint-Emilion

Rozier
Saint-Laurent-des-Combes
Saint-Christophe
Saint-Christophe-des-Bardes
Saint-Hubert
Saint-Emilion
Saint-Martial
Saint-Sulpice-de-Faleyrens
Saint-Pey
Saint-Pey-d'Armens
Saint-Pey "branche aînée"
Saint-Pey-d'Armens
Sarpe (Clos de)
Saint-Christophe-des-Bardes
Tour Baladoz
Saint-Laurent-des-Combes
Tour Berthonneau
Saint-Emilion
Tour des Combes
Saint-Laurent-des-Combes
Tour de Seme
Saint-Hippolyte
Tour Saint-Pierre
Saint-Emilion
Touzinat
Saint-Pey-d'Armens
Trapaud
Saint-Etienne-de-Lisse
Trimoulet (Clos)
Saint-Emilion
Truquet
Saint-Emilion
Union de Producteurs (q.v.
catalogue of crus)
Saint-Emilion
Val d'Or
Vignonet
Vieux Château Chauvin
Saint-Emilion
Vieux Fortin
Saint-Emilion
Vieux Grand Faurie
Saint-Christophe-des-Bardes
Vieux Moulin du Cadet
Saint-Emilion
Vieux Rivallon
Saint-Emilion
Vieux Sarpe
Saint-Christophe-des-Bardes

The Wines of Sainct-Milyon:
an invitation to good living

By comparison with the other vine-growing regions of Bordeaux, Saint-Emilion has always had an innovatory approach and for more than a century has distinguished itself by its creative originality. There are numerous examples. The Federation of Viticulturalists of Saint-Emilion was the first of its type in France, created in 1884, in the same year as the law on freedom of assembly. Like the viticultural co-operative movement of the thirties, this syndicalism was a "child of woe". It was born at the height of the phylloxera crisis, when the vineyards were devastated. It brought together in one huge body growers, coopers, tenant-farmers, cellar masters, etc. It created a group of people pledged to mutual self-help which, in 1905, became the first local Crédit Agricole bank in the department. It also set up an investment bureau and a centre for providing raw materials, a sort of co-operative purchasing centre. It protected its territory and the use of the name of Saint-Emilion long before the important law concerning the AOCs. And many a noisy lawsuit was brought against defrauders and usurpers.

In 1932, the first *cave coopérative* in the department of Gironde was creat ed, which today remains in the forefront of viti-vinicultural techniques and which in particular has just been equipped with an amazing computer system. Today, this *cave coopérative* controls a large proportion of the market and henceforth its role is essential for stabilizing prices. On September 13, 1948, the Jurade of Saint-Emilion took its place in the history of an intensely bacchic France as the first wine brotherhood of the Bordeaux region. It absorbed and destroyed a mediaeval past and the territorial powers of the *ancien régime* to assume the cultural right to wear the red robe with cape of white silk and to proclaim the merits of the *cru* loud and

long. At the time, it needed plenty of cheek and a certain chic to wear a robe! The business could easily have turned into a grotesque farce. It came through with flying colours thanks to three men: the *abbé* Bergey, the priest of Saint-Emilion, Jean Capdemourlin and Daniel Querre, the spiritual fathers of the Jurade. Their dignified solemnity communicated itself, silencing the disparagers and mockers who were waiting as they came out of the church to jeer at them. After high mass, they went to the town hall to be sworn in before the mayor. Then the twenty-two crimson jurats climbed to the top of the King's Tower and the mighty voice of the Chancellor Daniel Querre took the place of the sound of trumpets for the proclamation of the opening of the harvest: "Let the scissors snip in agile hands, line up the baskets side by side, let the vats heave and strain, let flow the must, let our songs rise to heaven that the blessèd wine fill the barrels, and bring us a life fruitful and vibrant!"

Two years later, the Jurade created a seal of quality, commonly called the "label", which was awarded after tasting. This initiative was to become a standard control and is today carried out in all

54

the Bordeaux AOCs. The first of these official controls came about in 1954. It created a fearful panic among the small growers who rushed to the *cave coopérative* in huge numbers. Many realized that to produce grapes was one thing, but to make good wine out of them was another. In the same operation, the terms of the Saint-Emilion appellation were re-defined according to the criteria cited above. Many people had cause to reproach themselves at the general meeting of the Federation for the Protection of the Appellation when it was decided that the whole of the 1963 and 1965 harvest and 95% of that of 1968 could not claim the name of Saint-Emilion. In 1972, ever at the spearhead of progress, the Federation proposed obligatory château bottling for the three "supérieures" AOC. This practice has been in force since the 1973 harvest.

The people of Saint-Emilion prize these aspects of independence. They bear witness to a strong professional solidarity which does not exclude minor internal conflicts. They are bound body and soul to their church tower and their "ancestral territory". It is true that several families have been firmly rooted there for four centuries or more. This explains the profusion of "gothic" labels or references to ancient history, often used by people who can in no way justify any claim thereto. It also explains the bombastic tone encountered in the

▲ *As everywhere else in France where vines are grown, the vignerons and cellar workers are fond of good food and the produce of their labours... often rewarded by medals.*

◄ *Between the two world wars, the war of the Saint-Emilion AOC took place, as witness these "political" posters.*

local way of speaking, which sometimes weighs down the advertising material with exuberant adjectives. Even the worthy Jurade, today under the moderate rule of Thierry Manoncourt, the proprietor of Figeac, does not remain untainted by this fervour: "By bringing back to life the majestic episodes of the glorious past, by exalting secular traditions which have made the fame of the city resound to the very limits of the earth, the Jurade of the present day intends to uphold and to blazon abroad the noble prestige of the honorific wine of Saint-Emilion." After such a declamation, if you do not feel a doctor *honoris causa* of Saint-Emilion when you take a sip of the *cru*, it is because you remain a philistine to the very limits of your mentality.

"Saint-Emilion is the quintessence of the wines from the hillsides." With my impertinent pertinence, I would add: "Yes, provided that it is not from the bottom of the slope!" In the book *Terroirs et Vins de France* (geological and oenological journeys, published under the direction of Charles Pomerol. BRGM Editions, 1948), we read: "The communes, eight in number, grouped around the Saint-Emilion appellation, represent about 5,000 hectares and produce a red wine, characteristic of a land full of history." Coming from a work which

▲ *An historic photograph: at the Town Hall of Bordeaux, the first reunion of the Jurats of Saint-Emilion and the Commanders of the Bontemps de Médoc.*

After high mass, following important council meetings, the Jurats go on parade. ▶

claims to be scientific, this string of statements would not appear to permit any contradiction. However, the eight communes in question are not "grouped around the Saint-Emilion appellation". They are included in the appellation. They "produce a red wine"? I beg to differ. They produce a thousand red wines. Of all the Bordeaux appellations, Saint-Emilion is the one which offers the greatest variety of types of wines, at least as many as the Côtes de Bourg. Here, the simplification is inapt because it is misleading. And how does

he describe this red wine? It is "characterized by a land full of history". That is a fine way for a geologist to avoid the question. Does the nature of the soil wear away beneath the footprints of those who have walked over it? The best definition of Saint-Emilion wines is to be found in Pierre Danche, and notably in his work *Blason des bons vins de France,* written at the beginning of the sixteenth century: "The Wines of Sainct-Milyon: an invitation to good living." I owe the next exquisite quotation to the erudition of the Burgundian Raymond Dumay who describes his tasting of a wine of Château Ausone, considered as the very archetype of the famous "wine from the hillsides", in this way: "Silently, we swirled the red liquor in our large glasses. The wine hollowed down in the centre as it rose up the sides. A luxuriant and subtle rose seemed to be blossoming between our fingers. It had more than one aroma, a slightly wild scent, highly pleasing to civilized people. We remained in front of this dark bottle for a while in meditation, a meditation which surpassed the pleasure of drinking. Mauriac's joyful panegyric came back to mind: *Every grape in every bunch is full of sunshine.*"

And here too is a short extract from a little book I am fond of because it says much in a few words. It is a rather rare work, with the title of *Vins de Bordeaux, Vins de Châteaux,* published in 1950 by IAC Editions in Lyons. To quote it here seems to me even more timely in that it was awarded the first literary prize of the Jurade of Saint-Emilion in the year of its publication. The author is addressing a visionary nymph, the modern Bordeaux version of Pygmalion:

"The wine of Saint-Emilion, Balbina, is a wine of the hillsides, and as such, deep in colour, warm, full-bodied and generous. Its slight hint of bitterness stimulates the appetite even after rich meats which its fullness and power make easy to digest. And here at the head of them all, is its first *Premier Cru*, Château Ausone, the oldest, but there remains no trace of the house of the orator and consul (*today such has been found at La Gaffelière. Editor's note*), save the great reputation which this wine deserves and which is preserved here as well as at Clos Fourtet, whose gates open out onto the church square in the centre of the village, and as at the Clos du Couvent and Château Canon, as ardent as a gunner, and as at Châteaux Bélair, Balestard, Beauséjour and Pavie, and at the Clos de la Magdelaine and the Angélus, but I cannot list them all for you, Balbina. I simply wish to draw your attention to the difference to be made between these and the ones called Graves Saint-Emilion. Their finesse, their bouquet, make them less self-assertive, but yet Château Cheval Blanc sticks in my memory and has all the distinction of Ausone as well as all the range of the Figeacs, with Château Figeac at the top of the list, along with their neighbours, including La Dominique." Shrewdly observed, reviewed and expressed, at least as far as the quintessence of the wines of Saint-Emilion is concerned, whether they are from the slopes or the "graves" regions. And how can the others be described? They are likeable table companions, younger brothers or else first cousins, sometimes simple family friends or just hangers-on. It takes all sorts to make a world. The microcosm of Saint-Emilion is a galaxy in which all the stars are not the largest but in which the golden rule is solidarity. And truthfully, I can tell you, this wine has a sort of flavour of fraternity.

*

Of all the *vigneron* villages in the Bordeaux area, Saint-Emilion is the most picturesque. The little old town, fixed on a hillside, presents the visitor with the sight of its pink roof tops of varying shapes which, according to the hour of the day, absorb or reflect the sunlight like an ever-changing jigsaw puzzle. In peaceful contemplation from the high terrace near the church tower and the Hostellerie Plaisance, the eye takes in the old houses overlapping one another in a logical disorder imposed by the nature of the site. The building material comes from beneath. Over the centuries, it has been taken from the subsoil, excavated stone by stone, creating a labyrinth of galleries whose twisting passages are today uncharted. For a long time, the quarry workers contributed very considerably to the prosperity of the commune. Saint-Emilion is not alone in being built from its own resources. The major part of Libourne and the villages round about, as well as nearly half the Bordeaux of the eighteenth century, were constructed thanks to the rock of Saint-Emilion (including the Great Theatre of Victor Louis). Several of the quarries have been reconverted into cellars for ageing wine. They ensure a cool and constant temperature, an important factor for the correct preservation of wine in casks, or a high level of hygrometry, reducing *consume,* or evaporation (excessive humidity in the atmosphere on the other hand can reduce the level of alcohol in the wine). Often the vines are planted above the cellars, some twenty-four, thirty, forty-five feet up. So it is surprising to see the radicles of the plants pierce the thickness of the rock and cling on to the ceiling. We can say that

---

A superb and surprising picture: the roots of vines planted twenty-four feet higher up
penetrate the rock and appear through the vaults of the cellars. ▶

in Saint-Emilion, these vines have become part of the fixtures, being part of the matrix of chalk to which they have clung for centuries; it will never be possible to remove them completely.

A subterranean wonder and *chef d'œuvre* of patient labour, the monolithic church is particularly worth a visit. We say in French "the work of a Benedictine" to mean "a work of laborious scholarship". But when we use this expression in the context of Saint-Emilion, we do not only mean the perseverance of a copier or a limner of prayer-books. For about three centuries, forsaking the quill for the pickaxe, the monks hollowed out this monument starting from the inside, a sort of defiance to the outside world, a cathedral deep down.

In Saint-Emilion, the passing ages are closely knit or interlock, creating a surprising continuity. Even certain contemporary anachronisms fit naturally into the picture. You should stroll through these pedestrian alleys, at the risk of twisting your ankle on the eroded cobble-stones, to discover the community spirit of the village of former times, in an age when the car did not isolate the passer-by from his immediate environment. You should climb to the top of the King's Tower to admire the calm, distant horizon. You should stop at the Collegiate Church, where an unaffected mastery of classic architecture reigns in silence. You can visit the Cordeliers' cloister, radiating the romanticism of Lamartine, where today a sparkling wine is made by the champagne method which can be drunk on the spot, particularly in the summer season, accompanied by macaroons, the speciality of Saint-Emilion.

▲ *The square, as seen from the top of the Saint-Emilion church tower, with the entrance to the monolithic church, hollowed out by the Benedictine monks.*

◄ *This 1905 postcard shows an interesting part of the monolithic church, the largest of its type.*

Take half a pound of ground almonds and the same amount of
granulated sugar. You will also need a glass of sweet white wine
(Loupiac, for example), four egg whites, one heaped tablespoonful
of butter and one of icing sugar. Mix the almonds and granulated
sugar together with the white wine and add a few drops of vanilla
essence. Beat the egg whites till they are stiff and add them to the
mixture. Pour into a saucepan, and reduce slightly over a gentle heat,
stirring all the time. When the preparation has lost its liquid and is
thoroughly blended, remove from the heat and continue to stir to
help it to cool. Then both you and the mixture can rest awhile until it

is cold. To finish, drop the mixture in small quantities from a baking spoon onto a well-greased oven tray. Dust with icing sugar and bake for about fifteen minutes at 180° centigrade (360° Fahrenheit, regulo N° 3 to 4), taking care that the sugar does not turn to caramel. In this way you will have successfully made an exquisite delicacy, Saint-Emilion macaroons.

▲ *The lie of the hillsides often necessitates stone walls to hold the land in place. These terraces contribute to the landscape's character.*

Gastronomy in the area is pleasurable. Several inns are to be found offering a warm welcome, the majority serving regional dishes with, here and there, original creations in a more modern style. As far as I am concerned, the wines of Saint-Emilion can find no better solid accompaniment than good charcuterie and either roast or grilled meats, especially grilled ones. Dishes which are too fussy harm the wine's subtlety. The most delicious way of appreciating a noble bottle of the *cru* is with a good entrecôte grilled on a fire of cabernet prunings or a leg of mutton of the Landes roasted on a fire of oak wood, accompanied by *cêpes* in the Bordeaux style, seasoned with parsley but not too much garlic (just a hint...). With the cheese, if you choose by preference a mild soft one (not goat cheese or Roquefort), your appreciation of the wine will be considerably heightened. The wine of Saint-Emilion has the particular distinction of being able to be drunk relatively young, yet having the potential for ageing well. I am speaking here of the wine from the hillsides, for those from the gravel slopes, like those from the Médoc, require longer in wood and more time in the bottle.

Lamprey is without any doubt the crowning glory of Saint-Emilion. This little prehistoric monster belongs to the group of agnathoi (without jaws). Its appearance is not very tempting but in a *matelote au*

▲ *Saint-Emilion macaroons are a delicious and traditional delicacy.*

A huge annual exhibition brings the craftsmen of Saint-Emilion together along with
other artisans of the region. Here, the potter Guy Jeanguyot at his wheel. ▶

vin rouge can be delicious. "Lampreys are vermicular; their skin is without scales and sticky; their round mouth, made for sucking, lacks jaws, but has several rows of horny teeth; on the side of their neck are several pairs of branchial orifices; their skeleton is completely cartilaginous. They are very inferior vertebrates to all others..." *(Grand Larousse encyclopédique).* This shortened description is not at all appetizing. Lampreys latch on to aquatic animals by their buccal suckers and they suck their blood. They are the vampires of the rivers. 67

They are caught in bow-nets in the river Dordogne and prepared in a *court-bouillon* with red wine, after collecting the blood to mix with the sauce. I do not recommend the neophyte lover of this fish to undertake its preparation, which demands Dracula-like manipulations. That is why I am not giving the recipe here. But it should also be known that it is essential that the backbone of the animal be removed, for it is poisonous. History tells that King Henry I died of a "surfeit of lamprey". None the less, lamprey is a dish for kings. You need young wine, which is first brought to the boil and flambéed. You also need the white flesh of large and tender leeks, a small amount of brandy and a pinch of cocoa. The fish is served with sippets, that is, small pieces of toast, and it is one of the rare fish which go really very well with a great red wine, probably because the lamprey is not a fish but an "aquatic vertebrate". It is also popularly known as *suce-caillou* (sucking head), *flûte sept-trous* (seven-holed flute) and *sept-oeil* (seven eyes). It often impresses women, doubtless because of the curse of the serpent in the Bible. Whatever the case, you should eat it in a restaurant or buy it ready prepared in tins or preserving jars. The best ones come from Monsieur Garde's restaurant in Libourne.

After the meal, the visitor wanting to take a trip round can make for the high plain to the north of Saint-Emilion, passing by the little country roads, walled in on either side, along the vineyards of Canon and Clos Fourtet, Beauséjour, etc. He will feel frustrated, for the countryside is obscured from the road. By foot or by bike, it will be a little better. This part of Saint-Emilion has an original character. The walls were constructed to dissuade marauders, to prevent animals from straying onto the vines and to stop grape thieves. The height of the walls has been carefully calculated and does not allow a person of ordinary height to see what is on the other side, whereas formerly, the growers had a complete panorama of the vine-growing countryside from their carts.

*

The panorama of the Saint-Emilion appellation is in three dimensions: in width, from the low valley of the river Dordogne; in height, from the hillsides on their rocky bed, and in depth from the gravel slopes of Figeac. They should not be confused; each sings its individual note, as well placed as can be and perfectly in tune, without ever coming together to make a real choir. The polyphony of Saint-Emilion is that of men. Not that of the wines. And to declare indiscriminately that all the *crus* are equal in merit as in objective value, would be to give the consumer a false image of the truth. On the other hand, I think that every "poetic" lover of the name Saint-Emilion should be able to distinguish the strata, even the coarse ones,

▲ *In Saint-Emilion, restaurants are welcoming and busy. From left to right and top to bottom: Le Logis de la Cadène (Tel. 57 24 71 40), Francis Goullé (Tel. 57 24 70 49), L'Hostellerie Plaisance (Tel. 57 24 72 32), Chez Dominique (Tel. 57 24 71 00).*

At Saint-Emilion's Maison du Vin, *the visitor can find a vast choice of wines.* ▶

which make up the normal – I should like to say "normative" – quality of each one. But the amateur can be wholly excused for his ignorance if we remember the enormous extent of the appellation and the compass of the economic interest which should never be brought into question!... except for a pretence of bringing things up to date. The revision of the classification has the effect of a pretentious or weary Swiss cuckoo... which flies out into a dead end and flops.

But the great wines of Saint-Emilion remain great. I call to mind the sage Rabindranâth Tagore who wrote, in round terms: "On the sands of worlds infinite, the children play. And thou stayest there, wreathed in smiles." Like love, Saint-Emilion wine is a passion for he who tastes it and an adventure for he who makes it. This proposition is sometimes reversible.

Catalogue of crus

The official classification of the *crus* of Saint-Emilion is subject to particular rules which are under the control of the INAO. The terms *Grand Cru, Grand Cru classé* and *Premier Grand Cru classé*, as they appear in this catalogue, are based on a compromise of the situation before and after the 1985 revision.

The number of coloured glasses beside a *cru* gives an idea of the value for money it represents. This estimation, while arrived at as objectively as possible, is naturally subject to discussion and to change. It is intended as a rough guide and has no official standing as a classification.

This symbol denotes an exceptional wine.

Certain châteaux have one or more different labels for other wines produced by the property (for example wines from young vines). Such wines are followed by an arrow which indicates the château of origin.
This symbol indicates that a particular name is a secondary wine of a larger estate.
This symbol denotes that the vinification of the *cru* is carried out at the *cave coopérative*, l'Union des Producteurs de Saint-Emilion.

CB   This denotes château-bottled.

Andron de Lescours (Château)

Commune: Saint-Sulpice-de-Faleyrens. **Proprietor:** Jean Charvet. Consultant oenologist: C.B.C. Libourne. **Size of vineyard:** 5 hectares. **Average age of vines:** 20 years. **Varieties:** 15% cabernet-sauvignon. 65% merlot. 20% cabernet-franc. **Production:** 20,000 bottles CB. **Sales by mail order:** Andron, 33330 Saint-Sulpice-de-Faleyrens. **Direct Sales:** Tel. 57 74 42 78. *Traditional methods are here employed in the production of this wine: a "good little bottle for Sunday lunch".*

Arcie (Château d')

→ Union de Producteurs

Grand Cru

Armens (Château d') → Bonnet

Arnaud de Jacquemeau (Château)

Commune: Saint-Emilion. **Proprietor:** Denis Dupuy. **Size of vineyard:** 4 hectares. **Average age of vines:** 45 years. **Varieties:** 25% cabernet-sauvignon. 55% merlot. 5% cabernet-franc. 15% malbec. **Production:** 8,000 bottles CB. **Visits:** Denis Dupuy. Tel. 57 24 73 09. **Direct sales and by mail order:** Denis Dupuy, Jacquemeau, 33330 Saint-Emilion. *Situated at the foot of the slope on the west side of Saint-Emilion, this estate's subsoil consists of sandy land on clay. An ancestral inheritance.*

Arthus (Château d')

Commune: Vignonet. **Proprietor:** Fournier Consorts. Director: Eric Fournier. Cellar master: Paul Cazenave. Consultant oenologist: G. Pauquet. **Size of vineyard:** 4.5 hectares. **Average age of vines:** 30 to 35 years. **Varieties:** mostly merlot. **Production:** 8,000 bottles CB. **Sales by mail order:** in France. S.E.V. Fournier, B.P. 28, 33330 Saint-Emilion. Tel. 57 24 70 79. **Retail sales:** Schröder & Schÿler.

It is out of family piety that the Fourniers continue to run this little property, along with the famous Château Canon which, as everybody knows, is a Saint-Emilion *Premier Grand Cru classé.* Darthus is a tiny locality of Vignonet but the name of the *cru* has always been written with an apostrophe. Eric Fournier reckons that he

Harvesting on the hill of Ausone.

makes a "good little wine" which is not too expensive. "Honesty first" is his publicity slogan. So any attempt to pass it off for what it is not is out of the question. This is sufficiently rare to be praised. However, no *vin de côte* will ever be produced from the vines of Vignonet.

Ausone (Château)

1er Grand Cru classé

Commune: Saint-Emilion. **Proprietors:** Madame Dubois-Challon & Vauthier Heirs. Cellar master: Marcel Lanau. Consultant oenologist: C.B.C. Libourne. **Size of vineyard:** 7.16 hectares. **Average age of vines:** 50 years. **Varieties:** 50% merlot. 50% cabernet-franc. **Production:** 30,000 bottles CB. **Visits:** Tel. 57 24 70 94 or 57 24 70 26. Direct sales and by mail order: in France Château Ausone. 33330 Saint-Emilion. **Retail sales:** through Bordeaux and Libourne.

"In the year 1783 on the seventeenth of October, Pierre Cantenat was born and baptized. He was the legitimate son of Jean Cantenat, a merchant cooper, and Jeanne Chatonnet, both inhabitants of La Madeleine, in the very place which is still today called Château Ausone. Godfather: Pierre Barat, uncle; godmother: Rose Malescot, an aunt from Brittany. Present: Michel and Elie Lacoste, who, being unable to sign, were witnesses through our intermediary. Vidal, priest." At the end of the eighteenth century, the idea of *cru* was slightly different from what it is today. The term "château" began to proliferate only after the classification of the wines of the Médoc and Sauternes, that is to say in the second half of the nineteenth century. Ausone is an exception. It is the only "château" of Saint-Emilion which dates from before the Second Empire. But this designation essentially applies to the dwelling, built in 1781 by Jean Cantenat, mentioned above. As for the wine, it bore the name of the locality it came from, together with that of the grower. So the Château Ausone of that period was called: Cantenat at La Madeleine. Whatever the case, Château Ausone has contemplated the hillside at Saint-Emilion for two centuries. Along with Beauséjour, Berliquet, Camfourtet (today, Clos Fourtet) and Canon, it is the most authentic of the historic *crus* of the "Haut Saint-Emilion". The respective destinies of Ausone and Bélair became united in 1916, when Jean Dubois-Challon bought the property from the Marignan family (see Bélair in the

Madame Dubois-Challon (on the left) personally supervises the quality of the grapes.

catalogue). But it is practically certain that there was confusion between the two during the preceding centuries. Historians prefer now the one, now the other. In the nineteenth century, Bélair was the most frequent to be cited at the head of the "first class" of Saint-Emilion. In 1850, Charles Cocks put Ausone in eleventh place. In 1868 it was fourth, behind Bélair, Troplong-Mondot and Canon. In 1886 it was second and, since the beginning of the century, Cocks and Féret have always put it at the top of the list. For several generations, the production of Ausone was minimal (in the order of 8 to 10 *tonneaux)* whereas the quality and the reputation of the *cru* were widely appreciated.

The estate is jointly owned by two branches of the Cantenat and Laffargue families which have descended side by side. The château is inhabited by Madame Jean Dubois-Challon, whose exquisite affability contributes to the charm of the place. But the Vauthier heirs are also to be found there, and in particular Alain, Marcel's son and the great-grandson of Edouard Dubois-Challon. Each of these two branches runs its own field of activity. Thus, Pascal Delbeck is only Madame Dubois-Challon's estate manager, whereas the Vauthiers look after their affairs themselves. The vineyard stretches unbroken round the château. Its land is typical: clayey chalk on a subsoil of Fronsac molasse with aeolian sand at the bottom of the hill. The slope provides natural drainage and gives rise to an erosion problem which is difficult to combat where the slope is steepest. Cultivation and vinification (in wooden vats) are traditional. Maturing in wood is in splendid cellars whose origins go back to the end of the sixteenth century when the Jurade of Saint-Emilion decided to restore the walls of the town by taking stones "from the rock under which lies the cemetery of La Magdelaine". The wines of Ausone are distinguished by their slender and elegant structure. They can become extremely subtle and sometimes surprise by their alcoholic strength, which makes one think of a fine Corton. With discreet but penetrating tannin, they perfectly illustrate a "wine from the hillsides" with delicate aromas and a "sunny" flavour. They can easily be distinguished from those of their rival Cheval-Blanc which are perfect examples of "wines from the gravel slopes". Their potential for ageing in the bottle is also surprising since they do not have a sturdy body, rather like those slender octogenarians who are always hale and hearty. No doubt the reason is due partly to an excellent resistance to oxidation and a level of volatile acidity which is sufficient to give vigour and vivacity without imposing its presence in a disagreeable manner. We can say that the wine of Ausone has a certain "eminence". That is normal for a wine from a hillside! We can also claim that "the very place which is still today called Château Ausone" does indeed correspond to the ancient villa of the famous Gallo-Roman poet although, to date, no historian has really settled the matter. But there is no need for archeological considerations to declare that the wine of Ausone is a great among the greats.

Austerlitz (Château)

Commune: Libourne. **Proprietor:** Gérard Audigay. Consultant oenologist: Gilles Pauquet. **Size of vineyard:** 6 hectares. **Average age of vines:** 40 years. **Varieties:** 25% cabernet-sauvignon. 50% merlot. 25% cabernet-franc. **Production:** 23 tonneaux. 1,000 bottles CB. **Direct sales and by mail order:** In France. Gérard Audigay, 170 avenue de l'Epinette, 33500 Libourne. Tel. 57 51 32 30. **Retail sales.** *Gérard Audigay not being the Napoleon of the vines, he will never know Waterloo.*

Aux Plantes (Clos)

Commune: Saint-Emilion. **Proprietor:** Gustave Venat. Director, vineyard manager and cellar master: Marie-Hélène Venat. Consultant oenologist: Michel Rolland. **Size of vineyard:** 0.77 hectares. **Average age of vines:** 10 years. **Varieties:** 10% cabernet-sauvignon. 80% merlot. 10% cabernet-franc. **Production:** 2,700 bottles CB. **Direct sales and by mail order:** In France. Clos aux Plantes, 33330 Saint-Emilion. Tel. 57 24 78 43. **Retail sales.** *The first harvest was in 1978. Harvesting is a family affair and is indeed a festive occasion. Several bottles remain for direct sales to a few customers.*

Badette (Château)

Grand Cru

Commune: Saint-Christophe-des-Bardes. **Proprietor:** William Arraud. Consultant oenologist: M. Chaine. **Size of vineyard:** 8.6 hectares. **Average age of vines:** 35 years. **Varieties:** 10% cabernet-sauvignon. 90% merlot. **Production:** 60,000 bottles CB. **Direct sales and by mail order:** In France and abroad. Château Badette, 33330 Saint-Christophe-des-Bardes. Tel. 57 74 42 13. **Retail sales:** a good three quarters of the production of this estate is sold through the trade.

During the course of the Second World War, Daniel Arraud saved the life of his friend who had been taken prisoner. A few years later in 1949, whilst he was walking in Saint-Emilion, William, his son, who was then a young apprentice mechanic, expressed the wish to work among vines and wines, like his father. But how to go about it? Daniel Arraud was a simple vigneron with no money behind him. The friend, a proprietor in Pomerol, came to hear of this and straight away advanced the money needed to buy Badette. Today, after the death of his father, William Arraud is at the head of the property. He keeps the name of his friend dark. But he welcomes with open arms any visitor who knocks at his door.

Badon (Clos)

Commune: Saint-Emilion. **Proprietor:** G.F.A. Badon Guérin. Director, estate manager, vineyard manager, manager and cellar master: Philippe Dugos. Consultant oenologist: M. Plomby. **Size of vineyard:** 8 hectares. **Average age of vines:** 25 years. **Varieties:** 20% cabernet-sauvignon. 40% merlot. 40% cabernet-franc. **Production:** 35,000 bottles CB. **Visits:** by appointment. Philippe Dugos. Tel. 57 24 71 03. **Direct sales and by mail order:** In France. Clos Badon, 33330 Saint-Emilion. **Retail sales.**

Clos Badon, at the foot of the hill of Pavie, was inherited by Philippe Dugos who, along with his wife, does everything from A to Z (to use his own terms). He is skilled in the use of the mechanical harvester which is quickly brought into service on the most suitable day of average maturity, and this at the lowest possible cost. He matures his wine in wood, for which he has calculated a depreciation period of eight years. And what is more, he has no cause for complaint, for he lacks wine rather than customers!

Badon Fleurus (Château)

Commune: Saint-Emilion. **Proprietor:** S.C.A. of Château Fouquet. Director, estate manager, vineyard manager and cellar master: Claude Mazière. **Size of vineyard:** 5 hectares. **Average age of vines:** 20 to 30 years. **Varieties:** 70% merlot. 30% cabernet-franc. **Production:** 30,000 bottles CB. **Retail sales:** through S.A.R.L. Mazière et Cie. Tel. 57 24 70 42. *Badon Fleurus seems to be a stand-by among Claude Mazière's numerous products. It was created in 1964.*

Badon la Garelle (Château)
→ *Peyrelongue*

Bagnols (Château) → *Viramon*

Baillarge (Château)

♈ ♈ ♈ ♈ ♈

Commune: Saint-Sulpice-de-Faleyrens. **Proprietor:** Michel Codognotto. Consultant oenologist: C.B.C. Libourne. **Size of vineyard:** 2.5 hectares. **Average age of vines:** 12 years. **Varieties:** 80% merlot. 20% cabernet-franc. **Production:** 13 tonneaux. **Retail sales:** in bulk. Tel. 57 24 77 91. *It seems that Michel Codognotto intends to sell his wine in the bottle. So much the better!*

sold in bulk

Balestard la Tonnelle (Château)

♈ ♈ ♈ ♈ ♈

Grand Cru classé

Commune: Saint-Emilion. **Proprietor:** G.F.A. Capdemourlin. Director and estate manager: Jacques Capdemourlin. Vineyard manager : Paul Jenck. Cellar master: Jean-Claude Bounias. Consultant oenologist: C.B.C. Libourne. **Size of vineyard:** 10.6 hectares. **Average age of vines:** 28 years. **Varieties:** 10% cabernet-sauvignon. 65% merlot. 20% cabernet-franc. 5% malbec. **Production:** 60,000 bottles CB. **Visits:** by appointment. Jacques Capdemourlin. Tel. 57 74 62 06. **Direct sales and by mail order:** in France. Jacques Capdemourlin, Château Roudier, Montagne, 33570 Lussac. **Retail sales:** through the Bordeaux trade. Exports: Belgium, Switzerland, Germany, Holland. Sole rights in the U.S.A.

"Wine is a form of human expression. You do not make it, you develop it." With each of his declarations, Jacques Capdemourlin exhales aestheticism just as a mignonette emits its lingering aroma. In 1963, after national service, this young man was torn between a natural inclination towards architecture and art school and a bond of fidelity to the vine-growing land that had been in the family for five centuries. He preferred to follow the second option, at the same time secretly reserving himself the right to allow the first one to have its say from time to time. It was in this way that he became a full-time grower and an experienced wine-maker. The architect lying dormant in him reveals itself in the structural work inside the house and cellars. In both these fields, his one concern is to "put the emphasis on the origins and their authenticity".

The origin of the name Balestard comes from a stout-hearted canon of Saint-Emilion who had a *penchant* for a bottle of this *cru*. He was not the only one. In the fifteenth century, the great French poet François Villon bewailed the fact that the nectar of Balestard was not within the reach of his purse:

"O Virgin pure, thou goddess chaste,
A seat in Heaven I sue;
Nor joy nor bliss on earth I taste:
Henceforth must I eschew
A costly wine of condign fame,
That blessèd Balestard by name...

"Bought but by men whom fortune crowns.
But I, poor and threadbare.
So if such wine in Heaven abounds,
Sweet Death, my soul now bear
Intrepid 'mongst the chosen throng,
This *cru* to sup for years endlong."

Could François Villon have imagined that four hundred years after his death, this wish expressed in his will would feature on the label of Château Balestard la Ton-

An old mill at Balestard. From Villon's time, perhaps?

nelle? Among those who have had the good fortune to taste this *cru* are people whose opinions are authoritative. When the Grand Jury chaired by Jacques Luxey was conducting one of its celebrated tastings, fourteen famous tasters placed Balestard in third place on an impressive list of the best wines of Saint-Emilion of the 1975 vintage. We should also quote the late Alexis Lichine's opinion when he wrote: "Among the seventy-two *Grands Crus,* there are two excellent ones which should merit promotion in the near future: Château Villemaurine and Château Balestard la Tonnelle." The wine lover who appreciates wine which has a good solid tannic base and a powerful structure owes it to himself to uncork a Balestard sooner or later.

Barail du Blanc

→ Union de Producteurs

Barberousse (Château)

Commune: Saint-Emilion. **Proprietor:** Jean Puyol. Consultant oenologist: Michel Rolland. **Size of vineyard:** 7 hectares. **Average age of vines:** 25 years. **Varieties:** 30% cabernet-sauvignon. 40% merlot. 30% cabernet-franc. **Production:** 58,000 bottles CB. **Direct sales and by mail order:** Tel. 57 24 74 24. **Retail sales:** Maison Lebègue. This name would sound appropriate in a drinking song.

Barberousse (Domaine de)

Commune: Saint-Emilion. **Proprietor:** Robert Chaubet. **Size of vineyard:** 0.59 hectares. **Average age of vines:** 22 years. **Varieties:** 20% cabernet-sauvignon. 80% merlot. **Production:** 4 to 5 tonneaux. **Visits:** 9 a.m. to 6 p.m. Robert Chaubet. Tel. 57 24 71 52. **Direct sales and by mail order:** in France and abroad. *A retired education inspector for the* département, *Robert Chaubet has taken up the torch of his father and adopted the Barberousse motto: "constant-healthy-good".*

Barbeyron (Château)

Grand Cru

Commune: St-Laurent-des-Combes. **Proprietor:** G.A.E.C. Bassilieaux Vineyards. Director and cellar master: Jean-Claude Bassilieaux. Estate and vineyard manager: Dominique Bassilieaux. Consultant oenologist: M. Hébrard. **Size of vineyard:** 7 hectares. **Average age of vines:** 35 years. **Varieties:** 75% merlot. 25% cabernet-franc. **Production:** 45,000 bottles CB. **Visits:** by appointment. G.A.E.C. Bassilieaux Vineyards, 33350 Saint-Magne-de-Castillon. Tel. 57 40 06 71. **Direct sales and by mail order:** in France and abroad (Switzerland, Belgium, West Germany, Great Britain).

In working gear, with his rough voice, and wearing a sailor's cap, Jean-Claude Bassilieaux is a man of the land and a man of action. As President of the Federation of the Côtes de Castillon, he protects the interests of the vineyards lovingly and honourably. The estate is run by the family. Before working on the vines, M. Bassilieaux was a nurseryman. Married at the age of twenty-one, he took his father-in-law's château in hand. At Saint-Magne where the Bassilieaux live, you can visit a modest but none the less very attractive cooperage museum whose tools have come down from his grandfather. The wine, ageing well, retains all its power.

Barde-Haut (Château)

Grand Cru

Commune: Saint-Christophe-des-Bardes. **Proprietor:** J.-C. Gasparoux. Consultant oenologist: Gilles Pauquet. **Size of vineyard:** 15.5 hectares. **Average age of vines:** 25 years. **Varieties:** 75% merlot. 25% cabernet-franc. **Production:** 70 tonneaux. 40,000 bottles CB. **Visits:** by appointment. J.-C. Gasparoux. Tel. 57 24 78 21. **Direct sales and by mail order.** *The buildings, set on the hillside, resemble a huge modern* bastide. *The wine has a deep colour, and is powerful with an agreeable hint of wood.*

Barrail des Graves (Château)

Commune: St-Sulpice-de-Faleyrens. **Proprietor:** G.A.E.C. Descrambe. Director and manager: Gérard Descrambe. Estate and vineyard manager: Philippe Fort. Consultant oenologist: Michel Rolland. **Size of vineyard:** 5.5 hectares. **Average age of vines:** 15 years. **Varieties:** 20% cabernet-sauvignon. 60% merlot. 15% cabernet-franc. 5% malbec. **Production:** 30,000 bottles CB. **Visits:** Tel. 57 74 94 77. **Direct sales and by mail order:** in France. Renaissance, Saint-Sulpice-de-Faleyrens, 33330 Saint-Emilion.

Gérard Descrambe alongside a label drawn by Reiser.

"What a fine Catholic he is!" This exclamation by Sancho Panza, as he was piously emptying a bottle, could equally well apply to Gérard Descrambe's personal collection. If, at Mouton, Philippe de Rothschild has had his labels designed by the greatest contemporary artists, Gérard Descrambe has acquired Rabelaisian illustrations, excellently executed by several famous humorists. Voltaire said: "On earth, the only serious thing I know is the cultivation of the vine". What the history of literature does not tell us is that "the old man of Ferney" was talking tongue in cheek when he recited his favourite apophthegm. Gérard Descrambe carries out his job as vigneron with absolute conscientiousness, but gladly consecrates the fruits of his labours to Bacchus, following the example of Ronsard:

"Fail not to grace this joyous fête,
O Bacchus, god of wine;
Our laughter gay we dedicate
And revels: all are thine."

The wines of Gérard Descrambe are ecological and theological. They treat effectively and respectively galloping consumption and chronic hypochondria.

Barry (Château du)

Grand Cru

Commune: Saint-Sulpice-de-Faleyrens. **Proprietor:** Noël Mouty. **Size of vineyard:** 8 hectares. **Average age of vines:** 40 years. **Varieties:** 10% cabernet-sauvignon. 80% merlot. 10% cabernet-franc. **Production:** 45,000 bottles CB. **Direct sales and by mail order:** in France and abroad. Noël Mouty, Château du Barry, Saint-Sulpice-de-Faleyrens, 33330 Saint-Emilion. **Retail sales.** *Held in unbroken line since before the First World War - 1911 to be precise - this* cru *has always lived up to the standards that it sets for itself.*

Basque (Château du)

→ Union de Producteurs

Grand Cru

Béard (Château)

Grand Cru

Commune: Saint-Laurent-des-Combes. **Proprietors:** Goudichaud Heirs. Consultant oenologist: M. Chaine. **Size of vineyard:** 8 hectares. **Average age of vines:** 30 years. **Varieties:** 65% merlot. 35% cabernet-franc. **Direct sales and by mail order:** in France and abroad. Belgium, Denmark. Château Béard. Tel. 57 24 72 96. **Retail sales:** through the Bordeaux trade.

Château Béard is an elegant dwelling dating from 1858 situated in the centre of Saint-Laurent-des-Combes. On January 1, 1983, Madame Corinne Dubos and her sister Véronique Goudichaud inherited the estate on the death of their father, who himself had inherited it from his father. Corinne Dubos, a young proprietor of dynamic approach, runs it. "I like to be in charge", she says with a composed smile. Before looking after vines, she used to sell wines of Saint-Emilion to the Circle of the Friends of the Vignerons. This experience enabled her to get to know French and foreign clients better. The vines are not treated with weed-killer. Harvesting is done by hand in a friendly atmosphere, and gradually *barriques* will replace the huge old vats in the cellars. The wine sometimes smells of violets.

Béard La Chapelle (Château)

Grand Cru

Commune: St-Laurent-des-Combes. **Proprietors:** Richard Moureau and Isabelle Desveaux. Estate manager, vineyard manager and manager: Richard Moureau. Consultant oenologist: C.B.C. Libourne. **Size of vineyard:** 15.5 hectares. **Average age of vines:** 30 years. **Varieties:** 5% cabernet-sauvignon. 80% merlot. 15% cabernet-franc. **Production:** 86,000 bottles CB. **Visits:** by appointment. R. Moureau. Tel. 56 52 21 46. **Direct sales and by mail order:** in France and abroad. R. Moureau, 11 rue de Marseille, 33000 Bordeaux. **Retail sales:** sole rights for Belgium and Denmark. The firm of Bordeaux Tradition.

Looking south down the road which runs along the hillsides and leads to Saint-Laurent-des-Combes, Béard La Chapelle has been a family estate for many generations. Traces of a cemetery have been found on the estate, whence the name "La Chapelle". The name of the little locality is called Béard, which perhaps does not quite justify the use of the illustration of the monolithic church of Saint-Emilion on the label. In 1980, when M. Armand Moureau was about to retire, he asked his son if he would take over. And so it was that at the age of thirty eight, Richard Moureau came back to the land. Supple, round and well-balanced, the wine has a nose of red fruits.

Beau-Mayne (Château) 🍶

→ *Couvent des Jacobins*

Beaurang (Château)

Commune: Saint-Emilion. **Proprietor:** Claude Puyol. Consultant oenologist: M. Chaine. **Size of vineyard:** 8.3 hectares. **Average age of vines:** 30 years. **Varieties:** 20% cabernet sauvignon, 60% merlot. 20% cabernet franc. **Production:** 40 tonneaux. 20,000 bottles CB. **Visits:** by appointment. Tel. 57 24 73 31. **Direct sales and by mail order:** in France. **Retail sales:** through the Bordeaux trade. *Father, mother, son and daughter-in-law run this vineyard without any outside help. Modern machinery and vat-house simplify the work.*

Beauséjour (Château)

1er Grand Cru classé

Commune: Saint-Emilion. **Proprietors:** Duffau-Lagarrosse Heirs. Estate manager: Jean-Michel Dubos. Cellar master: Bernard Oizeau. Consultant oenologist: Michel Rolland. **Size of vineyard:** 6.8 hectares. **Average age of vines:** 30 years. **Varieties:** 25% cabernet-sauvignon. 50% merlot. 25% cabernet-franc. **Production:** 35,000 bottles CB. **Visits:** by appointment. Tel. 57 24 71 62. **Direct sales and by mail order:** in France. **Retail sales:** (brokerage office in Belgium).

Trouble-free peoples have no history, nor have unharrassed proprietors. Certainly at Beauséjour all is order, peace, discretion, calm and stability. "We dislike flashy

Beauséjour Duffau-Lagarrosse: continuity triumphs.

publicity", whisper the Duffau-Lagarrosse Heirs, rather like a song learned off by heart a long time ago and intoned unaccompanied. This declaration of faith does not prevent them from having multi-coloured leaflets published on fine art-paper with views of bottles standing against a background of old stonework and rose trees... and from writing, for example: "In this way, the Heirs have managed to preserve for their vineyard its very long-standing fame among the most renowned *crus* of Saint-Emilion." I wonder why I think at this moment of Mauriac?

The estate has been in the family for more than 150 years. It was Toussaint Troquart who founded the genealogical line. Since 1847, the tree has been as straight as a yew and the Heirs (these latter seem to be particularly keen on the capital letter) have formed themselves into a limited company in order to create a better solidarity amongst themselves to resist the passing of time. Permanence and maintenance are the life-blood of Beauséjour (Duffau-Lagarrosse). The visitor will always be received most warmly and will be allowed to taste the most recent vintages at any time of the day. Jean-Michel Dubos, the estate manager, will be a knowledgeable and discreet guide. You will have a certain shivering impression of entering the heart of a secret sect, this feeling being even slightly intensified by the crypts hewn out of stone which serve as cellars for the bottles. But once you have been taken into the holy of holies, you can taste the most traditional, authentic and "ancestral" of all the wines of the Haut Saint-Emilion. It is from that moment, that you will indeed wish to show respect.

Beau-Séjour Bécot (Château)

1er Grand Cru classé

Commune: Saint-Emilion. **Proprietors:** Bécot & Fils. Director: Michel Bécot. Estate and vineyard manager: Dominique Bécot. Cellar master: Gérard Bécot. Consultant oenologist: Michel Rolland. **Size of vineyard:** 15 hectares. **Average age of vines:** 30 to 40 years. **Varieties:** 70% merlot. 30% cabernet-franc. **Production:** 70,000 bottles CB. **Visits:** by appointment. Tel. 57 74 46 87 or 57 24 61 60, daily. **Direct sales. Retail sales:** through the Bordeaux trade.

If you skim through the voluminous dossier of Beau-Séjour Bécot with a critical eye, you will be struck by the confusion between two words - a confusion resembling a typographical error and the fact of its being so ordinary would give rise to a smile had it not had such calamitous consequences for Michel Bécot and his children. For at the time of the last revision of the classification of the *crus* of Saint-Emilion, Château Beau-Séjour Bécot which was alphabetically at the head of the list of the Premiers Grands Crus classés, just after the super-greats, Ausone and Cheval-Blanc, found itself ignominiously downgraded into the cohort of the simple "crus classés"; rather as if a colonel were to be made a major. So what is the trouble? Constancy or consistency *(constance or consistance),* that is the question. Article number 6 of the rules concerning the classification, published by the *Journal officiel* of January 13, 1984, stipulates: "The commission bases its judgement on all factors which can be taken into consideration to justify or to annul the classification and among which can be cited in particular:

– **Consistency** of the property both as regards its size and qualitative characteristics;
– Marketing, presentation, reputation, range of promotional activities and sale price, **constancy** and quality of the wines submitted to testing along with others by tasting samples."

On February 14, 1985, the Viticultural and Agricultural Federation of Saint-Emilion

distributed worldwide to 300 journalists the "Provisional list of the châteaux in the classification of the *crus* of Saint-Emilion". This publication anticipated the official ratification of the new classification. It was at the very least over-hasty for the commission's opinion had to remain confidential until the signatures of the Minister of Agriculture and the Minister of Commerce had been appended. But it was accompanied by an explanatory letter which specified: "This latest revision conforms to an extremely precise set of rules; it is a charter of reference. The principal criteria are:
- Constancy of the property, both as regards its size and qualitative characteristics.
- Marketing, presentation (...) **constancy** and quality of the wines submitted to testing along with others by tasting samples".

Inasmuch as the Viticultural Federation of Saint-Emilion takes on its own shoulders all the terms of the official ruling, the use of the word "constancy" instead of the word "consistency" appears to be a serious oversight. For the consistency of a property means its being at the same time as its cohesion and its size, but not necessarily the unalterableness of its size. As to the consistency of the wine's quality, it is perfectly obvious that in this respect it is important to be constant! I know many a great *cru classé* in the Médoc which has carried out major surgery on its different parcels of land and which, notwithstanding considerable changes in the surface area both as regards dimension and the nature of the soil, has improved the qualitative consistency of its products. As I wrote in my book devoted to the Margaux appellation: "If it were necessary to deal the cards again to reform the 'hands' of 1855, the date of the famous classification, the viticultural Land Register would risk implosion. The numerous exchanges, mutations and acquisitions should be regarded as continuing improvements over the generations."

When Michel Bécot bought Château Beau-Séjour from Doctor Fagouet in 1969, he agreed to relinquish three hectares to the Boüard brothers to pacify Château L'Angélus. But he was already in possession through family inheritances of a good four hectares at La Carte, on the plateau of Saint-Martin, which largely compensated for the land forgeone at Mazerat both in surface area and in agrological quality. In 1979, he bought four and a half hectares at the side of his property on the plateau of Les Trois Moulins. That set tongues wagging in the area, for the price was extremely high, but Michel Bécot was aware that he was giving his estate a certain consistency by adding land of good quality, which history had recognized as belonging to the "first class". At the time, no official body turned a hair and Château Beau-Séjour Bécot continued to receive its certificates as and when necessary, approving it as a *Premier Grand Cru classé*. It seems that the downgrading of Beau-Séjour Bécot is an *a posteriori* sanction against an honest grower prudently managing his *cru*. It appears that no geological survey of the lands in question has been undertaken. The I.N.A.O. justifies its action, noting that "the absorbed land originally belonged to two *crus* which do not feature in the official list of the *Premiers Grands Crus classés*". Louis Orizet, the honorary inspector general for the I.N.A.O., spontaneously defended Michel Bécot, writing to him: "Your experience illustrates the dangers of including subjective criteria in the charter of the AOCs. This, among others, was one of the reasons for my premature resignation from the I.N.A.O. How can a *cru* of long-standing fame such as yours be disqualified and at the same time, a cohort of VDQS, which are technological wines and not wines from authentic and precise terrains, be admitted into the circle?" It should be said

Beau-Séjour Bécot: a splendid citadel, sheltering one of the best wines of the area.

that there is no text governing the expansion of a *cru*. The professor of law, Dominique Denis, has liberal views about such licence: "Legally speaking, nothing is to stop a château from expanding, even from moving about within the limits of the generic AOC, without losing the right to its qualification as a Saint-Emilion *Grand Cru, Grand Cru classé* or *Premier Grand Cru classé*, if it continues to meet the qualitative conditions required by law." It seems unthinkable to block any change or increase in land ownership which is beneficial to the rational production of a wine of quality by re-organization and consolidation of certain parcels of land. Of course if the proprietor of a *Premier Grand Cru classé* of Saint-Emilion were to start to produce wine on the plain, at Vignonet for example, there would be cause to make comment. But to annex a small parcel of land of less than five hectares lying by the side of the original vineyard and geologically irreproachable is an intelligent act which is of considerable benefit to the property economically. I have already had occasion to write that, before being great by reputation, a *cru* should be great

in respect of its total size. This means that the grower is free to spread out his different varieties judiciously, to plan re-planting in steady rotation to maintain an optimum age for the vines, to stagger the depreciation of his investments in the various installations and equipment as well as possible and to have at his disposal a choice of different vats to allow a selection policy. How I would have liked to know the opinion of Professor Enjalbert, who wrote: 'So the legislator will be obliged to seek in the delimitation of the different terrains a basic guarantee and to define in agrological terms what is meant by a vine-growing terrain of good quality.' In my book on Chablis, I call this doctrine "geo-viticulture". Today, we have extremely sophisticated investigation methods. No censor can claim to make or unmake the reputation of our *crus* from a basis of superficial allegations and say-so.

But at the end of the day, there is the wine to be tasted. The "sensory" control of quality as applied by the Federation of Saint-Emilion and the I.N.A.O. did not present all the guarantees of seriousness and efficacy which were to be expected.

After his downgrading, Michel Bécot sportingly proposed a blind tasting of the twelve *Premiers Grands Crus classés* covering different vintages. Of course, no-one accepted the challenge. And it is well known that several times his *cru* came out at the head or among the first few in similar tests. Inasmuch as I have tasted them carefully and impartially, I find that the last ten vintages of Beau-Séjour Bécot are entirely up to its reputation. This judgement is shared by many enlightened experts, among whom I will name Professor Emile Peynaud, the late Alexis Lichine and Hugh Johnson. In their authoritative works, the last two acknowledge the way Michel Bécot and his sons have restored the "tarnished reputation" of Beau-Séjour Bécot since they took over from the ineffable Doctor Fagouet.

So there we have the substance of the matter. As for the form, it seems to me that the Federation has not shown itself in its correct rôle. If the Bécots had committed a grave error, even an enormous blunder, the executive board would have had the right and duty to sanction them in an appropriate way and as far as possible without publicity. But it was a curious way of wanting to appear to be of irreproachable conduct and have a blameless image, to help to shoot down in flames one of its most illustrious members (Michel Bécot was the president of the said Federation from 1976 to 1979). This the more true in that the said Federation has not set an example of thorough rigidity. The board, in a meeting on October 12, 1985 (at the height of a thunderstorm), stipulated that "as the representative and protector of the profession's interests, the Federation has the duty to safeguard the fairness and correct procedure of the classification which it has instigated". Previously, on May 2, the same board declared itself "not qualified" to deal with M. Bécot's complaint. And, as we have seen further back, on February 14, it had published the new classification as a *fait accompli*. But the legislator had clearly stipulated that "the use of the terms *Grand Cru classé* or *Premier Grand Cru classé* is reserved for vine growing properties which have been granted an official classification, approved jointly by a decree of the Minister of Agriculture and the Secretary of State for Consumer Affairs, **after notification of the Federation concerned** on the proposition of the I.N.A.O. It was at the meetings of June 6 and 7 (that is nearly four months after the publication of the classification list) that the National Committee of the I.N.A.O perceived that "there was an essential element lacking in the dossier: **the formal notification of the federation concerned** as required by article 7 in paragraph 1 of the decree of January 11, 1984". It needed a waiting period lasting right up to the month of October for the "formal notification" to be given in favour by the board of the Federation. From it, I note "that the facts taken into consideration by the latter (the Commission) and the way the general procedure took place guarantee the promotion of *crus* of high quality". What about those downgraded? Would this perverse statement tend to mean that the guarantee is placed unilaterally on the side of those promoted? I read an implicit admission into this text and the Federation of Saint-Emilion which, in other respects, has outstanding merits, has in my view, been guilty of **inconsistency**.

If I were the Minister of Agriculture, I would say that the Saint-Emilion classification is highly irregular in both the spirit and the letter... from A to Z. Moreover, I would invite the Crédit Agricole to reimburse the interest paid by the Bécot family on the stocks unsold for a year. And I would award the Croix du Mérite Agricole to Michel Bécot to try to help him forget the torments of the purgatory he has suffered and to encourage him to continue to give wine lovers all over the world one of the twelve best wines of the distinguished terrain of Saint-Emilion. The most remarkable thing in the whole of this sorry tale is that Michel Bécot retains the morale of a warrior and the smile of an archangel.

Beau Vallon (Château du) ♟ → *Brun*

Bélair (Château)

1er Grand Cru classé

Commune: Saint-Emilion. **Proprietor:** Madame Helyett Dubois-Challon. Estate manager and vineyard manager: Pascal Delbeck. Cellar master: Marcel Laneau. Consultant oenologist: C.B.C. Libourne. **Size of vineyard:** 13 hectares. **Average age of vines:** 35 years. **Varieties:** 60% merlot. 40% cabernet-franc. **Production:** 60,000 bottles CB. **Visits:** tel. 57 24 70 94. **Direct sales and by mail order. Retail sales:** through the Bordeaux trade.

"Château Bélair is the Château Lafite of Saint-Emilion." This was how in 1867 A. Danflou affirmed the superiority of Bélair, formerly known by the name of Canolle. I have always liked observing the fortunes of words when they pass from one language to another. We know for example that "tennis" is the English pronounciation of the French imperative form "tenez" when the high-born used to play *jeu de paume* (real tennis). Another example is the area in London called the "Elephant and Castle" which takes its name from an inn which is today no longer in existence, whose signboard read "A l'Infante de Castille". For Bélair, the deformation has been inverted, for the venerable *cru* of Canolle, pronounced with a regional accent, takes its name from the seneschal Robert Knolles, the governor of Guienne (Aquitaine, English translation) under the orders of the English crown during the Hundred Years War. It was he who received Bertrand Du Guesclin's sword at the Battle of Auray in 1364. After the Battle of Castillon, the Canolles decided to stay in their adoptive province and they integrated into the nobility of Bordeaux whose fearsome fate they shared under the Reign of Terror. Several of

Until the beginning of this century, Bélair was put at the top of the Saint-Emilions.

them emigrated. Bélair was seized and sold, but the family recovered it during the Empire. At the same time the Goudichau family remained as estate managers of the property. Then, the daughter of the Marquis Victor de Canolle, Léontine, married Baron de Marignan, bringing Bélair with her as her dowry. The name of the *cru* then became "Bélair de Marignan". In 1850, Charles Cocks put Bélair at the head of the "Premiers Crus" of Saint-Emilion. For more than half a century, successive editions of *Bordeaux et ses vins* kept it in this position. In 1916, the family of Seissan de Marignan sold the estate to Edouard Dubois-Challon, who wanted particularly to ensure the promotion of his Château Ausone. Bélair then conformed to alphabetical order and it was probably at the express wish of the proprietor that Cocks and Féret wrote in their 9th edition (1922): "Formerly we had put Château Bélair at the head of the *crus* of Saint-Emilion. The quite exceptional and constant quality achieved by Château Ausone which results in the prices indicated further up obliges us to put this *cru* in the lead; but we consider the *cru* of Château Bélair quite as highly and it has in no way lost its worthy image thereby." In placing Ausone above Bélair, Dubois-Challon ensured a firm foothold for his ascent up the "hillside".

For centuries, the subsoil of Bélair's plateau was an important source for quarrying stone. The former owners of the château had had several support pillars marked as a guide through the labyrinth. It is said that there was direct access to the monolithic church by an underground passage. Today, Bélair has splendid cellars, which means that the wine ages under the very vines which have produced it. As to its quality, Bélair may be said to have suffered an eclipse in recent decades. None the less, the work carried out by Pascal Delbeck today is helping to restore its reputation. The style is entirely typical of a "wine from the hillsides": fine, rather light and sinewy, with a rose petal finish.

Bel-Air La Gravière (Château)   ♟♟♟♟♟

Commune: Libourne. **Proprietors:** M. and Madame René Lemoine. Consultant oenologist: Gilles Pauquet. **Size of vineyard:** 0.81 hectares. **Average age of vines:** 20 years. **Varieties:** 20% cabernet-sauvignon. 80% merlot. **Production:** 3 tonneaux. Tel. 57 51 48 55.

It was in 1957 that Robert Guillot, Madame René Lemoine's father, bought this property whose history can be traced back right to the middle of the eighteenth century. At that time, there was a royal pottery on the site. The estate has a microproduction exclusively reserved for the use of the family or friends.

Bel-Air Ouÿ (Château)
→ *Union de Producteurs*

Grand Cru

Belle Assise Coureau (Château)

Commune: Saint-Sulpice-de-Faleyrens. **Proprietor:** Yvan Brun. Consultant oenologist: Grézillac Laboratory. **Size of vineyard:** 13.2 hectares. **Average age of vines:** 15 to 30 years. **Varieties:** 30% cabernet-sauvignon. 60% merlot. 10% cabernet-franc. **Production:** 60,000 bottles CB. **Visits:** 8 a.m. to 7 p.m. daily. Yvan Brun. Tel. 57 24 61 62. **Direct sales and by mail order:** in France and abroad. *Belle Assise Coureau is an attractive estate in a single parcel which owes its name to a shallow vein of chalk, unusual in the plain.*

Bellefont-Belcier (Château)

Grand Cru

Commune: Saint-Laurent-des-Combes. **Proprietor:** S.C.I. of Château Bellefont-Belcier. Director and cellar master: Jean Labusquière. Vineyard manager: M. Nachit. Consultant oenologist: M. Chaine. **Size of vineyard:** 13 hectares. **Average age of vines:** 25 years. **Varieties:** 10% cabernet-sauvignon. 70% merlot. 20% cabernet-franc. **Production:** 60,000 bottles CB. **Visits:** by appointment. Jean Labusquière. Tel. 57 24 72 16. **Direct sales and by mail order:** in France and abroad. **Retail sales:** through Bordeaux and Libourne.

The dispute between ancient and modern has been settled. At Bellefont-Belcier, harvesting is done by machine. In the same spirit of "modern oenology", the wine will never have the slightest glimpse of wood. The result is a considerable evolution in the character of the *cru* relative to its former style, very classical, which had none the less earned it a good reputation. The property is graced by a charming manor house and by a quite unusual circular vat-house. The visitor can also admire plane-trees more than three hundred years old. The wine lover can appreciate the wines, which have a pronounced, youthful taste of fruit.

Bellegrave (Château)

Commune: Vignonet. **Proprietor:** G.F.A. of the Dangin Heirs. Director: G.A.E.C. of Château Bellegrave. Manager: Xavier Dangin. Consultant oenologist: Grézillac Laboratory. **Size of vineyard:** 12.5 hectares. **Average age of vines:** 25 years. **Varieties:** 30% cabernet-sauvignon. 55% merlot. 15% cabernet-franc. **Production:** 40,000 bottles CB. **Visits:** Xavier Dangin. Tel. 57 84 53 01. **Direct sales and by mail order. Retail sales.** *This cru can be justifiably considered as one of the best in the commune and really deserves its "three glasses".*

Bellegrave-Jaumard (Château)

Commune: Vignonet. **Proprietor:** André Boisseau. Tenant, vineyard manager and cellar master: Gilberte Gintrac. Consultant oenologist: M. Hébrard. **Size of vineyard:** 1.59 hectares. **Average age of vines:** 30 years. **Varieties:** 75% merlot. 25% cabernet-franc. **Production:** 1,200 bottles CB. **Sales by mail order:** Tel. 57 84 67 25. **Retail sales:** through the Bordeaux trade. *Madame Gilberte Gintrac is an extremely dynamic person who looks after the vines and makes her wine all according to the best traditions.*

Belle Rose (Clos)

Commune: Libourne. **Proprietors:** Jean-Pierre and François Faurie. **Size of vineyard:** 0.78 hectares. **Varieties:** 70% merlot. 20% cabernet-franc. 10% cabernet-sauvignon. **Production:** 2,000 bottles CB. **Direct sales and by mail order:** in France. François and Jean-Pierre Faurie, 13 boulevard de Garderose, 33500 Libourne. Tel. 57 74 07 03. **Retail sales through the trade:** sole rights in Belgium held by Maison Rodrigues in Zele.

This is a jewel set in the town, within the square formed by Avenue François-Mauriac and Rue Pierre-et-Marie-Curie in Libourne. Its proprietor, M. Jean-Pierre Faurie, is a photo-engraver by profession, a specialist in labels. His own label is modestly distinguished. It often adorns remarkable bottles which deserve to be discovered but which are not for everybody. Those who like the easy pleasures of modern vinification run a high risk of being disappointed. Those rare people privileged to have the chance of being able to buy one or two cases and who have the prudence to wait for several years before opening a bottle... they are the ones who will be rewarded a hundredfold, if indeed one can calculate the real value of such a high return in investment.

Bellevue (Château)

Grand Cru classé

Commune: Saint-Emilion. **Proprietor:** S.C. of Château Bellevue. Director: René de Coninck. Consultant oenologist: Michel Rolland. **Size of vineyard:** 6 hectares. **Average age of vines:** 25 years. **Varieties:** 70% merlot. 30% cabernet-franc. **Production:** 36,000 bottles CB. **Visits:** tel. 57 51 06 07. **Direct sales and by mail order. Retail sales:** through Libourne.

The Coninck family has long-standing and very close ties with the wine/vine economy of the Libourne area. M. René de Coninck is the chairman of the company which owns the six hectares of old land under vines. If we are to believe an engraved plaque on one of the walls of the Saint-Emilion town hall, Bellevue was formerly a *Premier Cru classé* of the commune, a position confirmed by the nineteenth century editions of *Bordeaux et ses vins*, including Charles Cocks who, in 1850, put it in fifteenth place. "Be in the classification? Whatever for?" - murmurs René de Coninck - "it would only serve to increase my taxes and it would not make a better wine. Moreover, any classification is made by the customer. I work for him because it is he who buys my wine." That is the voice of common sense and pragmatism. The wine of Bellevue has a fine colour and a subtle bouquet.

Bellevue Figeac (Château)

Grand Cru

Commune: Saint-Emilion. **Proprietor:** Jacques de Coninck. **Tel.** 57 51 98 02. **Size of vineyard:** 5.54 hectares. **Average age of vines:** 22 years. **Varieties:** 25% cabernet-sauvignon. 75% merlot. **Production:** 33 tonneaux. **Retail sales:** through Paris. *It seems that, in terms of production, too much has been asked of this vineyard!*

Belle-Vue Puyblanquet (Château)

Commune: Saint-Etienne-de-Lisse. **Proprietor:** Eliane Garnier. Vineyard manager and cellar master: Christian Garnier. Consultant oenologist: M. Chaine. **Size of vineyard:** 4.5 hectares. **Average age of vines:** 15 years. **Varieties:** 80% merlot. 20% cabernet-franc. **Production:** 30,000 bottles CB. **Visits:** tel. 57 40 35 18. **Direct sales and by mail order. Retail sales.** *He is a long-distance lorry driver. She meanwhile is the owner. They are both nice people. Their wine is agreeable.*

Bellile-Mondotte (Château)

Grand Cru

Commune: Saint-Laurent-des-Combes. **Proprietor:** G.F.A. Escure Heirs. Manager: Pierre Escure. Consultant oenologist: M. Pauquet. **Size of vineyard:** 4.5 hectares. **Average age of vines:** 25 years. **Varieties:** 60% merlot. 20% cabernet-franc. 20% cabernet-sauvignon. **Production:** 26,000 bottles CB. **Sales by mail order:** in France and abroad. G.F.A. Héritiers Escure, 54 rue Jean-Jaurès, 33500 Libourne. Tel. 57 51 07 59. **Retail sales:** through the trade in Bordeaux and Libourne. *A good* cru *in the little classical bourgeois style which produces agreeable wines that are easy to drink.*

Belregard-Figeac (Château) 🍷
→ *La Pignonne*

Benitey (Château)

→ *Union de Producteurs*

Bergat (Château)

Grand Cru classé

Commune: Saint-Emilion. **Proprietor:** Madame Clausse-Bertin. Managed by: Philippe Castéja. **Size of vineyard:** 3 hectares. **Average age of vines:** 20 years. **Varieties:** 15% cabernet-sauvignon. 60% merlot. 25% cabernet-franc. **Production:** 12 tonneaux. **Retail sales:** Ets. Borie-Manoux, 85 cours Balguerie-Stuttenberg, 33082 Bordeaux.

"The site of Château Bergat is one of the most picturesque, and from the height of its charming terrace, you look down over the valley of the Dordogne merging into one vast blue horizon, a superb backcloth for the distinguished vineyards of the surroundings, such as Château Ausone and Château Pavie." After this poetry from the beginning of the century, greatly inspired by the blue skyline of the Vosges, the *Revue vinicole* goes on: "It is one of the greatest among the great." But out of all the encomia addressed to Bergat, the most moving is doubtless the following, composed by a friend who had lost his sight and who wrote this acrostic:

> "**B**ergat, when I climb up thy hill from the wold,
> "**E**'en through my dark night thy fair walls I behold.
> "**R**eal yet a dream! Of thy grapes growing here
> "**G**leams e'er in my mind their rich hue without peer.
> "**A**nd so will I sing of this Saint-Emilion,
> "**T**hy *cru* which besotted our great poet Villon."

Philippe Castéja, the tenant of Madame Clausse-Bertin (whose family has owned Bergat for more than a hundred years), should try to get this *cru* better known, for despite its slender production, it deserves to be appreciated by a great number of wine lovers.

Berliquet (Château)

Grand Cru classé

Commune: Saint-Emilion. **Proprietors:** Viscount and Viscountess Patrick de Lesquen. Director: Patrick de Lesquen. Cellar master: Pierre Chaumet. Consultant oenologist: M. Callède (Coutras). **Size of vineyard:** 8.73 hectares. **Average age of vines:** 25 years. **Varieties:** 10% cabernet-sauvignon. 75% merlot. 15% cabernet-franc. **Production:** 45,000 bottles CB. **Visits possible. Retail sales:** *cave coopérative.*

"The estate's setting is one of the most attractive in Saint-Emilion. The château is in the finest discreet style of the eighteenth century. There are immense underground

After a generation in shadow, Berliquet is a brillant cru classé.

quarries which can in part be visited. The cellars are on two levels, one at ground level and the other underground. The gardens and the park have that charm of ancient residences. As you wander about, you can see wide horizons on every side, the plateau dominating the contour of Mazerat and the plain of the valley of the Dordogne. The green oak trees and the old windmill all announce in their own way a predominating Mediterranean climate at Berliquet whose vineyard and château carry their two hundred and twenty-five years magnificently well." This quotation is taken from the personal survey made by Professor Enjalbert. His memorandum on Château Berliquet was an influential element in the dossier for the classification of the *cru* at the time of the recent revision.

When Viscount Patrick de Lesquen decided to become a member of the *cave coopérative* of Saint-Emilion in 1953, the wine aristocrats of Saint-Emilion turned up their noses and the jungle telegraph of Libourne and the Chartrons pulled a long face. Berliquet among the anonymous flock of viticulturalists! Fifteen doleful years passed and then, little by little, Berliquet planted again, Berliquet bought equipment to make wine, Berliquet fitted out its cellars for ageing, in short, Berliquet lined itself up with the greatest *crus*. Under the enlightened management of Jacques-Antoine Baugier, the director of the *cave coopérative*, Château Berliquet equipped itself with a rational programme. In 1978, that is after twenty-five years of exile, the *cru*'s grapes took the road leading to its own vat-house and Viscount de Lesquen began to groom his request for a classification. He none the less remained firmly bound to the *cave coopérative,* of which he was the director and which would look after the marketing side after bottling the wine at the château. The jury for the new classification approved the venture and in fact Berliquet was the only one to be elected, whereas seven crowned heads fell. I do not make judgement here on those refused. But I consider that the rehabilitation of Berliquet is right and proper. When a viscount-banker and the director of a *coopérative* decide to work intelligently together, lovers of Berliquet are delighted.

Bertinat Lartigue (Château)

Commune: Saint-Sulpice-de-Faleyrens. **Proprietor:** Richard Dubois. Vineyard manager: Claude Dal-Piccol. Oenologists: Richard Dubois and Danielle Cugerone. **Size of vineyard:** 8 hectares. **Average age of vines:** 30 years. **Varieties:** 4% cabernet-sauvignon. 86% merlot. 10% cabernet-franc. **Production:** 15,000 bottles CB. **Visits:** Monday - Friday: 8 a.m. to noon and 2 p.m. to 7.30 p.m. Saturdays: tel. 57 24 72 75. **Direct sales and by mail order:** in France. **Retail sales:** 20% in bulk bottled by the trade for Japan and the United States. Variable quantities sold in the bottle.

Richard Dubois and his wife are both accomplished oenologists. That is to say that scientific knowledge has combined with experience acquired over the preceding generations. The family estate has just celebrated its hundredth anniversary and seems set to enjoy a renaissance. For the years to come, the Dubois are to steer their policy towards a rigorous selection of vats and the creation of a "Grand Cru" label, so expanding bottle sales. The recent vintages of their wine demonstrates that this course of action is well-founded. The 1980s have indeed seen years of exceptional sunshine which have allowed their very large proportion of merlot to reach a level of perfect maturity. Château Bertinat Lartigue is certainly a name to remember.

Bézineau (Château)

Commune: Saint-Emilion. **Proprietor:** Marguerite Faure. Consultant oenologist: Gilles Pauquet. **Size of vineyard:** 8.2 hectares. **Average age of vines:** 30 years. **Varieties:** 5% cabernet-sauvignon. 70% merlot. 25% cabernet-franc. **Production:** 30 tonneaux. 3,000 bottles. **Direct sales and by mail order:** Château Bézineau, 33300 Saint-Emilion. Tel. 57 24 72 50. **Retail sales:** in bulk, delivered at the time for bottling. *The Faure family has been at Bézineau for more than a hundred and fifty years. The réserve wine of the château ages in the wood.*

Bigaroux (Château)

Grand Cru

Commune: Saint-Sulpice-de-Faleyrens. **Proprietor:** Bernard Dizier. **Size of vineyard:** 23 hectares. **Average age of vines:** 20 years. **Varieties:** 18% cabernet-sauvignon. 60% merlot. 18% cabernet-franc. 4% malbec. **Production:** 100,000 bottles CB. **Visits:** Bernard Dizier. Tel. 57 24 71 97. **Direct sales and by mail order:** in France. *This is a relatively large estate, which is also relatively unknown to the French market: the reason is that ninety per cent of its production is bought directly by foreign distributors.*

Billeron-Bouquey (Château) 🛡 → Pailhas

Billerond (Château) 🏚
→ Union de Producteurs

Bois de Plince (Château)

Commune: Libourne. **Proprietor:** Jean-Claude Veyssière. Consultant oenologist: Gilles Pauquet. **Size of vineyard:** 2.5 hectares. **Average age of vines:** 30 years. **Varieties:** 15% cabernet-sauvignon. 70% merlot. 15% cabernet-franc. **Production:** 8,400 bottles CB. **Direct sales:** tel. 57 51 33 10. **Retail sales:** for export. *Cultivation and vinification are carried out in the most traditional way. The result is most commendable.*

Boisredon Grand Corbin (Château)

Commune: Saint-Emilion. **Proprietor:** Marcel Tartarin. Manager, vineyard manager and cellar master: Michel Lavandier. Consultant oenologist: Grézillac Laboratory. **Size of vineyard:** 2.3 hectares. **Average age of vines:** 40 years. **Varieties:** 70% merlot. 30% cabernet-franc. **Production:** 10,000 bottles CB. **Visits possible. Direct sales and by mail order:** tel. 57 24 71 14.

Bonnet (Château)

Grand Cru

Commune: Saint-Pey-d'Armens. **Proprietor:** G.A.E.C. of Château Bonnet. Director: Roger Bonnet. Cellar master: Patrick Bonnet. Consultant oenologist: M. Callède. **Size of vineyard:** 23 hectares. **Average age of vines:** 26 years. **Varieties:** 11% cabernet-sauvignon. 60% merlot. 27% cabernet-franc. 2% malbec. **Production:** 140,000 bottles CB. **Visits:** tel. 57 47 15 23. **Direct sales and by mail order:** in France and abroad. **Retail sales through the trade:** Maison Bordeaux Tradition.

The family's first vines were acquired by Pierre Bonnet and his son Francis between 1827 and 1864. Today, the estate is in the hands of the fifth generation. The bulk of the vineyard is situated around the commune of Saint-Pey-d'Armens, at the west and northwest boundaries of the village on soil of sandy chalk with a subsoil of iron-pan. There are about four hectares at Vignonet and the same number again around the commune of Saint-Etienne-de-Lisse, at the foot of the hillside. A quarter of the casks is renewed every year, and thanks to this, a fine hint of oak with notes of vanilla can be discerned and a bitter finish of good quality. Château Bonnet well deserves its *Grand Cru* appellation.

Bouquey (Château)

Grand Cru

Commune: Saint-Hippolyte. **Proprietor:** S.C.E. Château Bouquey. Managed by: Martine Pizzato. Vineyard manager: Yannick Arnaud. Consultant oenologist: Grézillac Laboratory. **Size of vineyard:** 5.6 hectares. **Average age of vines:** 17 to 25 years. **Varieties:** 10% cabernet-sauvignon. 65% merlot. 25% cabernet-franc. **Production:** 36,000 bottles CB. **Visits:** Madame Pizzato. Tel. 56 20 01 30. **Sales by mail order:** in France and abroad. **Retail sales:** United States, Switzerland, Ireland, Belgium, England. *A good "little"* Grand Cru *which will never be out of place in a corner of a big cellar.*

Boutisse (Château)

Grand Cru

Commune: Saint-Christophe-des-Bardes. **Proprietor:** Jean-François Carrille. Cellar master: J.-P. Regrenil. Consultant oenologist: Michel Rolland. **Size of vineyard:** 15 hectares. **Average age of vines:** 25 to 28 years. **Varieties:** 25% cabernet-sauvignon. 68% merlot. 5% cabernet-franc. 2% malbec. **Production:** 100,000 bottles CB. **Visits:** by appointment. Jean-François Carrille. Tel. 57 24 74 46. **Direct sales and by mail order:** in France and abroad. Maison d'Aliénor, place du Marcadien, 33330 Saint-Emilion. **Retail sales:** Ets. Vins de Crus.

With its fifteen hectares in one stretch, Boutisse is the perfect example of a family estate. Since 1975, it has been in the careful hands of Jean-François Carrille who has made a determined effort to reconstitute the vineyard. The late-lamented Professor Enjalbert gave a complete description of the unusual geology of the terrain, which finishes some three hundred feet up, on a rise of Aquitanian limestone with a content of quartz shingle and an interior layer of asteroidian limestone. These formations undoubtedly make for excellent vine-growing land. Several springs are to be found near the house. According to the old title deeds, they were formerly linked to retting rights for hemp and wool. In contrast, two ovens for baking bread, which are in the process of being restored, bear witness to its age and importance as a place of human habitation. Château Boutisse has all the characteristics of the "wines from the hillsides", with their light colour which quickly becomes brick-red, their delicate aromas with hints of gooseberry and their light tannic structure with notes of "burnt rock".

Bragard (Château) ⚑ → Haut-Cadet

Brieux-Chauvin (Château)

→ Millaud-Montlabert

Brisson (Château)  → Grand Destieu

Brun (Château)

Commune: St-Christophe-des-Bardes. **Proprietor:** G.F.A. of Château Brun. **Director:** Marc Brun. **Consultant oenologist:** M. Chaine. **Size of vineyard:** 7 hectares. **Average age of vines:** 15 years. **Varieties:** 20% cabernet-sauvignon. 80% merlot. **Production:** 27,000 bottles CB . **Visits:** tel. 57 24 77 06. **Direct sales and by mail order:** in France and abroad. **Retail sales:** through two traders in Bordeaux.

Château bottling was rare up to 1973. Now it is carried out systematically. This is to be welcomed in view of the high quality of this honourable wine. The Bruns are positive that their presence was known in 1600, but they think that their Saint-Emilion origins are lost in the mists of the early Middle Ages. Along with Michel Decazes, the proprietor at Saint-Sulpice-de-Faleyrens, they are the last descendants of the illustrious Decazes family (see Château du Cauze). The wines are deep in colour, rich and firm and fill the mouth.

Burlis (Château)

Commune: Vignonet. **Proprietor:** Christian Corbière. **Size of vineyard:** 3.3 hectares. **Varieties:** 75% merlot. 15% cabernet-sauvignon, 10% cabernet-franc. **Production:** 7,000 bottles CB. **Visits:** Sunday afternoons. Tel. 57 74 90 58. **Direct sales and by mail order:** in France. Christian Corbière, Micauleau, Vignonet, 33330 Saint-Emilion. *By and large, this is a 'good buy' for the wine-lover, as it offers fair value for money. This wine is not to be found through the Bordeaux trade.*

Cadet-Bon (Château)

Grand Cru classé

Commune: Saint-Emilion. **Proprietor:** François Gratadour. **Vineyard manager:** Paul Couderc. **Consultant oenologist:** M. Chaine. **Size of vineyard:** 4.17 hectares. **Varieties:** 60% merlot. 40% cabernet-franc. **Production:** 12,000 bottles CB. **Visits. Direct sales and by mail order:** tel. 57 24 71 29.

Before becoming a "Château", the name of the *cru* was "Le Cadet-Bon". The little vineyard stood out on the landscape to the north of Saint-Emilion because of its charming mill, which still adorns the label. It belonged to the Dubuch family up to 1931, the year in which it was sold to the Gratadours. Before, it was called "Cadet-Pinaud-Bon". Today, François Gratadour runs the estate successfully, congratulating himself on the relatively simple cultivation and the ideal ripening afforded by this plateau of clayey chalk which faces directly south. The wines have a rich colour, a robust body and an intense nose with hints of red fruits.

Cadet-Gratadour (Château) ⚱ → Cadet-Bon

Cadet-Peychez (Château)

♟♟♟♟♟

Grand Cru

Commune: Saint-Emilion. **Proprietor:** G.F.A. Jabiol-Sciard. Director: François Sciard. Consultant oenologist: C.B.C. Libourne. **Size of vineyard:** 1.10 hectares. **Average age of vines:** 20 years. **Varieties:** 70% merlot. 30% cabernet-franc. **Production:** 5,000 bottles CB. **Direct sales and by mail order:** Madame Sciard, B.P. 24, 33330 Saint-Emilion. **Retail sales through the trade:** Switzerland, Belgium, England. *An antique wooden press can still be seen. Good value for money.*

Cadet-Piola (Château)

♟♟♟♟♟

Grand Cru classé

Commune: Saint-Emilion. **Proprietor:** G.F.A. Jabiol. Managed by: Alain Jabiol. Consultant oenologist: C.B.C. Libourne. **Size of vineyard:** 7 hectares. **Average age of vines:** 20 years. **Varieties:** 28% cabernet-sauvignon. 51% merlot. 18% cabernet-franc. 3% malbec. **Production:** 36,000 bottles CB. **Visits:** afternoons only from 2 to 5.30 p.m. except Saturday and Sunday. **Direct sales and by mail order:** in France. Jabiol, B.P. 24, 33330 Saint-Emilion. Tel. 57 24 70 67 or 57 74 47 69. **Retail sales through the trade:** locally and abroad (Belgium, Switzerland, Germany, Netherlands, England, United States).

The previous proprietor, Robert Villepigue, was associated with Château Figeac. When he offered his wines to his customers, he used to establish the differences in price by basing it on tastings. It was in this way that several times he sold the wines of Cadet-Piola for a higher price than those of Figeac. Robert Villepigue, the founder of the *cave coopérative* of Saint-Emilion, was a highly colourful local figure. The Jabiol family leased the estate as from 1952 and bought it ten years later. There is no actual dwelling, for in the nineteenth century, Monsieur Piola, the mayor of Libourne, preferred to build his château on the plain of Condat, while giving all his attention to Cadet. This citizen Piola is said to have been the first to put a stop to working on the vines with a spade and introduce animal-drawn ploughing. A great pioneer of modern viticulture, he brought into Saint-Emilion the Guyot system of pruning, already known at that period in the Médoc. At one and the same time,

Three generations of the Jabiol family at the entrance to their estate.

he expanded the planting of the cabernet-sauvignon grape. In his time, the *cru* was quite simply called "Le Cadet", which corresponded to the oldest known name on the Land Register. It became "Cadet-Piola" only after his death. This locality enjoys a particularly temperate microclimate, making it invulnerable to both winter and spring frosts. The proof is that in 1956, after the terrible frost which decimated the major part of the Saint-Emilion vineyards, Cadet-Piola was one of the very rare *crus* to be able to harvest a decent crop. The soil is of clayey chalk, typical of the plateau, and the rocky subsoil is very shallow (from eight to twelve inches). As in several other places in the area, parallel furrows can be seen cut out in the rock by the growers of the Middle Ages, even of the Gallo-Roman period. Underneath the vineyards are cellars for ageing, comparable with those of Clos Fourtet. All these elements, typical of the area, are reflected in the wine – lively, intense even, and sunny with a slightly wild aromatic savour but not lacking in breeding.

Cadet-Pontet (Château)   ♟ ♟ ♟ ♟ ♟

Grand Cru

Commune: Saint-Emilion. **Proprietor:** Michel Mérias. Consultant oenologist: M. Rolland. **Size of vineyard:** 8 hectares. **Average age of vines:** 40 years. **Varieties:** 10% cabernet-sauvignon. 60% merlot. 30% cabernet-franc. **Production:** 4,800 bottles CB. **Visits:** by appointment. Michel Mérias. Tel. 57 24 72 66. **Direct sales and by mail order:** in France and abroad (Belgium and Switzerland).

Michel Mérias can remember well every Thursday and Saturday when he used to help his father on the vines. Sometimes he even helped on other days, after school. The work was done with horses. At Cadet-Pontet there were three of them. They used to set off for the whole day, taking their midday meal and fodder for the animals   103 with them. At night-fall, they returned without needing to look at any watch. It was a healthy physical tiredness. Nowadays, working with tractors is more testing. But the wine is still as good.

Caillou d'Arthus (Château)

Grand Cru

Commune: Vignonet. **Proprietor:** Jean-Paul Salvert. Tenant: Jean-Denis Salvert. Consultant oenologist: C.B.C. Libourne. **Size of vineyard:** 2.10 hectares. **Average age of vines:** 30 years. **Varieties:** 70% merlot. 30% cabernet-franc. **Production:** 9,600 bottles CB. **Visits:** by appointment. Jean-Paul Salvert. Tel. 57 84 63 29. **Direct sales and by mail order:** in France and abroad. *Jean-Paul's son, Jean-Denis Salvert, is the tenant of this estate and is developing a policy aimed at high quality. A new label will shortly appear on the market.*

Calvaire (Château du)

Commune: Saint-Etienne-de-Lisse. **Proprietor:** Roland Dumas (G. F. A. in process of being formed). **Size of vineyard:** 9.7 hectares. **Average age of vines:** 30 years. **Varieties:** 65% merlot. 35% cabernet-franc. **Production:** 60,000 bottles CB. **Retail sales through the trade:** Roland Dumas, wine merchant in Saint-Gervais, 33240 Saint-André-de-Cubzac. Tel. 57 43 90 01.

In rapid succession, Roland Dumas has just extended his land with the purchase from the S.A.F.E.R. of this estate at Saint-Etienne-de-Lisse for a price of about 8,000,000 francs, together with the 5.4 hectares of Château Le Roc at Saint-Sulpice-de-Faleyrens. These acquisitions will doubtless be bolstered by Château Quercy with its fifteen hectares spread out over the commune of Vignonet. If you ask him the reason for this consistent penetration into Saint-Emilion territory, he replies that firstly he could not regularly find sufficient wine to meet customers' requirements, and that secondly, he is getting ready for "retirement". In short, a "little job" to keep grandad occupied. But for him work has never been a cross to bear...

Cancet (Château)

Grand Cru

Commune: Saint-Sulpice-de-Faleyrens. **Proprietor:** M. Jacques de La Tour du Fayet. **Size of vineyard:** 9 hectares. **Average age of vines:** 15 years. **Varieties:** 15% cabernet-sauvignon. 70% merlot. 15% cabernet-franc. **Production:** 40,000 bottles CB. **Direct sales and by mail order:** in France. Tel. 57 24 72 08. *A good name; the wines of this estate are perfectly agreeable and well put together.*

Candale (Château de)

Grand Cru

Commune: Saint-Laurent-des-Combes. **Proprietor:** Jean Dugos. **Size of vineyard:** 4.10 hectares. **Average age of vines:** 15 to 35 years. **Varieties:** 10% cabernet-sauvignon. 50% merlot. 40% cabernet-franc. **Production:** 25,000 bottles CB. **Visits:** daily. M. Dugos. Tel. 57 24 72 97. **Direct sales and by mail order:** in France and abroad.

In the Middle Ages, the houses of Foix, Grailly and Candale were among the most powerful in the southwest. The dreaded Duke of Epernon, the first of the name, married Marguerite de Foix Candale, the last heiress of the dynasty after the English had harvested in Aquitaine. Candale's vineyard of today is a witness of those times for the vines are on the land formerly belonging to the counts of Candale. In between the rows of vines, fragments of terra cotta, mosaics and other remains are to be found. You can also see the entrance to a mysterious underground passage with a vaulted roof. The real origin of the settlement here is probably extremely old and must go back to the Gallo-Roman period. Jean Dugos's wine is "ancestral".

Canon (Château)

1er Grand Cru classé

Commune: Saint-Emilion. **Proprietor:** Société Fournier. Director: Eric Fournier. Cellar master: Paul Cazenave. Consultant oenologist: Gilles Pauquet. **Size of vineyard:** 18 hectares. **Average age of vines:** 35 years. **Varieties:** 3% cabernet-sauvignon. 55% merlot. 40% cabernet-franc. 2% malbec. **Production:** 80,000 bottles CB. **Visits:** tel. 57 24 70 79. **Direct sales and by mail order. Retail sales:** through the Bordeaux trade.

In 1856, the Paris Congress put an official stop to privateering, and the corsairs, finding themselves laid off, downed tools or ran the risk of finding themselves outlawed as pirates. But a century earlier, the spiritual heirs of Jean Bart, Duguay-Trouin or Forbin could be counted by the hundred. Jacques Kanon was one of these gallant musketeers of the sea. After being in command of the *Prince de Soubise*, a small boat of two hundred tons and sixteen cannon, he was named commander on board *La Valeur*. His second in command was Benjamin-Nicolas, the son of Pierre Bart. 1758 was a good year for him, for he captured an English corsair and, escorting a fleet carrying corn to Canada, he arrived in Quebec with another prize which was sold for more than 69,000 livres. When he returned, he began to think deeply about his life and wanted to find a haven and at the same time, an outlet for the investment of his capital. He was a sailor who liked good wine. He had a house in Blaye and knew the estuary and its two rivers very well. He sailed up the river Dordogne and, putting in at Condat, he explored the town of Saint-Emilion and set his heart on the property of Jean Biés, a former member of the King's bodyguard. The description of the vineyard, as it occurs in the title deeds dated April 1760, is not sufficiently precise to give us a clear idea. None the less, the vat-house was relatively well-equipped: "A press, a grape crusher, a huge vat containing ten ton-

The vat-house at Château Canon respects the tradition of using wood.

neaux, four other vats holding five to ten *tonneaux,* three kilderkins and pipettes and other small utensils". Production must have been about 40 *tonneaux* per year and the size of the vineyard was about twenty hectares, taking into account the yields of the time. In the context of the region, Jacques Kanon's *cru* was fairly important. The price was 40,400 livres, half of which was paid cash and the other half by promissory notes payable over three years with a yearly interest rate of 5%. The estate was then called "Bourdieu de Saint-Martin" and belonged to the parish of Saint-Martin de Mazerat. It seems that from the moment he was in possession of wine-making equipment, Jacques Kanon forsook the sea to some extent. In 1761, he had a little boat registered in Bordeaux under the name of *Colibri* but history has not related any great exploits it may have carried out at sea at this period. In all probability, the corsair developed his property, modernizing cultivation methods. The temperament of this successful self-made man brought him into conflict with his neighbour Berliquet, each rivalling the other for quality. Then he went back to sea, and set his course for the island of Santo-Domingo, which was then at the height of its prosperity, to take an interest in sugar, tobacco and coffee plantations. He brought back a servant to Saint-Emilion, who, being black, much impressed the parishioners. Undeniably, his love of the air of the open sea was too strong for him, for in 1767, when he had just finished building the château as we see it today, he set off for Santo-Domingo and, three years later, decided to sell his *cru* of Saint-Emilion to buy a colonial property in Gérémie. A purchaser presented himself in the person of Raymond Fontémoing, a rich bourgeois and wine merchant from Libourne, who paid the price of 80,000 livres. The estate remained in the Fontémoing family right

Tasting is still the best way to check quality.

up to 1857. It was at that moment, at the time of its sale to the Count of Bonneval, that it took on the name of Château Canon. After changing hands twice at the end of the century, Canon was bought by Gabriel Supan in 1919 for his daughter Henriette, the wife of André Fournier; Madame Fournier was a "great lady" of Saint-Emilion, whose stature and personality were comparable to those of Madame Loubat at Pétrus, Pomerol. Today, it is her grandson, Eric, who is mainly in charge of running the château. While remaining a resolute traditionalist, he has managed to imbue the old *cru* of Canon with a new youthfulness and his efforts to maintain a policy striving after high quality are undeniable. In this context, competition with his peers is keen. Canon is not always the best, but it is one of the best. The last three years appear particularly successful.

Canon-la-Gaffelière (Château)

Grand Cru classé

Commune: Saint-Emilion. **Proprietor:** S.C. Vignobles des comtes de Neipperg. Director, estate manager and consultant oenologist: Count Stephan de Neipperg. Vineyard manager: Paul Pétrou. Cellar master: Patrick Erésué. **Size of vineyard:** 19.5 hectares. **Average age of vines:** 30 years. **Varieties:** 5% cabernet-franc. 60% merlot. 35% cabernet-franc. **Production:** 120,000 bottles CB. **Visits:** by appointment. Count Stephan de Neipperg. Tel. 57 24 71 33. **Direct sales and by mail order. Retail sales:** through the Bordeaux trade.

Count Stephan de Neipperg.

Up to the last century, it was called Canon Boitard, from the name of its previous owners. The vineyard stretches out at the foot of the hill to the south of Château la Gaffelière and its designation on the Land Register gives it the right to use the name of this locality. Canon-la-Gaffelière was bought and restored by Pierre Meyrat, mayor of Saint-Emilion. From 1953, the date of the purchase, to 1969, the date of his death, Pierre Meyrat spared no pains to improve the reputation of the *cru*. It was a property in fine condition that Count Joseph-Hubert de Neipperg bought in 1971. But the family tradition of these great Austrian landowners, who have been growers for more than five centuries, demanded perfection. Joseph-Hubert de Neipperg, and today his son Stephan, perfected the work of Meyrat, providing Canon-la-Gaffelière with cultivation methods, wine-making equipment and an administrative approach and outlook all worthy of admiration. When Stephan de Neipperg speaks of the vineyard (in French, *vignoble*), he makes two words of it, saying "vigne noble", that is "noble vine", and you can feel all the respect that this young man in his thirties has for his family heritage in the world of wine. He also likes to recite his genealogy, not to vaunt his connections with the nobility, which go back to the beginning of the twelfth century, nor to claim the highest social status; rather, he uses this notion of direct descent from a line of people of quality as a foundation for his own personality. Today, they say in the area that he has become more Saint-Emilion-like than all the rest. In 1982, he came to live permanently at Canon-la-Gaffelière, renouncing the seductions of a diplomatic career, despite his brilliant university qualifications, and those of the meretricious European Gotha. But with a wink, he recalls that his ancestor Adam Albrecht, the Count Von Neipperg, was the lover, and then the second husband of Marie-Louise de Habsbourg-Lorraine, the Empress of the French. As for Stephan de Neipperg himself, he has made a love-match with Canon-la-Gaffelière. The products of their joint effort are elegant and distinguished; breeding will out.

Canon-Pourret (Château) ♟ → Franc-Pourret

Cantemerle (Château)   ♟♟♟♟♟

Commune: Saint-Emilion. **Proprietor:** Jean de Wilde. Tenant: Franck Grelot. **Size of vineyard:** 0.40 hectares. **Average age of vines:** 6 years. **Varieties:** 100% merlot. **Production:** 3 tonneaux. 1,800 bottles CB. **Direct sales and by mail order:** tel. 57 49 21 33. *No possible confusion between the Cantemerle of Saint-Emilion and the one which is a cru classé in the Haut-Médoc. The first has less than half a hectare, the second 53 hectares.*

*label
not
communicated*

Cantenac (Château)

Commune: Saint-Emilion. **Proprietors:** Brunot Heirs. Director and consultant oeonologist: Jean-Baptiste Brunot. **Size of vineyard:** 14 hectares. **Average age of vines:** 30 years. **Varieties:** 10% cabernet-sauvignon. 75% merlot. 15% cabernet-franc. **Production:** 50,000 bottles CB. **Visits:** Monday to Friday, 8 a.m. to noon and 2 to 6 p.m. Saturday, 9 a.m. to noon. **Direct sales and by mail order:** Tel. 57 51 35 22 in France. *Indeed, we really are still in Saint-Emilion, on the sandy gravel plain that lies to the southwest. The wines are characterized by their suppleness.*

Cantenac (Clos)

Commune: Saint-Emilion. **Proprietor:** Madame Linette Villatte. Directors: Linette and Jacques Villatte. Consultant oenologist: C.B.C. Libourne. **Size of vineyard:** 2.5 hectares. **Average age of vines:** 30 years. **Varieties:** 75% merlot. 25% cabernet-franc. **Production:** 12,000 bottles CB. **Direct sales and by mail order:** tel. 57 51 35 52.

Canterane (Château)

Commune: Saint-Etienne-de-Lisse. **Proprietor:** M. Trabut-Cussac. Consultant oenologist: C.B.C. Libourne. **Size of vineyard:** 10 hectares. **Average age of vines:** 35 years. **Varieties:** 75% merlot. 10% cabernet-sauvignon, 15% cabernet-franc. **Production:** 60 tonneaux. 40,000 bottles CB. **Sales by mail order:** tel. 57 40 18 14. *The estate has been in the same family for more than three centuries. In local dialect, the name means "singing frog". Not for those who drink water!*

Cap de Mourlin (Château)

Commune: Saint-Emilion. **Proprietor:** Jacques Capdemourlin. Estate manager: Paul Jenck. Cellar master: Bernard Oizeau. Consultant oenologist: Michel Rolland. **Size of vineyard:** 14 hectares. **Average age of vines:** 30 years. **Varieties:** 12% cabernet-sauvignon. 60% merlot. 25% cabernet-franc. 3% malbec. **Production:** 72,000 bottles CB. **Visits possible. Direct sales and by mail order:** tel. 57 74 62 06. **Retail sales.**

The Capdemourlin family has been present on the land of Saint-Emilion for more than five centuries. A very long time ago, the estate, whose name is written in three separate words, was called "Artuzan" (or Artugon?). In the middle of the seventeenth century it was already a well-known *cru*. The two brothers, Jean and Roger Capdemourlin, split their interests and each ran his own part separately for several years. Jean Capdemourlin was a notable figure in the Federation of Viticulturalists of Saint-Emilion and the Jurade. Since the 1983 vintage, the two separate harvests have fortunately been re-united by Jacques Capdemourlin and this has brought about a consolidation of quality. Old vines, cement vats, and oak casks all combine to make a wine worthy of note.

Capet (Château)

Grand Cru

Commune: Saint-Hippolyte. **Managers:** S.C. Château Le Couvent. **Size of vineyard:** approximately 10 hectares. **Average age of vines:** 25 years. **Varieties:** 5% cabernet-sauvignon. 83% merlot. 12% cabernet-franc. **Sales by mail order:** in France and abroad. Tel. 57 74 62 21. **Retail sales.** *The firm of Alexis Lichine & Co. (see Château Le Couvent), has the sole rights for this* cru, *whose origins go back to the seventeenth century.*

Capet-Guillier (Château)

Grand Cru

Commune: Saint-Hippolyte. **Proprietor:** S.C.I. Capet-Guillier. Directors: Madame Galinou and M. Bouzerand. Vineyard manager: M. Soulier. Consultant oenologist: M. Chaine. **Size of vineyard:** 15 hectares. **Average age of vines:** 30 years. **Varieties:** 10% cabernet-sauvignon. 60% merlot. 30% cabernet-franc. **Production:** 90,000 bottles CB. **Direct sales and by mail order:** tel. 57 24 70 21. **Retail sales.**

The estate of Capet-Guillier, which formed part of the "noble house and seigniory of Capet" belonged to the Countess de Guerchy, née d'Harcourt, and to her brother the Marquis de Beuvron; it was acquired in 1763 by the Taillade family, which already owned Château Lassègue. At the end of the eighteenth century, the Taillades already possessed all the vines along the chain of hills in the commune of Saint-Hippolyte. When the estate was split up between the four children on Frimaire 4 in the year XII (November 25, 1803), Capet-Guillier fell to the eldest son, an ancestor of the Charmolües (the present owners of Château Montrose at Saint-Estèphe) and the Guilliers. For two hundred years the estate of Capet-Guillier has been in the same family which, strongly attached to the reputation of its *cru*, has always succeeded in making excellent wine. Following M. Guillier, the senator, who was the owner for fifty years, and then his children, two of his grandchildren are anxious to maintain tradition, while keeping abreast of technical progress. I knew a Chartron wine merchant of my grandfather's generation who used to say to his broker in Saint-Emilion: "My dear friend, if you have a sample of Capet-Guillier, don't fail to think of me. You know that I always sell the wines I like."

Capet-Pailhas (Château) 🏰

→ Union de Producteurs

Cardinal (Château) 🏰 → Chante l'Alouette

Cardinal-Villemaurine (Château)

🍷🍷🍷🍷🍷

Grand Cru

Commune: Saint-Emilion. **Proprietors:** Jean-Marie and Jean-François Carrille. Consultant oenologist: Michel Rolland. **Size of vineyard:** 10 hectares. **Average age of vines:** 30 years. **Varieties:** 20% cabernet-sauvignon. 70% merlot. 10% cabernet-franc. **Production:** 60,000 bottles CB. **Visits:** by appointment. Tel. 57 24 74 46 or 57 24 73 35. **Direct sales and by mail order. Retail sales:** Ets. de Rivoyre & Diprovin.

What a curious combination of the two names this is! "Cardinal" recalls Gaillard de Lamothe, the nephew of Pope Clement V, who constructed the Palais Cardinal, whose ruins can still be seen near the property. "Villemaurine" evokes the camp the Moors struck here before the Battle of Poitiers. Jean-Marie and Jean-François

CHÂTEAU

CARDINAL-VILLEMAURINE

Saint-Emilion

Carrille took the estate in hand as from the 1983 harvest. They favour long maceration periods. After bottling, the wines are stored in splendid cellars hollowed out of the rock.

Carteau Côtes Daugay (Château)

🍷🍷🍷🍷🍷

Grand Cru

Commune: Saint-Emilion. **Proprietor:** Jacques Bertrand. Consultant oenologist: Michel Rolland. **Size of vineyard:** 12.3 hectares. **Average age of vines:** 25 years. **Varieties:** 10% cabernet-sauvignon. 65% merlot. 25% cabernet-franc. **Production:** 60,000 bottles CB. **Visits:** by appointment. Tel. 57 24 73 94. **Direct sales and by mail order:** in France. **Retail sales.**

This vineyard is situated on the southwest slope of Tertre Daugay. In 1985, the Bertrand family celebrated the château's centenary. Apart from his constant devotion to his *cru*, Jacques Bertrand is the secretary of the Syndicat viticole de Saint-Emilion and is particularly zealous in the defence of the appellation. His wines are full and reach their zenith after maturing for between ten and twenty years.

Carteau-Matras (Château)

Grand Cru

Commune: Saint-Emilion. **Proprietor:** Claude Bion. Vineyard manager: Jean-Marie Bion. Consultant oenologist: C.B.C. Cazenave-Mahé. **Size of vineyard:** 15 hectares. **Average age of vines:** 25 years. **Varieties:** 10% cabernet-sauvignon. 70% merlot. 20% cabernet-franc. **Production:** 75 tonneaux. 60,000 bottles CB. **Visits:** Weekdays. Tel. 57 24 72 35. **Direct sales and by mail order:** in France. **Retail sales.** *A wine of good quality. The cru has been handed down through successive generations of the same family for about two centuries.*

Cauze (Château du)

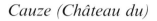

Grand Cru

Commune: Saint-Christophe-des-Bardes. **Proprietor:** Laporte Bayard family. Director, vineyard manager and cellar master: Bruno Laporte. Consultant oenologist: C.B.C. Libourne. **Size of vineyard:** 20 hectares. **Average age of vines:** 30 years. **Varieties:** 10% cabernet-sauvignon. 90% merlot. **Production:** 120,000 bottles CB. **Visits possible. Direct sales and by mail order:** tel. 57 74 62 47. **Retail sales through the trade:** Sichel; Marks & Spencer.

The *Histoire de Libourne* published in the last century by Raymond Guinodie gives precise details about the origins of this château which can be traced back to the seventeenth century. It was then a noble house belonging to the jurat François Decazes. His descendant, Pierre Elisée Decazes, was a brilliant diplomat, and was created a baron by Louis XVIII. On his retirement in 1834, he settled at Château du Cauze and successfully set his sights on the town hall of Saint-Christophe-des-Bardes. In 1851 he improved the buildings and constructed a round tower, the better to survey his lands. At that time he owned a fifth of the total area of the commune. Shortly before his death, he sold the estate to a rich person of some standing from Roubaix, Hector Wibaux. Three other proprietors followed in succession up to the private limited company of today successfully run by Bruno Laporte, who himself comes from an excellent family of growers of the Saint-Emilion region. The wine of Château du Cauze is honest and of regular quality. It is surprising not to find the least trace of cabernet-franc in the vineyard. Such an anomaly makes the wine untypical of Saint-Emilion.

Cauzin (Château)  → La Fleur Cauzin

Cazenave (Château)

→ Union de Producteurs

Champion (Château)

Commune: Saint-Christophe-des-Bardes. **Proprietor:** Jean Bourrigaud. **Size of vineyard:** 10 hectares. **Average age of vines:** 20 years. **Varieties:** 10% cabernet-sauvignon. 80% merlot. 10% cabernet-franc. **Production:** 30,000 bottles CB. **Visits:** by appointment, daily. Tel. 57 74 43 98. **Direct sales and by mail order:** in France and abroad. *A warm welcome has always been traditional in this family since the eighteenth century. It is a well-kept estate producing agreeable wines.*

Chante-Alouette (Château)

Commune: Saint-Emilion. **Proprietor:** Madame Jeanine Barbary. Tenant, vineyard manager and consultant oenologist: Alain Berjal. **Size of vineyard:** 5 hectares. **Average age of vines:** 25 years. **Varieties:** 30% cabernet-sauvignon. 70% merlot. **Production:** 24,000 bottles CB. **Visits:** tel. 57 74 60 06 or 57 75 42 55. **Direct sales and by mail order:** in France. *Monsieur Barbary's dream came true the day his daughter married a man from Saint-Emilion - Alain Berjal.*

Chante Alouette Cormeil

Commune: Saint-Emilion. **Proprietor:** Yves Delol. Consultant oenologist: Gilles Pauquet. **Size of vineyard:** 8 hectares. **Average age of vines:** 25 years. **Varieties:** 20% cabernet-sauvignon. 60% merlot. 20% cabernet-franc. **Production:** 42,000 bottles CB. **Visits:** by appointment. Tel. 57 51 02 63. **Direct sales and by mail order:** in France and abroad. *Sandy soil laid over a subsoil of iron-pan. This estate has been in the family for more than a century but has gradually increased in size over the generations.*

Chante l'Alouette (Clos)

Commune: Saint-Emilion. **Proprietor:** François Ouzoulias. Estate manager and cellar master: Pierre Ouzoulias. Consultant oenologist: Michel Rolland. **Size of vineyard:** 3 hectares. **Average age of vines:** 25 years. **Varieties:** 90% merlot. 10% cabernet-franc. **Production:** 14 tonneaux. 10,000 bottles CB. **Visits:** tel. 57 51 07 55. **Sales by mail order:** in France. **Retail sales:** Ets. Ouzoulias S.A. *A rather elusive label which may offer pleasant surprises.*

Chauvin (Château)

Grand Cru classé

Commune: Saint-Emilion. **Proprietors:** Béatrice Raynaud and Marie-France Février. **Director:** Henri Ondet. Consultant oenologist: Michel Rolland. **Size of vineyard:** 13 hectares. **Average age of vines:** 20 years. **Varieties:** 10% cabernet-sauvignon. 60% merlot. 30% cabernet-franc. **Production:** 70,000 bottles CB. **Visits:** by appointment. Tel. 57 51 33 76. **Direct sales and by mail order:** in France. **Retail sales:** through the Bordeaux trade.

This fair-sized, trim vineyard is situated in the heart of the sandy glacis, halfway between Cheval Blanc and the butte of Rol. It is a property in one stretch which, during the Second Empire, belonged to the Fourcaud-Laussac family, whose descendants still reign at Cheval Blanc. At that time, they carried out the drainage of the land on the two estates, a considerable job which, even with the mechanical and technical aids of today, would be a long and exacting undertaking.

In 1891, Victor Ondet managed to buy his first parcel. Fifteen years later, it was increased to seven hectares. His two children, Georges and Georgette, inherited it in 1911. Henri, Georges's son, finally became the sole proprietor in 1934 and by successive purchases brought the total size up to thirteen hectares. So it is the fourth generation on site today, represented by Béatrice Raynaud and Marie-France Février.

Château Chauvin is a good product with a high reputation and has the advantage of being widely distributed. Its name is often to be found on wine lists of high-class restaurants. It will always be a judicious purchase, giving value for money which will never disappoint anybody. It is better to choose slightly older vintages, but not too old.

Cheval Blanc (Château)

1er Grand Cru classé

Commune: Saint-Emilion. **Proprietor:** S.C. of Château Cheval Blanc. **Director:** Jacques Hébrard. Vineyard manager: Pierre Perdigal. Cellar master: Gaston Vaissière. Consultant oenologist: Gilles Pauquet. **Size of vineyard:** 36 hectares. **Average age of vines:** 34 years. **Varieties:** 33% merlot. 66% cabernet-franc. 1% malbec. **Production:** 140,000 bottles CB. **Visits:** 9 to 11.30 a.m. and 3 to 5.30 p.m. Tel. 57 24 70 70. **Retail sales.**

"At Cheval Blanc, the gravel is strictly gunz", concludes Professor Enjalbert. There is gunz gravel over more or less all the Bordeaux region, and especially on the right bank of the Garonne and the estuary of the Gironde. But what appears most remarkable of all to this scientist is the presence of decalcified rubble over "the southern sector of the vineyards of Cheval Blanc from Chauvin to Bourrue. This roughly fractured rubble is mixed with a matrix of clayey sand and lies on the molasse." And he adds a little further on: "Quality was assured". Already on the map of the geographer Belleyme, drawn up in 1764, this terrain was planted with a sizeable

vineyard. But it was an almost abandoned estate which president Ducasse bought

Jacques Hébrard is the current Chancellor of Bordeaux's Wine Academy.

in 1832 from Félicité de Carle-Trajet, a widow of seven years and up against appalling financial difficulties (see Figeac in the catalogue). The new proprietor started out with his acquisition in a deplorable state, with its dilapidated house and barn, and a land essentially given over to "inter-cropping". I have already had occasion, notably in my book on the Côtes de Bourg, to speak of the tiresome rôle played by agricultural advisers of the Romantic period when they recommended widening the vine-rows to allow growing fodder, cereal or vegetable crops in between. Because of the increased yields, the immediate profit tempted more than one grower, but ruin was on the other hand inevitable because of the excessive production of a wine of pitiful quality. Ducasse took the time to reflect and to measure his land. In 1834, when he had plans of the present château drawn up, he knew that he would be buying other land to perfect the estate. Henri Enjalbert supposes that it was he who

Cheval Blanc: relatively modest buildings for such a distinguished label.

instigated the extensive drainage work before establishing the "contemporary" vineyard. In 1852, Jean Laussac-Fourcaud married the daughter of president Ducasse, taking on the administration of the estate at the same time. The preparation of the vine-growing terrain by modern drainage was then in its early stages. It is probable that the father-in-law prompted his son-in-law to undertake such work and financed its execution himself. As far as I know, this was the very first work of its type in the Gironde along with that done at Château Lagrange in Saint-Julien, carried out

at the same time by the progressive estate manager Galos for Charles Tanneguy, Count Duchâtel. Moreover in 1868, that is sixteen years later, Cocks and Féret paid tribute to the event: "On this type of terrain, Monsieur Laussac-Fourcaud had the happy idea of adopting the Médoc system of cultivation and pruning (...). For the fifteen years that Monsieur Laussac-Fourcaud has been proprietor of this estate, he has never ceased making considerable improvements to it. Extensive drainage work has protected all the vines from becoming waterlogged." In 1870, the estate of Cheval Blanc amounted to 42 hectares. This size was not to change. But the *cru*'s rise to fame was prodigious. The first gold medal obtained at the Paris Exhibition in 1878 inaugurated the early and brilliant fame of Cheval Blanc. In 1893, Albert, who had changed his name at the public registry office to Fourcaud-Laussac, succeeded his father. He rigorously selected his grape varieties after the phylloxera crisis and adopted an outward-looking promotional policy, one of the first in Saint-Emilion to do so. Cheval Blanc then took the lead and was at the head of the "premiers grands crus des graves Saint-Emilion" according to Cocks and Féret, who constantly remind us that these wines "rather resemble those of the Médoc".

CHEVAL-BLANC

After Albert Fourcaud-Laussac's death, his five children formed a private limited company amongst themselves, directed by Jacques. I often came across this country squire from Libourne, with his stiff-starched collar and neatly laced ankle-boots. He was a man who was sparing of words, always listening to the person speaking to him as if he were learning something new. But his personal style had long been established, and he could be totally intransigent, though with the most extreme courtesy. Today, the three branches of the family which have retained an interest are the Fourcaud-Laussacs, Lanauzes and Carennes. The director is Jacques Hébrard, a man of imposing stature and expansive gesture and whose speech is sometimes halting. He is the chancellor of Bordeaux's Wine Academy. Ever imperturbable, he is the very embodiment of the *cru*'s excellence and the distinction attained by its illustrious label.

Cheval Blanc is a great wine for a great connoisseur. Its greatness has several dimensions, for it involves that of the wine lover's bank account. The *cru*'s relationship to the best Médoc wines can often be noted. I confess that at blind tastings I have often confused Cheval Blanc and Château Margaux... and that if tasting of the first ten Bordeaux is done "horizontally", one can be hard put to place "Cheval" in the land of its origin. All the latest vintages appear to me to be worthy of praise. Although I have not undertaken to enter into this sphere of activity (which I leave without demur to "specialist" journalists), I must mention Cheval Blanc 1982, which I consider one of the best bottles of Bordeaux of that vintage. I am pleased to pay tribute to the young oenologist Gilles Pauquet who works with the cellar master Gaston Vaissière to produce this king of kings.

Cheval Brun (Château) ♟♟♟♟♟

Commune: Saint-Emilion. **Proprietor:** Pierre Ternoy. Director: Monique Ternoy. Consultant oenologist: C.B.C. Libourne. **Size of vineyard:** 5 hectares. **Average age of vines:** 40 years. **Varieties:** 70% merlot. 30% cabernet-franc. **Production:** 20 tonneaux. 5,000 bottles CB. **Direct sales and by mail order:** tel. 57 51 46 10. *We prefer the white one (Cheval Blanc) but need much more money to buy it. There is the black one too (Cheval Noir), but neither of them will take you for a ride.*

Cheval Noir

Commune: Saint-Emilion. **Proprietor:** Mähler-Besse. **Size of vineyard:** 4.5 hectares. **Average age of vines:** 10 years. **Varieties:** 25% cabernet-sauvignon. 50% merlot. 25% cabernet-franc. **Production:** 25 tonneaux. **Visits:** tel. 56 52 16 75. **Sales by mail order. Retail sales:** Mähler-Besse S.A., 49 rue Camille Godard, 33000 Bordeaux.

This is an exception to the rule. The commercial name of Cheval Noir features in this catalogue because it really and truly comes from a parcel of Saint-Emilion land which belonged to the Uzac brothers. These latter sold the name, and the little vineyard, to the old established and respectable firm of Mähler-Besse in Bordeaux who made this the war-horse for their better Saint-Emilion blends, the wine of this *cru* being always the basis for each blend. Today, it is the best selling of all of Mähler-Besse's products. It can be found more or less everywhere in Europe and an intensely dynamic commercial strategy is afoot to break into the Anglo-Saxon markets. My personal opinion is that this wine is excellent value for money, often

greatly superior to the "authentic little *crus*" bottled... when it rains. For the wine lover, it is a question of choosing between the labels of these, with all their potential variations in quality, or the guaranteed level of quality offered by a wine which can be counted on to live up to its own standards.

Clos des Jacobins (Château)

Grand Cru classé

Commune: Saint-Emilion. **Proprietors:** Domaines Cordier. Director: Jean Cordier. Estate manager: P. Frédéric. Manager and oenologist: Georges Pauli. **Size of vineyard:** 7.5 hectares. **Average age of vines:** 30 years. **Varieties:** 5% cabernet-sauvignon. 85% merlot. 10% cabernet-franc. **Production:** 55,000 bottles CB. **Visits:** tel. 56 31 44 44. **Sales by mail order:** in France and abroad. Ets. Cordier, 10 quai de Paludate, 33800 Bordeaux. **Retail sales:** Ets. Cordier.

It is probable that this vineyard was once the property of this religious order. The "Couvent des Jacobins" is yet another example in Saint-Emilion. Scattered about at the time of the Revolution and sold by the Nation, lands belonging to religious communities often came into the hands of local people of note. The Clos des Jacobins belonged to the Cordes and Vauthier families before becoming part of the Cordier estates.

119

Its site stretches out on the plateau of tertiary asteroidian limestone on the other side of the hill of Saint-Emilion, covered with a thin layer of fine gravel and aeolian sands. Like the Cordier vineyards of the Médoc or Sauternes (Gruaud Larose, Talbot, Meyney, Lafaurie-Peyraguey), the Clos des Jacobins is looked after in an irreproachable, even spectacular, manner. You would think it had come, with immediate vacant possession, straight out of a catalogue of "General manufacturers of luxury vineyards". This particular model is not big, but it is in the style of "a pretty jewel for someone who has already got everything". The wine's appearance does not lie and it has a distinguished elegance with a floral touch of wild rose.

Clos Haut Cabanne (Château)

Commune: Saint-Emilion. **Proprietor:** Juliette Amblard. Consultant oenologists: Messieurs Legendre and Pauquet. **Size of vineyard:** 1.05 hectares. **Average age of vines:** 25 to 30 years. **Varieties:** "There's a mixture of everything" (sic!). **Production:** 4 tonneaux. **Retail sales:** in bulk.

The term "Clos" is perfectly correct here for the land, the house and the vineyard form a charming little enclosure to the north of Saint-Emilion going towards Pomerol. Juliette Amblard runs her inheritance with zeal and is greatly attached to her old vines which make "the best". Her mother, who is now nearly ninety, still prunes despite her advanced age "because I do it better". It is a pity that Juliette Amblard has not made up her mind to bottle her own wine.

Clos Jean Voisin (Château)

Commune: Saint-Emilion. **Proprietor:** G.F.A. Sautarel. Directors: Jacques and André Sautarel. Consultant oenologist: Gilles Pauquet. **Size of vineyard:** 3.17 hectares. **Average age of vines:** 20 years. **Varieties:** 15% cabernet-sauvignon. 70% merlot. 15% cabernet-franc. **Production:** 12 tonneaux. 5,000 bottles CB. **Direct sales and by mail order:** Château Tournefeuille, Néac, 33500 Libourne. Tel. 57 51 18 61. **Retail sales.**

Clos Saint-Emilion Magnan (Château)

Commune: Saint-Emilion. **Proprietor:** Simone Philippe. Vineyard manager and cellar master: Marc Philippe. Consultant oenologst: Mademoiselle Cazenave. **Size of vineyard:** 7.3 hectares. **Average age of vines:** 30 years. **Varieties:** 30% cabernet-sauvignon. 40% merlot. 30% cabernet-franc. **Production:** 36,000 bottles CB. **Retail sales:** Maison Lebègue. Tel. 57 51 48 92.

Comte des Cordes (Ch.) ⚱ → Fonrazade

Corbin (Château)

♟♟♟♟♟

Grand Cru classé

Commune: Saint-Emilion. **Proprietor:** Société Civile des Domaines Giraud. **Director:** Madame J. Blanchard. **Manager:** Philippe Giraud. **Cellar master:** Emmanuel Giraud. **Size of vineyard:** 13.38 hectares. **Average age of vines:** 25 years. **Varieties:** 30% cabernet-sauvignon. 65% merlot. 5% cabernet-franc. **Production:** 90,000 bottles CB. **Retail sales through the trade:** exclusively. Tel. 57 24 70 62.

Henri Enjalbert points out that Edouard Féret, in his 1868 edition, qualifies Cheval Blanc, Bélair, Mondot, Figeac and Corbin as "châteaux". He adds: "For Corbin, the word château is surprising. In 1868, the estate was only in the second *crus*, the residence was nondescript, and the production barely average: twenty tonneaux including those from Jean Faure. But the Chaperons, the proprietors, took care with their wines. Edouard Féret was not unaware of this."

The phylloxera crisis affected the Corbin estate, which was restored with French rootstock treated with carbon disulphide. This ended in a ruinously expensive failure and, after being planted all over again with American stock, the estate was merged with that of Jean Faure. The 1922 edition of Féret's *Bordeaux et ses Vins* puts it among the first *crus* of the Saint-Emilion graves. It was subsequently taken in hand by Joseph Giraud who ran this old estate prudently and it is his heirs who administer it today.

Corbin truly deserves to be called "château".

121

Corbin Michotte (Château)

Grand Cru classé

Commune: Saint-Emilion. **Proprietor:** Jean-Noël Boidron.
Size of vineyard: 7.6 hectares. **Average age of vines:**
35 years. **Varieties:** 5% cabernet-sauvignon. 65% merlot.
30% cabernet-franc. **Production:** 33,000 bottles CB. **Visits:**
by appointment. Tel. 59 96 28 57. **Sales by mail order:** in
France. **Retail sales:** through the Bordeaux trade.

Château Corbin Michotte lies at a height of between 90 and 135 feet. It is a single
vineyard on gravelly, sandy ridges and situated at the limit of the Saint-Emilion and
Pomerol appellations. These terrains are very poor and act as a filter. Jean-Noël
Boidron lectures in oenology at Bordeaux University and, already the proprietor
of Château Calon in Montagne, he acquired Corbin Michotte in 1959. He put into
practice his knowledge as an oenologist which is to understand the terrain, that is the
intrinsic nature of the land on which the vines grow. At Corbin Michotte, the vines
are stripped of leaves thirty days before harvesting for the grapes to take the sun
better. Harvesting is of course done by hand. The work is carried out very rapidly in
two days by a large team of pickers. Before being put into vat, the grapes are sorted,
still by hand. Ageing is carried out half in the vat and half in new wood. Corbin
Michotte is a *cru* of constant quality, which is outstandingly successful in years
of rain and which, in great years, can attain an amazing degree of concentration.
Recently Jean-Noël Boidron's *cru* has made spectacular progress. The number of
glasses attributed to him here reflects rather an average judgement over twenty years
than a recognition of its present remarkable quality.

Cormeil-Figeac (Château)

Grand Cru

Commune: Saint-Emilion. **Proprietor:** G.F.A. Cormeil-
Figeac. Director and manager: Claude Moreaud. Estate manager: Richard Moreaud. Consultant oenologist:
C.B.C. Libourne. **Size of vineyard:** 10 hectares. **Average
age of vines:** 23 years. **Varieties:** 65% merlot. 35% cabernet-
franc. **Production:** 48,000 bottles CB. **Visits:** by appointment. Richard Moreaud. Tel. 57 24 70 53. **Direct sales and
by mail order:** in France. **Retail sales** through the trade:
for export only.

Cormeil-Figeac is within the old limits of the huge estate of Figeac. In 1850, Charles
Cocks listed it in his hundred *crus* of Saint-Emilion. Right up to the beginning of
this century, it featured among the names of the most famous "graves". When René
Moreaud bought it in 1980, the property was in a pitiful state of dilapidation, and
it was he who restored the vineyard to hand it down to his son Robert in perfect
condition. This latter continued the work of his father, a perfectionist, notably in
carrying out extensive drainage work on the land. The third generation, Claude and
Richard Moreaud, are now in the vines and in the cellars, both fired by the same
wish to succeed. They are particularly keen to call themselves "vignerons" and
not "growers cum producers cum managers", so distinguishing strongly between
what is for them pure tradition and what they consider has become merely a job

motivated by profit. "That is how we work, we rebel against modernization when it affects quality", they say together in chorus. And indeed, the Moreauds hold fast to this approach with success. They readily cite the poets to illustrate the virtues of their wine. "One evening the soul of wine sang in the bottle", they print on their advertising material, much in the style of Gault and Millau. The French poet Baudelaire, who wrote this verse, was also capable of observing life with a more jaundiced eye. Elsewhere in his works, we find the following remark: "For the trader, honesty is speculating for profit." I shall not insist any further because in this case the owners can prove their sincerity. The yield per hectare, for example, is only 32 hectolitres on average. The 1972, 1973, 1977 and 1984 vintages were not judged worthy of being château bottled. On the other hand, recent successful years are gaining a richness and an extraordinary fullness. "Our wines are not appreciated by people tasting in haste" the Moreauds reply, like an air they learnt by heart. We can confirm that the affair Cormeil-Figeac and the Moreauds is one of the heart and moreover a sound affair.

Côte Baleau (Château)

Grand Cru classé

Commune: Saint-Emilion. **Proprietor:** S.C.E. des Grandes Murailles. Tenants: M. and Madame Reiffers. Vineyard manager and cellar master: Jean Brun. Consultant oenologist: Michel Rolland. **Size of vineyard:** 17 hectares. **Average age of vines:** 30 years. **Varieties:** 20% cabernet-sauvignon. 70% merlot. 10% cabernet-franc. **Production:** 100,000 bottles CB. **Direct sales and by mail order:** tel. 57 24 71 09. **Retail sales.**

This was one of the victims of the I.N.A.O.'s new classification. Indeed, Château Côte Baleau lost its title as a Grand Cru classé. This *cru* might perhaps have been able to keep its position if it had kept entirely separate means of vinification and ageing, instead of grouping together with the other estates of Monsieur and Madame Reiffers: Grandes Murailles and Clos Saint-Martin.

With 17 fine hectares in production, there is no doubt at all that Côte Baleau would merit and justify autonomous equipment. But here too, I think that the commission for the new classification was severe and heavy handed. But let the traditional lovers of this label be assured. The quality of the wine of Côte Baleau, be it *classé* or not, remains the same.

Côte de la Mouleyre (Château)

Grand Cru

Commune: Saint-Etienne-de-Lisse. **Proprietors:** Emile and Pierre Roques. Director, estate and vineyard manager, manager and cellar master: Pierre Roques. Consultant oenologist: Michel Rolland. **Size of vineyard:** 5.6 hectares. **Average age of vines:** 45 years. **Varieties:** 20% carbernet-sauvignon. 70% merlot. 10% cabernet-franc. **Production:** 36,000 bottles CB. **Visits:** by appointment. Pierre Roques. Tel. 57 40 16 48. **Direct sales and by mail order:** in France and abroad.

Emile and Pierre Roques set foot on the soil of Bordeaux in December 1963. They arrived from their native, trouble-stricken Algeria, having as their principal qualifications a knowledge of the vine-growing profession, which they had previously carried out in one of the best regions of North Africa, Mascara, which was then called "the Saint-Emilion of Algeria". Is it because of this correlation? Whatever the case, after looking for a place to anchor, they set their heart on Côte de la Mouleyre and its 5.6 hectares of premium vines. Before that, they had journeyed 17,500 miles which, if what I learned at school is correct, represents 28 times the length of France crossed in a straight line. "We had more or less to learn everything all over again." they say modestly. But they and Côte de la Mouleyre were made for each other. They took on the old vines and worked them to ensure the production of a good wine. "Harvesting by hand... I absolutely insist." declares Emile Roques almost passionately. And he adds: "For a quality vineyard, the machine is a massacre. It is botched work!" The Roques know what work is. Their work is a splendid achievement and well done.

Côte de Tauzinat (Château)
→ Union de Producteurs.

Côtes Bernateau (Château)

Grand Cru

Commune: Saint-Etienne-de-Lisse. **Proprietor:** Régis Lavau. **Size of vineyard:** 16 hectares. **Average age of vines:** 25 years. **Varieties:** 10% cabernet-sauvignon. 65% merlot. 20% cabernet-franc. 5% petit-verdot. **Production:** 80,000 bottles CB. **Visits:** by appointment. Tel. 57 40 18 19. **Direct sales and by mail order:** in France.

"The land loves me; it sticks to my feet." This is one of Régis Lavau's professions of faith. Personally, I would like to give a true picture of this man by switching his sentence the other way round: "My feet love the land; they stick to it." By that, I mean to say that love is shared between the man and his land, and that their child is a robust wine, which promises to show itself loveable.

Côtes du Gros Caillou (Château)

Commune: Saint-Sulpice-de-Faleyrens. **Proprietor:** Jean Tourenne. Consultant oenologist: M. Chaine. **Size of vineyard:** 6 hectares. **Average age of vines:** 15 to 30 years. **Varieties:** 20% cabernet-sauvignon. 80% merlot. **Production:** 30 tonneaux. **Direct sales and by mail order:** Tel. 57 24 75 17. **Retail sales:** sold partly in bulk. *The 1982 vintage obtained a gold medal at the Concours Général de Paris.*

Coudert (Château)

Grand Cru

Commune: Saint-Christophe-des-Bardes. **Proprietor:** Jean-Claude Carles. Consultant oenologist: Michel Rolland. **Size of vineyard:** 5 hectares. **Average age of vines:** 20 years. **Varieties:** 10% cabernet-sauvignon. 70% merlot. 20% cabernet-franc. **Production:** 30,000 bottles CB. **Visits:** by appointment. Jean-Claude Carles. Tel. 57 24 78 92. **Direct sales and by mail order:** in France and abroad. **Retail sales:** through Libourne. A little *cru,* rather light in character, which will not harm a sensitive palate.

Coudert-Pelletan (Château)

Grand Cru

Commune: Saint-Christophe-des-Bardes. **Proprietor:** Jean Lavau. Administered by: G.A.E.C. Jean Lavau & Fils. **Size of vineyard:** 6.15 hectares. **Average age of vines:** 24 years. **Varieties:** 20% cabernet-sauvignon. 60% merlot. 20% cabernet-franc. **Production:** 40,000 bottles CB. **Visits:** Messieurs Lavau. Tel. 57 24 77 30. **Direct sales and by mail order:** in France and abroad. **Retail sales.**

Before the Revolution, several ancestors of the Lavaus were to be found as jurats of Saint-Emilion. They were a family of coopers and cellar masters. Jean Lavau's two sons, Philippe and Christophe, both work on the estate, each following his own specialization – one in cultivation and vinification, and the other in administration and marketing. They appear greatly attached to their inheritance and family tradition. The wines are keenly appreciated by wine merchants but also by their private clients.

Coutet (Château)

Grand Cru classé

Commune: Saint-Emilion. **Proprietor:** S.C.I. Château Coutet. Director: Jean David-Beaulieu. Consultant oenologists: Michel and Danielle Rolland. **Size of vineyard:** 11 hectares. **Average age of vines:** 40 years. **Varieties:** 5% cabernet-sauvignon. 45% merlot. 45% cabernet-franc. 5% malbec. **Production:** 45 tonneaux. **Visits:** by appointment. Tel. 57 24 72 27. **Direct sales and by mail order:** in France. **Retail sales:** abroad.

In 1808, the young and brilliant barrister Jean David married Marie-Caroline Lavau whose family had long been in the Libourne region. He made a brilliant career for himself, becoming a deputy under Louis-Philippe and the mayor of Libourne. Since this time, Château Coutet has remained in the David-Beaulieu family. The main building is a *chartreuse* with a mansard roof, which has a romantic and rather nostalgic appearance.

To the west of Saint-Emilion, the vineyard stretches its eleven hectares of clayey chalky land over the first slope to be seen when coming from Libourne. The surrounding area contains a whole string of *crus classés*. The vines are kept in production up to an advanced age and are tended traditionally. The bulk of the production is destined for export, so this good wine is rather difficult to find on the French market.

Couvent des Jacobins

Grand Cru classé

Commune: Saint-Emilion. **Proprietors:** Messieurs Joinaud-Borde. Director: M. Borde. Cellar master: M. Oizeau. Consultant oenologist: M. Cassignard. **Size of vineyard:** 9.3 hectares. **Average age of vines:** 40 years. **Varieties:** 5% cabernet-sauvignon. 65% merlot. 30% cabernet-franc. **Production:** 45,000 bottles CB. **Visits:** by appointment. Tel. 57 24 70 66. **Retail sales:** through Saint-Emilion.

In the heart of the ancient town, the Couvent des Jacobins presents its venerable stones for the visitor to admire. As restored by the Joinaud-Borde family, the owners since 1902, they create a happy marriage between the past and the present. The origin of the monastery goes back to the thirteenth century. The order of the preaching Jacobin friars settled there in the fourteenth century and we know that the Duke of Lancaster, the lieutenant-general of Guienne (or Aquitaine if you prefer), confirmed the donation in 1389.

These monks should not be confused with the "Jacobin club", a political society which was formed at the time of the Revolution. The Jacobin friars had been so called when Philippe-Auguste gave the disciples of Saint Dominique the hospice in the rue Saint-Jacques in Paris which used to take in pilgrims from Compostella. This name gradually proliferated all over France as the Dominican monasteries were progressively set up in the provinces. It is highly likely that the Couvent des Jacobins in Saint-Emilion was for several centuries a religious education centre as well as a staging-post for Compostella. In order to guarantee means of subsistence for the community, the monks used to grow vines on terraces at the foot of the ramparts of the town. When the Crown of England took over, it set its (lion-)heart on ensuring an outlet for the production of its protégés. According to a certain tradition, the wines of the Jacobins were served at royal banquets after being transported by specially chartered English ships. At the time of the Revolution, the goods of the Jacobins were confiscated and the land dispersed by sales at auction. Today, the Couvent des Jacobins is a vineyard at the foot of the hill on the south side and split up into three parcels. It produces elegant and distinguished wines which are generally more soft than tannic.

Couvent des Jacobins

Grand Cru

Commune: Saint-Emilion. **Proprietor:** Gabrielle Semelin. Director, vineyard manager and cellar master: Alain Borde. **Size of vineyard:** 0.36 hectares. **Average age of vines:** 80 years. **Variety:** 100% merlot. **Production:** 1,200 bottles CB. Tel. 57 24 71 23.

Croix de Mazerat (Château) ♟ → Beauséjour

Croix Figeac (Château)

Commune: Saint-Emilion. **Proprietor:** Jean Guimberteau. **Size of vineyard:** 4 hectares. **Average age of vines:** 24 years. **Varieties:** 70% merlot. 30% cabernet-franc. **Production:** 20 tonneaux. **Direct sales:** tel. 57 24 60 12. **Retail sales.**

Croque Michotte (Château)

Grand Cru classé

Commune: Saint-Emilion. **Proprietor:** Madame Hélène Rigal-Geoffrion. Estate manager: Jean Brun. **Size of vineyard:** 15 hectares. **Average age of vines:** 30 to 40 years. **Varieties:** 5% cabernet-sauvignon. 75% merlot. 20% cabernet-franc. **Production:** 80,000 bottles CB. **Visits possible. Direct sales and by mail order:** tel. 57 51 13 64.

When the little estate of Croque Michotte changed hands in 1852, it was in a pitiful state and there was less than half a hectare under vines. It should be said that Croque Michotte was one of the leased farms in the fief of Corbin, given over to growing cereal crops. It was only in the second half of the nineteenth century that, following in the footsteps of Cheval Blanc and La Dominique, this area became a vineyard. The name of Croque Michotte, which has a charming connotation with children's fairy stories, takes its name from the little bread oven attached to the ancient farm.

Despite its mediaeval name, Croque Michotte has an ultra-modern vat-house.

Reinstated by the rules of the art by the then proprietor, a certain Dubois, Croque Michotte's vineyard stood up to phylloxera in an exceptional way. At the time, it was called quite simply, Michotte. Samuel Geoffrion became its proprietor in 1906 and it is his daughter, Hélène Rigal-Geoffrion who today reigns over the 15 hectares of excellent vines, under the supervision of Jean Brun, one of the best estate managers in Saint-Emilion. Stainless-steel vats and other equipment have been introduced to modernize the undertaking. Croque Michotte is an excellent wine which I have often tasted and which has never disappointed me. Is that not right, Pierre Castéja? Today, in my opinion, it deserves four glasses.

Cros-Figeac (Château)

Grand Cru

Commune: Saint-Emilion. **Proprietor:** Christian Cassagne. **Size of vineyard:** 5 hectares. **Average age of vines:** 20 years. **Varieties:** 15% cabernet-sauvignon. 70% merlot. 15% cabernet-franc. **Production:** 35,000 bottles CB. **Direct sales and by mail order:** tel. 57 24 76 32. *A perfectly charming label for a wine from sandy terrain. It develops as quickly as a child's sandcastle, and disappears as rapidly too.*

Cruzeau (Château)

Commune: Libourne. **Proprietors:** Messieurs Jean, Lucien, Georges Luquot. **Size of vineyard:** 5 hectares. **Average age of vines:** 20 years. **Varieties:** 10% cabernet-sauvignon. 70% merlot. 20% cabernet-franc. **Production:** 24,000 bottles CB. **Visits:** tel. 57 51 18 95. **Direct sales and by mail order:** in France. **Retail sales:** Maison A. Luquot Fils.

Local report has it that the lords of Cruzeau and Chantenac grew vines here in 1788. It was at this time that the château was built. It is situated between Libourne and Saint-Emilion, to the south of Pomerol. The vineyard, in one stretch, is planted on a sandy gravelly soil with a subsoil rich in iron-pan. The wines are very characteristic of the terrain, having a fine colour, a rather generous body and tannins which do not rule out finesse.

Curé Bon La Madeleine (Château)

Grand Cru classé

Commune: Saint-Emilion. **Proprietor:** Maurice Landé. **Size of vineyard:** 5 hectares. **Average age of vines:** 25 years. **Varieties:** 5% cabernet-sauvignon. 90% merlot. 5% malbec. **Production:** 24,000 bottles CB. **Visits:** mornings only from Tuesday to Friday. Tel. 57 24 70 95. **Direct sales and by mail order:** in France and abroad. **Retail sales.**

Once upon a time, there was a priest called Bon who lived at La Madeleine ...

Pierre Bon was the mayor of Saint-Emilion in 1323. Since this time, the vineyard has been handed down in direct line or through marriage. I think that this is a record in any château's history. In the last century, there really was a priest (*curé*) called Bon. It was he who gave the *cru* its "contemporary" reputation. On his death, his nephew Camille Lapelleterie inherited it. That was in 1874. Since then, the family Landé-Lapelleterie continues the work of the holy man with devotion. Enshrined between Ausone, Bel-Air and Canon, Curé Bon La Madeleine is entirely typical of the wines of the "Haut Saint-Emilion". All authoritative authors are in agreement and pay tribute to its firmness and suppleness. Breeding and finesse are sure to be found. I will even go further: this *cru* is on the level of the greatest. The only thing is that its small size prevents everyone from knowing it. Never forget that!

Dassault (Château)

Grand Cru classé

Commune: Saint-Emilion. **Proprietor:** Château Dassault S.A.R.L. Director: M. Massing. Estate manager and steward: A. Vergriette. Vineyard manager: Claude Barge. Consultant oenologist: Michel Rolland. **Size of vineyard:** 24 hectares. **Average age of vines:** 20 years. **Varieties:** 10% cabernet-sauvignon. 65% merlot. 25% cabernet-franc. **Production:** 115,000 bottles CB. **Visits:** by appointment. Tel. 57 24 71 30. **Sales by mail order:** in France. **Retail sales:** excellent and reliable distribution can be depended upon from Michel Querre (Libourne), SEA-GRAM (United States), SEVES (Benelux).

Re-established by Marcel Dassault, this cru *holds a very honorable place to-day.*

At the very beginning of the fifties, Marcel Dassault decided to start a new factory for assembling aeroplanes. First of all, he bought an enormous stretch of land near Bordeaux-Mérignac airport. There were hardly any buildings on the various sites, but they were in the vine-growing region of the Graves. Formerly, a large part of the diocesan vineyards encircled the city of Bordeaux, in Le Bouscat, Caudéran, Mérignac, Pessac and Talence. The preparation of the ground for the future aeronautic hangars scarcely presented any problems but a parcel of vines had to be uprooted. Marcel Dassault was greatly troubled by this, so much so that he felt he should atone for this shameful act. This was how he came to buy Château Couprie, a little Saint-Emilion *cru* representing an intestate succession lacking inheritors. And, while his new factory was assembling Mirages, the industrialist put in hand a plan to re-establish his estate, rechristened Dassault, so that no one should be unaware of the fact. He devoted the time and money necessary to it. In 1969, after the complete restoration of the vineyard, the working buildings and the château, and after making several overtures in high places, Château Dassault was admitted to the ranks of *cru classé*. For the record, I should mention that my father, Pierre Ginestet, acted as the aircraft manufacturer's intercessor against certain tiresome people – others might say "jealous" people – who were opposed to its being classified. "When a man of that calibre takes such an interest in vines and wine, it benefits everybody." From that time, there is no doubt that Château Dassault holds its place perfectly among its peers. At several blind tastings, it has proved that it could rival the greatest *crus*. Generally, it has a highly concentrated bouquet with notes of plum and a rich structure which guarantees that it matures excellently.

Despagnet *(Château)* 🏰

→ *Union de Producteurs*

Destieux (Château)

Grand Cru

Commune: Saint-Hippolyte. **Proprietors:** Madame F. Dauriac, Messieurs C. and C. Dauriac. Consultant oenologist: Michel Rolland. **Size of vineyard:** 8 hectares. **Varieties:** 10% cabernet-sauvignon. 65% merlot. 25% cabernet-franc. **Production:** 40 – 45,000 bottles CB. **Visits:** daily by appointment. Tel. 57 24 77 44 or 57 40 25 05. **Direct sales and by mail order:** in France. **Retail sales.**

The vineyard lies on the hillside of Saint-Emilion and, facing south, it benefits from a maximum amount of sunshine. The land is of compact clayey chalk, a guarantee of quality, but particularly difficult to work. Of the two Dauriac brothers, one is in charge of a haematological clinic and the other is a biologist. However, they worship the family estate and are passionately fond of vinification for which scientifically they are highly competent, striving for a type of wine which is as tannic and powerful as possible. I will say that the methods of vinification at Château Destieux are at the peak of our knowledge of oenology. The lover of good wine will for the most part find this *cru* extremely full-bodied and will want to treasure it in his cellar, bequeathing it to his grandchildren along with the family's most precious possessions.

Destieux Berger (Château)

→ *Union de Producteurs*

Grand Cru

Divin Pasteur (Clos)

Commune: Libourne. **Proprietor:** Yvonne Delage. Vineyard manager: Pierre Delage. Consultant oenologist: Michel Rolland. **Size of vineyard:** 2 hectares. **Average age of vines:** 15 years. **Varieties:** 65% merlot. 35% cabernet-franc. **Retail sales:** in bulk.

sold in bulk

Doumayne (Château)

Commune: Libourne. **Proprietor:** Francis Robin. Estate manager: J.-L. Robin. Vineyard manager and cellar master: D. Robin. Consultant oenologist: Michel Rolland. **Size of vineyard:** 1.5 hectares. **Average age of vines:** 30 years. **Varieties:** 70% merlot. 30% cabernet-franc. **Production:** 8,000 bottles CB. **Visits:** tel. 57 51 03 65. **Direct sales and by mail order:** in France and abroad. **Retail sales:** for export. *The Robins have been proprietors in the Libourne area since 1750.*

131

Doumayne (Clos)

Commune: Libourne. **Proprietor:** Roland Bel. Consultant oenologist: M. Chaine. **Size of vineyard:** 1.5 hectares. **Average age of vines:** 40 years. **Varieties:** 50% merlot. 50% cabernet-franc. **Production:** 9,000 bottles CB. **Direct sales and by mail order:** in France. Tel. 57 51 00 88. *Lovers of a really good little wine will never be disappointed by this one.*

Fagouet Jean-Voisin (Château) ☖ → Jean Voisin

Faleyrens (Château)

Commune: Saint-Sulpice-de-Faleyrens. **Proprietor:** Jeanine Brisson. Consultant oenologist: C.Œ de Grézillac. **Size of vineyard:** 4 hectares. **Varieties:** 15% cabernet-sauvignon, 40% merlot, 45% cabernet-franc. **Production:** 13 tonneaux. 12,000 bottles CB. **Direct sales and by mail order:** Madame Brisson, Mondou, Saint-Sulpice-de-Faleyrens, 33330 Saint-Emilion. Tel. 57 74 45 10. **Retail sales.**

Faleyrens (Château de)

Commune: Saint-Sulpice-de-Faleyrens. **Proprietors:** Simon Père et Fils. Director, vineyard manager and cellar master: Claude Simon. Consultant oenologist: Michel Rolland. **Size of vineyard:** 3.85 hectares. **Average age of vines:** 30 years. **Varieties:** 40% cabernet-sauvignon. 60% merlot. **Production:** 17 tonneaux. 10,000 bottles CB. **Direct sales and by mail order:** Tel. 57 24 74 28. **Retail sales.** *Cultivation, harvesting and vinification are rationalized as much as possible to ensure an economic output. This may explain why this wine lacks personality.*

Faurie (Domaine de)

Commune: Saint-Emilion. **Proprietor:** Bernard Oizeau. Consultant oenologist: Michel Rolland. **Size of vineyard:** 0.2 hectares. **Average age of vines:** 35 years. **Varieties:** 60% merlot. 40% cabernet-franc. **Production:** 18,000 bottles CB. **Retail sales:** M. Maurice Lalande (Clos du Roy, Barsac). Tel. 57 24 60 76. *Proprietor since 1967, Bernard Oizeau has practised his talents as cellar master in several Saint-Emilion grands crus.*

Faurie de Souchard (Château)

Grand Cru classé

Commune: Saint-Emilion. **Proprietor:** G.F.A. Jabiol-Sciard. Director: Françoise Sciard. Consultant oenologist: C.B.C. Libourne. **Size of vineyard:** 11 hectares. **Average age of vines:** 27 years. **Varieties:** 9% cabernet-sauvignon. 65% merlot. 26% cabernet-franc. **Production:** 50,000 bottles CB. **Visits:** tel. 57 24 72 55. **Direct sales and by mail order.**

Faurie, which originally was a family name, is a very old locality of Saint-Emilion. The English must remember it well, since a battle – rather less decisive, it is true, than that of Castillon – was fought here during the Hundred Years War. Afterwards, the land of Faurie belonged to the Courbrets and, in the eighteenth century, to the Souchard family. In 1933, Faurie de Souchard was bought by Monsieur and Madame Maurice Jabiol who have a taste for fine and beautiful things. Their daughter Françoise Sciard leased the estate as from the beginning of 1983. The vineyard is in a single stretch on the north hillside of the commune. The proportion of merlot grapes gives the wine an unctuous suppleness. This *Grand Cru classé* holds a very honourable place among its peers.

Ferrand (Château de)

Grand Cru

Commune: Saint-Hippolyte. **Proprietor:** Baron Bich. Director: Jean-Pierre Palatin. **Size of vineyard:** 28 hectares. **Average age of vines:** 25 years. **Varieties:** 18% cabernet-sauvignon. 68% merlot. 14% cabernet-franc. **Production:** 150,000 bottles CB. **Visits:** tel. 57 74 47 11. **Direct sales and by mail order. Retail sales:** through the Bordeaux trade.

In the course of recent years, two great industrialists have set foot on Saint-Emilion territory. The first was Marcel Dassault, whose *cru* henceforth bears his name. The second is Baron Bich, who bought Château Ferrand in 1978 and whose coronet now decorates the label. It is an extremely fine estate in one stretch, set on a plateau of clayey chalk and flanked by a charming holiday residence which is in the styles of the sixteenth and seventeenth centuries. As for the style of the wine, it tends to be robust in body and to have a rich tannin content, making it suitable for long ageing.

Figeac (Château)

1er Grand Cru classé

Commune: Saint-Emilion. **Proprietor:** Thierry Manoncourt. Estate manager: Clément Brochard. **Size of vineyard:** 40 hectares. **Average age of vines:** 35 years. **Varieties:** 35% cabernet-sauvignon. 30% merlot. 35% cabernet-franc. **Production:** 125 tonneaux. **Visits:** Weekdays: 9 a.m. to noon and 3 to 5 p.m. Tel. 57 24 72 26. **Retail sales.**

Figeac's gravelly ridge is a characteristic element of the cru.

To sum up the situation in a nutshell, Figeac as such could be an *appellation d'origine contrôlée* in its own right. This idea seems sound to me. It helps one to understand better the fundamental difference which distinguishes the hillsides, the *graves* and the other terrains. If, because of the haphazard way human settlements are created, Figeac had been established as a village, or better, as a parish, a local borough would have been created and the fate of the Manoncourts would accordingly have been changed. Even if it were to mean encroaching on the land of Pomerol, delineated simply by an artificial frontier of bituminous asphalt some eighteen feet wide and not recognized by Professor Enjalbert himself, the vine-growing territory of the appellation would contain some fifty estates (there are about thirty in Saint-Julien). Cheval Blanc and Figeac would be the *premiers crus* (perhaps La Dominique, too) and, with regard to these, instead of speaking of the wines of Saint-Emilion, we would say: "I prefer the Figeacs to the Saint-Emilions," or vice versa. Once the distinction has been made, personal preference is simply a matter of taste. In an attempt to clarify the topography, Cocks and Féret, back in the second third of

the last century, had drawn up two lists: that of the Haut Saint-Emilion, in which the *crus* of the hillsides and the plateau featured, and that of the Saint-Emilion Graves which they never wanted to assimilate with the former. This was shrewd, in any event, much more subtle than the list of Lecoutre de Beauvais, published in 1841, and reprinted by Charles Cocks in 1850, which listed all the *crus* of Saint-Emilion "horizontally", whether they came from the top or the bottom. At the time of the second edition of *Bordeaux et ses Vins, classés par ordre de mérite* (1868), the editors enumerated the *premiers crus,* which were some twenty in number, from Bélair to Balleau. There then followed a special mention: "The following *crus* have a particular character; they are like the Saint-Emilion wines and those of Pomerol and much resemble the Médocs. The *crus* Château Figeac and Cheval Blanc sell like all the *premiers crus* of these two communes."

From the beginning of this century, the comparison with the *crus* of the Médoc is made less peremptorily (doubtless because these latter made representations to the honourable editor with a few distinguished gasps of protest): "The Saint-Emilions and Pomerols have an aromatic savour, a finesse and a highly developed bouquet. They recall the Médocs somewhat." It was at this time that Cheval Blanc bolted, racing away in front of all the others, a breakaway which is still going strong.

And yet, when Thierry Manoncourt crosses his legs, sitting learnedly in his armchair of crimson velvet, and raises his index finger in solemn gesture, history is restored to its true dignity: "Cheval Blanc was neither more nor less than Figeac's leased farm!" At the beginning of the nineteenth century, the estate of Figeac had about 200 hectares. Henri Enjalbert described it thus: "In 1807–1810, Château Figeac had all the advantages of that of a 'Great' of the Médoc: a huge estate on privileged terrain of fine gravel, a beautiful château and a vast park, an almost secular viticultural tradition." We know that after this, its proprietor, André de Carle-Trajet, speculated in the cultivation of crops other than the grape, such as clover or madder. When he died in 1825, he bequeathed to his wife, Félicité de Gères, a difficult financial situation which the young widow only succeeded in aggravating. For ten years she sold off land in order to survive, and this was how Cheval Blanc found its personality and how many parcels of land were scattered about. The second half of the century saw seven proprietors in succession. In 1892, Henri de Chevremont allowed himself to be convinced by his son-in-law, André Villepigue, to offer Figeac to his daughter. Thierry Manoncourt is her great grandson.

The vines of Figeac half-share, along with those of Cheval Blanc, practically all the sixty hectares of gunz gravel which is responsible for the fame of these *crus*. The agronomic model of the estate is copied from that of a great Médoc *cru*. The cabernets (sauvignon or franc) predominate, representing 70% of the grapes. This gives the wine a remarkable individuality. It is always very powerful, rich, even opulent, with a generous aromatic savour. Since 1947, Thierry Manoncourt and his wife, Marie-France (née Duboys de Labarre) have given Figeac meticulous attention which could even be called devotion. The constancy of its quality is proved even in the off-years which bear witness to the keen demands of the proprietor. We would not have expected less from the Premier Jurat of Saint-Emilion.

Fleur Cardinale (Château) ♟♟♟♟♟

Grand Cru

Commune: Saint-Etienne-de-Lisse. **Proprietor:** G.F.A. Château Fleur Cardinale. Director: Madame Claude Asséo. Cellar master: Alain Asséo. Consultant oenologist: Michel Rolland. **Size of vineyard:** 9.3 hectares. **Average age of vines:** 30 years. **Varieties:** 15% cabernet-sauvignon. 70% merlot. 15% cabernet-franc. **Production:** 45 tonneaux. **Visits:** tel. 57 40 14 05. **Direct sales and by mail order:** in France. **Retail sales:** through the Bordeaux trade.

"I draw my greatest satisfaction from the telephone calls or the letters I receive from my clients", declares Claude Asséo without false modesty. "We settled here permanently in March 1983 after selling our textile business in Paris and our house. We wanted to change our life. For people who were over fifty, it was not easy. I wanted to make the best wine possible with the help of a famous oenologist." The results obtained by these newly-imported citizens have been hailed by many connoisseurs, including one of the greatest in the United States, Robert Parker. La Fleur Cardinale is in fact a good wine for enlightened wine-lovers: aromas of black cherries and liquorice, a solid structure, an agreeable suppleness. It can equally well be drunk soon after bottling or after many years of ageing.

Flouquet (Château)

Grand Cru

Commune: Saint-Emilion. **Proprietors:** Bernard & Fils. **Size of vineyard:** 20 hectares. **Average age of vines:** 25 years. **Varieties:** 10% cabernet-sauvignon. 60% merlot. 30% cabernet-franc. **Production:** 100 tonneaux. 70,000 bottles CB. **Direct sales and by mail order:** in France. Tel. 57 24 72 48. **Retail sales.** *From father to son over five generations. At the foot of the hillside to the south of Saint-Emilion.*

Flouquet Madeleine (Château)

Grand Cru

Commune: Saint-Emilion. **Proprietors:** M. and Madame Jean Penchaud. **Size of vineyard:** 1 hectare. **Average age of vines:** 50 years. **Varieties:** 60% merlot. 40% cabernet-franc. **Production:** 6,000 bottles CB. **Visits:** weekends only. Tel. 57 24 73 61. **Direct sales and by mail order:** in France.

Five different parcels to make up one hectare! What matter where they are, or their geological formations and exposure, seeing that I am telling you that they are excellent and that Jean Penchaud's father, who was a connoisseur, bought one of them simply for his personal consumption. It should also be mentioned that Jean Penchaud is a cooper by trade and did not want to make tonneaux for the rest of his life with the firm of Demptos without filling three or four for the sole pleasure of being responsible for the container and the contents. In 1983, his wish came true. For him, it is a great satisfaction. For his future customers, it will be a revelation. And the vines are only fifty years old!...

Fombrauge (Château)

Grand Cru

Commune: Saint-Christophe-des-Bardes. **Proprietor:** Bordeaux Château Invest. **President:** Flemmin Kaarberg. **Advisor:** Charles Bygodt. **Technical director:** Stéphane Savigneux. **Cellar master:** Ugo Arguti. **Consultant oenologist:** C.B.C. M. Chaine. **Size of vineyard:** 50 hectares. **Average age of vines:** 25 years. **Varieties:** 10% cabernet-sauvignon. 60% merlot. 30% cabernet-franc. **Production:** 300,000 bottles CB. **Visits:** tel. 57 24 77 12. **Direct sales and by mail order. Retail sales.** *Particuly easy to find in Denmark for obvious reasons.*

Fombrauge: a beautiful estate over which henceforth flies the flag of Denmark.

This is a vast estate of seventy-five hectares which is split up over two areas. One is in the commune of Saint-Christophe-des-Bardes and the other straddles Saint-Etienne-de-Lisse and Saint-Hippolyte. Their area is equal, each having twenty-five hectares of vines at the present time. Such a large area, rare in the Saint-Emilion appellation, is *a priori* a guarantee of quality, because it gives the grower a wide range of soils and exposures which, together with the different varieties of grapes, provide complementary characteristics. The secret consists of using the right proportion of each element and in making rigorous selections from the different vats. And this is how Charles Bygodt runs his estate. When his father died in 1973, this intelligent businessman took the property in hand, as he might have done any industrial enterprise. But he soon discovered the real value of the product, that is, its noble quality. It was a revelation which dictated a policy of high quality. "It always pays in the end," he likes to say, adding that if profit is an encouragement, the real reward is the customer's satisfaction.

Today, Château Fombrauge enjoys a fine reputation. It is often served at official and important banquets, so recovering its fame of the last century. In 1978, Monsieur Bygodt received a letter from an old firm of wine-merchants in the Netherlands, accompanied by a label of Château Fombrauge 1893. Business relations were at once cemented, to the great satisfaction of the importer and exporter. Indeed Fombrauge is one of the oldest *crus* of Saint-Emilion. It is also a cradle of man's earliest labours, for Bordeaux University recently discovered a palaeolithic site there. I warmly recommend mammoth trunk roasted on old roots of *vitis vinifera* and washed down with a Fombrauge of the 11,985 B.C. vintage. On March 18, 1987, the estate of Fombrauge was bought by a Danish group controlled by the firm of Hans Just of Copenhagen. The price was more than 60,000,000 francs. From that time, Fombrauge has become a sort of institution in the manner of some of the greatest *crus* of the Médoc. Its management is very active in seeking all forms of publicity. Will this make the wine any better?...

Fonplégade (Château)

Grand Cru classé

Commune: Saint-Emilion. **Proprietors:** Armand Moueix heirs. Director and cellar master: Armand Moueix. Consultant oenologist: Bernard Crébassa. **Size of vineyard:** 18 hectares. **Average age of vines:** 25 years. **Varieties:** 5% cabernet-sauvignon. 60% merlot. 35% cabernet-franc. **Production:** 90,000 bottles CB. **Visits:** by appointment. Tel. 57 51 50 63. **Sales by mail order:** in France. **Retail sales:** S.A. Moueix et Fils.

When Jean-Marie Moueix, Armand's father, bought Fonplégade in 1953, Mademoiselle de Rochefort-Lavie handed him a lamentable vineyard, pitiful cellars and vat-house, and a derelict residence fit only for phantoms. She had inherited it from her adoptive father, Paul Boisard. This man had a well-established reputation as an enlightened grower. He struggled brilliantly against phylloxera at the end of the last century and was one of the champions of the cabernet-sauvignon in the Saint-Emilion region. But after him, the fine estate of Fonplégade, which had been considered as a very model of agronomy at the time, gradually declined until the Moueix came to save it. Formerly, Fonplégade was not lacking in letters patent of nobility, since the estate had been in the aristocratic hands of the Duke de Morny and his sister, the Countess de Galard. As for Mademoiselle de Rochefort-Lavie, her principal claim to fame was that of having been the ward of the priest Bergey, which explains why Armand Moueix is in possession of a part of the holy man's

Fonplégade: a fountain which every year fills up with ... good wine!

library. In 1962, this dogged man from the department of Corrèze bought some of the land of Le Tertre Daugay so completing the work of consolidation carried out by Boisard. The locals claim that Fonplégade means "refluent fountain" because the springs are to be found at the top of the hill. I find this explanation absurd. If the prefix "fon" means simply "fountain", the suffix "plégade" derives from the Gascon *plear* or *plenhar*, which in its guttural form becomes *plegar* which expresses the idea of the verb "to fill". *Que s'a plegat la pança* does not mean: "he bowed from the waist" but "he ate his fill". Fonplégade means quite simply "fountain filled to overflowing" – that 'springs' clearly into evidence. I hope that with this little lesson I have helped to confirm the Gascon authenticity of the site and I will add that today, the wines of Fonplégade are well-made and delicious. They are undoubtedly in the leading group of *Grands Crus classés*, one of those which one day or another will break away, catch up with and join the *Premiers*.

Fonrazade (Château)

Grand Cru

Commune: Saint-Emilion. **Proprietor:** Guy Balotte. Consultant oenologist: Grézillac Laboratory. **Size of vineyard:** 13 hectares. **Average age of vines:** 25 years. **Varieties:** 20% cabernet-sauvignon. 80% merlot. **Production:** 70,000 bottles CB. **Visits:** tel. 57 24 71 58. **Direct sales and by mail order:** in France and abroad. **Retail sales.**

Formerly belonging to the Comte des Cordes for several years, Fonrazade came into Guy Balotte's hands at the very time that General de Gaulle was taking into his own the destiny of France. Since 1958, he has modernized, improved and rationalized his estate, which is now in an impeccable state, including the reception room which is capable of holding 150 people. The vineyard is contiguous with Château L'Angélus and faces south.

Fonroque (Château)

Grand Cru classé

Commune: Saint-Emilion. **Proprietor:** G.F.A. Château Fonroque. Director: Jean-Jacques Moueix. Estate manager: Michel Gillet. Cellar master: Jean Veyssière. Consultant oenologist: Jean-Claude Berrouet. **Size of vineyard:** 18 hectares. **Average age of vines:** 30 years. **Varieties:** 5% cabernet-sauvignon. 75% merlot. 20% cabernet-franc. **Production:** 100,000 bottles CB. **Retail sales:** Ets. Jean-Pierre Moueix. Tel. 57 51 78 96.

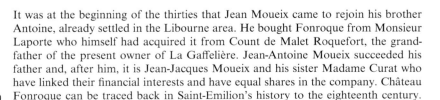

It was at the beginning of the thirties that Jean Moueix came to rejoin his brother Antoine, already settled in the Libourne area. He bought Fonroque from Monsieur Laporte who himself had acquired it from Count de Malet Roquefort, the grandfather of the present owner of La Gaffelière. Jean-Antoine Moueix succeeded his father and, after him, it is Jean-Jacques Moueix and his sister Madame Curat who have linked their financial interests and have equal shares in the company. Château Fonroque can be traced back in Saint-Emilion's history to the eighteenth century.

A stone lintel in the cellar bears the inscription: "1756". The vineyard is spread out on a chalky plateau and a hill of chalky clay with a contribution of sandy silt at the foot of the slope. It is a fine estate whose production is perfectly organized. The wines have a generous tannic structure and have powerful aromas. On ageing, the great years can attain a perfectly remarkable fullness and distinction. Although it may not reach the peak of quality, this *cru* is nevertheless very dependable.

Fontenelle (Château)

Commune: Saint-Etienne-de-Lisse. **Proprietors:** The Bigarette brothers (Edgar and Hubert). Consultant oenologist: M. Hébrard. **Size of vineyard:** 1.65 hectares. **Average age of vines:** 25 years. **Varieties:** 15% cabernet-sauvignon. 50% merlot. 20% cabernet-franc. 15% malbec. **Production:** 8,400 bottles CB. **Direct sales and by mail order:** in France and abroad. Tel. 57 40 08 86. *La Fontenelle is a (miraculous) little fountain which most obligingly provides a steady flow of wine.*

Fortin (Château) ♟
→ La Grâce Dieu des Prieurs

Fougueyrat (Château)

Grand Cru

Commune: Saint-Emilion. **Proprietor:** Daniel Nicoux. Consultant oenologist: M. Rolland. **Size of vineyard:** 5.18 hectares. **Average age of vines:** 35 years. **Varieties:** 80% merlot. 20% cabernet-franc. **Production:** 30,000 bottles CB. **Direct sales and by mail order:** in France. Tel. 57 24 70 64. *Conservative methods and an old trick: a dessert spoonful of salt per tonneau at the time of fining with egg-whites.*

Fourney (Château)

Grand Cru

Commune: Saint-Pey-d'Armens. **Proprietor:** Jean-Pierre Rollet. Vineyard manager: Marcel Zamparo. Cellar master: Luca Zamparo. Consultant oenologist: François Maurin. **Size of vineyard:** 12 hectares. **Varieties:** 6% cabernet-sauvignon. 64% merlot. 30% cabernet-franc. **Production:** 76,000 bottles CB. **Direct sales and by mail order:** B.P. 23, 33300 Saint-Emilion. Tel. 57 47 15 13.

If the term "Château" in the Bordeaux region often does not mean very much architecturally speaking, we must allow nevertheless that Fourney fully deserves this epithet both because of the quality of its construction and because of its vine-growing 141 function. Indeed, it is an extremely elegant dwelling, in the style of Louis XVI, said to have been designed by the famous Victor Louis, the architect of the Grand Théâtre in Bordeaux. It is the home of Jean-Pierre Rollet and his family who bought the estate more than twenty years ago. The Rollets have been growers in Saint-Emilion since the beginning of the eighteenth century. The wines of Fourney are full of tannin with notes of very ripe red fruits. The great years are particularly successful.

Fourtet (Clos)

1er Grand Cru classé

Commune: Saint-Emilion. **Proprietor:** Lurton Frères. (Société Civile du Clos Fourtet). Estate manager: Pierre Lurton. Cellar master: Daniel Alard. Consultant oenologists: E. Peynaud and M. Hébrard. **Size of vineyard:** 18 hectares. **Average age of vines:** 30 years. **Varieties:** 10% cabernet-sauvignon. 70% merlot. 20% cabernet-franc. **Production:** 80,000 bottles CB. **Visits:** Monday to Friday 9 a.m. to noon and 2 to 6 p.m. Tel. 57 24 70 90. **Direct sales and by mail order:** in France. **Retail sales:** through the Bordeaux trade.

Although it has a large bourgeois dwelling constructed before the Revolution, this *Premier Grand Cru classé* of Saint-Emilion did not shape its style after the model of the "Châteaux" and its label has retained its ancient discretion. As regards ancient history, Clos Fourtet can boast deep roots. Already in the Middle Ages "Camfourtet" was an important site in Saint-Emilion. In the seventeenth century, it was inherited by the Rulleau family, of whom Henri Enjalbert says that it sired a line of great growers. He says that "if the Rulleaus were the first to make great wines at Clos Fourtet, this was primarily because they were able to change the grape varieties and in so doing turned this small traditional estate with many weaknesses and poor wines into a new vineyard with uniform stock of long life, thereby establishing a vineyard with a high percentage of old vines."

As regards deep roots and old vines, you should see the roof of the cellars at Clos Fourtet. Ancient stone quarries, these monolithic cellars go down to some forty-five feet underground, and the roots of the cabernet-franc can be seen hanging from the rock like fragile creepers. What prodigious vitality to have driven the plant to bore through the rock, using the smallest natural fissure to seek its way to find the least nourishment! In Saint-Emilion, and particularly at Clos Fourtet, this type of viticultural speleology is surprising us. The body of the terrain of Clos Fourtet is made up of a very thin layer of arable land, just enough to permit young plants to strike root. From the second or third year, the vines must fruit with difficulty. This is rather in the style of the viticulture of Burgundy, confirmed in some measure by the walled enclosures which justify the term "Clos".

My grandfather, Fernand Ginestet, owned Clos Fourtet from the end of the First World War up to the end of the Second. In 1948, he exchanged the *cru* for François Lurton's shares in Château Margaux. The following twenty years did not particularly heighten the good reputation of the name. Since that time, his descendants: Madame Noël, Messieurs André, Lucien and Dominique Lurton have run the estate, and Clos Fourtet has returned to its former glory. Technically, vinification has evolved and metal vats are in use, but maturing in wood is rigorously preserved. The proprietors take advantage of their famous monolithic cellars to ensure a constant temperature and atmospheric humidity of 85% to guarantee high quality. As regards the first

A bourgeois mansion whose garden is a vineyard.

point, I am entirely in agreement: wine which is developed without any variation in temperature evolves gradually. As regards the second point, I am less enthusiastic. Such a high hygrometric saturation level can lower the degree of the wine. But all this is merely small talk. For without any possible dispute, the wines of Clos Fourtet are at the very peak of quality. They are highly representative of the vine-clad hill which is the true soul of Saint-Emilion – and when I say highly, I mean in terms of both altitude and of breeding and cultivation. This is especially true of recent vintages.

Franc (Château) ☖ → Franc Patarabet

Franc Bigaroux (Château)

Commune: Saint-Sulpice-de-Faleyrens. **Proprietor:** Yves Blanc. Estate manager: Michel Martrinchard. Cellar master: Jean-François Vergne. Consultant oenologist: M. Hébrard. **Size of vineyard:** 9 hectares. **Average age of vines:** 19 years. **Varieties:** 20% cabernet-sauvignon. 60% merlot. 20% cabernet-franc. **Production:** 60,000 bottles CB. **Visits:** weekdays from 8 a.m. to noon and 2 to 5.30 p.m. Tel. 57 51 54 73. **Sales by mail order:** Vignobles Yves Blanc, 167 avenue Foch, 33501 Libourne Cédex B.P. 170. **Retail sales:** 90% for export to United States, England, Denmark, Belgium.

This is a label which has shown constant progress over recent years. Part of the vineyard of Château Franc Bigaroux is at the foot of the clayey chalky slope and the other part on warm sandy land. Vinification is carefully controlled thanks to equipment for cooling the musts. The result is a wine with a rich bouquet, with aromas of crystallized fruits. Its body is ample, rich and unctuous. It is an excellent "typical Saint-Emilion" which can sometimes compete with much better known *crus*. Moreover, foreign connoisseurs are well aware of this. All the principal export 143 markets appreciate this wine, which is to be found in the best European and American restaurants. Today Yves Blanc has come to regret that his vineyard is not larger so that his label might be better known.

Franc-Cros (Château)

Commune: Saint-Emilion. **Proprietors:** M. and Madame André Lafarge. **Size of vineyard:** 3.3 hectares. **Average age of vines:** 30 years. **Varieties:** 20% cabernet-sauvignon. 60% merlot. 20% cabernet-franc. **Production:** 12 tonneaux. 3,000 bottles CB. **Visits:** tel. 57 24 60 14. **Direct sales and by mail order:** in France. **Retail sales.** *Several parcels, neighbours to estates of good quality form the estate of this vigneron family which can count back more than five generations.*

Franc-Fongaban

Commune: Saint-Emilion. **Proprietor:** Jean-Louis Bigaud. **Size of vineyard:** 0.36 hectares. **Average age of vines:** 25 years. **Varieties:** 40% merlot. 25% cabernet-franc. 25% malbec, 10% cabernet-sauvignon. **Production:** 1.5 tonneaux.

Formerly, the valley of Fongaban was made up of a few vineyards, but more especially by a host of little gardens which were cultivated by the inhabitants of the nearest town. In view of their number, the area of each was small. Originally Jean-Louis Bigaud's maternal grandfather had one such which he was able to increase by buying a parcel alongside. Gaston Bigaud, his son, managed to add another plot and began to plant vines. Then two or three more microscopic additions and the concern reached the present area of 0.36 hectares. Jean-Louis Bigaud treasures this little vine-growing kingdom in his heart. His wine is principally destined for his own personal consumption and that of his friends. Sometimes, he consents to sell a few bottles to those "in the know". You should try to be one of their number, but no businessmen, please!

Franc Grâce-Dieu (Château)

Grand Cru

Commune: Saint-Emilion. **Proprietor:** Germain Siloret. Tenant: S.E.V. Fournier. Cellar master: Paul Cazenave. Consultant oenologist: Michel Rolland. **Size of vineyard:** 8.27 hectares. **Average age of vines:** 25 years. **Varieties:** 7% cabernet-sauvignon. 52% merlot. 41% cabernet-franc. **Production:** 40,000 bottles CB. **Visits:** tel. 57 24 70 79. **Direct sales and by mail order:** B.P. 28, 33330 Saint-Emilion. **Retail sales.**

This is one of the estates of Saint-Emilion that is richest in history, in the sense of daily life as it has been lived through the ages. It is intimately linked to the Guadets, a family whose local fame has featured widely in all the old chronicles and gazettes since the seventeenth century. This family gave the town no fewer than five mayors. In 1692, Pierre Guadet, the lord of La Grâce-Dieu, was elected the first jurat. The family estates extended from Saint-Martin de Mazerat to the Porte Bourgeoise in Sansonnet, near the Porte Bouqueyre at La Grâce-Dieu and even into the parish of Saint-Hippolyte. In 1930, Germain Siloret, a Breton by origin, married a daughter of the Siloret family, the heiress of the aforementioned estate of the Guadets. In the Middle Ages, it was a Cistercian monastery which, by the grace of God, was exempt from taxes – whence its name. Germain Siloret, today retired, held the highly responsible post of technical advisor to the Department of Highways, Rivers and Forests. It was he notably who was responsible for the siphoning of the water-tables in the department of the Landes to make possible and to further the cultivation of maize. In Saint-Emilion, Germain Siloret presents the image of a wise old man, crowned with a fine career as a great servant of the state but happily retired in discreet modesty. He has never sought personal stardom but he has always listened to and readily advised all those who think that they have something to say or write. Henri Enjalbert would never have dreamed of not consulting him in his survey of the Libourne vineyards. His estate is leased to the Fourniers of Château Canon; but he is still to be found on his vines and in the cellars. The wine of La Grâce-Dieu can be drunk with your eyes closed.

Franc Jaugue Blanc (Château)
→ Union de Producteurs

Franc-Laporte (Château)

Commune: Saint-Christophe-des-Bardes. **Proprietor:** Max Rollet. Consultant oenologist: C.B.C. Libourne. **Size of vineyard:** 6.59 hectares. **Average age of vines:** 20 years. **Varieties:** 50% merlot. 50% cabernet-franc. **Production:** 30 tonneaux. 5,000 bottles CB. **Direct sales:** tel. 57 24 77 03. **Retail sales.**

Franc Lartigue (Château)
→ Union de Producteurs

Grand Cru

Franc Le Maine (Château)
→ Union de Producteurs

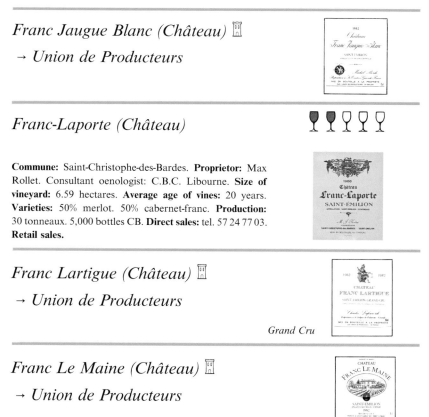

Franc-Mayne (Château)

Grand Cru classé

Commune: Saint-Emilion. **Proprietor:** Société Civile Agricole du Château Franc-Mayne. Director: Nicole Butaud. Vineyard manager: Raphaël Herrera. **Size of vineyard:** 6.82 hectares. **Average age of vines:** 20 years. **Varieties:** 15% cabernet-sauvignon. 70% merlot. 15% cabernet-franc. **Production:** 43,000 bottles CB. **Visits:** tel. 57 24 62 61. **Direct sales and by mail order:** in France and abroad.

The large firm of Libourne wine-merchants, Theillassoubre, became the proprietors of this *cru* in 1903. Formerly, Franc-Mayne belonged to Baron G. des Cordes and the vineyard, which at that time had an area of eight hectares, had become detached from the mediaeval estate of La Gomerie. In 1984, a private company was formed, with the Axa Group (Mutuelles Unies) as the principal shareholders, but it is Madame Butaud, the heiress of the Theillassoubres, who still runs the estate. Traditionally, Franc-Mayne is a well-known and highly appreciated name in the Benelux countries. The three parcels which make up the vineyard on the plateau, on the hillside and at the foot of the slope ensure the wine a good variety of complementary qualities. Hugh Johnson describes it as "a small, well-run estate on the west slopes." I would add that the wines of Franc-Mayne are agreeably supple and easy to drink.

Franc-Mazerat (Château)

Commune: Saint-Emilion. **Proprietor:** Pierrette Koch. Consultant oenologist: Michel Rolland. **Size of vineyard:** 2 hectares. **Average age of vines:** 30 years. **Varieties:** 50% merlot. 50% cabernet-franc. **Production:** 7,000 bottles CB. **Direct sales and by mail order:** tel. 57 24 73 07. **Retail sales.** *Pierrette Koch has worked on the vines since she was twenty. Her mother, who is approaching eighty, still gives her a hand.*

Franc Patarabet (Château)

Grand Cru

Commune: Saint-Emilion. **Proprietor:** G.F.A. Faure Barraud. Directors: Mesdames Barraud & Guschlbauer. Estate manager: M. Terras. Cellar master: M. Fontaniol. Consultant oenologist: M. Chaine. **Size of vineyard:** 5.5 hectares. **Varieties:** 30% cabernet-sauvignon. 40% merlot. 30% cabernet-franc. **Production:** 20 tonneaux. **Visits:** tel. 57 24 70 36 or 57 24 60 91. **Direct sales and by mail order. Retail sales:** Nouvelles-Halles and Vinothèque de Bordeaux. *People still speak of Grandfather Barraud's 1929s, but the recent vintages are far from being a disgrace. You can buy the 1967s too.*

Franc Petit Figeac (Château)

Commune: Saint-Emilion. **Proprietors:** M. and Madame Gilbert Dumon. Consultant oenologist: M. Rolland. **Size of vineyard:** 4.5 hectares. **Average age of vines:** 20 years. **Varieties:** 85% merlot. 15% cabernet-franc. **Production:** 12,000 bottles CB. **Visits:** tel. 57 24 73 42. **Direct sales and by mail order:** in France. *The Dumons' table is large but never large enough: it appears to shrink when they put all their bottles of old vintages on it for friends and clients to taste.*

Franc Pineuilh (Château)

Commune: Saint-Christophe-des-Bardes. **Proprietor:** Jean-Paul Deson. Consultant oenologist: C.B.C. Libourne. **Size of vineyard:** 1.38 hectares. **Average age of vines:** 25 years. **Varieties:** 5% cabernet-sauvignon. 60% merlot. 35% cabernet-franc. **Production:** 10,000 bottles CB. **Visits:** tel. 57 24 77 40. **Direct sales and by mail order.** *A discreet little* cru *which can be poured without problems and which slips down nicely.*

Franc Pipeau (Château)

Grand Cru

Commune: Saint-Hippolyte. **Proprietor:** Jacqueline Bertrand Descombes. Director: Jacques Bertrand. Consultant oenologist: Michel Rolland. **Size of vineyard:** 4.5 hectares. **Average age of vines:** 30 years. **Varieties:** 10% cabernet-sauvignon. 70% merlot. 20% cabernet-franc. **Production:** 25,000 bottles CB. **Sales by mail order:** in France. Tel. 57 24 73 94. **Retail sales:** France and abroad. *A very lively alcoholic wine. Rather closed up and short on the palate. Sometimes, a bitter finish.*

Franc-Pourret (Château)

Grand Cru

Commune: Saint-Emilion. **Proprietor:** François Ouzoulias. Estate manager and cellar master: Pierre Ouzoulias. Consultant oenologist: Michel Rolland. **Size of vineyard:** 5 hectares. **Average age of vines:** 40 years. **Varieties:** 10% cabernet-sauvignon. 80% merlot. 10% cabernet-franc. **Production:** 21,000 bottles CB. **Visits:** Monday to Friday from 3 to 6 p.m. Tel. 57 51 07 55. **Sales by mail order:** in France. François Ouzoulias, 17 rue du Colonel Picot, 33500 Libourne.

"Quality comes from the little extras. It is more than a job, it is a passion." On his own vines, Pierre Ouzoulias practises a method of cultivation which might be called "gardening". Chemical weed-killer or pesticides are not allowed. In the vat-house maceration with carbonic protection and daily vat-recycling, passing the wine over the solids, are practised. Personally, I am highly in favour of this procedure, which makes the major aromas very agreeable. Franc-Pourret is found mainly in Europe among a select clientele. Generally, the wines have a highly developed bouquet, are full of body with mellow tannins and are long in the mouth.

Franc-Robin (Château)

Commune: Saint-Christophe-des-Bardes. **Proprietor:** Michel Laudu. Consultant oenologist: C.B.C. Libourne. **Size of vineyard:** 10.85 hectares. **Average age of vines:** 20 years. **Varieties:** 50% merlot. 50% cabernet-franc. **Production:** 1 tonneau. Tel. 40 83 23 84. *Difficult... if you can manage to get a taste of this wine, you must be one of Michel Laudu's old army friends.*

label
not
communicated

Francs Bories (Château)
→ *Union de Producteurs*

Gaillard (Château)

Grand Cru

Commune: Saint-Hippolyte. **Proprietor:** M. J.-J. Nouvel. Consultant oenologists: Mademoiselle Cazenave and M. Chaine. **Size of vineyard:** 18 hectares. **Average age of vines:** 30 years. **Varieties:** 40% cabernet-sauvignon. 40% merlot. 20% cabernet-franc. **Production:** 90,000 bottles CB. **Visits:** by appointment. Tel. 57 24 72 05. **Direct sales and by mail order:** in France. *Six generations!... The Gaillards were there before the Revolution. Those of today like their wines to be supple.*

Gaillard de la Gorce (Château)

Grand Cru

Commune: Saint-Etienne-de-Lisse. **Proprietor:** Jean-Pierre Rollet. Vineyard manager: Marcel Zamparo. Cellar master: Luca Zamparo. Consultant oenologist: François Maurin. **Size of vineyard:** 8 hectares. **Varieties:** 29% cabernet-sauvignon. 46% merlot. 25% cabernet-franc. **Production:** 50,000 bottles CB. **Visits:** on weekdays and by appointment only. **Direct sales and by mail order:** B.P. 23, 33330 Saint-Emilion. Tel. 57 47 15 13.

On May 29, 1729, Léon Roulleau, known as Rollet, and his wife, Marie Thibaut, proprietors at Saint-Etienne-de-Lisse, made their will. Together they decided to disinherit their two daughters as far as possible and to share the vines out between their two sons. Jean-Pierre Rollet is a direct descendant of the younger, Pierre Roulleau, also known as Rollet. Over the generations, the little estate has grown and it is one of the four pride and joys belonging to Jean-Pierre Rollet in the Saint-Emilion appellation. Moreover, gold, silver and bronze medals regularly reward this ancestral production. The vineyard is set at the limit of the terrain of clayey chalk and siliceous clay with iron-pan. This gives the wines a rather harmonious balance: full and rich without being excessively heavy. The table of the Grand Duchy of Luxembourg, those of the Palais de l'Elysée or of many French diplomats have often endorsed the fine reputation of this likeable Gallant.

Gaubert (Château)

Grand Cru

Commune: Saint-Christophe-des-Bardes. **Proprietor:** Jean Ménager. **Managed by:** G.A.E.C. Ménager. Vineyard managers and cellar masters: Joëlle and Gérard Ménager. Consultant oenologist: M. Hébrard. **Size of vineyard:** 8 hectares. **Average age of vines:** 40 years. **Varieties:** 70% merlot. 30% cabernet-franc. **Production:** 24,000 bottles CB. **Direct sales and by mail order:** tel. 57 24 70 55. *An altitude of some 290 feet to the east of Saint-Emilion and an ecological cultivation to give a strictly honest and typical wine.*

Gerbaud (Clos)

Commune: Saint-Pey-d'Armens. **Proprietor:** Ginette Chabrol. Cellar master: Jean Chabrol. Consultant oenologist: M. Hébrard. **Size of vineyard:** 2.5 hectares. **Average age of vines:** 20 years. **Varieties:** 15% cabernet-sauvignon. 70% merlot. 15% cabernet-franc. **Production:** 18,000 bottles CB. **Visits:** by appointment. Tel. 57 47 12 39. **Direct sales and by mail order.** *A production that appears overgenerous for such a small vineyard.*

Gessan (Château)

Commune: Saint-Sulpice-de-Faleyrens. **Proprietor:** Bernard Gonzalès. Vineyard manager and consultant oenologist: Ets. Bonneau. **Size of vineyard:** 7.19 hectares. **Average age of vines:** 20 years. **Varieties:** 35% cabernet-sauvignon. 65% merlot. **Production:** 50,000 bottles CB. **Visits:** mornings only. Tel. 57 74 44 04. **Direct sales. Retail sales:** Ets. Bonneau in Branne. *The proprietors do not run the estate themselves but they look after the marketing side. The wines are easy to drink...and to forget.*

Ghildes (Clos des)

Commune: Libourne. **Proprietor:** Gérard Faisandier. Cellar master: Jean Michaud. Consultant oenologist: M. Rolland. **Size of vineyard:** 1.12 hectares. **Average age of vines:** 80 years. **Varieties:** 30% cabernet-sauvignon. 40% merlot. 30% cabernet-franc. **Production:** 6,000 bottles CB. Tel. 57 51 20 79.

A musician at heart, Gérard Faisandier had none the less always had the idea that one day he would retire from the world of music to enter that of wine. He was already the owner of Château La Bassonnerie in Pomerol when he bought the Clos des Ghildes in 1962. The vineyard of the Clos des Ghildes is in the Grand Circle, opposite Pomerol. One fine sunny evening, strolling along the sands of Saint-Emilion across the vines, you can still hear an air on the bassoon. The wines of Gérard Faisandier are not lacking in harmony.

Godeau (Château)

Grand Cru

Commune: Saint-Laurent-des-Combes. **Proprietor:** S.C.I. du Château Godeau. Director: Georges Litvine. Estate manager: J.-F. Galhaud. Consultant oenologist: Michel Rolland. **Size of vineyard:** 4.25 hectares. **Average age of vines:** 25 years. **Varieties:** 35% cabernet-sauvignon. 60% merlot. 5% cabernet-franc. **Production:** 20,000 bottles CB. **Visits:** by appointment. Tel. 57 74 08 48. **Direct sales and by mail order:** in France and abroad.

It was a Belgian industrialist, M. Georges Litvine, who in 1978 made himself a present of this polished gem – clay over underlying limestone. The vineyard has undergone a thorough restoration and the vat-house resembles an exhibition model. The wines are very deep in colour, owing to their virile tannins, and are an excellent "typical Saint-Emilion". The designation of "Grand Cru" is in no way an exaggeration and corresponds to a real quality.

Gombaud Ménichot (Château)

→ *Union de Producteurs*

Gourdins (Domaine des)

Commune: Libourne. **Proprietor:** Madame Coudreau. Tenant: J.-P. Estager. Consultant oenologist: Gilles Pauquet. **Size of vineyard:** 1.5 hectares. **Average age of vines:** 15 years. **Varieties:** 80% merlot. 20% cabernet-franc. **Production:** 7 tonneaux. 3,600 bottles CB. **Sales by mail order:** in France. Tel. 57 51 04 09. **Retail sales:** J.-P. Estager, Libourne.

Several proprietors of the Libourne area have one foot in Saint-Emilion and the other in Pomerol. Such is the case of Jean-Pierre Estager who runs some twelve hectares at Château La Cabane in Pomerol. In Saint-Emilion, he is notably to be found as the tenant of Madame Coudreau, on one-and-a-half hectares situated in the old appellation "Sables Saint-Emilion". He describes his wine himself as "fruity, with a supple attack, whose even balance allows it to develop rather rapidly, while retaining its potential for ageing". The wine of the Domaine des Gourdins is always sold at reasonable prices.

Grand Barrail Lamarzelle Figeac

Grand Cru classé

Commune: Saint-Emilion. **Proprietor:** Association Carrère. Consultant oenologist: Michel Rolland. **Size of vineyard:** 19 hectares. **Average age of vines:** 25 years. **Varieties:** 20% cabernet-sauvignon. 70% merlot. 10% cabernet-franc. **Production:** 100,000 bottles CB. **Direct sales and by mail order:** tel. 57 24 71 43.

The Carrère family trust also owns the Châteaux Lamarzelle in Saint-Emilion, Cambon La Pelouse in the Haut-Médoc and Ladevigne in Bergerac. Six members of the family divided the tasks out among themselves to run this large inheritance. Along with Cheval Blanc and Figeac, Grand Barrail Lamarzelle Figeac is one of the largest estates of the Graves of Saint-Emilion. Separated from Figeac about the middle of the last century, this *cru* was reconstituted in 1895, after the phylloxera crisis, by an industrialist from the department of the Nord called Bouchard (Enjalbert says Boitard). It was he who had the eighteenth century monastery, which made up the principal dwelling, demolished in order to construct the château of today. The most amusing thing about it is that at the same time he built two dwellings in the same style. One in the department of the Nord, in the centre of a brewery he owned (the construction material was brick) and the other, in stone, on his new estate in Saint-Emilion. History sentimentally has it that his legitimate wife lived in the first and his mistress in the second. So this happy mortal was able to lead a double life in his twin châteaux without ever going into the wrong bedroom and he drank to Cupid and Bacchus with March beer in the north, and with Saint-Emilion wine in the south.

Anticonstitutionnellement, which is supposed to be the longest word in the French language, does not take up the typographical space required by Château Grand Barrail Lamarzelle Figeac. The first has 20 letters, the second 35. I have often cited 151 it as an example of the complexity of certain Bordeaux labels. It must be confessed that foreign wine lovers sometimes deserve praise for being able to memorize them. However, this *cru* produces an excellent wine perfectly in the style of those from the best areas of Figeac; that is to say, very complex, consistent and of great substance wherein the merlots dominate, as the nose discerns from the aromas of blackcurrant, and the mouth from a fine flattering unctuousness on the palate. Has this wine got its address wrong? I seem to be describing a *grand cru* of Pomerol!

Grand Bert (Château)   ♟♟♟♟♟

Commune: Saint-Sulpice-de-Faleyrens. **Proprietor:** Philippe Lavigne. Consultant oenologist: M. Maugein in Puisseguin. **Size of vineyard:** 8 hectares. **Average age of vines:** 15 years. **Varieties:** 5% cabernet-sauvignon. 65% merlot. 30% cabernet-franc. **Production:** 50,000 bottles CB. **Visits:** from 10 a.m. Monday to mid-day Saturday. Tel. 57 40 60 09. **Direct sales and by mail order:** in France and abroad. Philippe Lavigne, Saint-Philippe d'Aiguille, 33350 Castillon-la-Bataille. *With a name like Philippe 'Lavigne', the expression "family tradition" takes on a real meaning.*

Grand Bigaroux (Château)   ♟♟♟♟♟

Grand Cru

Commune: Saint-Sulpice-de-Faleyrens. **Proprietor:** Jean-Louis Fayard. **Size of vineyard:** 4 hectares. **Average age of vines:** 25 to 30 years. **Varieties:** 5% cabernet-sauvignon. 90% merlot. 5% cabernet-franc. **Production:** 12,000 bottles CB. **Direct sales and by mail order:** in France and abroad. Tel. 57 24 75 18. **Retail sales.**

Bigaroux is a hamlet cut in two by the road which runs from Libourne to Bergerac, and the crossroads gives almost direct access to Saint-Emilion, passing close by the *cave coopérative*. It was in 1978 that Jean-Louis Fayard acquired this estate, being already a grower at Moulin de Pierrefitte (see that name), also situated in the commune of Saint-Sulpice-de-Faleyrens. The label of "Grand Bigaroux" seems to me to be intelligent and many Bordeaux "châteaux" could well use it for inspiration. It is a reproduction of the National Geographical Society's official map enabling the position of the *cru* to be pinpointed. At any rate, it adorns honest wines which reveal their charms particularly in the great years, the off-years sometimes seeming rather thin and bitter.

Grand Bouquey (Château)

→ *Union de Producteurs*

Grand Corbin (Château)

Ⓨ Ⓨ Ⓨ Ⓠ Ⓠ

Grand Cru classé

Commune: Saint-Emilion. **Proprietor:** Family Company of Alain Giraud. Director: Geneviève Giraud. **Size of vineyard:** 12.76 hectares. **Average age of vines:** 25 years. **Varieties:** 30% cabernet-sauvignon. 65% merlot. 5% cabernet-franc. **Production:** 80,000 bottles CB. **Visits:** strictly by appointment. Tel. 57 24 70 62. **Direct sales and by mail order.**

"Viticulture gives more satisfaction than law." This well-expressed aphorism is the profession of faith made by Philippe Giraud, the grandson of Joseph who was the proprietor of Trotanoy in Pomerol, and whose descendants owned Châteaux Certan-Giraud and Clos du Roy in that area. The family originates from Normandy, but came to live in the region of Corbin, which should not be confused with the Corbin in Saint-Georges Saint-Emilion and which, up to the eighteenth century, was "noble land".

The vine made its appearance there in the middle of the nineteenth century, as in the major part of the region of the Graves of Saint-Emilion, which is very similar, geomorphologically, to the Pomerol appellation. The wines are also akin to what is usually called the "Pomerol type". They are firm, robust and round. They develop rather quickly and give fine notes of red fruits.

Grand-Corbin-Despagne (Château)

Ⓨ Ⓨ Ⓨ Ⓠ Ⓠ

Grand Cru classé

Commune: Saint-Emilion. **Proprietor:** Despagne Consorts. Estate manager and vineyard manager: Guy Despagne. Consultant oenologist: Michel Rolland. **Size of vineyard:** 26 hectares. **Average age of vines:** 60 years. **Varieties:** 70% merlot. 25% cabernet-franc. 5% cabernet-sauvignon. **Production:** 100 tonneaux. **Visits:** Tel. 57 51 74 04. Guy Despagne. **Direct sales and by mail order:** in France. **Retail sales.**

At the time of the "nuptials" of the wines of Bordeaux and those of Burgundy, the 1947 Grand-Corbin-Despagne was served at Clos Vougeot; what an outstanding privilege for a Bordeaux wine to be admitted into the holy of holies of Burgundy! On this memorable occasion, which took place in the fifties, the husband was the wine of Burgundy. The bride he won was no consolation prize and he made no complaints about her excessive beauty. He found the wedding, it was said, rather to his liking, but he soon returned to his first love in the region of La Romanée and Le Clos de Bèze, whereas the bride, brought up in the odour of sanctity thanks to the good wine of Saint-Emilion, decided to return demurely into the bosom of the family to avoid household squabbles. But was the marriage really ever consummated? It seems that Master Burgundy – what a rake! – had already led the ham of Mayence to the altar long before, whereas Mistress Bordeaux started her life anew with Gouda cheese. From that time, Grand-Corbin-Despagne takes itself for a Pomerol *grand cru*, the Burgundy of the wines of Bordeaux.

Grand Corbin Manuel (Château)

Grand Cru

Commune: Saint-Emilion. **Proprietor:** Pierre Manuel. **Size of vineyard:** 12 hectares. **Average age of vines:** 20 years. **Varieties:** 40% cabernet-sauvignon. 45% merlot. 15% cabernet-franc. **Production:** 70,000 bottles CB. **Visits:** Pierre Manuel. Tel. 57 51 12 47. **Direct sales and by mail order:** in France and abroad. **Retail sales:** Coste & Fils. *Given the fact that the cabernets (sauvignon and franc) are predominant among the vines, Pierre Manuel's wines have remarkable breeding.*

Grand Destieu (Château)

Commune: Saint-Sulpice-de-Faleyrens. **Proprietor:** Claude Thibaud. Consultant oenologist: M. Rolland. **Size of vineyard:** 9.6 hectares. **Average age of vines:** 30 years. **Varieties:** 20% cabernet-sauvignon. 80% merlot. **Production:** 50 tonneaux. 6,000 bottles CB. **Direct sales and by mail order:** in France. Tel. 57 24 73 48. **Retail sales.**

In the year of grace 1445, Captain d'Estieu, an officer of the regiment of Navarre, decided to make the first and last retreat in his life – his retirement. He settled at Saint-Sulpice-de-Faleyrens, giving his name to the place. For five generations, Château Grand Destieu has been the property of the Thibaud family, who are also growers at Vignonet (Château Brisson). The wines have body with an agreeable aromatic savour and are rich in alcohol. The best are aged in wood for two years. The Thibauds keep them for their faithful private clients.

Grandes Murailles (Château)

Grand Cru classé

Commune: Saint-Emilion. **Proprietor:** S.C. des Grandes Murailles. Tenants: M. & Madame Reiffers. Vineyard manager and cellar master: Jean Brun. Consultant oenologist: Michel Rolland. **Size of vineyard:** 2 hectares. **Average age of vines:** 30 years. **Varieties:** 20% cabernet-sauvignon. 60% merlot. 20% cabernet-franc. **Production:** 12,000 bottles CB. **Direct sales and by mail order:** Château Côte Baleau, 33330 Saint-Emilion. Tel. 57 24 71 09. **Retail sales.**

Crash! Bang! Wallop! Collapsing like dominoes, Grandes Murailles and Château Côte Baleau fell on the field of battle – declassified. They belong to the Reiffers family, heirs of the Malens, who are also the proprietors of Clos Saint-Martin. The I.N.A.O. Commission took a malicious pleasure in blowing with all its force on these labels which made up a pretty house of cards. The great walls ("grandes murailles") are the oldest, the most picturesque... perhaps the most famous of any wall in Saint-

Despite the censors' huffing and puffing, the Great Walls are still standing.

Emilion. What glory is there in demolishing a wall? Obviously, my image is to be taken in the figurative sense. But I had my heart set on choosing these great walls to illustrate the jacket of this book. It was not for the originality of the idea, but for what it represented. I shall be charged again with provocation. And yet the Grandes Murailles today represent a symbol which has become legend. Legends should not be destroyed. In my book on Chablis, I quoted the poet Patrice de La Tour du Pin:

"A country which has no legends left is condemned to die of cold." To declassify two hectares of historic land is an outrage! And now I have a personal word to say to the wine lover:

"Now warm up your heart with a wine pure and true, come, drink down a glass of Grandes Murailles' *cru*."

Grand Faurie (Domaine du)

Grand Cru

Commune: Saint-Emilion. **Proprietor:** René Bodet. Consultant oenologist: M. Chaine. **Size of vineyard:** 4 hectares. **Average age of vines:** 15 years. **Varieties:** 20% cabernet-sauvignon. 70% merlot. 10% cabernet-franc. **Production:** 18 to 20 tonneaux. **Sales by mail order:** in France and abroad. Tel. 56 85 81 42. *René Bodet took over in 1957. He has established a good clientele to whom he sells direct.*

Grand Fortin (Château)

🍷🍷🍷🍷🍷

Commune: Saint-Emilion. **Proprietor:** S.C.E. des Vignobles A. Janoueix. Director: Michel Janoueix. Cellar master: Guy Janoueix. Consultant oenologist: C.B.C. Libourne. **Size of vineyard:** 6 hectares. **Average age of vines:** 20 years. **Varieties:** 25% cabernet-sauvignon. 50% merlot. 25% cabernet-franc. **Production:** 25 tonneaux. 2,500 bottles CB. **Retail sales:** through Bordeaux. Tel. 57 51 06 99 or 57 51 41 24.

Grand Lartigue (Château)

🍷🍷🍷🍷🍷

Grand Cru

Commune: Saint-Emilion. **Proprietors:** M. and Madame Daudier de Cassini. Cellar master: M. Oizeau. Consultant oenologist: M. Rémy Cassignard. **Size of vineyard:** 7 hectares. **Average age of vines:** 25 years. **Varieties:** 10% cabernet-sauvignon. 60% merlot. 30% cabernet-franc. **Production:** 42,000 bottles CB. **Sales by mail order:** in France. Tel. 57 24 73 83. *It was the quality of the wines of Saint-Emilion and the charm of the region which, in 1977, decided Monsieur and Madame Daudier de Cassini to become proprietors and growers.*

Grand Mayne (Château)

🍷🍷🍷🍷🍷

Grand Cru classé

Commune: Saint-Emilion. **Proprietor:** Jean-Pierre Nony. Vineyard manager: René Venat. Consultant oenologist: Michel Rolland. **Size of vineyard:** 16.87 hectares. **Average age of vines:** 25 years. **Varieties:** 10% cabernet-sauvignon. 50% merlot. 40% cabernet-franc. **Production:** 80 tonneaux. **Visits:** Jean-Pierre Nony. Tel. 57 74 42 50. **Direct sales and by mail order:** in France. **Retail sales.**

During the wood-pigeon shooting season, which also corresponds to that of harvesting, the virgin vine which clothes the walls of Grand Mayne is dressed in purple like a sumptuous evening gown made by a great dress designer. Several centuries have been needed to create the model. The manor has scarcely gone out of fashion since the fifteenth century, thanks to several alterations in style, and the cellars were finished in the eighteenth century. At that time, Mayne belonged to the Laveaus, a powerful Libourne family whose fortune was made from trade with the overseas dependencies. At the beginning of the nineteenth century, Jacques Laveau's son was the largest landowner in Saint-Emilion, having nearly 300 hectares, of which the vineyards of Soutard and Mayne were part. On Jean Laveau's death in 1836, this little empire was split up among numerous heirs, but the whole of the land of Mayne was kept more or less intact. The vineyard and its château are to the west of Saint-Emilion in one unbroken stretch on land of clayey chalk and sandy gravel. The choice of varieties seems particularly well adapted to the nature of the geology

Château Grand Mayne is an extremely elegant dwelling.

and various exposures of the terrain. Jean Nony succeeded his father in 1975. Since then, he has seen to all aspects concerning the administration of the estate and uses the most modern methods of vinification. Harvesting is done by hand. Depending on the vintage, removal of the stalks can be total or done in part. Fermentation takes place in a series of stainless steel vats which have a total capacity of 1,920 hectolitres. Temperatures are rigorously monitored and controlled. The wine is drawn off into casks of which half are renewed yearly. The wines of Château Grand Mayne have a deep colour thanks to a long period in the vat. They have body but are distinguished especially by their delicate aromas and the finesse which comes from their tannins. The evenness in quality from one vintage to another should be mentioned. For example, the 1977s, 1980s and 1984s produced bottles entirely worthy of this *Grand Cru classé*.

Grand Mirande (Château)

Grand Cru

Commune: Saint-Emilion. **Proprietor:** Christian Junet. Consultant oenologist: Gilles Pauquet. **Size of vineyard:** 9 hectares. **Average age of vines:** 20 years. **Varieties:** 5% cabernet-sauvignon. 60% merlot. 35% cabernet-franc. **Production:** 30 tonneaux. 12,000 bottles CB. **Direct sales and by mail order:** in France and abroad. Tel. 57 51 34 91. **Retail sales:** through Bordeaux and Libourne. *The great-grandfather was six-and-a-half feet tall and was called Mirande. That is the ancestral origin of Château Grand Mirande, which has cement vats.*

Grand-Pey-Lescours (Château)

Grand Cru

Commune: Saint-Sulpice-de-Falyerens. **Proprietor:** G.F.A. Escure Heirs. Director and manager: Pierre Escure. **Size of vineyard:** 27 hectares. **Average age of vines:** 15 years. **Varieties:** 65% merlot. 35% cabernet-franc. **Production:** 150,000 bottles CB. **Direct sales and by mail order:** in France. Tel. 57 51 07 59. **Retail sales.** *The Escure family also owns Château Bellile-Mondotte in Saint-Laurent-des-Combes. This vineyard, large by the standards of Saint-Emilion, is capable of producing wines of great charm.*

Grand-Pontet (Château)

Grand Cru classé

Commune: Saint-Emilion. **Proprietor:** S.A. Grand-Pontet. Director and manager: Claude Pourquet. Estate managers: Gérard and Dominique Bécot. Consultant oenologist: Michel Rolland. **Size of vineyard:** 14 hectares. **Average age of vines:** 50 years. **Varieties:** 10% cabernet-sauvignon. 75% merlot. 15% cabernet-franc. **Production:** 65,000 bottles CB. **Visits:** by appointment. Tel. 57 74 46 87. **Direct sales and by mail order. Retail sales:** through Bordeaux 'en primeur'.

On Saint-Emilion's famous west plateau, Grand-Pontet spreads out its fourteen chalky hectares, some half a mile from the collegiate church and 500 yards from the old church of Saint-Martin de Mazerat. For several years, the property belonged to the wine-merchants, Barton and Guestier, who distributed its wines mainly in Anglo Saxon countries. In 1980, the Pourquet, Bécot (Beau-Séjour Bécot) and Berjal families pooled their resources to buy the estate. The wines are both solid and sinewy.

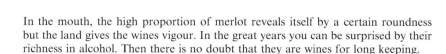

In the mouth, the high proportion of merlot reveals itself by a certain roundness but the land gives the wines vigour. In the great years you can be surprised by their richness in alcohol. Then there is no doubt that they are wines for long keeping.

Grangey (Château)
→ Union de Producteurs

Grand Cru

Graves (Château des) 🛈 → Moulin Bellegrave

Gravet (Château)

Ỵ Ỵ Ỵ Ợ Ợ

Grand Cru

Commune: Saint-Sulpice-de-Faleyrens. **Proprietor:** Jean Faure. **Size of vineyard:** 8.5 hectares. **Average age of vines:** 25 years. **Varieties:** 80% merlot. 20% cabernet-franc. **Production:** 54,000 bottles CB. **Visits:** M. Faure. Tel. 57 24 75 68. **Direct sales and by mail order:** in France and abroad.

Here too, family tradition bears its fruits, for the recent vintages of Château Gravet have won many gold medals at exhibitions. The estate is protected from the north winds by the hill of Château Tertre Daugay and it benefits from a very favourable microclimate. Thanks to its proportion of merlot, the wine is fruity, has a good bouquet and a suppleness characterized by mellow tannins. All the working buildings and the residence alongside speak of order and tidiness which inspire confidence. For a wine lover anxious to deploy his wine budget prudently, I recommend Gravet as a well-made wine at a reasonable price. The minor vintages for simple meals, the average ones for Sundays, and the great ones for important occasions.

Gravet-Renaissance (Château)

Ỵ Ỵ Ợ Ợ Ợ

Grand Cru

Commune: Saint-Sulpice-de-Faleyrens. **Proprietor:** Albert Peuch. Consultant oenologist: Jean-François Chaine. **Size of vineyard:** 9 hectares. **Average age of vines:** 30 years. **Varieties:** 7% cabernet-sauvignon. 60% merlot. 30% cabernet-franc. 3% malbec. **Production:** 72,000 bottles CB. **Retail sales:** direct bottle (exclusively) sales through the family firm of Peuch & Besse. Distributed throughout France and exported, especially to Belgium, Switzerland and the U.S.A.

Graviers d'Elliès (Château des)

Ỵ Ỵ Ỵ Ợ Ợ

Grand Cru

Commune: Saint-Sulpice-de-Faleyrens. **Proprietor:** Max Elliès. Director: Jean-Pierre Rollet. Vineyard manager: Marcel Zamparo. Cellar master: Luca Zamparo. Consultant oenologist: François Maurin. **Size of vineyard:** 7 hectares. **Varieties:** 25% cabernet-sauvignon. 75% merlot. **Production:** 46,700 bottles CB. **Direct sales and by mail order:** in France and abroad. Vignobles Rollet, B.P. 23, 33330 Saint-Emilion. Tel. 57 47 15 13. *The Rollets have been vignerons from father to son for more than 250 years. That is what you can call 'having a profession!'*

Gravillon (Château du)

Commune: Saint-Sulpice-de-Faleyrens. **Proprietor:** Georges Lavaud. Consultant oenologist: Michel Rolland. **Size of vineyard:** 3.5 hectares. **Average age of vines:** 25 years. **Varieties:** 20% cabernet-sauvignon. 60% merlot. 20% cabernet-franc. **Production:** 17,000 bottles CB. **Visits:** tel. 57 24 52 73. **Direct sales and by mail order.** *Brought up on the vines, Georges Lavaud has left the vineyards to take up a responsible position with the Fédération des Cadres Agricoles.*

Gros-Caillou (Château)

Commune: Saint-Sulpice-de-Faleyrens. **Proprietor:** Jacques Dupuy. Consultant oenologist: Gilles Pauquet. **Size of vines:** 18 hectares. **Average age of vines:** 20 years. **Varieties:** 5% cabernet-sauvignon. 90% merlot. 5% cabernet-franc. **Production:** 80 tonneaux. 55,000 bottles CB. **Direct sales and by mail order:** Tel. 57 24 74 91 or 57 24 75 69. **Retail sales:** through Bordeaux. *Jacques Dupuy succeeded his father, Geaorges Dupuy, in 1981. His wine tends to be supple and round.*

Guadet-Saint-Julien (Château)

Grand Cru classé

Commune: Saint-Emilion. **Proprietor:** Robert Lignac. Consultant oenologist: P.F. Chenard. **Size of vineyard:** 6 hectares. **Average age of vines:** 25 years. **Varieties:** 75% merlot. 25% cabernet-franc. **Production:** 24,000 bottles CB. **Visits:** Robert Lignac. Tel. 57 74 40 04. **Direct sales and by mail order:** in France and abroad. **Retail sales.**

Recalling former times, the little estate of Saint-Julien in Saint-Emilion also bears the name of Marie Elie Guadet, a barrister and a deputy for the department of Gironde, who was guillotined in June 1794. Less than a century later, the vineyard was bought by Mathieu Garitey, the great-grandfather of today's proprietor. It is

very well situated at the northern entrance to the town, on the plateau near the Burgesses' Gate. The visitor can admire the magnificent cellars. The wines are rich in alcohol and tannins. They have fine aromas and are perfectly suitable for ageing over several years.

Gueyrosse (Château)

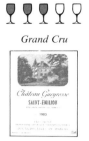

Grand Cru

Commune: Libourne. **Proprietor:** Yves Delol. Consultant oenologist: M. Pauquet. **Size of vineyard:** 4.70 hectares. **Average age of vines:** 25 years. **Varieties:** 20% cabernet-sauvignon. 60% merlot. 20% cabernet-franc. **Production:** 24,000 bottles CB. **Visits:** by appointment. Tel. 57 51 02 63. **Direct sales and by mail order:** in France and abroad.

In the heart of the suburbs of Libourne, with its feudal appearance and its foundations deep in the clay, overlooking the river Dordogne, Château Gueyrosse takes the visitor by surprise. The estate came into the Delol family through Madame Delol, née Magen. Her great-uncle, M. Jean Paillet, a wine merchant in Libourne, was the first to acquire it. At the time of the purchase in 1855, Château Gueyrosse was a huge mansion. Twenty years later, after extensive alterations, the architecture of the old dwelling presented the anachronistic appearance of a mediaeval château.

Yves Delol had been the tenant of the estate from 1973 when in 1982, on the death of his father (who had originally come from the Sauternes region) he became its proprietor. Yves Delol receives visitors warmly. He does not sell his production through any wine merchants. He is anxious to have direct contact with his customers. Moreover, Château Gueyrosse and Yves Delol form an inseparable unit welded together by something akin to love. Domaine Chante Alouette Cormeil is his second property. He runs his estates with paternal benevolence, not forgetting however to exert his authority from time to time, as any manager should. That is part of the tradition, as is harvesting by hand (with a team of students which increases the family for a few days), or fining with egg-whites four months before bottling. Since 1987, Château Gueyrosse has become a *Grand Cru*.

Gueyrosse (Domaine de)

Commune: Libourne. **Proprietor:** Robert Mignon. Consultant oenologist: M. Pauquet. **Size of vineyard:** 0.62 hectares. **Average age of vines:** 15 years. **Varieties:** 75% merlot. 25% cabernet-franc. **Production:** 2,000 bottles CB. **Retail sales:** in bulk. Tel. 57 51 37 78. *What remains of a vineyard of four hectares on which father used to live but which has now been split up between five children.*

Gueyrot (Château)

Grand Cru

Commune: Saint-Emilion; **Proprietors:** de La Tour du Fayet Frères. **Size of vineyard:** 8.5 hectares. **Average age of vines:** 25 years. **Varieties:** 20% cabernet-sauvignon. 60% merlot. 20% cabernet-franc. **Production:** 40,000 bottles CB. **Direct sales and by mail order:** in France. Tel. 57 24 72 08.

Guignan la Tonnelle (Château)

Commune: Saint-Sulpice-de-Faleyrens. **Proprietor:** Arlette Rambeaud. Vineyard manager: Gérard Jayle. Consultant oenologist: Michel Rolland. **Size of vineyard:** 2.16 hectares. **Average age of vines:** 15 years. **Varieties:** 50% cabernet-sauvignon. 50% merlot. **Production:** 1,500 bottles CB. **Direct sales and by mail order:** in France. Madame Rambeaud, Les Bigaroux, 33330 Saint-Sulpice-de-Faleyrens. Tel. 57 24 76 66. **Retail sales.**

Guillemin La Gaffelière (Ch.)

Grand Cru

Commune: Saint-Emilion. **Proprietor:** S.C.E. des Vignobles Fompérier. Director and manager: Yves Fompérier. **Size of vineyard:** 9.5 hectares. **Average age of vines:** 35 years. **Varieties:** 15% cabernet-sauvignon. 65% merlot. 15% cabernet-franc. 5% malbec. **Production:** 60,000 bottles CB. **Direct sales and by mail order:** in France. Tel. 57 74 46 92. *One-third of the land is sandy, one-third of chalky alluvium and one-third on a hillside of limestone. This is a satisfactory balance.*

Guillemot (Château)

Commune: Saint-Christophe-des-Bardes. **Proprietor:** Pierre Lavau. Consultant oenologist: C.B.C. Libourne. **Size of vineyard:** 8 hectares. **Average age of vines:** 20 years. **Varieties:** 30% cabernet-sauvignon. 40% merlot. 30% cabernet-franc. **Production:** 30 tonneaux. 12,000 bottles CB. **Direct sales:** tel. 57 24 77 21. **Retail sales:** Ets. Quancard.

Haut-Badette (Château)

Commune: Saint-Emilion. **Proprietor:** Jean-François Janoueix. Vineyard manager: Max Chabrerie. Cellar master: Paul Cazenave. Consultant oenologists: Messieurs Legendre & Pauquet. **Size of vineyard:** 4.5 hectares. **Average age of vines:** 30 years. **Varieties:** 10% cabernet-sauvignon. 90% merlot. **Production:** 30,000 bottles CB. **Visits:** by appointment: tel. 57 24 70 98 or 57 51 41 86. **Direct sales and by mail order:** in France and abroad. *The vineyard of Haut-Badette stretches out at the foot of Châteaux Haut-Sarpe and Balestard la Tonnelle. The wine develops rapidly.*

Haut-Brisson (Château)

Grand Cru

Commune: Vignonet. **Proprietor:** Yves Blanc. Vineyard manager: Michel Martrinchard. Cellar master: Jean-François Vergne. Consultant oenologist: M. Hébrard. **Size of vineyard:** 13 hectares. **Average age of vines:** 18 years. **Varieties:** 30% cabernet-sauvignon. 60% merlot. 10% cabernet-franc. **Production:** 86,000 bottles CB. **Visits:** tel. 57 51 54 73. **Sales by mail order:** 167 av. Foch, B.P. 170, 33501 Libourne Cédex.

In 1974, Yves Blanc decided to leave the *coopérative* to work for himself. Three years later, he set off to conquer the markets, linking his knowledge of viticulture with a real talent as a salesman. Today, 90% of his sales go for export. The name of his wine is to be found on many wine lists in famous restaurants. Robert Parker considers that Haut-Brisson should be promoted to the rank of *Grand Cru classé*.

Haut-Bruly (Château) 🏠 → Union de Producteurs

Haut-Cadet (Château)

Grand Cru

Commune: Saint-Emilion. **Proprietor:** S.C.I. du Château Haut-Cadet. Director: Jean Lafaye. Vineyard manager and cellar master: Gabriel Audebert. Consultant oenologist: M. Chaine. **Size of vineyard:** 12 hectares. **Average age of vines:** 25 years. **Varieties:** 65% merlot. 35% cabernet-franc. **Production:** 66,000 bottles CB. **Visits:** tel. 57 40 08 88. **Retail sales.**

The vineyard of "Cadet" stretches out over three areas: in le Cadet, the soil is made up of asteroidian limestone; in le Bragard, it is siliceous with a subsoil of clay; in Jean Voisin, it is clay mixed with iron-pan, which dominates. Since July 1985, Dutch capital has been invested in this fine property.

Haut-Corbin (Château)

Commune: Saint-Emilion. **Proprietor:** S.C.A. Haut-Corbin. Director: M. Parment. Estate manager and cellar master: D. Teyssou. Manager and consultant oenologist: G. Pauli. **Size of vineyard:** 6.5 hectares. **Average age of vines:** 25 years. **Varieties:** 19% cabernet-sauvignon, 70% merlot, 11% cabernet-franc. **Production:** 40,000 bottles CB. **Visits:** Madame Malbec. Tel. 56 31 44 44. **Sales by mail order:** in France. Château Haut-Corbin, 33330 Saint-Emilion. **Retail sales:** Ets. Cordier.

Haute-Nauve (Château)

→ *Union de Producteurs*

Grand Cru

Hautes Graves du Rouy (Château)

Commune: Vignonet. **Proprietor:** Guy Bouladou. Vineyard managers: B. and G. Bouladou. Consultant oenologist: M. Hébrard. **Size of vineyard:** 19.7 hectares. **Average age of vines:** 30 years. **Varieties:** 75% merlot. 25% cabernet-franc. **Production:** 80 tonneaux. 25,000 bottles CB. **Direct sales and by mail order:** tel. 57 84 55 92. **Retail sales:** through the *cave coopérative* and Maison Cordier. *Despite its relatively high levels of production, this label is not very easy to find.*

Hautes Versannes (Château)

→ *Union de Producteurs*

Haut-Ferrandat (Château)

Commune: Saint-Emilion. **Proprietor:** Christian Goujou. Consultant oenologist: C.B.C. Libourne. **Size of vineyard:** 6.5 hectares. **Average age of vines:** 30 years. **Varieties:** 1% cabernet-sauvignon. 80% merlot. 19% cabernet-franc. **Production:** 34 tonneaux. 15,000 bottles CB. **Direct sales and by mail order:** tel. 57 24 74 62. **Retail sales:** in bulk. *Christian Goujou is a good grower who ought to take the trouble to bottle his wine himself.*

Haut-Fonrazade (Château)

Grand Cru

Commune: Saint-Emilion. **Proprietor:** Jean-Claude Carles. Consultant oenologist: M. Rolland. **Size of vineyard:** 11 hectares. **Average age of vines:** 15 years. **Varieties:** 10% cabernet-sauvignon. 70% merlot. 20% cabernet-franc. **Production:** 72,000 bottles CB. **Visits:** by appointment. Tel. 57 24 78 92. **Direct sales and by mail order:** in France and abroad. Château Coudert, Saint-Christophe-des-Bardes. **Retail sales:** through Libourne. *Harvesting by hand but vinification in vats of cement and no ageing in wood.*

Haut-Grand-Faurie (Château) 🛡 → Larmande

Haut-Gravet (Château)   ♟♟♟♟♟

Commune: Saint-Sulpice-de-Faleyrens. **Proprietor:** Alain Aubert. **Size of vineyard:** 4.51 hectares. **Average age of vines:** 25 years. **Varieties:** 10% cabernet-sauvignon. 60% merlot. 30% cabernet-franc. **Production:** 25,000 bottles CB. **Visits:** tel. 57 40 04 30. **Direct sales and by mail order:** possible in France and abroad. *A powerful, rounded wine with an aromatic savour which is indeed very suitable for ageing.*

Haut Gros Caillou (Château)   ♟♟♟♟♟

Commune: Saint-Sulpice-de-Faleyrens. **Proprietor:** Paul Lafaye. **Size of vineyard:** 6.40 hectares. **Average age of vines:** 30 years. **Varieties:** 5% cabernet-sauvignon. 70% merlot. 25% cabernet-franc. **Production:** 35 tonneaux. 12,000 bottles CB. **Visits:** Paul Lafaye. Tel. 57 24 75 75. **Direct sales and by mail order:** in France. **Retail sales:** *through the trade.*

Haut-Gueyrot (Château)   ♟♟♟♟♟

Commune: Saint-Laurent-des-Combes. **Proprietor:** Jean-Marcel Gombeau. Consultant oenologist: M. Chaine. **Size of vineyard:** 8 hectares. **Average age of vines:** 25 years. **Varieties:** 15% cabernet-sauvignon. 70% merlot. 15% cabernet-franc. **Production:** 40 tonneaux. 24,000 bottles CB. **Direct sales and by mail order:** in France. Tel. 57 24 60 53. **Retail sales.** *In grandfather Delbos's time, they used to cultivate 4 to 5 journaux of corn (about 1.5 hectares). Jean-Marcel Gombeau has turned them into a larger vineyard tended like any garden.*

Haut-Jaugue-Blanc (Château)   ♟♟♟♟♟

Commune: Saint-Emilion. **Proprietor:** Joseph Debacque. Consultant oenologist: M. Hébrard. **Size of vineyard:** 1.5 hectares. **Average age of vines:** 15 years. **Varieties:** 50% merlot. 50% cabernet-franc. **Production:** 10 tonneaux. 1,000 bottles CB. **Visits:** by appointment. Tel. 57 51 27 44. **Direct sales. Retail sales.** *It could yield excellent quality, given the necessary will on the part of the proprietor.*

Haut-Jonqua (Château)

Commune: Saint-Sulpice-de-Faleyrens. **Proprietor:** Georges Ripes. **Size of vineyard:** 4.25 hectares. **Average age of vines:** 10 to 30 years. **Varieties:** 10% cabernet-sauvignon. 70% merlot. 20% cabernet-franc. **Production:** about 22 to 25 tonneaux. **Visits:** daily. Tel. 57 24 75 92. **Direct sales and by mail order:** in France and abroad. **Retail sales.** *Georges Ripes encourages his private clients to bottle the wine themselves, delivering it to them in plastic containers. An interesting experience if you have never tried before!*

Haut-Jura (Château)

Commune: Saint-Emilion. **Proprietor:** Société Civile d'Exploitation Andrieu & Fils. Vineyard manager: René Andrieu. Cellar master: Christian Andrieu. Consultant oenologist: M. Callède. **Size of vineyard:** 0.49 hectare. **Average age of vines:** 16 years. **Varieties:** 100% merlot. **Production:** 3,000 bottles CB. **Visits:** tel. 57 74 66 07. **Direct sales and by mail order:** S.C.E. Andrieu & Fils, 33230 Saint-Denis de Pile.

Haut-Lavallade (Château)

Grand Cru

Commune: Saint-Christophe-des-Bardes. **Proprietors:** Jean-Pierre Chagneau & Fils. Consultant oenologist: M. Maugein. **Size of vineyard:** 12 hectares. **Average age of vines:** 35 years. **Varieties:** 15% cabernet-sauvignon. 65% merlot. 20% cabernet-franc. **Production:** 60,000 bottles CB. **Visits:** daily from 8 a.m. to noon and 2 to 6 p.m. Sundays, by appointment. Tel. 57 24 77 47. **Direct sales and by mail order:** in France and abroad. *A good size for an estate handed down over the decades from generation to generation in unbroken line from the great-great-grandfather of the present owner.*

Haut-Lavergne (Château)
→ Union de Producteurs

Haut-Matras Côte Daugay (Château)
→ Franc-Cros

Haut-Mazerat (Château)

Grand Cru

Commune: Saint-Emilion. **Proprietor:** G.A.E.C. Goutey-ron Frères. Directors: Francis and Christian Goutey-ron. Consultant oenologist: M. Rolland. **Size of vineyard:** 11.3 hectares. **Average age of vines:** 25 years. **Varieties:** 10% cabernet-sauvignon. 60% merlot. 30% cabernet-franc. **Production:** 80,000 bottles CB. **Visits:** by appointment. Tel. 57 74 44 69 or 57 24 71 15. **Direct sales and by mail order:** in France and abroad. **Retail sales.**

To the west of the village of Saint-Emilion, Haut-Mazerat lies in a gorge between Bellevue-Contet and Daugay and has its own microclimate. It enjoys an exceptionally high number of hours of sunshine, and the subsoil is characterized by an abundant water-table not very far below the surface. This combination of heat and cold gives substantial yields and high degrees of alcohol in great years. Part of the vineyard is planted on rubbly clayey limestone which is called "terre clappe". I mention this fact in order to urge the taster to show his appreciation by clapping his approval.

Haut-Mazerat (Clos) ⚲ → Haut-Mazerat

Haut-Montil (Château) ▦
→ Union de Producteurs

Grand Cru

Haut-Moureaux (Château) ▦
→ Union de Producteurs

Haut-Patarabet (Domaine du)

Grand Cru

Commune: Saint-Emilion. **Proprietor:** François and Pierre Ouzoulias. Estate manager: Pierre Ouzoulias. Consultant oenologist: Michel Rolland. **Size of vineyard:** 3.5 hectares. **Average age of vines:** 25 years. **Varieties:** 90% merlot. 10% cabernet-franc. **Production:** 13,000 bottles CB. **Sales by mail order:** in France. 17 rue du Colonel Picot, 33500 Libourne. Tel. 57 51 07 55. **Retail sales:** Ets. Ouzoulias S.A. 10 av. du Parc, 33500 Libourne. *Patarabet, in dialect, means "the bottom of the ravine". And indeed, it is next to La Gaffelière at the bottom of the hillside of Pavie.*

Haut-Peyroutas (Château)

Grand Cru

Commune: Vignonet. **Proprietor:** Guy Labécot. Consultant oenologist: Michel Rolland. **Size of vineyard:** 5.5 hectares. **Average age of vines:** 15 years. **Varieties:** 50% merlot. 50% cabernet-franc. **Production:** 27 tonneaux. 8,000 bottles CB. **Visits:** daily. Tel. 57 84 53 31. **Direct sales and by mail order:** in France. **Retail sales:** through the Bordeaux trade.

Guy Labécot will not continue the work of his father M. André Labécot, a blacksmith in Vignonet. After his military service, during a shooting party, Guy Labécot spotted a parcel of vines which his father bought straight away. That happened in 1950. Then, spurred on by his friends, he extended his vineyard as much as he could, and so, five years later the name of Haut-Peyroutas was registered. Guy Labécot likes hunting. When you enter Haut-Peyroutas, a pack of thirty hounds welcomes you. Madame Labécot is dynamic and energetic with a radiant smile. At harvesting, it is she who is in charge of the team. Her son Fabien helps out too. A haunch of wild boar and a bottle of Haut-Peyroutas will always go well together.

Haut-Plantey (Château)

Grand Cru

Commune: Saint-Emilion. **Proprietor:** Michel Boutet. Vineyard manager and cellar master: Jean-Claude Micoine. Consultant oenologist: Rémy Cassignard. **Size of vineyard:** 9 hectares. **Average age of vines:** 30 years. **Varieties:** 80% merlot. 20% cabernet-franc. **Production:** 48,000 bottles CB. **Visits:** by appointment. Tel. 57 24 70 86. **Direct sales and by mail order:** in France. **Retail sales:** through Bordeaux. *Formerly a seat of the Marquaux abbots. The vineyard is greatly split up. Its harvest is vinified in the cellars of Château Petit Val, which is also owned by Michel Boutet.*

Haut-Pontet (Château)

Grand Cru

Commune: Saint-Emilion. **Proprietor:** G.F.A. du Château Haut-Pontet. Director and cellar master: Yves Limouzin. Vineyard managers: M. and Madame Grasseau. Consultant oenologist: M. Hébrard. **Size of vineyard:** 5 hectares. **Average age of vines:** 35 years. **Varieties:** 10% cabernet-sauvignon. 80% merlot. 10% cabernet-franc. **Production:** 35,000 bottles CB. **Direct sales and by mail order:** in France. Tel. 57 24 76 77. **Retail sales:** Jean-Pierre Moueix. *Having given up his pâtisserie and hung up his chef's hat in favour of returning to the family vineyard, this former pastry-cook no longer uses fresh eggs, save for fining.*

Haut-Puyblanquet (Château)

→ *Tour Puyblanquet*

Haut-Rocher (Château)

Grand Cru

Commune: Saint-Etienne-de-Lisse. **Proprietor:** Jean de Monteil. Consultant oenologist: M. Hébrard. **Size of vineyard:** 8 hectares. **Average age of vines:** 22 years. **Varieties:** 15% cabernet-sauvignon. 60% merlot. 20% cabernet-franc. 5% malbec. **Production:** 42,000 bottles CB. **Visits:** by appointment. Tel. 57 40 18 09. **Direct sales and by mail order:** in France and abroad. **Retail sales:** 40% through the Bordeaux trade.

The history of Haut-Rocher began when Château du Rocher planted several acres lower down. M. de Monteil used to live at Château du Rocher. In 1870, he had Haut-Rocher constructed. His son Adhémar came into the estate. Today, Jean de Monteil, a direct descendant, is a representative of the Knights of Monteil. He has worked on the estate since 1972. Half of the vineyard, which covers a total of thirteen and a half hectares, is planted on the hillside of Castillon. The vines spread out on a gentle slope facing southeast. Harvesting is done by hand. Long fermentation periods are favoured, in concrete vats, fitted out with a hot and cold temperature control.

Haut-Saint-Brice (Château)

Commune: Vignonet. **Proprietor:** Jacques Thibaud. Consultant oenologist: M. Plomby. **Size of vineyard:** 2.72 hectares. **Average age of vines:** 10 years. **Varieties:** 100% merlot. **Production:** 12 tonneaux. 2,000 bottles CB. **Direct sales:** tel. 57 84 68 01. **Retail sales.** *A wine which most of the time loses its own identity in the vats of the trade.*

Haut-Sarpe (Château)

Grand Cru classé

Commune: Saint-Emilion. **Proprietor:** Joseph Janoueix. Estate manager: Max Chabrerie. Cellar master: Paul Cazenave. Consultant oenologists: Messieurs Legendre and Pauquet. **Size of vineyard:** 12 hectares. **Average age of vines:** 30 years. **Varieties:** 70% merlot. 30% cabernet-franc. **Production:** 75,000 bottles CB. **Visits:** by appointment. J. Janoueix. Tel. 57 51 41 86 or M. Chabrerie. Tel. 57 24 70 98. **Direct sales and by mail order:** in France and abroad. J. Janoueix, 37 rue P. Parmentier, 33500 Libourne.

169

In 1898, just before the preceding century turned its final pages, a man from the *département* of Corrèze by the name of Jean Janoueix left the plateau of Millevaches to join the hill of a thousand *crus*. He did not suffer from the change of climate. Where he came from, winters were harsh and cultivation austere. Here, the climate was moderate and the vines seemed to be stretching out their branches to welcome him. Of course it was not easy; he had his work cut out but it was not a fruitless task. Like many others of his fellow-countrymen, he took a business in Libourne, made sure that several suppliers would work with him simply on the strength of a verbal agreement – my word is my bond – and set off for the pasture-lands of Normandy with his pilgrim staff in the form of good wine... which, when it came to business, turned into a marshal's bâton. His children followed in his footsteps. One of them, his son Joseph, wanted to strengthen family ties with the area they had chosen to settle in. In 1930, when the viticultural world of Bordeaux was in stagnation, he bought Château Haut-Sarpe, and the more clearly to reveal his intentions, he proposed to, in nicely-turned phrases, and later married Marie-Antoinette Estrade, the daughter of a worthy wine merchant. Moving from conquest to conquest, he founded his own business and gradually ensured its ongoing viability (as the modern term has it) in order to enable it to supply unimpeachable products. My purpose here is not to draw up a list of Joseph Janoueix's estates but to take Château Haut-Sarpe as an exemplary model.

Many others before me have acknowledged the splendid origin of the vineyard and the high quality of its wines. Henri Enjalbert quotes it as being "one of the oldest in Saint-Emilion and of long-standing renown. Even in 1750, Pierre Beylot, a wine merchant in Libourne, spoke of the *cru* of Sarpe. In 1807, his son Mathieu bought wines of Sarpe for a very high price which left by road for Bruxelles." It is very rare to see the professor practise pleonasm, so if he mentions at one and the same time the age of the *cru* and its reputation, it is because he is anxious to underline both these facts. Nowadays, many vineyards claim distant origins – sometimes unjustifiably – without being able to back up such claims with quality. In the middle of the eighteenth century, the famous "*cru* de Sarpe" belonged to Count Jacques Amédée de Carles, the king's lieutenant general. In the nineteenth century, it passed into the hands of Count d'Allard then to the barons du Foussat de Bogeron who retained it right up to its acquisition by Joseph Janoueix. The château as such, and as we see it today, was built at the very beginning of the Romantic period, to plans by Léon Droyn who went to seek creative inspiration from the Trianons at Versailles. The park, covering three hectares, was traced out on the edge of the limestone plateau. Here we must speak of the good fairy of the house, Marie-Antoinette Janoueix, who has only to look at a garden plot, saying "I wish", to see it immediately spring into flower, and who with taste and a sure touch chooses the curtain-loops as a perfect match for the wallpaper. With a wave of a magic wand, the old windmill was restored and the harvesters' lodging areas began to resemble an offshoot of the Club Méditerranée. If by chance you go to harvest at Haut-Sarpe, not only will you be fed and lodged like wealthy holiday-makers, but you can also slip into your photograph album a picture in which you are to be seen alongside a cinema star, an Olympic champion, the wife of a government Minister, an ambassador, a duchess or a member of the *Institut*. Much later, uncorking that bottle of Château Haut-Sarpe 1985 with emotion in front of your wide-eyed grandchildren, you will say to them, with a little quiver in your voice: "Yes, this wine is one that I harvested!".

The wines of Haut-Sarpe, generally speaking, are remarkable. Made and aged under the eye of the cellar master Paul Cazenave, they have a splendid colour and a

The windmill at Haut-Sarpe: a successful restoration.

bouquet which is an olfactory tapestry of a thousand fruits and is rich in the mouth, full of well-absorbed tannins. In great vintages, after a few years, they can stand up to all the best *crus* of the area and even outclass them. For the Janoueix, the development of great wine is truly a work of art. Moreover, I will leave the final word to a famous artist, the painter Foujita: "Delacroix used to say that the merit of any picture is that it is a feast for the eye; Haut-Sarpe is a feast for the eye, but one for the nose and the palate too." In conclusion let me add "for the heart and the intellect as well".

Haut-Segottes (Château)

Grand Cru

Commune: Saint-Emilion. **Proprietor:** Danielle André. Consultant oenologist: M. Chaine. **Size of vineyard:** 8.6 hectares. **Average age of vines:** 25 years. **Varieties:** 10% cabernet-sauvignon. 50% merlot. 40% cabernet-franc. **Production:** 50,000 bottles CB. **Visits:** Monday to Saturday from 9 a.m. to noon and 2 p.m. to 6 p.m. Tel. 57 24 60 82. **Direct sales and by mail order:** in France. **Retail sales.** *Strictly traditional methods faithfully handed down over four generations of expert wine makers are used exclusively in making this great little* cru.

Haut-Simard (Château)

Commune: Saint-Emilion. **Proprietor:** Claude Mazière. **Size of vineyard:** 10 hectares. **Average age of vines:** 20 years. **Varieties:** 70% merlot. 30% cabernet-franc. **Production:** 60,000 bottles CB. **Visits:** by appointment. Tel. 57 24 70 42. **Direct sales and by mail order:** in France. *Between La Gaffelière, Canon-la-Gaffelière and Pavie, a vineyard in one stretch, the property of Claude Mazière since 1947. The wine is typical of the terrain and deserves to be known.*

Haut Vachon La Rose (Château)

Commune: Saint-Emilion. **Proprietor:** André Quenouille. **Size of vineyard:** 2.44 hectares. **Average age of vines:** 20 to 25 years. **Varieties:** 75% merlot. 25% cabernet-franc. **Production:** 10 tonneaux. 3,000 bottles CB. **Direct sales and by mail order:** tel. 57 24 78 93. **Retail sales:** in bulk. *Some of the wine is château-bottled but it is a matter of regret that the entire production is not sold through the same channels.*

Haut-Veyrac (Château)

sold in bulk

Commune: Saint-Etienne-de-Lisse. **Proprietor:** Société Civile du Château Haut-Veyrac. Directors: Jacqueline Castaing and Gérard Claverie. **Size of vineyard:** 7.3 hectares. **Average age of vines:** 18 years. **Varieties:** 60% merlot. 40% cabernet-franc. **Production:** 35 tonneaux. **Retail sales:** Société de Luze, Bordeaux. Tel. 57 51 61 80. *The Claverie family has been established in this area for at least five generations. What then has happened to the dynamism and drive of former times?*

Jacques Blanc (Château)

Grand Cru

Commune: Saint-Etienne-de-Lisse. **Proprietor:** G.F.A. du Château Jacques Blanc. Director: Pierre Chouet. Cellar master: Christian Zamparo. Consultant oenologist: M. Hébrard. **Surface area of vineyard:** 20 hectares. **Average age of vines:** 30 years. **Varieties:** 10% cabernet-sauvignon. 64% merlot. 26% cabernet-franc. **Production:** 100,000 bottles CB. **Visits possible. Direct sales and by mail order:** in France. Tel. 57 40 18 01. **Retail sales:** France and abroad.

At the end of the fourteenth century, Jacques Blanc was an eminent jurat of Saint-Emilion. Tradition has it that he was extremely demanding as regarded the quality of his wines. Six centuries later, his memory is perpetuated by the name of this *grand cru,* in the attentive hands of M. Pierre Chouet. This unusual wine maker, of delicate health, has now put aside chemically based medicines forever. Today he is a convinced follower of homeopathy and gentle medicines which have become his new religion. As he never does anything by halves, since 1978 he has carried out on his vineyards the natural biological methods which worked for him. So all the treatments, both on the vines and in the cellars alike, are of direct vegetable or mineral extraction. As a member of the "Nature and Progress" society, he keeps a faithful record of all the treatments. The Ministry of Agriculture is beginning to show an interest in this type of practical experiment especially in a true working environment. For example, extensive work on the drainage has been carried out, and has indisputably improved the condition of the vineyard. Of course, all this is expensive and the yields are not destined for the book of records. But Château Jacques Blanc deserves to be cited as one of the good *crus.*

Jacques Noir (Château)

Commune: Saint-Etienne-de-Lisse. **Proprietor:** Rémy Daut. Consultant oenologist: M. Rolland. **Size of vineyard:** 5.37 hectares. **Average age of vines:** 20 years. **Varieties:** 10% cabernet-sauvignon. 60% merlot. 30% cabernet-franc. **Production:** 36,000 bottles CB. **Direct sales and by mail order:** in France and abroad. M. Daut, Château des Demoiselles, 33350 Saint-Magne. Tel. 57 40 11 88.

Lying in one unbroken stretch at the bottom of the slope, the vineyard of Château Jacques Noir forms a triangle whose apex points towards the south. The regular rows of vines surround the little railway station of Saint-Etienne-de-Lisse. What were the true origins of the story of the knight known as Jacques Noir who, according to legend, haunted Saint-Emilion and its surroundings, no one knows. But it may be supposed that this sinister unknown warrior was simply the shade of Jacques Blanc, his immediate neighbour. You can also buy a few bottles of Château Jacques Noir at the Château des Demoiselles, a sales point situated one mile away from Castillon-la-Bataille on the road from Libourne.

Jauma (Château) → Union de Producteurs

Jean Blanc (Château)   ♙♙♙♙♙

Commune: Saint-Pey-d'Armens. **Proprietor:** Yvonne Brette.
Size of vineyard: 6.5 hectares. **Average age of vines:**
25 years. **Varieties:** 60% merlot. 40% cabernet-franc. **Pro-**
duction: 25 tonneaux. 10,000 bottles CB. **Direct sales and**
by mail order: in France. Tel. 57 47 15 21. **Retail sales:** in
bulk. *A good wine of constant quality, much appreciated by*
wine merchants and a small private clientele, especially in
the north of France.

Jean du Mayne (Château)  → L'Angélus

Jean Faure (Château)   ♙♙♙♙♙

Grand Cru classé

Commune: Saint-Emilion. **Proprietor:** G.F.A. du Château
Jean Faure. Director and cellar master: Michel Amart.
Consultant oenologist: Madame Rolland. **Size of vineyard:**
17 hectares. **Average age of vines:** 30 years. **Varieties:**
30% merlot. 60% cabernet-franc. 10% malbec. **Production:**
96,000 bottles CB. **Visits:** daily. Tel. 57 51 49 36. **Direct**
sales and by mail order: in France. **Retail sales:** through
Bordeaux.

When Michel Amart took over the administration of Château Jean Faure in 1976,
he was bent on demonstrating his ability, by raising this old name out of the cohort
of the *Grands Crus classés* gaining it recognition as a *Premier.* This laudable intention
was never realized. Worse still, for at the time of the revision of the classification
in 1985, Château Jean Faure was thrown out of the club of the *crus classés.* The
sanction was severe and what is more was justified, in a vexatious way: "Notorious
deficiencies in the running of your *cru*'s estate, principally as regards oenology. This
opinion has been entirely justified by the tasting of different vintages provided in
support of your demand. They are not of a corresponding quality not corresponding
to that of a *Grand Cru classé.*"

And yet, Michel Amart, following his father-in-law, Michel de Wilde, had given
back to Château Jean Faure its individuality, which was previously firmly linked
with that of Château Ripeau. He though he had left no stone unturned, had over-
looked no investment necessary, both on the vines and in the cellars, to give his *cru*
better attention and better equipment: ploughing four times in the traditional way,
organic and mineral fertilizer, tested treatments for the health of the vines, harvesting by hand, rose trees at the end of the vine rows and begonias at the entrance to

Should the I.N.A.O. Commission be disqualified for de-classifying Jean Faure?

the property, a three week vinification period in metal vats, ageing in *barriques* of oak from the Allier, fining with the whites of fresh eggs, no filtering, but more than four rackings per year over the two years' ageing period! Professor Emile Peynaud in person had tasted three recent vintages, making the following comments: "1981, deeply coloured, already opening out, striking the nose with its tannin and good wood, rich, full-bodied with an agreeable bitter tannin and a pleasing finish. 1982, still violet in colour, with little evolution, blocked in its early youth. Very full-bodied with rather severe tannin. 1983, deeply coloured, ripe fruit, rich, full-bodied, good quality tannin." Michel Amart tells us: "It was for this very 1983 vintage that I bought new *barriques* of the best quality which cost me a fortune!" So then, what does this accusation with which he is so gravely charged mean: "notorious deficiencies"? Michel Amart understands it even less since his estate has never been subjected to any inspection, nor even simply visited by a representative of the I.N.A.O. Truth to say, before him the oenological work was not of the best. From 1970 to 1975, the wines are hard and astringent with high levels of volatile acidity. But since 1976, these unfortunate traits of character have been removed. Rolland, the oenologist from Libourne, has done a good job. Michel Amart was hoping to blush with pleasure on hearing the jury's congratulations. He blushed with shame when he heard the censorious criticisms being read out. And of course, he has lodged an appeal with the Minister of Agriculture against the judgement of the censors.

Without leaping directly into the controversy, I will venture to declare that the debate is ill-conceived. For, with these gravelly soils, his extremely Médoc-like methods and especially his 60% cabernet-franc and 10% malbec, Michel Amart makes wines which have an undeniable "left bank" style. It is not surprising either that the pure, rounded Saint-Emilions do not recognize one of their own region. It is not surprising that Emile Peynaud should appreciate the tannic structure of Jean Faure and note its rather austere character in the early stages. Michel Amart's challenge has been to make Saint-Julien wine in Saint-Emilion. If I were Saint Peter, I would gladly welcome him into the paradise of great wines, whether the wines be classified or not.

Jean Voisin (Château)

Grand Cru

Commune: Saint-Emilion. **Proprietor:** S.C. Chassagnoux. Director: Pierre Chassagnoux. Consultant oenologist: Gilles Pauquet. **Size of vineyard:** 14 hectares. **Average age of vines:** 10 to 25 years. **Varieties:** 15% cabernet-sauvignon. 60% merlot. 25% cabernet-franc. **Production:** 70,000 to 75,000 bottles CB. **Visits:** tel 57 24 70 40. **Direct sales and by mail order.** Ets. Chassagnoux & Fils 114 route de Saint-Emilion, 33500 Libourne. **Retail sales:** Chassagnoux & Fils.

The estate is situated in what is commonly called the "graves" of Saint-Emilion. Jean Voisin's wines are extremely supple and can be tasted almost immediately after bottling. "We are very near Pomerol" says Pierre Chassagnoux... as if he wanted to apologize.

Juguet (Château)
→ Union de Producteurs

Jupille (Château)

Commune: Saint-Sulpice-de-Faleyrens. **Proprietor:** Régis Visage. **Size of vineyard:** 7 hectares. **Average age of vines:** 25 years. **Varieties:** 65% merlot. 35% bouchet. **Direct sales and by mail order:** in France. Tel.57 24 62 92. **Retail sales:** Ets Bordeaux Tradition. *The most notable characteristics of the wines made by Régis Visage are, generally, a certain elegance and fruitiness.*

Jupille Carillon (Château) → Jupille

La Barde (Château de)

Grand Cru

Commune: Saint-Laurent-des-Combes. **Proprietor:** Michel Bergey. Consultant oenologist: Soussac Laboratory. **Size of vineyard:** 4 hectares. **Average age of vines:** 15 years. **Varieties:** 85% merlot. 15% cabernet-franc. **Production:** 23,000 bottles CB. **Sales by mail order:** tel. 56 63 71 42. **Retail sales.** *The Gascon word* la barde *means "lark" whereas* le barde *is of course a Celtic minstrel. This little* cru *is Michel Bergey's big success. He also grows wines at Saint-Macaire.*

Labarde (Clos)

Commune: Saint-Laurent-des-Combes. **Proprietor:** Jacques Bailly. Consultant oenologist: C.B.C. Libourne Saint-Emilion. **Size of vineyard:** 4.5 hectares. **Average age of vines:** 40 years. **Varieties:** 5% cabernet-sauvignon. 80% merlot. 15% cabernet-franc. **Production:** 22,000 bottles CB. **Visits:** tel. 57 74 40 26. **Direct sales and by mail order:** in France and abroad. Jacques Bailly, Bergat, 33330 Saint-Emilion. **Retail sales.**

There is no age for love. At fifty-four (that was in 1978) Jacques Bailly decided to work in the sun. For the previous twenty years he had worked as a mushroom grower in the cellars contiguous with those of Ausone, Bélair, Clos Fourtet and Canon. "The vine showed itself to me by its roots hanging above my head, and the wine by its aromas, which it breathed through the walls separating us." Thus, the wine lover wanted to become a creator, working above ground instead of below it. When he bought his estate, it was in a more than pitiful state, being the subject of family wranglings arising from a joint inheritance among several dozen people. The vineyard, perfectly restored, reigns over a hillside facing south, sweeping from east to west. The natural drainage of the soil composed of asteroidian limestone is ideal. After several installations aimed at improving the wine, Jacques Bailly has constructed reception buildings for his customers including a tasting room, rustic and simple, which can receive thirty or so visitors. You will often be able to congratulate the proprietor on the quality of his production.

La Boisserie (Château)

→ Union de Producteurs

Grand Cru

La Bonnelle (Château)

→ Union de Producteurs

Grand Cru

La Bonté (Domaine de)

Commune: Libourne. **Proprietor:** Robert Labonté. Consultant oenologist: M. Legendre. **Size of vineyard:** 0.32 hectares. **Average age of vines:** 30 years. **Varieties:** 50% merlot. 50% cabernet-franc. **Production:** 2,500 bottles CB. **Direct sales:** 220 av. de l'Epinette, 33500 Libourne. Tel. 57 51 28 02. *A vestige of Libourne's vine-growing past, this diminutive cru is destined to be expropriated.*

La Bourrue (Château) ♟ → *Grand Fortin*

Labrie (Château) 🏰

→ *Union de Producteurs*

La Carte (Domaine de)

Commune: Saint-Emilion. **Proprietor:** Bernard Loménie. **Size of vineyard:** 0.223 hectares. **Average age of vines:** 5 years. **Varieties:** 100% merlot. **Production:** 1,200 bottles CB. **Direct sales and by mail order:** in France. Tel. 57 74 42 09. *A tiny vineyard planted very recently, which should do well in the future.*

La Carte de Beau-Séjour ♟

→ *Beau-Séjour Bécot*

La Caze Bellevue (Château)

Commune: Saint-Sulpice-de-Faleyrens. **Proprietor:** Philippe Faure. Consultant oenologist: C.B.C. Libourne. **Size of vineyard:** 7 hectares. **Average age of vines:** 18 years. **Varieties:** 80% merlot. 20% cabernet-franc. **Production:** 28 tonneaux. 16,000 bottles CB. **Visits:** tel. 57 74 41 85. **Direct and retail sales.** *Philippe Faure also leases Château Gravet from his father. Some of his vintages are of excellent quality and make one regret that all is not entirely château-bottled.*

La Chapelle-Despagnet (Château)

Grand Cru

Commune: Saint-Sulpice-de-Faleyrens. **Proprietor:** Ginette Gagnaire. **Size of vineyard:** 7.01 hectares. **Average age of vines:** 30 years. **Varieties:** 70% merlot. 30% cabernet-franc. **Production:** 30 to 35 tonneaux. **Sales by mail order:** in France. Ginette Gagnaire, Margot, 33330 Saint-Emilion. Tel. 57 51 35 20. **Retail sales.**

Château bottling is carried out by the firm of Maison Lebègue, which has its own mobile bottling plant. This is a good system, freeing the grower from anxiety and the expenses of equipment and labour. The wines are agreeable.

La Chapelle-Lescours (Château)

Grand Cru

Commune: Saint-Sulpice-de-Faleyrens. **Proprietor:** Pierre Quentin. Vineyard managers and cellar masters: Pierre and Jacques Quentin. Consultant oenologist: M. Hébrard. **Size of vineyard:** 7.36 hectares. **Average age of vines:** 100 years. **Varieties:** 10% cabernet-sauvignon. 70% merlot. 15% cabernet-franc. 5% malbec. **Production:** 48,000 bottles CB. **Direct sales:** tel. 57 74 41 22. **Retail sales.** *Perhaps one of the oldest vineyards in the commune if we take account of the archeological remains.*

La Clide (Château)

sold in bulk

Commune: Saint-Sulpice-de-Faleyrens. **Proprietor:** Antoine Suils. Consultant oenologist: Mademoiselle Cazenave-Mahé. **Size of vineyard:** 4.09 hectares. **Average age of vines:** 20 years. **Varieties:** 40% cabernet-sauvignon. 50% merlot. 10% cabernet-franc. **Production:** 20 tonneaux. **Retail sales:** a large part is sold for export. Tel. 57 24 76 91. *A traditional supplier to the wine trade, Antoine Suils has never had any marketing problems. But nevertheless it seems to me that it must be frustrating not to have your own label.*

La Clotte (Château)

Grand Cru classé

Commune: Saint-Emilion. **Proprietor:** Chailleau heirs. Estate manager: Michel Gillet. Cellar master: Jean Veyssière. Oenologist: Jean-Claude Berrouet. **Size of vineyard:** 3.7 hectares. **Average age of vines:** 35 years. **Varieties:** 80% merlot. 20% cabernet-franc. **Production:** 19,000 bottles CB. **Direct sales. Retail sales:** Ets. Jean-Pierre Moueix.

"Our pride is to carry on gladly the genuine artisan traditions which make the 'great wines', the fame and honour of our region." When Georges Chailleau opened his mouth, it was to eat and drink or to express his frank opinion. In either case you gave him your attention. This man of generous proportions (I think he used to weigh 20 stone) had a large personality to match. Without any hesitation, I can say that Daniel Querre and Georges Chailleau were, for the last generation the best bards of Saint-Emilion. They were both present at the time the Jurade was created in 1948. The second carried out the office of Grand Vinetier up to his death in 1973. This title had been created specially for him and he bore it proudly with an undeniable natural authority. We say that certain children are born with a silver spoon in their mouth. He was born with a fork and a tasting cup in his. One of the finest palates that I ever knew, he had a passion for anything which could be tasted. Comparing *crus* and vintages was an everlasting game of which he never tired. And in addition, you had to sit with him at his table to understand the real meaning of the word con- 179

A splendid survival from the past...

viviality. He had had a charming new house built and he used to take you round the kitchen, of course, before going into the drawing-room. He called it his own Palais de Chailleau. Along with his family, his *cru* of La Clotte was what he held most dear in this world. He had inherited it from his father in 1932, this latter having acquired it from the Marquis Archambault de Grailly in 1913. For several years, the *cru* was called "La Clotte de Grailly". Over four modest hectares, the vines are cultivated in terraces facing directly south along the ramparts, from the Porte Brunet to the Porte Bouqueyre, at the foot of the watchtower. It is one of the most authentic old vineyards in Saint-Emilion. It is protected, in the old style, by walls of dry stone, calculated to dissuade grape thieves. The wines of La Clotte never betray the love which is given them. Today, the Chailleau heirs have entrusted the estate to the Etablissements Jean-Pierre Moueix as tenants, which is an extra guarantee of high quality, if it were needed. A tourist can taste the wines in excellent conditions in the Logis de la Cadène restaurant in Saint-Emilion, kept by Georges Chailleau's son-in-law and granddaughter, Madame Mouliérac having died a few years back. You will appreciate the fullness and the olfactory complexity of Château La Clotte as well as the differences in the vintages, which do not indicate any irregularity in the intrinsic quality but are the most precise reflection of climatic variations from one year to another. And then you will recall Georges Chailleau's sparkling eye and epicurean palate, remembering his words: "... and now, all that remains is for you to watch this limpid Saint-Emilion wine being poured out; observe its *moiré* reflections of old velvet in a clear, fine glass. The taster should then gently swirl it round in a circular movement and lift it towards the light to see its ruby colour. Already he is intoxicated with the bouquet which captivates his sense of smell with its aromas of autumnal undergrowth. Then, with his eyes closed, he inhales it and

Ploughing at Château La Clotte is still carried out "in the old style".

finally savours it, taking small sips in order to keep its perfumes in his mouth, while his taste-buds start to open up and his palate judges and appreciates. And the appraisal of any connoisseur will always be flattering, for our wine should not only be drunk for its breeding but because it is recommended for good health on account of its powerful tannin and because it promotes digestion, as Doctor Yves André of the Institut Pasteur said so well in his outstanding Treatise on Gastronomy." As to the physiology of tasting, Brillat-Savarin could teach Georges Chailleau nothing whatever.

La Clusière (Château)

Grand Cru classé

Commune: Saint-Emilion. **Proprietor:** Consorts Valette S.C.A. Director: Madame Antoinette Valette. Estate manager: Patrick Valette. Manager: Jean-Paul Valette. Cellar master: Pierre Rabeau. Consultant oenologist: Pascal Ribéreau-Gayon. **Size of vineyard:** 3.5 hectares. **Average age of vines:** 30 years. **Varieties:** 10% cabernet-sauvignon. 70% merlot. 20% cabernet-franc. **Production:** 10 tonneaux. 9,600 bottles CB. **Visits:** by appointment. Tel. 57 24 72 02. **Direct sales and by mail order:** in France and abroad: mainly in Belgium, Switzerland and the Netherlands. **Retail sales:** through the Bordeaux trade.

An old property of the Thibeauds who restored the vineyard, this little *cru* is practically dovetailed into that of Château Pavie. So it was logical that the Valette brothers, the owners of that *Premier Cru classé*, should take possession of it on the first possible occasion, which presented itself in 1953. Today, La Clusière is cultivated,

vinified and aged in the same administrative spirit as Pavie. To the extent that the casks which serve for ageing the second are used again for the first. I will not go as far as to say that the two wines resemble each other like two drops from the same tonneau, but both understand that every year the famous elder brother commands the right of seniority to assert and maintain his rank. The younger brother will always remain "the youngster".

La Commanderie (Château)

Grand Cru

Commune: Saint-Emilion. **Proprietor:** M. Marcel Roger. Consultant oenologist: C.B.C. Libourne. **Size of vineyard:** 3.4 hectares. **Average age of vines:** 25 years. **Varieties:** 5% cabernet-sauvignon. 85% merlot. 10% cabernet-franc. **Production:** 20,000 bottles CB. **Visits:** from 9 a.m. to noon and 2 p.m. to 6 p.m. Tel. 57 24 60 44 and 68 42 23 23. **Direct sales. Retail sales:** Belgium, Luxemburg, United States, Great Britain, France.

Pierre Brasseur has just sold his estate to a likeable architect from Narbonne who is in love with vines, wines and the Bordeaux region. In fact, he is already a grower on his family property in the heart of the Saint-Chignan AOC. But he has just made an old dream come true in being able henceforth to count his venerable vines in Saint-Emilion, near Figeac and Cheval Blanc. A specialist in vinicultural architecture, Pierre Brasseur has designed cellars and vat-houses as far away as Moldavia. So here is an infusion of new blood and a creative spirit in our old wine-making province. We welcome him and will be happy to taste the fruit of his bacchic labours. The wines of La Commanderie are to be highly estimated.

La Couspaude (Château)

Grand Cru classé

Commune: Saint-Emilion. **Proprietor:** G.F.A. La Couspaude (Vignobles Aubert). Director and consultant oenologist: Daniel Aubert. **Size of vineyard:** 7.01 hectares. **Average age of vines:** 25 years. **Varieties:** 25% cabernet-sauvignon. 50% merlot. 25% cabernet-franc. **Production:** 48,000 bottles CB. **Visits:** everyday in July, August and in September, up to the 15th. Tel. 57 40 15 76 or 57 40 01 15. **Direct sales and by mail order:** in France and abroad. **Retail sales:** England, Denmark, Luxembourg and the United States.

The underground cellar of La Couspaude is remarkably well equipped.

Since the first edition of Charles Cocks's *Bordeaux et ses Vins* in 1850, and right up to the beginning of this century, La Couspaude always figured on top of the list of the "premiers crus" of Saint-Emilion. In 1867, when it took part in an exhibition, the *cru* was judged particularly worthy of praise, so much so that an engraved marble plaque notes this fact at the entrance to the town hall. In point of fact, La Couspaude has collected a large number of medals. Over the years, they have been added one after the other onto the label, crowning it with glory and resembling a shop-window full of *Louis-d'Or*. As this display was becoming too cumbersome, Daniel Aubert put them into storage from the 1975 vintage on, so restoring to his wine a discreet and sober presentation. The vineyard of La Couspaude has remained unchanged for one-and-a-half centuries. Only the working buildings have changed and been improved, their highly functional character revealing an impeccable constancy in the running and maintenance of the estate. The underground cellar and the vast reception room are remarkably well equipped. Proprietors of the *cru* since 1908, the Auberts have been growers from father to son from 1750. La Couspaude is the jewel among their large range of vineyards. They know how to make good wine.

La Croix Chantecaille (Château)

♈ ♈ ♈ ♈ ♈

Grand Cru

Commune: Saint-Emilion. **Proprietor:** Marie-Madeleine Angle. Consultant oenologists: M. Chaine and Mademoiselle Cazenave-Mahé. **Size of vineyard:** 7 hectares. **Average age of vines:** 25 years. **Varieties:** 70% merlot. 30% malbec. **Production:** 30 tonneaux. 15,000 bottles CB. **Visits:** tel. 57 51 11 51. **Direct sales and by mail order:** in France. *An estate lying on the boundary between Château Gazin in Pomerol and Château Croque-Michotte. A select neighbourhood for these fruity wines.*

La Croix de Jaugue (Château)

Commune: Libourne. **Proprietor:** Georges Bigaud. Consultant oenologist: Gilles Pauquet. **Size of vineyard:** 4.35 hectares. **Average age of vines:** 30 years. **Varieties:** 80% merlot. 20% cabernet-franc. **Production:** 18 tonneaux. 5,000 bottles CB. **Direct sales:** Château La Croix de Jaugue, 150 av. Général de Gaulle, 33500 Libourne. Tel. 57 51 51 29. **Sales by mail order:** in France and abroad. **Retail sales:** through Libourne.

From spring to early autumn you can call in at Georges Bigaud's to taste and buy his most recently bottled wines. They are robust and tannic and undergo a long maceration period: three to four weeks' fermentation. They mature in wood and have their roots as deeply in the clay as in tradition. The young oenologist Gilles Pauquet displays his talents to the full in extracting the best from this average *terroir*.

La Croix Fourney (Château)

Grand Cru

Commune: Saint-Pey-d'Armens. **Proprietor:** G.F.A. du Château La Croix Fourney (Madame Marie-Louise Sauterel). Cellar master: Benoît Turbet-Delof. Consultant oenologist: André Vaset. **Size of vineyard:** 10 hectares. **Average age of vines:** 18 years. **Varieties:** 50% cabernet-sauvignon. 35% merlot. 15% cabernet-franc. **Production:** 50,000 bottles CB. **Direct sales:** Château La Croix Fourney, 36 avenue Haldimand, 1400 Yverdon (Switzerland). Tel. 57 24 51 20 or 57 47 15 75. **Sales by mail order:** in France and abroad. **Retail sales.** *Madame Sauterel gives her closest attention to this Grand Cru which matures in wood for one year.*

La Croix Montlabert (Château) ⌂ → Montlabert

La Croizille (Château)

Grand Cru

Commune: Saint-Laurent-des-Combes. **Proprietor:** Société du Château La Claymore. Vineyard manager: Louis Marin. Manager: Raymon Marin. Consultant oenologist: Société Laffort in Bordeaux. **Size of vineyard:** 4.95 hectares. **Average age of vines:** 30 years. **Varieties:** 85% merlot. 15% cabernet-franc. **Production:** 30,000 bottles CB. **Visits:** Louis Marin. Tel. 57 51 53 37. **Direct sales and by mail order:** in France. Château Canon Chaigneau. B.P. 1, Pomerol. **Retail sales:** through Bordeaux and abroad.

I have known Raymond Marin for some fifteen years and as a friend have witnessed his tenacity and professionalism at work and I know he likes things to be straight and clear-cut. I know too his liking for supple wines which are well made and strike a happy balance between the traditional and modern approach. For some time now he has devoted more attention to the promotion of his production. He is an connoisseur and collector of paintings. He has an original work of art printed on his labels in the style of Mouton Rothschild at Pauillac and Siran at Margaux. Château La Croizille is not the largest estate of the Marin-Audra family as regards the total size, but it is undoubtedly the gem. It was bought in 1977 from Barton and Guestier in Bordeaux. Its good reputation continues to progress. In my opinion Château La Croizille is a typical example of a well-made wine at reasonable price.

La Cure (Clos de)

Grand Cru

Commune: Saint-Christophe-des-Bardes. **Proprietor:** Christian Bouyer. **Size of vineyard:** 6 hectares. **Average age of vines:** 35 years. **Varieties:** 13% cabernet-sauvignon. 75% merlot. 12% cabernet-franc. **Production:** 30,000 bottles CB. **Visits possible. Direct sales and by mail order:** tel. 57 24 77 18.

Christian Bouyer, the proprietor of this little vineyard since 1967, has gradually discovered the high quality of this land, whereas his predecessor, an old man, weary of life, had let the estate degenerate into the most anonymous "generic" type. Under the *ancien régime,* this land belonged to the priest of Saint-Christophe-des-Bardes who drew much satisfaction therefrom, both for his palate... and for his pocket. Once the work had been taken over by Christian Bouyer and his wife, née Françoise Arteau (a jurat called Arteau was to be found in Saint-Emilion in the Middle Ages), they started to build a reputation quite naturally without the need for any blaring publicity but by a still small voice whispered down the line. Today, they export directly to many countries and their customers are faithful. The wines are well made and have a flattering and charming character. The son, who is almost sixteen, drives the family tractor as well as any seasoned vigneron. He has already earned his sail-board. The motor-scooter is due at any moment. And afterwards?... why not a micro-computer to help mum and dad with running the estate?

La Dominique (Château)

Grand Cru classé

Commune: Saint-Emilion. **Proprietor:** Société des Vignobles Dominique Pichon. Director: Clément Fayat. Estate and vineyard manager: Michel Musset. Cellar master: Jacques Chambaud. Consultant oenologist: Michel Rolland. **Size of vineyard:** 18.5 hectares. **Average age of vines:** 25 years. **Varieties:** 12% cabernet-sauvignon. 70% merlot. 12% cabernet-franc. 6% malbec. **Production:** 72,000 bottles CB. **Visits:** by arrangement with the office of Clément Fayat in Libourne (which might require some persistance...): Tel. 57 51 92 00. **Direct sales and by mail order:** in France. **Retail sales:** through the Bordeaux trade.

"La Dominique enjoys exactly the same conditions as Cheval Blanc, one of the best *crus* of the area, as regards the land wherein dominate gravel, clay and ferruginous sand. A straight line, drawn by the proprietors, divides the two estates. La Dominique has approximately twenty-one hectares, almost entirely planted with premium vines and, in an average year, producing 35 to 80 *tonneaux*. Combining the generosity of the Saint-Emilion wines with the aromatic savour of those of Pomerol, the wines of La Dominique are among the most famous of the Libourne region." This description, which dates from 1870, comes from the pages of the *Ginestet Guide* of the period, Charles de Lorbac. It is still valid today, since the *cru*'s situation is exactly the same and eighteen and a half out of twenty-one hectares are currently in production. Of course, meanwhile, the yields have increased, here as everywhere else, thanks to the progress made in viticultural agronomy. Much water has flowed under the bridges, or as we say in our area, much wine has flowed in the butts. For the avatars of Vishnu can be considered as small beer when compared with the fortunes and misfortunes of La Dominique. When Bordeaux was prospering

from business with France's overseas dependencies, the rich merchant who bought this vineyard "for his personal satisfaction" gave it the name of the island in the West Indies where his fortune had been made and which the English had annexed by the Treaty of Paris, 310 years after the battle of Castillon, as good a way as any of taking revenge on history. After two more centuries, we arrive at the eve of today when Professor Enjalbert completely assimilated the terrain of Cheval Blanc, Figeac and La Dominique. As far as the geological morphology was concerned, science was of course on his side. As for the physiology of the vineyard however, he left certain things unsaid. But that was not his problem. Speaking of problems, there have been quite a few at La Dominique. Without giving a detailed list, I will simply indicate for the edification of present and future generations the condition in which the estate was to be found after the 1956 frosts: a deep coma. In conflict with a joint family trust of four people, Etienne de Baillencourt could do nothing but hope to survive. No one was willing (or able) to endorse a cheque against the future by contributing to any replanting. He himself was prepared (or wanted) to hope that, with time on his side, he would retrieve his land from the frost as others might pull their chestnuts out of the fire, by successfully recovering the frost-burnt land. But things are not always that simple, and fingers can get burned, even in the family circle and in Saint-Emilion. After thirteen years of despair, Batman arrived in the shape of Clément Fayat. A successful industrialist, this man from Argentat in the *département* of Corrèze still retained for the land a certain nostalgia, which he inherited from his peasant ancestors. As he carried out his activities at Libourne as a bridge-builder and motorway constructor, he became irritated by the proliferation of his compatriots, who had been installed in Saint-Emilion and Pomerol for several generations. In point of fact, he was not jealous, but envious. Unravelling the juridical web of rightful ownership, he devoted the time and money necessary to conquer fair La Dominique. But it was not so easily to be conquered, he knew. Batman turned into a Prince Charming to awaken the Beauty of the sleeping vines.

This attempt to give the kiss of life lasted nearly twenty years. Replanting a little less than one hectare every year, he gave back new life to the vineyard. During this time, he demolished the wooden vats, which were too old. But you are not born in Corrèze to waste coal and wood in any old way... and the money which they can provide. The wooden vats were piously salvaged and entrusted to the best carpenter, in order to restore the doors and windows of the old buildings according to the rules of the art. There was a vat-house, but no cellars. The Baillencourts used to sell in bulk and, in accordance with the deplorable practices encouraged by the dinosaurs of the Chartrons, they even negotiated their crop before it was harvested, like a pig in a poke. Clément Fayat, a good Prince Regent, did all he could to protect each harvest right up to the time of bottling at the château. Today, from the stainless steel vats to the *barriques* of best oak and the bottle cellars, the wine of La Dominique thrives in a royal jewel casket. Its sovereign, the proprietor, waited for five years before letting others judge the effect. It was only in 1975 that he decided to put his vintages out to the wine merchants in Bordeaux. Brokers and merchants scratched their heads: "Bless me! La Dominique... er... still exists?" Of course, they were told. "Well then, let's see if the wine is all right.", they replied. Result: 80% of the 1985 vintage, put up for sale at mid-day, was sold for the asking price before 4 p.m., while the proprietor was still having lunch. Every buyer wanted to have even more.

The moral of the story? Clément Fayat gives it himself: "In the same year, 1969, I bought La Dominique in a state of utter neglect, as well as a factory in full production. I paid approximately the same price for each. Today, I might sell the factory for one franc, but I would not sell La Dominique for all the gold in the world." Clément Fayat is no longer an industrialist. He is an impassioned grower who makes the wine of your dreams. Maybe, but why did he not give the award of the Merite Agricole to old Monsieur Musset, who has been a great vigneron on this land for fifty-five years?

La Fagnouse (Château)

Grand Cru

Commune: Saint-Etienne-de-Lisse. **Proprietor:** Madame Coutant. Consultant oenologist: M. Chaine. **Size of vineyard:** 10 hectares. **Average age of vines:** 15 years. **Varieties:** 85% merlot. 15% cabernet-franc. **Production:** 50,000 bottles CB. **Visits possible. Direct sales and by mail order. Retail sales.** *Most of the vineyard has recently been replanted, but on this land the vines gain in strength and vigour as they age. Rendez vous in the twenty-first century.*

La Fleur (Château)

Grand Cru

Commune: Saint-Emilion. **Proprietor:** Madame Lily P. Lacoste Loubat. Director: Jean-Pierre Moueix. Estate manager and vineyard manager: Michel Gillet. Cellar master: Jean Veyssière. Oenologist: Jean-Claude Berrouet. **Size of vineyard:** 6.5 hectares. **Average age of vines:** 30 years. **Varieties:** 70% merlot. 30% cabernet-franc. **Production:** 30,000 bottles CB. **Retail sales:** Ets. Jean-Pierre Moueix. *Madame Lily P. Lacoste is also in association with Jean-Pierre Moueix at Château Pétrus and Latour in Pomerol. She inherited this estate from her mother.*

La Fleur Cauzin (Château)

Commune: Saint-Christophe-des-Bardes. **Proprietor:** Raynal Demur. **Size of vineyard:** 8 hectares. **Average age of vines:** 30 years. **Varieties:** 20% cabernet-sauvignon. 80% merlot. **Production:** 50 tonneaux, 10,000 bottles CB. **Visits:** by appointment: *tel. 57 24 77 58.* **Direct sales and by mail order:** in France. *Eighty per cent of this vineyard is planted on the hillside and benefits from its southern exposure. This estate produces wines which have a certain panache.*

La Fleur Cravignac (Château)

Grand Cru

Commune: Saint-Emilion. **Proprietors:** Lucienne and André Beaupertuis. Cellar master: M. Oizeau. Consultant oenologist: Gérard Gendrot. **Size of vineyard:** 7.5 hectares. **Average age of vines:** 30 years. **Varieties:** 10% cabernet-sauvignon. 60% merlot. 30% cabernet-franc. **Production:** 36,000 bottles CB. **Visits:** tel. 56 28 09 96 or 57 74 44 01. **Direct sales and by mail order:** Château Cravignac, 10 rue César Franck, 33320 Eysines. **Retail sales:** Coste et Fils, Langon. Nony-Borie, Bordeaux. Audy, Libourne.

Madame Lucienne Beaupertuis inherited this property from her uncle Maxime Noël. The name of Cravignac is closely linked to the history of Saint-Emilion, for Jean-Baptiste Lavau de Cravignac, a barrister at the Parlement and Jacques Lavau de Cravignac, a banker, were mayors of the commune one after the other towards the middle of the eighteenth century. Local history has it that Raymond Poincaré particularly appreciated the wine of La Fleur Cravignac at the *Congrès national des anciens combattants* in 1929. A political tradition which is happily maintained: the '80, '81 and '82 vintages are served in the restaurant of the *Assemblée nationale*. It is quite obvious that all who drink it are excellent members of the Parlement with a high level of assiduity.

La Fleur Figeac (Clos)

Commune: Saint-Emilion. **Proprietors:** Marcel Moueix heirs. Director and manager: Armand Moueix. Consultant oenologist: M. Crébana. **Size of vineyard:** 3.43 hectares. **Average age of vines:** 35 years. **Varieties:** 70% merlot. 30% cabernet-franc. **Production:** 19,000 bottles CB. **Sales by mail order:** A. Moueix & Fils, Château Taillefer, 33500 Libourne. Tel. 57 51 50 63. **Retail sales:** A. Moueix & Fils. *Entirely typical of the wines from the graves of Saint-Emilion, this little cru can pride itself on having crus classés as neighbours.*

La Fleur Gueyrosse (Château)

Commune: Libourne. **Proprietor:** Robert Simon. Consultant oenologist: Mademoiselle Cazenave. **Size of vineyard:** 2.16 hectares. **Average age of vines:** 22 years. **Varieties:** 10% cabernet-sauvignon. 60% merlot. 30% cabernet-franc. **Production:** 10 tonneaux. 2,000 bottles CB. **Direct sales.** **Retail sales:** through Langon. *The wine for private customers matures in wood, that which goes to the trade in cement vats.*

La Fleur Peilhan (Château) ♟ → Bellegrave

La Fleur Picon (Château)

Grand Cru

Commune: Saint-Emilion. **Proprietors:** Monsieur and Madame Christian Lassègues. **Size of vineyard:** 6 hectares. **Average age of vines:** 25 years. **Varieties:** 70% merlot. 30% cabernet-franc. **Production:** 30,000 bottles CB. **Visits:** preferably on Saturdays and Sundays. Tel. 57 24 70 56. **Direct sales and by mail order:** in France. **Retail sales.** *A recently created name for a pretty little vineyard bordering on Pomerol. Indeed the resemblance is so marked that you might think the wine had come from just across the road.*

La Fleur Pourret (Château)

Grand Cru

Commune: Saint-Emilion. **Proprietor:** Domaines Prats. Director: Bruno Prats. Vineyard manager and cellar master: Gilbert Xans. Manager: Robert Hallay. Consultant oenologist: Professor Pascal Ribéreau-Gayon. **Size of vineyard:** 4.5 hectares. **Average age of vines:** 20 years. **Varieties:** 10% cabernet-sauvignon. 57% merlot. 33% cabernet-franc. **Production:** 18,000 bottles CB. **Sales by mail order:** in France. Domaines Prats, 84 rue Turenne, 33000 Bordeaux. Tel. 56 44 11 37. **Retail sales:** Domaines Prats.

After the First World War, Fernand Ginestet, the grandfather of the present owners (and of the author of this book), united the little vineyard of Haut-Pourret with that of La Fleur Pourret, not far from "Petit-Figeac", another family estate. At that time they enjoyed a symbiotic relationship with the famous Clos Fourtet. Bruno Prats has developed cultivation and vinification in a modern style which is not without charm. Without ever being sublime, La Fleur Pourret has a certain worth.

La Fleur Puyblanquet (Château) ♟ → Robin

Lafleur Vachon (Château)

Commune: Saint-Emilion. **Proprietor:** Raymond Tapon. Consultant oenologist: Mademoiselle Cazenave. **Size of vineyard:** 2.5 hectares. **Average age of vines:** 20 years. **Varieties:** 15% cabernet-sauvignon. 70% merlot. 15% cabernet-franc. **Production:** 7,000 bottles CB. **Visits:** by appointment. Tel. 57 74 46 42. **Direct sales and by mail order:** in France and abroad: Germany. **Retail sales:** through Libourne.

In the Tapon family, the work of the vineyard has always been linked with that of the nurseryman. In the last century, M. Tapon, the grandfather, learned to graft vines with Macquin and Galhaud in Montagne. And still today, the grandson, Raymond Tapon, continues the family tradition. He produces rootstock at Pernes-les-Fontaines in the Vaucluse, because of the favourable climatic conditions. Château Gazin in Pomerol is an old customer, for it was already being supplied in the time of the grandfather. In marvellous little underground cellars, attractively equipped, the vines of tomorrow, full of promise, are piled up in earth.

La Forterie (Clos) ⚱ → La Commanderie

La Gaffelière (Château)

1er Grand Cru classé

Commune: Saint-Emilion. **Proprietor:** Count de Malet Roquefort. Director: Léo de Malet Roquefort. Vineyard manager: Edouard Garin. Cellar master: J.-M. Galeri. Consultant oenologist: M. Guimberteau. **Size of vineyard:** 22 hectares. **Average age of vines:** 40 years. **Varieties:** 10% cabernet-sauvignon. 65% merlot. 25% cabernet-franc. **Production:** 80,000 bottles CB. **Visits:** Monday to Friday from 8 a.m. to noon and 2 to 6 p.m. Tel. 57 24 72 15. **Direct sales and by mail order:** in France. **Retail sales:** through Bordeaux in the traditional way.

It is difficult to imagine that this country gentleman with his polished manners is a descendant of a barbarian companion of Roland the Viking who took part in the invasion and pillage of Normandy at the end of the ninth century. At that time, the ancestor warrior of Count Léo de Malet Roquefort used to make his libations to the god Thor, the son of Odin, by pouring the terrible eau-de-vie (akvavit), distilled by moonlight and mixed with reindeer's blood, into the skull of an enemy killed in battle. Several years later, his son gave help to William the Conqueror against the infamous Harold who, as everybody knows, was defeated at Hastings in 1066. Then the Norman was ennobled and his move to the south made him less bellicose. He crossed the Périgord to settle at the château of Roquefort, situated at Lugasson, near Rauzan. From the Hundred Years War on, the family name was established once and for all as Malet Roquefort. On which side were they at the time of the Battle of Castillon? History remains discreet and the memory of the Malet Roque-

190

Halfway up the hill, La Gaffelière has a privileged situation and attractive grounds.

forts is not sufficiently long to say whether they fought with Charles VII or Talbot. But immediately afterwards, one of them settled in Saint-Emilion. In the old town on the present site of the museum, the family house became the "Dwelling of the Malets". Towards the end of the seventeenth century, a Malet Roquefort married a daughter of the Leroy family and became the lord of La Gaffelière. Léo, Count de Malet Roquefort, is the direct descendant of the elder branch; all of which tells us how deeply rooted this family is in the area. In Saint-Emilion, the Capdemourlins too share this ancient connexion with the land, traced in direct line. Obliged to take up the reins at an early date following the death of his father, Léo de Malet wasted no time in bringing his personal touch to the estate's production. La Gaffelière – which was called La Gaffelière-Naudes for a long time – was in some measure a victim of its own ancestral weight. The prevailing mentality, based for generations on the maintenance of tradition, could sometimes show itself as a deadening force in the face of progress. The everlasting reply: "But, Sir, we have always done it like that!" was an impregnable fortress of habits elevated into rules. It needed patience and perseverance to bring about an evolution in the development of things. Without denying his subjective approach in any way, Léo de Malet has given his *cru* that objective rigour which is the rule today in any Bordeaux château of high standing, especially since universities have taken an active interest in the vineyard, the vat-house and cellars, after sportingly backing the wine's label as they might have endorsed a glorious T-shirt. Here is the proof. The sixties generally produced astringent wines showing more volatile acidity than floral bouquet. The seventies are marked by a continuing improvement in quality, the vintages all being equal in other respects; since the beginning of the eighties, La Gaffelière has raised itself to the very summit. Léo de Malet, an experienced horseman, has perfectly mastered his mount, and ventures to give demonstrations of advanced horsemanship. Now an approach seeking perfection also prevails among the vines and with the wine. The Malet Rocqueforts' motto: *in arduis fortior* could also be complemented by the maxim *semper altum*. In the winter of 1985, La Gaffelière studied the work of each season of the year. Everything was looked at in the closest detail. Messieurs Cordeau, of the I.N.R.A., Guimberteau, the eminent oenologist, Compin, the agronomist, Thienpont, the former estate manager, Garin, from the famous school at Montpellier, and the proprietor tackled everything which might possibly improve the working of the estate: graft-stock, methods of improving the soil, treatments to improve the state of the vines and the land, study of the yields (between 35 and 45 hectolitres, neither more nor less), the way of pruning the vines to be used on this estate, thinning out the grape-stalks (also called "false harvest" because it "harvests" grapes which will never mature), long vinification periods with prolonged maceration (the *vins de presse* become "clairets": professionals will understand), a systematic introduction of new vats, selecting wines to determine three different levels of quality, the first being kept for the principal wine of the *cru*, fining with egg-whites, cask by cask, in the style of the greatest wines of the Médoc, and all filtering ruled out; in short, Léo de Malet took a radical approach to the factors affecting quality in the complex matter of making wine, which for all that no longer has any resemblance to the mysteries of alchemy.

To the side of the château there is a little locality called "Palat". Since 1969, archeological excavations have revealed the site of a rich *palatium*, dated today with certainty as belonging to the Gallo-Roman period of the third and fourth centuries, that is to say at the time of Ausonius. The layout of this villa has been more or less determined, except for a part buried under the main road. There is no doubt that it was the secondary residence of a high-ranking person of note and the mosaics on the floor depict, here and there, the fertile vine. Moreover, the layout of the dwelling is strangely akin to that of the villas known around Trèves, in the countryside of the *département* of La Moselle. Knowing that good old Ausonius lived in this region for several years before returning to Burdigalan (Bordeaux) territory, the presumption is very strong that we have finally discovered one of his seven residences in the southwest. Whatever the case, the evidence is clear: La Gaffelière has been an important growing and wine-producing site in Saint-Emilion from the first days when men grew *Vitis vinifera* in our area. I confess that I am touched by the cumulative effect of all this, without speaking of that resulting from the superb quality of the wine. La Gaffelière has everything in its favour: the land, the men and "romance". As Jacques Bouzerand wrote in *Le Point:* "And here's the wonder of it! Every bottle is enriched by its own history, which increases the pleasure of the palate." As for the Roman agronomist Columella, he declared his admiration for the *palatum eruditum*. Among the joys of life one thing is certain: it is a great pleasure to be able to savour culture in this way.

La Gaffelière (Clos) 🗝 → La Gaffelière

La Gaffelière (Domaine de)

Commune: Saint-Emilion. **Proprietor:** Claude Mazière. **Size of vineyard:** 10 hectares. **Average age of vines:** 20 to 30 years. **Varieties:** 70% merlot. 30% cabernet-franc. **Production:** 60,000 bottles CB. **Visits:** by appointment. Tel. 57 24 70 42. **Direct sales and by mail order:** in France and abroad: Belgium and England. *One of Claude Mazière's many labels which, although adorning bottles of agreeable wine, should not be confused with the château of the same-sounding name.*

La Garelle (Château)

Commune: Saint-Emilion. **Proprietor:** Guy Thibeaud. **Size of vineyard:** 8.7 hectares. **Average age of vines:** 20 years. **Varieties:** 5% cabernet-sauvignon. 85% merlot. 10% cabernet-franc. **Production:** 50 tonneaux. **Direct sales and by mail order:** in France. Tel. 57 40 05 32. **Retail sales:** in bulk.

La Gomerie (Château)

Grand Cru

Commune: Saint-Emilion. **Proprietor:** Marcel Lescure. **Size of vineyard:** 3 hectares. **Average age of vines:** 20 years. **Varieties:** 5% cabernet-sauvignon. 90% merlot. 5% cabernet-franc. **Production:** 17,000 bottles CB. **Direct sales and by mail order:** in France and abroad. Tel. 57 24 71 35.

"In the year 1276, Dom Bertrand, the *abbé* of Fayze, received the manor of La Gomerie with all its appurtenances and revenues as a donation from Hélie, Viscount of Castillon. Edward I, the king of England confirmed this donation by letters patent dated December 7, 1289" (Gallia Christiana, vol II. p. 888). For more than 193 four centuries, La Gomerie remained attached to the abbey of Fayze, which had a priory built there. At the time of the Revolution, the estate, which covered some 200 hectares, was split up. The modest vineyard of today represents the ancient site of the priory. Marcel Lescure treats his vines, wine and customers lovingly.

La Grâce Dieu (Château)

Commune: Saint-Emilion. Proprietor: Société Château La Grâce Dieu. Director, vineyard manager and cellar master: Christian Pauty. Consultant oenologist: M. Chagneau. **Size of vineyard:** 12 hectares. **Average age of vines:** 20 years. **Varieties:** 15% cabernet-sauvignon. 70% merlot. 15% cabernet-franc. **Production:** 72,000 bottles CB. **Direct sales:** tel. 57 24 71 10. **Retail sales.** *A good name of long standing which is moving towards progressive methods. La Grâce Dieu has been converted to the sect of modern oenology. Amen.*

La Grâce Dieu des Prieurs (Château)

Grand Cru

Commune: Saint-Emilion. **Proprietors:** M and Madame Laubie. Consultant oenologist: Mademoiselle Cazenave-Mahé. **Size of vineyard:** 7 hectares. **Average age of vines:** 30 years. **Varieties:** 5% cabernet-sauvignon. 80% merlot. 15% cabernet-franc. **Production:** 36,000 bottles CB. **Sales by mail order:** Madame Laubie, 35 avenue Georges Clemenceau, 33500 Libourne. Tel. 57 51 07 87. **Retail sales:** for export. *The acquisition of the property goes back to the fifties. The wine is full and fruity, resembling a wine of Pomerol.*

La Grâce Dieu Les Menuts (Château)

Grand Cru

Commune: Saint-Emilion. **Proprietor:** G.F.A. des Vignobles Xans-Pilotte. Director: Max Pilotte. Consultant oenologist: Michel Rolland. **Size of vineyard:** 13 hectares. **Average age of vines:** 25 to 30 years. **Varieties:** 10% cabernet-sauvignon. 60% merlot. 30% cabernet-franc. **Production:** 60 to 70,000 bottles CB. **Visits:** weekdays and by appointment at weekends. Tel. 57 24 73 10. **Direct sales and by mail order. Retail sales.**

The origins of this *cru* go back to the last century, to the time of the first sale to Jean Thibeau, a grower, of two parcels totalling approximately 0.90 hectares in the area of La Grâce Dieu. Each succeeding generation bought successive plots of land here and there, the total size today being thirteen hectares. This has resulted

in considerable fragmentation, with the advantage of having a wide range of soils

The fifth generation confirms its attachments to bygone days.

and microclimates. The fifth generation by marriage is now in charge to the estate. As for the sixth, notably represented by Madame Audier, who has just finished her studies in viticulture and oenology and was"baptized" in the font of the family vats at the time of the 1985 vintage. Her father, Max Pilotte, having her to help out, can devote a little more of his time to his passion for collecting tools and instruments connected with vines and wines. The Thibeau-Xans-Pilotte clan claims the honour of being called peasant-vignerons. In the best years, maceration lasts nearly a month. Then a dense colour, a concentrated bouquet, a wine of great substance and with an extremely long finish await the taster. This is truly splendid work.

Lagrange de Lescure (Château)

Grand Cru

Commune: Saint-Sulpice-de-Faleyrens. **Size of vineyard:** approximately 10 hectares. **Varieties:** 37% cabernet-sauvignon. 25% merlot. 37% cabernet-franc. **Sales by mail order:** in France and abroad. Tel. 57 74 62 21. **Retail sales.** *See Château Le Couvent with which this label has close links, as much in its management as for its marketing.*

La Grave Figeac (Château)

Grand Cru

Commune: Saint-Emilion. **Proprietor:** Odette Ornon. Manager and cellar master: Georges Meunier. Consultant oenologist: Gilles Pauquet. **Size of vineyard:** 4.5 hectares. **Average age of vines:** 30 years. **Varieties:** 20% cabernet-sauvignon. 60% merlot. 20% cabernet-franc. **Production:** 24,000 bottles CB. **Direct sales and by mail order:** tel. 57 51 38 47. **Retail sales.**

195

La Grezolle (Domaine de)

Commune: Saint-Sulpice-de-Faleyrens. **Proprietor:** S.C.E. Vignobles Michel Decazes. **Size of vineyard:** 4 hectares. **Average age of vines:** 15 years. **Varieties:** 80% merlot. 20% cabernet-franc. **Production:** 16 tonneaux. 10,000 bottles CB. **Direct sales and by mail order:** in France. Vignobles Michel Decazes, Château Compassant, Génissac, 33420 Branne. Tel. 57 24 47 60. *The Decazes family has been on this land for five centuries, but has there been any advance?*

La Madeleine (Clos)

Grand Cru classé

Commune: Saint-Emilion. **Proprietor:** Hubert Pistouley. **Size of vineyard:** 2 hectares. **Average age of vines:** 18 years. **Varieties:** 50% merlot. 50% cabernet-franc. **Production:** 11,000 bottles CB. **Direct sales and by mail order:** in France. H. Pistouley, La Gaffelière, 33330 Saint-Emilion. Tel. 57 24 71 50.

A little estate in the style of "a family jewel", this vineyard faces south on the hillside of La Madeleine, of great historical importance in the Haut Saint-Emilion. Hemmed in by *Premiers Grands Crus classés,* its dimensions do not allow it to reign with the princes. But this wine is a real find for the wine lover. Fine, well-bred, supple and sinewy, the Clos La Madeleine is capable of enchanting the most delicate palate.

Lamartre (Château) 🏰

→ *Union de Producteurs*

Grand Cru

La Marzelle (Château)

Grand Cru classé

Commune: Saint-Emilion. **Proprietor:** Association Carrère. **Director:** M. Carrère. **Consultant oenologist:** Michel Rolland. **Size of vineyard:** 13 hectares. **Average age of vines:** 20 years. **Varieties:** 20% cabernet-sauvignon. 70% merlot. 10% cabernet-franc. **Production:** 80,000 bottles CB. **Sales by mail order:** in France and abroad. **Retail sales.**

It was perhaps a lisping child who gave it this labio-sibyllant name for all time. Under the *ancien régime,* La Marzelle was a feudal benefice which belonged to the

Cistercians of Fayze for a while, like La Gomerie. But it seems that the disciples of Saint Bernard never made much of these two donations. And yet, as from 1760, vines were to be found here, entirely justified by the terrace of high gunz gravel which emerges from the surrounding sands. The Belliquets, Chauvins and Longas, bourgeois families of Libourne, followed one after the other up to the Revolution. Then there was total eclipse and the name of the *cru* reappeared only at the beginning of this century. Château La Marzelle figures worthily in today's list of the *crus classés*. Could it do even better?

Lamarzelle Cormey (Domaine de)

Grand Cru

Commune Saint-Emilion. **Proprietors:** Nouvel Heirs. Manager: Claude Moreaud. Estate manager: Richard Moreaud. Consultant oenologist: C.B.C. Libourne. **Size of vineyard:** 5 hectares. **Average age of vines:** 11 years. **Varieties:** 100% merlot. **Production:** 24,000 bottles CB. **Sales by mail order:** S.C.E.A. Domaines Cormeil Figeac-Magnan, Cormeil Figeac, 33330 Saint-Emilion. Tel. 57 24 70 53. *The vineyard was completely restored between 1969 and 1980. It is planted on a superficial vein of clay (as at Pétrus!) – rare in Saint-Emilion.*

La Mélissière (Château)

Grand Cru

Commune: Saint-Hippolyte. **Proprietor:** Patrick Bernard. **Size of vineyard:** 12 hectares. **Average age of vines:** 20 years. **Varieties:** 33% cabernet-sauvignon. 33% merlot. 33% cabernet-franc. **Production:** 60 tonneaux. 20,000 bottles CB. **Visits:** tel. 57 24 60 81. **Direct sales and by mail order:** Patrick Bernard, Mitrotes, Saint-Laurent-des-Combes, 33330 Saint-Emilion. *This* cru *belongs to one of the oldest families in the area but today the wine is drunk younger and younger.*

La Mondotte (Château)

Grand Cru

Commune: Saint-Emilion. **Proprietor:** S.C.E. Vignobles des Comtes de Neipperg. Director: Count Stephan de Neipperg. Vineyard manager: Paul Pébou. Cellar master: Patrick Erésué. **Size of vineyard:** 4 hectares. **Average age of vines:** 35 years. **Varieties:** 7% cabernet-sauvignon. 65% merlot. 28% cabernet-franc. **Production:** 20,000 bottles CB. **Direct sales and by mail order:** in France. Château Canon La Gaffelière, 33330 Saint-Emilion. Tel. 57 24 71 33. **Retail sales:** for export. *This little property appears as a second label of Château Canon La Gaffelière. It enables a selection to be made to the advantage of this latter.*

Lamour (Château)

Commune: Saint-Emilion. **Proprietor:** S.C. du Château Lamour. Managers: Jacques de Coninck, Serge Feuillatte. **Size of vineyard:** 3.68 hectares. **Average age of vines:** 17 years. **Varieties:** 35% cabernet-sauvignon. 65% merlot. **Production:** 20 tonneaux. **Sales by mail order.** *The lightness of this wine from the "sands" is compensated for by a four to five weeks' maceration period.*

La Nauve (Clos)

Commune: Saint-Laurent-des-Combes. **Proprietor:** Madame Guion-Bénard. Vineyard manager and cellar master: M. Bénard. Consultant oenologist: M. Chaine. **Size of vineyard:** 0.256 hectares. **Average age of vines:** 20 years. **Varieties:** 100% merlot. **Production:** 1,200 bottles CB. **Direct sales and by mail order:** tel. 57 24 70 32. *A very confidential production reserved for a small circle of friends and acquaintances.*

L'Ancien Moulin (Château)

Commune: Libourne. **Proprietor:** M. Gilbert Favrie. Consultant oenologist: Gilles Pauquet. **Size of vineyard:** 4 hectares. **Average age of vines:** 25 years. **Varieties:** 10% cabernet-sauvignon. 50% merlot. 40% cabernet-franc. **Production:** 16,000 bottles CB. **Visits:** by appointment. Tel. 57 51 29 02. **Direct sales and by mail order:** in France and abroad. Gilbert Favrie, 11 chemin du Ruste, 33500 Libourne.

With its soil of siliceous clay and subsoil of iron-pan, this *cru* is closest to the terrain of Pomerol than to most traditional Saint-Emilions. In fact, L'Ancien Moulin is adjacent to the Pomerol appellation and is to the extreme west of that of Saint-Emilion, on either side of the brook of Tailhas. Cultivation is extremely traditional

(four types of ploughing with no herbicides) and harvesting is done by hand. Classical vinification and maturing in wood, of which one-sixth is of new wood. An agreeable wine: fruity, lively, light, honest.

L'Angélus (Château)

Grand Cru classé

Commune: Saint-Emilion. **Proprietors:** Messrs de Boüard de Laforest. Director: Jacques de Boüard. Estate manager: Hubert de Boüard. Consultant oenologists: Hubert de Boüard and Pascal Ribéreau-Gayon. **Size of vineyard:** 23 hectares. **Average age of vines:** 25 years. **Varieties:** 5% cabernet-sauvignon. 45% merlot. 50% cabernet-franc. **Production:** 144,000 bottles CB. **Visits:** by appointment. Tel. 57 24 71 39. **Direct sales and by mail order:** in France. **Retail sales:** through the Bordeaux trade.

Today, L'Angélus rings out the good word of Saint-Emilion over all points of the globe. Formerly, according to oral tradition, it was the one place from where the angelus-bell of the other three churches of the area could be heard: Mazerat, Saint-Martin-de-Mazerat and Saint-Emilion. In 1909, Maurice de Boüard inherited the estate from his aunt. The main part of the estate was the 13 hectares of vines whose wine went under the name of "Mazerat". This legacy must have helped to settle the eldest son of a large family, who had to emigrate to America at the age of 16. He served in the dragoons and distinguished himself by his fiery temperament. In 1924, he did not let the opportunity slip of buying the three hectares called "L'Angélus" from the Gurchy family. He was fifty-four at that time. Twelve years later he had his right hand crushed by the wheel of a cart which, being drawn by a horse that had bolted, he tried to stop. Stolidly, he learned to write with his left hand and died in 1959 at the age of 89, having heard the angelus-bell for the last time. His three sons had taken on the running of the estate at the end of the last Great War. They

Jacques, Christian, Hélène and Hubert de Boüard de Laforest.

decided that, as the best bells give but one note, they would group together the productions of Mazerat and the little vineyard under the one name of L'Angélus. It was under this name that the vineyard was classified in 1954.

In 1960, the youngest brother, Alain, left the family firm. In 1969, the property was increased by three neighbouring hectares, bought from Château Beauséjour. All is now in one stretch and is situated at the foot of a southern slope benefiting from a maximum amount of sunshine. The average age of the vines is maintained at twenty-five years. Vinification is traditional with fermentation periods of about three weeks. Ageing is carried out in new casks for two-thirds of the vintage over a period of fourteen to sixteen months. The rest retains the freshness of its original fruit in vats. A complete blending of each vintage takes place a little before bottling. The whole of the production is put into wooden cases. I must confess my already long-standing personal soft spot for the wines of L'Angélus. They can open up rapidly while remaining consistent and profound. This distinctive character is not as frequent as might be thought when it comes to the difficult matter of judging between the spontaneous charms of adolescence and the subtle virtues of maturity. L'Angélus has the secret of olfactory analogies such as cachou, liquorice, vanilla and crystallized fruits. It is a wine which rarely disappoints and whose distinctive personality can always be rediscovered with pleasure. The good reputation enjoyed by this *cru* throughout the world is wholly justified.

Langrane (Château) 🍾

→ *Saint-Pey "Branche Aînée"*

Laniote (Château)

Grand Cru classé

Commune: Saint-Emilion. **Proprietors:** Freymond-Rouja heirs. Director: M. de la Filolie. Estate manager: M. Jean Brun. Oenologist: Florence Ribéreau-Gayon. **Size of vineyard:** 5 hectares. **Average age of vines:** 25 years. **Varieties:** 10% cabernet-sauvignon. 70% merlot. 20% cabernet-franc. **Production:** 30,000 bottles CB. **Visits:** M. Bombeau. Tel. 57 24 70 80. **Direct sales and by mail order:** in France and abroad. **Retail sales.**

To the northwest very close to the town, this five hectare vineyard is planted on heavy land, of clayey limestone type with ferruginous veins in the lowest part. It is undoubtedly the *cru* which is the most authentically representative of the good Saint Emilion, for the famous Trinity Chapel is to be found here, built in the twelfth century above the grotto where Emilion lived four centuries earlier. The tourist should not fail to visit the pious hermitage with its picturesque charm. It is cut out of the rock like a troglodyte bed-sitter whose "furniture" is part of the fixtures. An altar, a bed, and an armchair are of the same rock. Undeniably Saint Emilion had a sense of rustic design when he fitted out his small quarters. An atmosphere of pious simplicity reigns and you cannot enter without a certain emotion. On the left as you go in, protected by ancient but anachronistic balustrades, you can see the pure spring which incited the holy man to make his dwelling here. Lovers, pious pilgrims, the devout and the superstitious never fail to throw a pin into it, while making a wish which will come true in the course of the year if it falls to form the shape of a cross with another pin already submerged therein. Seeing that the pins at the bottom of the pool can be counted by the thousand, if you have a wish you want to come true, go and throw your pin into the limpid waters of the hermitage. Your short fervent prayer will be heard. It works better than any game of chance. Those who have nothing (or everything) to ask for should throw a coin in. There are already tons upon tons. Perhaps in a thousand years, an archeologist from another galaxy will discover the Saint-Emilion "treasure" and destroy the legend of the Saint's poverty. Another special benediction of the spot: women who want to have a child should

sit in the stone armchair thinking hard of their dearest wish. Less than three moons later, they will have a little Jesus in the crib. Especially if the future father has taken of the waters of Saint-Emilion – in the shape of Château Laniote, for example!

L'Annonciation (Château de)

Commune: Saint-Emilion. **Proprietor:** Bruno Callégarin. Consultant oenologist: Mademoiselle Cazenave. **Size of vineyard:** 4.5 hectares. **Average age of vines:** 30 years. **Varieties:** 33% cabernet-sauvignon. 33% merlot. 33% cabernet-franc. **Production:** approximately 30,000 bottles. **Visits:** tel. 57 51 74 50. **Direct sales and by mail order:** in France and abroad. Bruno Callégarin, 11 avenue de l'Europe, 33500 Libourne. **Retail sales.**

Lapelletrie (Château)

Grand Cru

Commune: Saint-Christophe-des-Bardes. **Proprietor:** GFA Lapelletrie (Pierre Jean family). Director: Christian Lassegues. Cellar master: Monsieur Gagnaire. Consultant oenologist: Monsieur Pauquet. **Size of vineyard:** 12 hectares. **Average age of vines:** 50 years. **Varieties:** 80% merlot. 20% cabernet-franc. **Production:** 66,000 bottles CB. **Direct sales and by mail order:** in France and abroad. Tel. 57 24 77 54.

Perched on two ridges of clayey limestone, the vineyard of Château Lapelletrie dominates the commune of Saint-Christophe-des-Bardes. On his marriage in 1930, M. Pierre Jean (the mayor of Saint-Christophes-des-Bardes for thirty-two years) bought Château Lapelletrie. Today, Lapelletrie is the centre of a not inconsiderable vine and wine business. Huge cellars enable ordinary wines to be stored and despatched, notably for sale in plastic containers. Large underground cellars present favourable conditions to preserve the château's folklore, of which some customers are very fond.

Lapeyre (Château)

Grand Cru

Commune: Saint-Etienne-de-Lisse. **Proprietor:** Simone Tauziac. Tenant, vineyard manager and cellar master: Hubert Tauziac. Consultant oenologist: Max Jumin. **Size of vineyard:** 12 hectares. **Average age of vines:** 25 years. **Varieties:** 10% cabernet-sauvignon. 50% merlot. 40% cabernet-franc. **Production:** 70,000 bottles CB. **Visits:** by appointment. Tel. 57 40 18 24. **Direct sales and by mail order:** in France and abroad. **Retail sales.**

Simone Tauziac is a very capable woman. The proprietor of Châteaux Lapeyre and Guinot (a second label), she retired from work in 1983 at the age of 65. To replace her, she entrusted the estate to her son Hubert, but none the less keeps a watchful eye on it. In her time, Madame Tauziac was both on the vineyard and in the cellars. It was she who first did the château bottling here. When she started to market her wine, she was particularly astute. She extracted the names of Lapeyre and Guinot from telephone directories covering the whole of France, and wrote off to them proposing the sale of her wine. She remembers and smiles: "People took the bait... often, but they were pleased! You know, there are more Lapeyres then you would have imagined."If you have an uncle by the name of Lapeyre, you know now how to give him pleasure. Otherwise, give your grandfather a case of it. In any case this fresh and light wine will give pleasure to eveybody.

La Pierre du Maréchal (Château)

Commune: Saint-Christophe-des-Bardes. **Proprietor:** Max Iteï. **Size of vineyard:** 1 hectare. **Average age of vines:** 20 years. **Varieties:** 70% merlot. 30% bouchet. **Production:** 6,000 bottles CB. **Direct sales and by mail order:** in France. Tel. 57 24 62 36. *Since 1955, this little vineyard has managed to stabilize Max Iteï, formerly a globe-trotter and an adventurer.*

La Pignonne (Clos)

Commune: Libourne. **Proprietor:** Denis Pueyo. Directed by: GAEC Pueyo Frères. Consultant oenologist: M. Pauquet. **Size of vineyard:** 3 hectares. **Average age of vines:** 25 years. **Varieties:** 70% merlot. 30% cabernet-franc. **Production:** 18 tonneaux. 8,000 bottles CB. **Visits:** by appointment. Tel. 57 51 13 26. **Direct sales and by mail order:** in France and abroad: Germany, Belgium. Denis Pueyo, 15 avenue de Gourinat, 33500 Libourne. **Retail sales:** in bulk. *The three generations of the Pueyos make their wine in cement vats in a happy atmosphere. These is no danger of being importuned by an excess of tannins.*

La Pointe Bouquey (Château)

Grand Cru

Commune: Saint-Pey-d'Armens. **Proprietor:** René Bentenat. Vineyard manager and cellar master: Philippe Bentenat. Consultant oenologist: M. Hébrard. **Size of vineyard:** 6.85 hectares. **Average age of vines:** 30 years. **Varieties:** 75% merlot. 25% cabernet-franc. **Production:** 25 tonneaux. 6,000 bottles CB. **Direct sales and by mail order:** tel. 57 47 15 34. **Retail sales:** through the Bordeaux trade. *The mayor of Saint-Pey-d'Armens should show an example and bottle more of his wine.*

Larcis Ducasse (Château)

Grand Cru classé

Commune: Saint-Laurent-des-Bardes. **Proprietor:** Hélène Gratiot Alphandéry. Estate manager and cellar master: Philippe Dubois. Consultant oenologist: J.-F. Chaine. **Size of vineyard:** 10 hectares. **Average age of vines:** 20 to 30 years. **Varieties:** 10% cabernet-sauvignon. 65% merlot. 25% cabernet-franc. **Production:** 50 to 60,000 bottles CB. **Visits:** by appointment. Philippe Dubois. Tel. 57 24 70 84. **Direct sales and by mail order:** in France and abroad. **Retail sales:** through Bordeaux and Libourne.

Château Larcis Ducasse was acquired in 1893 by Henry Raba, a direct descendant of an old family of ship-owners and wine merchants, installed in Bordeaux since the eighteenth century and close relatives of the Foulds, the Gradises and the Péreires.

Larcis Ducasse is of the two crus classés lying outside the commune of Saint-Emilion.

In 1936, André Raba, one of the five children of Henry, who had been a medical auxiliary in the army during the First World War, set up at Larcis Ducasse, so succeeding his mother. 1941: the Nazi troops invaded the estate. André Raba was imprisoned in Libourne, accused of listening to the English radio. He died soon after, the result of brutal treatment, leaving the property to his niece, Madame Gratiot Alphandéry. She too was menaced in her own turn by the occupying forces and fled to unoccupied France with her two children. She came back to Larcis Ducasse after the Liberation in 1944, and from that date she has run the estate, at the same time holding down an important position in education in Paris.

During the war, the estate and the harvest were safeguarded thanks to the devotion and the outstanding competence of the estate manager, M. Pharaon Roche. Today he has been replaced (since 1978) by Philippe Dubois, born at Larcis Ducasse where his parents were employed. It was a long time ago that my friend Pierre Castéja, the owner of Maison Joanne, converted me to the aromatic subtleties of this wine.

Larguet (Château) 🏚 → Union de Producteurs

Larmande (Château)

🍷🍷🍷🍷🍷

Grand Cru classé

Commune: Saint-Emilion. **Proprietor:** Jean-Fernand Mèneret Capdemourlin. Estate and vineyard manager: Philippe Mèneret-Capdemourlin. Cellar master: Roland Dudilot. Consultant oenologists: Messieurs Peynaud and Guimberteau. **Size of vineyard:** 19.5 hectares. **Average age of vines:** 35 years. **Varieties:** 5% cabernet-sauvignon. 65% merlot. 30% cabernet-franc. **Production:** 90,000 bottles CB. **Visits:** by appointment. Tel. 57 24 71 41 or 57 74 40 77. **Sales by mail order:** in France. Château Larmande, rue Guadet, 33330 Saint-Emilion. **Retail sales:** through Bordeaux and Libourne.

Larmande is a locality on the north side of Saint-Emilion. The vines grow on a wide variety of soils. This geological diversity is reflected in the wine which presents a fine, rich structure. The average age of the vineyard is maintained at 35 years, and the yields per hectare are very reasonable. There is one parcel of cabernet-franc of unknown exact age, but it is more than a hundred years old.

A hundred years ago, Larmande belonged to the Saint-Genis family who had succeeded the Pion de Cases. At that time, the *cru* was rated by Cocks and Féret

In the old town, Larmande is an ancient manor-house of the fourteenth century.

with the seconds of Saint-Emilion. The estate manager of the property then was called Germain Mèneret. Towards the end of the preceding century, he wanted to buy the estate from his employer. As he could not find the necessary sum by himself, he called on his friend Amédée Capdemourlin. The two families were very close to each other, so much so that the following generation saw them linked by marriage. Germain Mèneret (junior) and his wife (née Capdemourlin) inherited the property in 1935. It is their son Jean-Fernand (known as Jean) who has succeeded them and is in charge of running the estate with the help of his two sons. I am very fond of the wines of Larmande. They are of a fine consistency which fills the mouth.

La Rocaille (Château)

Commune: Libourne. **Proprietor:** François Florit. **Size of vineyard:** 5.47 hectares. **Average age of vines:** 20 years. **Varieties:** 20% cabernet-sauvignon. 70% merlot. 10% cabernet-franc. **Production:** 30 tonneaux. **Direct sales and by mail order:** François Florit, Gueyrosse, 33500 Libourne. Tel. 57 51 01 23. *Well made wine, without excessive acidity which usually will give real pleasure to the genuine wine lover.*

Laroque (Château)

Grand Cru

Commune: Saint-Christophe-des-Bardes. **Proprietor:** SCA Château Laroque. Estate manager: Bruno Sainson. Manager: Franck Allard. Consultant oenologist: Michel Rolland. **Size of vineyard:** 44 hectares. **Average age of vines:** 25 years. **Varieties:** 15% cabernet-sauvignon. 65% merlot. 20% cabernet-franc. **Production:** 250,000 bottles CB. **Visits:** tel. 57 24 77 28. **Direct sales:** Château Laroque, 33 rue de Saint-Genès, 33000 Bordeaux. **Retail sales:** Alexis Lichine & Co.

The first stones of Laroque date from the Middle Ages, of which the round tower is a vestige. Reconstructed in the eighteenth century in pure Louis XIV style, it is one of the most imposing and magnificent châteaux of the region. For several centuries it was the property of the Counts of Rochefort Lavie, whose monogram still adorns the ornamental wrought iron gateway. In the thirties, the Beaumartin family bought up all the Rochefort estates. Château Laroque had to wait until 1960 before being put back into good condition. With nearly 45 hectares

The imposing architecture of Château Laroque.

in production, it is one of Saint-Emilion's large vineyards. Today, the *cru* is distributed exclusively by the firm of Alexis Lichine & Co. The recent vintages have all the characteristics of the wines from the hillsides and are not lacking in elegance.

La Rose (Clos)

Grand Cru

Commune: Saint-Emilion. **Proprietor:** Jean-Claude Carles. Consultant oenologist: Michel Rolland. **Size of vineyard:** 2 hectares. **Average age of vines:** 15 years. **Varieties:** 10% cabernet-sauvignon. 70% merlot. 20% cabernetfranc. **Production:** 12,000 bottles CB. **Visits:** by appointment. Tel. 57 24 78 92. **Direct sales and by mail order:** in France and abroad. Château Coudert, Saint-Christophe-des-Bardes. **Retail sales:** through Libourne. *A pleasant and unpretentious wine which is both supple and fruity.*

La Rose Blanche (Château)

Commune: Saint-Christophe-des-Bardes. **Proprietor:** Mme Lisette Fritegotto. Consultant oenologist: M. Hébrard. **Size of vineyard:** 6 hectares. **Average age of vines:** 20 years. **Varieties:** 20% cabernet-sauvignon. 60% merlot. 20% cabernet-franc. **Production:** 20,000 bottles CB. **Visits:** tel. 57 24 62 26. **Direct sales and by mail order:** Lisette Fritegotto, La Brièche, 33330 Saint-Christophe-des-Bardes. **Retail sales:** Borie-Manoux, Barrière. *Madame Fritegotto divides her time between the general post office in Bordeaux and her vineyard, which bears the stamp of a good wine.*

La Rose Côtes Rol (Château)

Grand Cru

Commune: Saint-Emilion. **Proprietor:** Yves Mirande. **Size of vineyard:** 8.5 hectares. **Average age of vines:** 25 years. **Varieties:** 15% cabernet-sauvignon. 65% merlot. 15% cabernet-franc. 5% malbec. **Production:** 42,000 bottles CB. **Visits:** daily; groups by appointment. Tel. 57 24 71 28. **Direct sales and by mail order:** in France and abroad. *Several gold and silver medals have rewarded this successful grower. None the less the wines sometimes lack a certain substance and presence on the palate.*

La Rose-Pourret (Château)

Commune: Saint-Emilion. **Proprietors:** B. & B. Warion. Director: Madame Warion. Consultant oenologist: Mademoiselle Cazenave-Mahé. **Size of vineyard:** 8.14 hectares. **Average age of vines:** 30 to 50 years. **Varieties:** 75% merlot. 25% cabernet-franc. **Production:** 40,000 bottles CB. **Visits:** weekdays. Tel. 57 24 71 13. **Direct sales and by mail order:** in France and abroad. **Retail sales.** *Wines with a pleasant bouquet and a light, supple character which can be drunk relatively young but which, logically enough, are not well-disposed towards long ageing.*

La Roseraie (Château)

Commune: Saint-Emilion. **Proprietor:** Christian Lasfargeas. Consultant oenologist: J.-F. Chaine. **Size of vineyard:** 4.5 hectares. **Average age of vines:** 25 years. **Varieties:** 5% cabernet-sauvignon. 80% merlot. 15% cabernet-franc. **Production:** 18 tonneaux. 7,000 bottles CB. **Direct sales and by mail order:** in France, C. Lasfargeas, Vachon, 33330 Saint-Emilion. Tel. 57 74 40 38. **Retail sales.** *Settled on a hillside, Raymond Lasfargeas does not burden himself with literature. He makes a good wine and it sells well. That is the tradition.*

La Rose Rol (Château) → Petit Bigaroux

La Rose-Trimoulet (Château)

Commune: Saint-Emilion. **Proprietor:** Jean-Claude Brisson. Consultant oenologist: C.B.C. Libourne. **Size of vineyard:** 5 hectares. **Average age of vines:** 25 years. **Varieties:** 10% cabernet-sauvignon. 70% merlot. 20% cabernet-franc. **Production:** 25 tonneaux. **Visits:** tel. 57 24 73 24. **Direct sales and by mail order. Retail sales:** French and Belgian wine merchants.

In 1834, distant "cousins" of Jean-Claude Brisson bought a parcel of vines of 2.6 hectares, which had been detached from Château Trimoulet. This acquisition was concluded for a consideration of 4,000 francs payable over eight years at an annual interest rate of 5%. During the second half of the nineteenth century, the working buildings were gradually constructed and two new parcels were added to increase the size of the estate. Since 1967, Jean-Claude Brisson has leased the estate from his parents. Tannic without being excessively so, the wine is one revealing finesse rather than power. Highly recommended for delicate palates.

La Rouchonne (Château)

→ Union de Producteurs

Laroze (Château)

 Ŷ Ŷ Ŷ Ŷ Ŷ

Grand Cru classé

Commune: Saint-Emilion. **Proprietor:** S.C.E. Château Laroze. Director: Georges Meslin. **Size of vineyard:** 30 hectares. **Average age of vines:** 20 years. **Varieties:** 10% cabernet-sauvignon. 45% merlot. 45% cabernet-franc. **Production:** 158,000 bottles CB. **Visits:** tel. 57 51 11 31. **Sales by mail order:** in France. S.C.E. Château Laroze, 62 quai du Priourat, 33500 Libourne. **Retail sales:** through the Bordeaux trade.

With thirty hectares, Château Laroze is one of the larger estates in Saint-Emilion. The vineyard was created in 1882 when Madame G. Gurchy united the estates of Camus-La Gomerie and Lafontaine. The château was constructed in 1885 and all the working installations were the object of admiration of the observers of the time. Straight away the *cru* gained fame with the name of Laroze-Gurchy, which Cocks and Féret ranked with the "first seconds" of Saint-Emilion. Doctor Meslin became the next proprietor in the course of the twenties. Georges Meslin succeeds him today.

L'Arrosée (Château)

 Ŷ Ŷ Ŷ Ŷ Ŷ

Grand Cru classé

Commune: Saint-Emilion. **Proprietor:** G.F.A. du Château l'Arrosée. Tenant and vineyard manager: François Rodhain. Consultant oenologist: Pascal Ribéreau-Gayon. **Size of vineyard:** 10 hectares. **Average age of vines:** 25 years. **Varieties:** 35% cabernet-sauvignon. 45% merlot. 20% cabernet-franc. **Production:** 60,000 bottles CB. **Retail sales:** tel. 57 24 70 47.

The terrain is characterized by its wide variety of soils, whose nature, incline, drainage and lower layers can change within the space of a few rows. The old vines draw their water from twenty-four to thirty feet down where the water-table never dries up. The name of the *cru* takes its origin from this. In 1958, the highly respected firm of wine merchants, Barrière Brothers, in Bordeaux, drew up a contract. L'Arrosée gained considerable fame from that time, but this *cru* was already greatly appreciated in the nineteenth century. François Rodhain maintains traditional cultivation methods. He is an unflinching partisan of harvesting at the latest possible date. For example, in 1980, they were still gathering the grapes on Hallowe'en. Professor Pascal Ribéreau-Gayon adds his oenological knowledge to the vinification. The result is agreeable. It can be superb: taste the 1983.

Lartigue Naude (Château) ☿ → Bigaroux

La Sablière (Château)

Commune: Saint-Emilion. **Proprietors:** M. and Mme Robert Avezou. Consultant oenologist: Rolland Frères. **Size of vineyard:** 10 hectares. **Average age of vines:** 20 years. **Varieties:** 10% cabernet-sauvignon. 70% merlot. 20% cabernet franc. **Production:** 50 tonneaux. 20,000 bottles CB. **Visits:** tel. 57 24 73 04. **Direct sales and by mail order:** in France and abroad. **Retail sales:** Bordeaux trade. *This estate, whose vines are on good gravel, has been run by tenant farmers from father to son since 1956. The wines are closer to the style of Pomerol than of Saint-Emilion.*

La Sablonnerie (Château)

Commune: Saint-Sulpice-de-Faleyrens. **Proprietors:** Messieurs Robert Lavigne & Fils. Manager: Michel Lavigne. Consultant oenologist: M. Rolland. **Size of vineyard:** 10.5 hectares. **Average age of vines:** 28 years. **Varieties:** 5% cabernet-sauvignon. 60% merlot. 35% cabernet-franc. **Production:** 50 tonneaux. **Visits:** tel 57 24 75 35. **Direct sales and by mail order:** in France. **Retail sales.**

Split up into five different parcels, the vineyard of La Sablonnerie is situated between the village of Saint-Sulpice-de-Faleyrens and the Tertre de Daugay. In 1956, the vines were destroyed by frost. On the eve of taking his *baccalauréat*, Michel Lavigne left school to help his father replant from scratch. This grower has always plenty of confidence and zeal and in good years keeps his best wine for his private clients. This is why it is better not to buy this wine through the trade.

La Salle (Domaine de) ☿ → Sansonnet

La Seigneurie (Château de)

Grand Cru

Commune: Saint-Etienne-de-Lisse. **Proprietor:** the Laporte-Bayard family. Directed by: Laporte Père & Fils. Consultant oenologist: Michel Rolland. **Size of vineyard:** 10 hectares. **Average age of vines:** 25 years. **Varieties:** 15% cabernet-sauvignon. 70% merlot. 15% cabernet-franc. **Production:** 60,000 bottles CB. **Visits:** tel. 57 74 62 47. **Retail sales.** *The Laportes bought the property in 1978 "in order to move up in the world and to be nearer to Saint-Emilion's church tower".*

La Serre is an attractive family-sized estate.

La Serre *(Château)*

Commune: Saint-Emilion. **Proprietor:** M. B. d'Arfeuille. Director: Luc d'Arfeuille. Consultant oenologist: M. Rolland. **Size of vineyard:** 7 hectares. **Average age of vines:** 35 years. **Varieties:** 20% cabernet-sauvignon. 80% merlot. **Production:** 36,000 bottles CB. **Visits:** tel. 57 51 17 57. **Sales by mail order. Retail sales.**

Two hundred yards from the ramparts of Saint-Emilion, between Villemaurine and Trottevieille, the vineyard of Château La Serre spreads out its seven hectares over clayey gravelly land. The dwelling was constructed towards the end of the seventeenth century by Romain de Labayme, whose family included a large number of jurats, barristers in the Parlement and five mayors of Bordeaux from the sixteenth to the eighteenth centuries. Today the d'Arfeuille family owns this estate. Vinification is highly traditional, with a fermentation period of about three weeks. The high proportion of merlot makes the wines very round and extremely rich. This good label deserves a sales drive.

Lassègue *(Château)*

Grand Cru

Commune: Saint-Hippolyte. **Proprietors:** M. and Madame Jean-Pierre Freylon. Consultant oenologist: Centre Informations Œnologiques, chambre d'agriculture de la Gironde. **Size of vineyard:** 22.5 hectares. **Average age of vines:** 20 years with some plots replanted quite recently. **Varieties:** 25% cabernet-sauvignon. 40% merlot. 35% cabernet-franc. **Production:** 150,000 bottles CB. **Visits:** M. Freylon. Tel. 57 24 72 83. **Direct sales and by mail order:** in France. **Retail sales.**

Good terrain situated along the south hills of the Saint-Emilion appellation, continuing on from Château Pavie and Larcis Ducasse. Madame Freylon's mother, Madame Belliquet, had this *cru* from her family from the middle of the eighteenth century. For once, I shall leave the final appreciation to come from the mouth of the oenologist who has made a pertinent commentary on four recent vintages:

Vintage	1979	1981	1982	1983
Colour	Mature carmine.	Intense and mature carmine.	Intense ruby.	Deepest garnet-red.
Bouquet	Delicate. Notes of ripe grape and a hint of wood.	Powerful. Hints of leather, a touch of wood. Very persistent cabernet.	Very fine nose. Floral notes of merlot and berries.	Intense overtones of berries and kernels.
Flavour	Supple on the palate. Ready for drinking.	Fine and elegant, well balanced. Ready for drinking.	Full-bodied. Harmonious. Powerful. Good tannins. A great future.	Solid. Well structured. Very good tannins. A great future.

Conclusions: good all round. The 82s and 83s are typical of Saint-Emilion – Grézillac Study and Oenological Information Centre.

La Tonnelle (Château)

→ Union de Producteurs

La Tonnelle (Clos de) ⚑ → Soutard

La Tour du Guetteur (Château)   ♟♟♟♟♟

Commune: Saint-Emilion. **Proprietor:** Antoinette Andrieux. Manager: François Morin. Consultant oenologist: Michel Rolland. **Size of vineyard:** 0.35 hectares. **Average age of vines:** 50 years. **Varieties:** 50% merlot. 50% cabernet-franc. **Production:** 1,200 bottles CB. **Retail sales:** tel. 57 84 38 52.

This rare and charming label announces that "this very small vineyard in the heart of Saint-Emilion has terraces entirely cultivated by hand. From exceptional terrain of exceptional quality, the wine it produces is limited in quantity and is not available on the open market, being reserved for the privileged few."

La Tour du Pin Figeac (Château)

Grand Cru classé

Commune: Saint-Emilion. **Proprietor:** G.F.A. Giraud Bélivier. Tenant: André Giraud. **Size of vineyard:** 10.5 hectares. **Average age of vines:** 35 to 40 years. **Varieties:** 75% merlot. 25% cabernet-franc. **Production:** 50 tonneaux. **Visits:** Madame Giraud. Tel. 57 51 06 10. **Direct sales and by mail order:** in France and abroad. G.F.A. Giraud Bélivier, Château Le Caillou, Pomerol. *An excellent* cru *yielding a quality remarkable for its consistency.*

La Tour du Pin Figeac Moueix

Grand Cru classé

Commune: Saint-Emilion. **Proprietors:** Marcel Moueix heirs. Director and cellar master: Armand Moueix. Consultant œnologist: Bernard Crébassa. **Size of vineyard:** 9 hectares. **Average age of vines:** 20 years. **Varieties:** 5% cabernet-sauvignon. 60% merlot. 30% cabernet-franc. 5% malbec. **Production:** 48,000 bottles CB. **Visits:** tel. 57 51 50 63. **Sales by mail order:** in France. S.A. Moueix & Fils. Château Taillefer, 33500 Libourne. **Retail sales:** S.A. Moueix & Fils.

The two châteaux – twin brothers – cited above extend the resemblance even to having the same name. The tower (La Tour) disappeared a long time ago and the umbrella pine (le Pin) no longer exists. These vineyards are situated on the sandy gravel at the boundary of Saint-Emilion and Pomerol and in the immediate neighbourhood of Cheval Blanc. They have a good reputation which goes back to

the beginning of this century. The wines frequently develop rapidly and can easily be confused with those of Pomerol.

La Tour Figeac (Château)

Grand Cru classé

Commune: Saint-Emilion. **Proprietor:** S.C. du Château La Tour Figeac. Director: Michel Boutet. Vineyard manager: Jean Beyly. Consultant oenologist: Rémy Cassignard. **Size of vineyard:** 13.63 hectares. **Average age of vines:** 35 years. **Varieties:** 60% merlot. 40% cabernet-franc. **Production:** 72,000 bottles CB. **Visits:** by appointment. Tel. 57 24 70 86. **Direct sales and by mail order:** in France only. **Retail sales:** through the Bordeaux trade. *This label is highly sought after by the entire Bordeaux trade.*

Corbière, Lassèverie, Martin-Boiteau, Rapin and, today, Michel Boutet, these are the names of the successive proprietors of La Tour Figeac since 1879, that is at the time of its being detached from Château Figeac. The *cru* underwent an eclipse during the last war. It was then reorganized and the estate now covers 40 hectares. The previous owners had the eighteenth century tower reconstructed and they built an elegant mansion standing on a balustraded perron. The vineyard of today is in one unbroken stretch, situated on a high point of the graves of Saint-Emilion next to Cheval Blanc on the east side and Figeac on the south, the boundary of the Pomerol appellation lying to the west. Michel Boutet, the proprietor since 1973, is an expert in the field of agriculture and he became a grower out of the love of wine. At the age of eighteen he was already a collector of fine bottles. He remains a partisan of harvesting by hand and a vinification which emphasizes suppleness.

Latte de Sirey (Château) ♟♟♟♟♟

Commune: Saint-Laurent-des-Combes. **Proprietor:** M. Neycenssas. Director: Michèle Neycenssas. Consultant oenologist: M. Chaine. **Size of vineyard:** 5 hectares. **Average age of vines:** 30 years. **Varieties:** 10% cabernet sauvignon. 80% merlot. 10% cabernet franc. **Production:** 30 tonneaux. 18,000 bottles CB. **Visits:** tel. 57 24 74 05. **Direct sales and by mail order:** in France and abroad. Max Neycenssas, Petit Gueyrot, 33330 Saint-Laurent-des-Combes. **Retail sales.**

Of abrupt manner and sarcastic address, Max Neycenssas is a sensitive vigneron who likes to pour out his feelings on his wine and his job. A defender of tradition, he does not use herbicides on the vines. He ploughs in the four traditional ways and fines with egg-whites. But the secret of his wine does not lie therein. Only Max knows it and it will never come out in his forceful way of speaking. You have to go and knock at his door. This proprietor is as genuine as his wine and both merit a detour. The 82 obtained a gold medal in Paris in 1984 and, more recently, his 86 was also awarded a distinction. This is possibly one of the most traditional *crus* to be found in the whole of Saint-Emilion: all the methods used both in the vineyard and in the cellar have proved their worth over more than a century.

Lavallade (Château) ♟♟♟♟♟

Grand Cru

Commune: Saint-Christophe-des-Bardes. **Proprietor:** Pierre Gaury. Consultant oenologist: C.B.C. Libourne. **Size of vineyard:** 12 hectares. **Average age of vines:** 40 years. **Varieties:** 65% merlot. 35% cabernet-franc. **Production:** 84,000 bottles CB. **Visits:** tel. 57 24 77 49. **Direct sales and by mail order. Retail sales:** Libourne.

Half the vineyard is ploughed, the other half treated with herbicides. Harvesting is done half by machine and half by hand. Yes, but are they the same halves? Whatever the case, everything comes together in cement vats.

La Vieille Eglise (Domaine de)

Grand Cru

Commune: Saint-Hippolyte. **Proprietors:** M. Palatin and M. Micheau-Maillou. Consultant oenologist: C.B.C. Libourne. **Size of vineyard:** 13 hectares. **Average age of vines:** 18 years. **Varieties:** 5% cabernet-sauvignon. 65% merlot. 30% cabernet-franc. **Production:** 70,000 bottles CB. **Visits:** tel. 57 24 77 48 or 57 24 61 99. **Direct sales and by mail order:** in France and abroad. **Retail sales:** Savour-Club. *A generally well-made wine which can be counted on to reach a good average standard. In good years it can be excellent.*

Lavignère (Château)

→ Union de Producteurs

Le Blanquey (Château) → Touzinat

Le Bois du Loup (Château)

Grand Cru

Commune: Vignonet. **Proprietors:** M. and Madame Raymond Lenne. Consultant oenologist: M. Plomby. **Size of vineyard:** 0.62 hectares. **Average age of vines:** 55 years. **Varieties of vine-stock:** 50% merlot. 50% cabernet-franc. **Production:** 2,000 bottles CB. **Visits:** by appointment. Tel. 57 40 07 87. **Direct sales and by mail order:** Raymond Lenne, Château du Bois, 33350 Saint-Magne-de-Castillon. **Retail sales.**

Château Le Bois du Loup belongs to M. and Madame Raymond Lenne, already the proprietors of Château du Bois in Saint-Magne-de-Castillon. The vineyard of Le Bois du Loup stretches out over sandy land. Harvesting is traditional. Vinified in cement vats, the wine matures in wood.

Le Brégnet (Clos)

Commune: Saint-Sulpice-de-Faleyrens. **Proprietors:** Jean-Michel and Arlette Coureau. Consultant oenologist: C.B.C. Libourne. **Size of vineyard:** 7 hectares. **Average age of vines:** 30 years. **Varieties:** 5% cabernet-sauvignon. 85% merlot. 10% cabernet-franc. **Production:** 35 tonneaux. 20,000 bottles CB. **Visits:** tel. 57 24 76 43. **Direct and retail sales.**

This is an attractive little estate, tastefully and discreetly ensconced in its vineyard. Everything is a very model of correctness and I cite Jean-Michel and Arlette Coureau as perfect examples of young growers. They should be encouraged to do more château bottling, even if it means buying a *barrique* or a tonneau *en primeur*. It will be money well invested and very good value for money, with the possibility of choosing the exact number of half-bottles, bottles or magnums that you want.

Le Castelot (Château)

Grand Cru

Commune: Saint-Sulpice-de-Faleyrens. **Proprietor:** G.F.A. J. Janoueix. Vineyard manager: Max Chabrerie. Cellar master: Paul Cazenave. Consultant oenologists: Messieurs Legendre and Pauquet. **Size of vineyard:** 5.5 hectares. **Average age of vines:** 45 years. **Varieties:** 20% cabernet-sauvignon. 60% merlot. 20% cabernet-franc. **Production:** 35,000 bottles CB. **Visits:** by appointment. Tel. 57 51 41 86. **Direct sales and by mail order:** in France and abroad. Exclusive worldwide distribution through M. Janoueix, 37 rue Pline Parmentier, 33500 Libourne.

It is thanks to Henri IV that the corner turret was built.

In the spirit of friendship and with a ready will, the clients and their children come to give a hand with the harvests of the Janoueix, who have added this *Grand Cru* to the list of their products. Exactly four centuries ago, good King Henri IV of Navarre, surprised by a storm, took refuge in the hostelry of the Bosquet. The innkeeper and his wife waited on him hand and foot and the Gascon *au panache blanc* was soon tucking in to an exquisite boiled chicken washed down with many a hearty glassful from the best cask. The charming hostess spoiled him so much that in the small hours, when the storm had abated, King Henri permitted a "little château" to be built in this place, that is a manor-house with a turret having a cone-shaped roof and a weathercock, symbols of lordly rank. Among the quotations of Henri IV, one has been forgotten: "You should always look to see which way the hurricane is blowing." This was inspired at Castelot. Since then, the *cru* benefits from a serene microclimate. Its wine is purple and bright, with a fruity bouquet which is not lacking in panache or courage. Its proprietor even goes so far as to assert that it has "guts".

Le Chatelet (Château)

Grand Cru classé

Commune: Saint-Emilion. **Proprietors:** H. and P. Berjal. **Size of vineyard:** 6 hectares. **Average age of vines:** 15 to 20 years. **Varieties:** 33% cabernet-sauvignon. 33% merlot. 33% cabernet-franc. **Production:** 30 tonneaux. **Visits:** by appointment. Tel. 57 24 70 97. **Direct sales and by mail order:** in France and abroad. M. Berjal, B.P. 16, 33330 Saint-Emilion. **Retail sales.**

Three hundred yards from the collegiate church on the west of the town, this estate stretches out over the limestone plateau, worn away by erosion, which makes up part of the history of Haut Saint-Emilion. Its distinguished neighbours are Clos Fourtet and Beau-Séjour Bécot. Moreover, Madame Berjal inherited this property from her father, M. Bécot. The terrain is excellent and has an advantageous exposure. Classical vinification confers distinction, often revealed as when a pretty young woman approaches, by perfumes full of promise. You have then only to raise the glass to your lips. And your mouth will fill with delicate fragrances at which your memory will have no cause to blush.

Le Conte Marquey (Château)

Commune: Saint-Hippolyte. **Proprietor:** Jean-Paul Borderie. Tenant, vineyard manager and cellar master: Irène Bouyer. Consultant oenologist: Mademoiselle Cazenave. **Size of vineyard:** 4.96 hectares. **Average age of vines:** 17 years. **Varieties:** 35% cabernet-sauvignon. 30% merlot. 35% cabernet-franc. **Production:** 23 tonneaux. 10,000 bottles CB. **Visits:** by appointment. Tel. 57 24 62 28. **Direct sales and by mail order:** J.-P. Borderie, Haut-Piney, 33330 Saint-Hippolyte. **Retail sales.** *The proprietor's son is a pilot with Air France but it is mother who is at the controls. The balanced proportions of the varieties should be noted: they give the wine its harmonious if rather light character.*

Le Couvent (Château)

Grand Cru

Commune: Saint-Emilion. **Proprietor:** S.C. Château Le Couvent. Director: M. François-M. Marret. **Size of vineyard:** approximately 10 hectares. **Average age of vines:** 50 years. **Varieties:** 20% cabernet-sauvignon. 55% merlot. 25% cabernet-franc. **Sales by mail order:** in France and abroad. Tel. 57 74 62 21. **Retail sales:** for export.

You would think that the Saint-Emilion vineyards which belong to the "Marne and Champagne" group are the estate of a secret sect. For everything is shrouded in mystery here: those in charge (the manager or cellar master have had strict instructions to remain anonymous), the oenologists (it appears that there are three), the total area in production, etc. M. François-M. Marret arrived in Saint-Emilion in 1981. His first acquisition was Château Pontet-Clauzure in October 1981, followed by Château Le Couvent in December of the same year. Every year has been marked by a fresh purchase; 1982: Lagrange de Lescure; 1983: Capet and Les Baziliques; 1984: Petit-Bert. The noisy echoes of the rumours this started up were to be heard all over the countryside. As too was the droning of the owner's personal helicopter flying over his lands and sometimes going to cast rather too close an eye over his neighbours'. And you know, a light coloured three-piece suit was something worn more than twenty years ago on the Left Bank in Paris. In short, the discretion of the Société Civile du Château Le Couvent does not go unnoticed! But the management hopes to develop its export business, and, when all is said and done, wherever they may come from, the wines are not as bad as all that.

Le Freyche (Château)

Commune: Saint-Pey-d'Armens. **Proprietor:** Henri Domezil. Consultant oenologist: Mademoiselle Cazenave. **Size of vineyard:** 4 hectares. **Average age of vines:** 15 years. **Varieties:** 50% merlot. 50% cabernet-franc. **Production:** 20 tonneaux. 15,000 bottles CB. **Visits possible. Direct sales and by mail order. Retail sales.** *This* cru *is good enough to merit being exclusively château-bottled.*

Le Grand Faurie (Château)

Grand Cru

Commune: Saint-Emilion. **Proprietor:** Charles Bouquey. **Size of vineyard:** 4 hectares. **Average age of vines:** 35 years. **Varieties:** 60% merlot. 40% cabernet-franc. **Production:** 24,000 bottles CB. **Visits:** by appointment. Tel. 57 51 35 27. **Direct sales and by mail order:** in France and abroad. Charles Bouquey, Le Rivallon, 33330 Saint-Emilion. **Retail sales.** *A family and ancestral estate like Vieux-Rivallon. Excellent terrain and vines carefully tended. Perhaps the racking off of the wines is a little too hasty.*

Le Jurat (Château)

Commune: Saint-Emilion. **Proprietor:** S.C.A. Haut-Corbin. **Director:** M. Parment. Estate manager and cellar master: D. Teyssou. Manager and consultant oenologist: Georges Pauli. **Size of vineyard:** 7.5 hectares. **Average age of vines:** 25 years. **Varieties:** 25% cabernet-sauvignon, 75% merlot. **Production:** 40,000 bottles CB. **Visits:** Madame Malbec. Tel. 56 31 44 44. **Sales by mail order:** in France. Madame Gonzales, Ets. Cordier, 10 quai de la Paludate, 33800 Bordeaux Cédex. **Retail sales:** Ets. Cordier.

Le Loup (Château) → Union de Producteurs

Le Maine (Château)

Commune: Saint-Pey-d'Armens. **Proprietor:** Pierre Veyry. Consultant oenologist: M. Rolland. **Size of vineyard:** 5.15 hectares. **Average age of vines:** 20 years. **Varieties:** 15% cabernet-sauvignon. 66% merlot. 18% cabernet-franc. 1% malbec. **Production:** 20,000 bottles CB. **Visits:** daily. Tel. 57 24 60 75 or 57 24 74 09. **Direct sales and by mail order:** in France. Château Le Maine, Raynaud, 33330 Saint-Pey-d'Armens.

The house is in the commune of Saint-Pey-d'Armens but the vineyard is situated in that of Saint-Laurent-des-Combes. Greatly spread out over a radius of a mile, it lies in six different areas, each with its own type of soil. Cultivation and vinification are conducted in the traditional fashion and excessive maturity is systematically sought after. The average age of the vines is maintained at about twenty-five years. For ten years, Pierre Veyry has been expanding his direct sales and he very readily receives visitors in his renovated cellars.

Le Mayne (Château)

Commune: Libourne. **Proprietor:** Jean-Claude Dupuy. Consultant oenologist: M. Pasquier. **Size of vineyard:** 1.35 hectares. **Average age of vines:** 10 years. **Varieties:** 25% cabernet-sauvignon. 75% merlot. **Production:** 6,000 bottles CB. **Direct sales:** Jean-Claude Dupuy, Saint-Raphaël, 33480 Avensan. Tel. 56 58 17 41. **Sales by mail order.**

Jean-Claude Dupuy succeeded his father, Max, a proprietor and wine-merchant in Libourne. He is also to be found in Pomerol on the three hectares of Château La Providence and in Villegouge in the Fronsac region in the *cru* of La Bruyère. But he is from Saint-Raphaël in the Médoc, the little homeland of the famous archbishop Pey-Berland. Up to now, his estate in Saint-Emilion has withstood urbanization. Jean-Claude Dupuy blends the traditional with the modern.

Le Mont d'Or (Château)

Commune: Saint-Emilion. Proprietor: Consorts Lavandier. Tenant: Thierry Lavandier. Consultant oenologist: Laboratoire de Grézillac. Size of vineyard: 3 hectares. Average age of vines: 30 years. Varieties: 60% merlot. 40% cabernet-franc. Production: 15 tonneaux. 8,000 bottles CB. Direct sales and by mail order. Consorts Lavandier, Saupiquet, 33330 Saint-Emilion. Tel. 57 74 46 64. Retail sales: Sichel & Co.

L'Epine (Château)

Commune: Libourne. Proprietors: Jean and Monique Ardouin. Vineyard manager and cellar master: Monique Ardouin. Consultant oenologist: Mademoiselle Mahé. Size of vineyard: 2.13 hectares. Average age of vines: 25 years. Varieties: 60% merlot. 40% cabernet-franc. Production: 12,000 bottles CB. Visits: by appointment. Tel. 57 51 07 75. Direct sales and by mail order: in France and abroad. Jean and Monique Ardouin, 4 quai du Priourat, 33500 Libourne.

As in Courgis, in the Chablis region, there was once supposed to have been on the present site of the vineyard of Château L'Epine, a stone holding a thorn from Christ's crown. This was the legendary origin of the name of Château L'Epine, a little estate in the suburbs of Libourne and bordered lower down by the Lour. Formerly a teacher, Jean Ardouin has never really concerned himself with the vineyard. It is his wife who runs the family concern. Monique Ardouin is a woman who loves nature and likes to watch the flowering of the vines. She is also a woman of the land, who climbs on the tractor, supervises the harvesting, vinifies and looks after the bottling. In all her comings and goings, she is followed and helped by her young son Gabriel, a genius of a grower in the making.

L'Epinette (Domaine de)

Commune: Libourne. Proprietor: Thierry Lavandier. Consultant oenologist: Laboratoire de Grézillac. Size of vineyard: 1 hectare. Average age of vines: 25 years. Varieties: 50% merlot. 50% cabernet-franc. Production: 6,000 bottles CB. Visits: tel. 57 74 46 64. Direct sales and by mail order. *The whole of the production is sold to direct customers whose faithfulness demonstrates their satisfaction.*

Le Prieuré (Château)

Grand Cru classé

Commune: Saint-Emilion. **Proprietor:** Olivier Guichard. Estate manager and cellar master: Jacques Rougier. Consultant oenologist: C.B.C. Libourne. **Size of vineyard:** 5.44 hectares. **Average age of vines:** 21 years. **Varieties:** 60% merlot. 40% cabernet-franc. **Production:** 24,000 bottles CB. **Sales by mail order:** in France and abroad. S.C.E. Baronne Guichard, Château Siaurac, Néac, 33500 Libourne. Tel. 57 51 64 58. **Retail sales.**

Facing Ausone on the opposite slope near Trottevieille and Troplong-Mondot, there is no doubt that the vineyard of Le Prieuré has an advantageous situation with its southern exposure. Monsieur Olivier Guichard's maternal grandfather bought the estate in 1897. It was the result of the division out of the real estate of the *cru* of Les Cordeliers which was still in existence at the end of the last century – a survival of an ecclesiastical inheritance of the *ancien régime*. Baroness Guichard has the larger part of her land in the Lalande de Pomerol appellation, but there are considerable portions in Pomerol and Saint-Emilion. The combined terrains represent a production which does honour to the family.

Les Baziliques (Château)

Grand Cru

Commune: Saint-Christophe-des-Bardes. **Size of vineyard:** about 10 hectares. **Average age of vines:** 25 years. **Varieties:** 25% cabernet-sauvignon. 39% merlot. 36% cabernet-franc. **Sales by mail order:** in France and abroad. Tel. 57 74 62 21. *See Château Le Couvent. The annual production of this label varies according to commercial factors.*

Lescours (Château de)

Grand Cru

Commune: Saint-Sulpice-de-Faleyrens. **Proprietor:** S.A.E. du Château Lescours. Director: Pierre Chabriol. Cellar master: Daniel Julliot. Consultant oenologist: M. Gendrot. **Size of vineyard:** 34 hectares. **Average age of vines:** 20 years. **Varieties:** 5% cabernet-sauvignon. 70% merlot. 25% cabernet-franc. **Production:** 180,000 bottles CB. **Visits:** daily. Saturday and Sunday by appointment. Tel. 57 24 74 75. **Direct sales and by mail order:** in France and abroad (United States and Japan). **Retail sales:** Lescours.

Château de Lescours was built in 1341 by a certain Pey de Lascortz, an equerry of King Edward I of England. It was in the sixties that Monsieur Pierre Chariol, a doctor, gave up his profession to take the fate of Lescours in hand. A lover of travel, he set sail for the New World and created his first clientèle. Even to-day, Château de 221

Lescours exports more than 80% of its production to the U.S.A. Its second market is Japan. (One Sunday, as usual, Pierre Chariol went to the bookmakers to "place his bet". He came back to his estate accompanied by a Japanese. This unexpected visitor was a famous sommelier in his own country.) Today, Château de Lescours is run by the son, Pierre Chariol, but several of his sisters and one of his brothers-in-law make an active contribution in furthering the already high reputation of this *cru*. This is undoubtedly one of the best wines produced in the commune of Saint-Sulpice-de-Faleyrens.

Les Fougères (Château) 🏠 → *Bouquey*

Les Grandes Versannes (Château) 🏠 → *Gravet-Renaissance*

Les Grandes Versannes (Clos)

Commune: Saint-Emilion. **Proprietor:** M. and Madame Sylvain. Consultant oenologist: C.B.C. Libourne. **Size of vineyard:** 1.38 hectares. **Average age of vines:** 35 years. **Varieties:** 25% cabernet-sauvignon. 50% merlot. 25% cabernet-franc. **Production:** 7,000 bottles CB. **Direct sales and by mail order:** tel 57 51 13 51. *A cooper to the* Grands Crus classés *who has his own little* cru *and who produces the best wine he can for his many friends and relations.*

Les Graves d'Armens (Château) 🏰 → *Union de Producteurs*

Lespinasse (Château)

Grand Cru

Commune: Saint-Pey-d'Armens. **Proprietor:** Roger Bentenat. Consultant oenologist: Mademoiselle Cazenave. **Size of vineyard:** 7.5 hectares. **Average age of vines:** 25 years. **Varieties:** 80% merlot. 20% cabernet-franc. **Production:** 35 tonneaux. 18,000 bottles CB. **Direct sales and by mail order:** tel. 57 47 15 08. **Retail sales.**

Four different ways of ploughing during the year, cultivation and harvesting by hand; tradition is sacrosanct among the vines. In the vat-house and the cellars, concessions have been made to modern times. Vinification and storage in cement vats but the wine does pass through casks and is fined with egg-whites. All is done conscientiously and the good reputation of this château is well deserved.

Le Tertre Rotebœuf (Château)

Grand Cru

Commune: Saint-Laurent-des-Combes. **Proprietors:** F. and E. Mitjavile. Consultant oenologist: M. Chaine. **Size of vineyard:** 4.5 hectares. **Average age of vines:** 20 years. **Varieties:** 80% merlot. 20% cabernet-franc. **Production:** 24,000 bottles CB. **Visits:** tel. 57 24 70 57. **Direct sales and by mail order:** in France. **Retail sales.**

François Mitjavile.

Before the days of the tractor, the vigneron used to use the horse on the plain and the ox on the hillside. When the slope was steep, the ruminant used to breathe stertorously. That is the exact origin of the name Roteboeuf on the Land Register ("Roter" in French meaning "to belch" and "bœuf" meaning "ox"). François Mitjavile and his wife have been settled here for some ten years. They have considerably improved the state of the vineyard and the cellars, and accordingly, the quality of the wine. A third of the casks is renewed every year. Le Tertre Roteboeuf is an ideal small vine-growing estate, entirely typical of Saint-Emilion. With its rustic, pure eighteenth century style, the château is a charming illustration of the vineyard countryside as it existed 250 years ago. The Mitjaviles always keep a few bottles for their friends and passing clients. Both they and their reasonably priced wine deserve to be known. They are cordial and healthy.

Leydet-Figeac (Château)

Grand Cru

Commune: Saint-Emilion. **Proprietor:** S.C.E.A. des Vignobles Leydet. Directors, vineyard managers and cellar masters: Bernard Leydet and Jean-Gérard Chazeau. **Size of vineyard:** 1.25 hectares. **Average age of vines:** 23 years. **Varieties:** 60% merlot. 40% cabernet-franc. **Production:** 6,000 bottles CB. **Visits:** daily. **Direct sales:** Château Leydet-Figeac, Rouilledinat, 33500 Libourne. Tel. 57 51 19 77. **Sales by mail order:** in France and abroad. *The wine of this estate has a minimum fermentation period of twenty days in stainless steel vats and is then aged in wood. It is more in the style of Pomerol than Saint-Emilion. It is supple and aromatic.*

223

Leydet-Valentin (Château)

Commune: Saint-Emilion. **Proprietor:** Bernard Leydet. Consultant oenologist: C.B.C. Libourne. **Size of vineyard:** 5.06 hectares. **Average age of vines:** 20 years. **Varieties:** 5% cabernet-sauvignon. 60% merlot. 30% cabernet-franc. 5% malbec. **Production:** 24,000 bottles CB. **Visits:** daily. Tel. 57 24 73 05. **Direct sales and by mail order:** in France and abroad. **Retail sales:** Coste in Langon. *Well made wines.*

L'Hermitage (Château)

Commune: Saint-Emilion. **Proprietor:** G.F.A. du Château Matras. Tenant: Véronique Gaboriaud. Consultant oenologist: Michel Rolland. **Size of vineyard:** 3.5 hectares. **Average age of vines:** 30 years. **Varieties:** 30% cabernet-sauvignon. 30% merlot. 30% cabernet-franc. 10% malbec. **Production:** 23,000 bottles CB. **Visits:** tel. 57 51 52 39. **Retail sales:** 20% goes for export. *It is quite rare to find four different varieties in such a small domain.*

L'Housteau-Neuf (Clos de)

Commune: Libourne. **Proprietor:** Jean Fortin. Consultant oenologist: Michel Rolland. **Size of vineyard:** 1 hectare. **Average age of vines:** 19 years. **Varieties:** 25% cabernet-sauvignon. 50% merlot. 25% cabernet-franc. **Production:** 5 tonneaux. **Retail sales:** in bulk. *It is undoubtedly a pity that this little* cru *does practically no bottling.*

Lianet (Château) ♟ → Trapaud

Lisse (Château de)

Commune: Saint-Etienne-de-Lisse. **Proprietor:** S.C. des Vignobles Jean Petit. Vineyard manager and cellar master: Didier Parrot. **Size of vineyard:** 12 hectares. **Average age of vines:** 30 years. **Varieties:** 15% cabernet-sauvignon. 50% merlot. 35% cabernet-franc. **Production:** 72,000 bottles CB. **Visits:** by appointment. Tel. 57 40 18 23. **Direct sales and by mail order:** in France and abroad. **Retail sales.** *Also see Château Mangot which belongs to the same proprietor in the same commune. The label, printed in imitation of a medieval parchment, none the less adorns honest wine.*

L'Oratoire (Clos de)

Grand Cru classé

Commune: Saint-Emilion. **Proprietor:** S.C. du Château Peyreau. **Director:** Michel Boutet. **Consultant oenologist:** Rémi Cassignard. **Size of vineyard:** 9.45 hectares. **Average age of vines:** 32 years. **Varieties:** 75% merlot. 25% cabernet-franc. **Production:** 48,000 bottles CB. **Visits:** by appointment. Tel. 57 24 70 86. **Direct sales and by mail order:** in France. S.C.E. du Château Peyreau. **Retail sales:** through the Bordeaux trade.

Its ancient history is intimately linked with that of Château Peyreau. The vineyard lies on the sandy glacis which stretches out at the foot of Soutard and Sarpe. At the end of the last century it belonged to the Beylot family who had a charming residence built in wooded parkland. Since 1971, a limited company administered by Michel Boutet has taken over from the Lenne family. Count de Neipperg (Château Canon La Gaffelière) is a shareholder. The wines are made in the "old style" with eighteen months in wood, racking every three months and fining with egg-whites. They are generally vigorous and with a long life in front of them. They need to be kept for at least four to five years before beginning to develop and the great vintages can be kept for one or two generations.

Magdelaine (Château)

1er Grand Cru classé

Commune: Saint-Emilion. **Proprietor:** Ets. Jean-Pierre Moueix. **Estate and vineyard manager:** Michel Gillet. **Cellar master:** Jean Veyssière. **Consultant oenologist:** Jean-Claude Berrouet. **Size of vineyard:** 10.5 hectares. **Average age of vines:** 25 years. **Varieties:** 80% merlot. 20% bouchet. **Production:** 45,000 bottles CB. **Retail sales:** Ets. Jean-Pierre Moueix, Libourne.

"The Chatonnets reigned for two centuries (up to 1953) over La Magdelaine. They perpetuated its renown which, up to the Second Empire, was due to the vineyard on the plateau. When the Hill showed itself capable of producing great wines in the middle of the nineteenth century, the Chatonnets bought five hectares on the hillside, detached from the vineyard of Fonplégade and they constructed the château of today." This is how Henri Enjalbert sums up the history of Château Magdelaine. Obviously, things were not as simple as that, but this gives the story in a nutshell. In fact, after having had part of their landed estate for two centuries in the locality called La Madeleine (that is the land near the chapel of the same name) and having come through the Revolution relatively unscathed, the Chatonnets found their real estate threatened with division as the result of marriages. Already in 1850, there were three distinct estates using the name "La Magdelaine". (Enjalbert is wrong when he says that the *cru*'s spelling was changed by Georges Jullien, the son-in-law of one of the Chatonnets, at the end of the last century. The present spelling of the

Château La Magdelaine, an engraving dating from the end of the nineteenth century.

name conforms perfectly with the original.) Twenty years later, these estates were four in number and were known thus: Chatonnet, Chatonnet-Crépin, Bon Barat (which created the *cru* of Curé Bon La Madeleine) and Domecq Cazaux, which later became Malineau-la-Madeleine, a name which has disappeared today. It was at this time that the names were spelt in different ways in order to distinguish between them: Magdelaine, Madeleine, La Madeleine, La Magdeleine, and so on. Meanwhile, the elder branch of the Chatonnets, anxious to reconstitute its heritage, had acquired five hectares on the slope of Fonplégade, in order to become economically viable. Georges Jullien, a notary in Saint-Emilion, appears as a Sunday grower who was very gifted at public relations and able to maintain the reputation of the *cru* at its highest level. In 1922, Féret's *Bordeaux et ses Vins* puts it in third place, just behind Ausone and Bélair. Under what exact conditions was the individual spelling of the names negotiated? I do not know, but from the twenties, the distinction became clearly established.

In 1952, Jean-Pierre Moueix bought Château Magdelaine from Georges's son, Jean Jullien, who although a brilliant academic in the field of law, seems never to have lifted a finger in his life. He used to spend the majority of his time, especially

226

when it was fine, behind the wall of his father's study in his bowler hat watching people go by with an indifferent air. The reincarnation of Diogenes, perhaps? The annual great event was the trip to Bordeaux to buy his New Year's suit. The weekly event was the market in Libourne and lunch at the Pigeon Blanc, opposite the Hôtel de France. He never married and lived under the protective wing of a housekeeper who did nothing to treat the chronic gout with which he was afflicted. A true eccentric, way out on the fringe, he seized every opportunity to cock a snook at the establishement, for example, by donating *piquette* (a drink made by steeping in water grape-skins crushed under pressure), in bottles bearing his own label, for the banquet of the Syndicat viticole which used to take place in a spirit of conviviality at the Guirauds at Le Palais Cardinal. Coming one hundred years after Balzac, this character surpasses caricature.

Jean-Pierre Moueix came on the scene, as only he knows how to on great occasions. He first took the estate on a lease, then he bought it. And Magdelaine changed its serenity without losing any of its authenticity. Staged by the oenologist Jean-Claude Berrouet, with Michel Gillet in the vines and Jean Veyssière in the cellars, the show is perfect. We have an annual festival of the Moueix productions:

The pigeon-cot was formerly a privilege reserved for those of lordly rank.

a wine which is theatrical and sublime, classical and audacious like Wagner staged by Chéreau. Every label is a complete playbill. Is this the best show in town? Not necessarily, but everybody rushes there. Indeed, everybody is right. Ring down the curtain. Bravo! Encore!

Magnan (Château)

Grand Cru

Commune: Saint-Emilion. **Proprietor:** G.F.A. Cormeil-Figeac. Tenant: Claude Moreaud. Estate manager: Richard Moreaud. Consultant oenologist: C.B.C. Libourne. **Size of vineyard:** 10 hectares. **Average age of vines:** approximately 22 years. **Varieties:** 85% merlot. 15% cabernet-franc. **Production:** 48,000 bottles CB. **Sales by mail order:** S.C.E.A. Domaines Cormeil-Figeac-Magnan, Cormeil-Figeac, 33330 Saint-Emilion. Tel. 57 24 70 53. **Retail sales:** for export.

Until 1978, the previous proprietors used to take the harvest to the *cave coopérative*. Since 1979, Robert Moreaud has buckled down to the job of restoring his new estate. He himself readily concedes that at the moment the vineyard is unbalanced, half the vines being old and at the end of their life, and the other half being young stock. The undisguised ambition of this competent grower is to put Château Magnan back in the place of *premier cru* which it occupied exactly one century ago in Cocks and Féret's *Bordeaux et ses Vins*. For the moment, the wines are fairly well structured and pleasant. But come back in fifteen years from now!

Magnan La Gaffelière (Château)

Grand Cru

Commune: Saint-Emilion. **Proprietor:** Hubert Pistouley. **Size of vineyard:** 8 hectares. **Average age of vines:** 14 years. **Varieties:** 10% cabernet-sauvignon. 50% merlot. 40% cabernet-franc. **Production:** 43,000 bottles CB. **Direct sales and by mail order:** in France. Tel. 57 24 71 50.

One of Hubert Pistouley's ancestors, Transon, was a cooper at La Gaffelière in the eighteenth century. We know that in 1777, he sold his wine to Horeau Beylot, the Libourne wine merchant. This gives a glimpse into the background of the present owner of this family vineyard increased over the generations and bordering famous names. The wines are well structured and very suitable for ageing. Although of an affable nature, Hubert Pistouley does not receive visitors. Write to him.

Mangot (Château)

Commune: Saint-Etienne-de-Lisse. **Proprietor:** G.F.A. du Château Mangot. **Director:** Jean Petit. Vineyard manager and cellar master: Didier Parrot. **Size of vineyard:** 35 hectares. **Average age of vines:** 40 years. **Varieties:** 80% merlot. 20% cabernet-franc. **Production:** 210,000 bottles CB. **Visits:** by appointment. Tel. 57 40 18 23. **Direct sales and by mail order:** in France and abroad. **Retail sales:** Vignobles Jean Petit.

Château Mangot is one of Jean Petit's recent acquisitions. But the firm known as Vignobles Jean Petit is a concern of long standing. Monsieur Marcelin Petit, the grandfather, was its founder. Today, the vines are spread out over a total area of eighty hectares, half of which is planted on the hills of Castillon. Although the vineyard is of this imposing size, Jean and Jacqueline Petit maintain a family atmosphere in their relations with their employees. The latter usually call them Mum and Dad. The prices fixed by these growers appear to be very reasonable for a quality of wine which will not disappoint the connoisseur.

Marquey (Château)

Grand Cru

Commune: Saint-Emilion. **Proprietor:** Alain Berjal. **Size of vineyard:** 4 hectares. **Average age of vines:** 20 years. **Varieties:** 40% cabernet-sauvignon. 60% merlot. **Production:** 24,000 bottles CB. **Visits:** tel. 57 74 60 06 or 57 74 42 55. **Direct sales and by mail order:** in France. Alain Berjal, B.P. 16, 33330 Saint-Emilion. **Retail sales:** abroad. *A property belonging to Alain Berjal, situated at the foot of the hill of Pavie.*

Marquis de Mons (Château du) ♟
→ La Vieille Eglise

Marrin (Château)

Commune: Saint-Christophe-des-Bardes. **Proprietor:** René Chêne. Vineyard managers: Françoise et René Chêne. Consultant oenologist: C.B.C. Libourne. **Size of vineyard:** 16.37 hectares. **Average age of vines:** 50 years. **Varieties:** 85% merlot. 15% cabernet-franc. **Production:** 65 tonneaux. 10,000 bottles CB. **Direct sales and by mail order:** tel. 57 24 77 60. **Retail sales.** *The property of René and Françoise Chêne since 1975, this* cru *belonged at the end of the last century to M. Bouquey, a notable figure from Saint-Emilion.*

Marsolan (Château de)

Commune: Saint-Christophe-des-Bardes. **Proprietor:** Jean Cheminade. Consultant oenologist: M. Hébrard. **Size of vineyard:** 0.64 hectares. **Average age of vines:** 20 years. **Varieties:** 70% merlot. 30% cabernet-franc. **Production:** 4,500 bottles CB. **Direct sales and by mail order:** Jean Cheminade, Beynat, 33350 Saint-Magne-de-Castillon. *One of the smallest vineyards of Saint-Emilion.*

Martinet (Château)

Commune: Libourne. **Proprietor:** de Lavaux. Consultant oenologist: M. Pauquet. **Size of vineyard:** 17 hectares. **Average age of vines:** 20 years. **Varieties:** 15% cabernet-sauvignon. 85% merlot. **Production:** 100 tonneaux. **Visits:** tel. 57 51 06 07. **Sales by mail order:** in France and abroad. **Retail sales:** Horeau Beylot.

This is one of the largest vineyards today in the commune of Libourne. It is of long-standing reputation and has been associated for many years with the Decazes, Saint-Genis and de Lavaux families, this latter being the present proprietor. Its traditional clientele is particularly in the Benelux countries. Without reaching the heights of finesse, its wine is a very honest representative of the "sables de Saint-Emilion" and certainly one of the best of this area. But do not expect to be drinking a Saint-Emilion from the hillsides! The annexation of the "Sables Saint-Emilion" by the main appellation comes about in fact as a result of the reduction of this area following the urbanization of Libourne. For the growers of the region, it was not a bad deal.

Matignon (Château)

Commune: Libourne. **Proprietor:** Henri Matignon. Consultant oenologist: M. Rolland. **Size of vineyard:** 1.45 hectares. **Average age of vines:** 15 years. **Production:** 8 tonneaux. 4,000 bottles CB. **Direct sales:** Henri Matignon, 60 chemin de la Lamberte, 33500 Libourne. Tel. 57 51 12 86. **Sales by mail order:** in France. **Retail sales:** through the Bordeaux trade.

Château Matignon is set in Libourne behind the last houses, which announce the first vines of Pomerol. This tiny vineyard is rather like the garden of a pretty little house in the suburbs. Unfortunately, it risks disappearing, for it is about to be the victim of the construction of an outer ring-road. But for want of a Saint-Emilion from Château Matignon, you are always at liberty to drink a Pomerol from Château des Jacobins, belonging to the same proprietor, Monsieur Henri Matignon. Moreover there is a good family resemblance between the two wines.

Matras (Château)

Grand Cru classé

Commune: Saint-Emilion. **Proprietor:** G.F.A. Château Matras. Tenant: Véronique Gaboriaud-Bernard. **Size of vineyard:** 14 hectares. **Average age of vines:** 20 years. **Varieties:** 30% cabernet-sauvignon. 35% merlot. 30% cabernet-franc. 5% malbec. **Production:** 60,000 bottles CB. **Visits:** daily by appointment. Tel. 57 51 52 39. **Direct sales:** Château Matras, B.P. 127, 33501 Libourne Cédex. **Sales by mail order:** in France. Madame Gaboriaud-Bernard, Château Bourseau, 33500 Lalande de Pomerol. **Retail sales:** through Bordeaux and Libourne.

"This vineyard dominates the valley. It is protected from the north winds and is situated 1,000 yards from Saint-Emilion's church tower. Because of this, it was spared the terrible frosts of 1956." So there you have the explanation of Matras's miraculous microclimate! Convincing, do you not think? When I tell you that this plot of verdant vineland belonged for a while to Cardinal de Sourdis, the Archbishop of Bordeaux, you will be reassured as to the divine protection which sheltered Matras from every sort of adversity. According to its owner, the oenologist Jean Bernard-Lefebvre, the name of Matras takes its origin from the paraphernalia of warfare of the Middle Ages: "Either the bolt of a crossbow or the crossbowman's large arrow, it also designated the warrior who used it." With the *Grand Robert* coming to the help of the *Grand Bernard,* with *Grand Albert* in between, I have another equally plausible explanation to suggest: the matrass is a glass or earthenware vessel with a long neck, once used in alchemy but nowadays in chemistry and pharmacy for various procedures, but notably for distillation. Do you agree? In alternate years, the coat of arms adorning Château Matras's label will display a crossbow one year, and the year after, a distillation flask.

For several years, Château Matras was leased by Monsieur Vauthier. When the proprietor, Madame de Fremond (née Carle), wanted to sell the estate, she realized

231

that her tenant had not asked for the *cru* to be classified in 1954, the date the classification was determined. In fact, Matras had more or less fallen into oblivion. The affair had noisy repercussions which were discreetly muffled. The dossier was compiled and Château Matras had the honour of featuring on the first page of the 1969 edition of Cocks and Féret's *Bordeaux et ses Vins*, under the heading "Late entries and errata". Along with seven other *crus* of Saint-Emilion (including Château Dassault), it had just been finally recognized as a *Grand Cru classé*. It must be said that oblivion is a contagious spell. Professor Henri Enjalbert himself, describing the valleys and pockets on the south side in detail, particularly the valley of Mazerat, did not mention Matras, which none the less featured on Belleyme's map in 1785! But Madame Véronique Gaboriaud, the current mistress of the estate and the daughter of Jean Bernard-Lefebvre, is now trumpeting the fame of her *cru* so loudly that she will be heard in all the four corners of the earth. News for wine-lovers: Matras is back on the scene.

Maurens (Château) ☖ → Fombrauge

Maurins du Boutail (Château)

Commune: Saint-Sulpice-de-Faleyrens. **Proprietors:** Monsieur and Madame Bourée. **Size of vineyard:** 4 hectares. **Average age of vines:** 20 years. **Varieties:** 25% cabernet-sauvignon. 50% merlot. 25% cabernet-franc. **Production:** 25,000 bottles CB. **Visits:** tel. 57 24 74 47. **Direct sales and by mail order:** in France. *Aromatic, rounded, smooth and easy to drink, these are wines which can be appreciated either young or old.*

Mauvezin (Château)

Grand Cru classé

Commune: Saint-Emilion. **Proprietor:** GFA Cassat & Fils. Consultant oenologist: Libourne. **Size of vineyard:** 3.20 hectares. **Average age of vines:** 10 to 100 years. **Varieties:** 10% cabernet-sauvignon. 35% merlot. 55% cabernet-franc. **Production:** 16,000 bottles CB. **Visits:** tel. 57 24 72 36 or 57 24 62 57. **Direct sales and by mail order:** G.F.A. Cassat & Fils, B.P. 44, 33330 Saint-Emilion. **Retail sales:** for restaurants.

On a plateau of asteroidian limestone, the arable land is only two or three feet deep. Mauvezin is an old little locality. The Fontémoings were proprietors there in the eighteenth century. Enjalbert relates that the estate measured eight acres and that the wine was of the highest quality. It was a satellite of the parish of Saint-Martin. The etymology of the name is Latin, *malum vicinium* meaning sometimes "evil quarter" and sometimes "wicked neighbour". But that in no way impinges on the excellence of the limited quantity of wine made by Pierre Cassat, which can be found with pleasure on the wine-list of many good restaurants. Not to be confused with the Château Mauvezin of the Haut-Médoc appellation.

Mauvinon (Château)

→ *Union de Producteurs*

Grand Cru

Mayne-Figeac (Château)

Grand Cru

Commune: Saint-Emilion. **Proprietor:** Jean-Jaime Chambret. Consultant oenologist: M. Rolland. **Size of vineyard:** 1 hectare. **Average age of vines:** 30 years. **Varieties:** 65% cabernet-sauvignon. 35% cabernet-franc. **Production:** 5,000 bottles CB. **Visits:** Jean-Jaime Chambret, 30 chemin de la Corbière, 33500 Libourne. Tel. 57 51 06 81. **Sales by mail order:** in France.

Formerly, each of the most outstanding members of any family had his "eke name", that is to say, his nickname. Jean-Jaime Chambret's great grandfather was called "Vieux Cadiche" or local old peasant-vigneron. The grandfather, who must have been a lady-killer, answered to the name of "Chéri". Jean-Jaime Chambret lives in Libourne but he remains greatly attached to his vineyard and his cellars. In spring, he likes to go to smell the flowering vines: "It is a delight!" Mayne-Figeac is a pure wine.

Mazeran (Château)

→ *Vieux Château Peymouton*

Mazouet (Château)

→ *Union de Producteurs*

Mélin (Château)

Commune: Libourne. **Proprietor:** S.C. Debacque René & Fils. Consultant oenologist: Gilles Pauquet. **Size of vineyard:** 13 hectares. **Average age of vines:** 25 years. **Varieties:** 75% merlot. 25% cabernet-franc. **Production:** 70 tonneaux. (20,000 bottles). **Direct sales and by mail order:** S.C. Debacque & Fils, 17 rue des Réaux, 33500 Libourne. Tel. 57 51 00 66. **Retail sales:** Ets. De Rivoyre & Diprovin. *Young Vincent Debacque seems to have found the road leading to consistent high quality. Well done! Here is a* cru *which has made spectacular progress over the last five years.*

233

Menuts (Clos des)

Grand Cru

Commune: Saint-Emilion. **Proprietor:** Pierre Rivière. Cellar master: Serge Beau. Consultant oenologist: M. Chaine. **Size of vineyard:** 23.60 hectares. **Average age of vines:** 30 years. **Varieties:** 30% cabernet-sauvignon. 70% merlot. **Production:** 156,000 bottles CB. **Visits:** tel. 57 24 70 59 or 57 24 73 90. **Direct sales and by mail order:** in France. **Retail sales.**

This is the best of Pierre Rivière's wines. The Rivières have been growers in Saint-Emilion for three generations. The firm of Rivière, founded in 1875, also owns properties in Lussac, Montagne and in the Bordeaux Supérieur area. The vineyard of the Menuts is divided into two parts, one near the ramparts of Saint-Emilion and the other at the foot of the hillsides. Ageing is carried out in the cool of deep underground cellars hewn out of the rock. They deserve a visit and can easily be found opposite the post office. The wines of the Rivières are a worthwhile purchase.

Merlin (Château)

Grand Cru

Commune: Libourne. **Proprietor:** Alain Debacque. Consultant oenologist: M. Hébrard. **Size of vineyard:** 2.06 hectares. **Average age of vines:** 20 years. **Varieties:** 70% merlot. 30% cabernet-franc. **Production:** 10 tonneaux. 6,000 bottles CB. **Visits:** by appointment. Tel. 57 74 14 90. **Direct sales and by mail order:** Alain Debacque, Domaine de Ridet, Condat, 33500 Libourne. **Retail sales.**

It was perhaps the wizard Merlin in person who described the wines of this *Grand Cru* in this way: "With a bouquet of brambles and hawthorn and an after-smell of truffles." Recently acquired by M. and Mme. Alain Debacque, Château Merlin, on the fringe of Libourne, has started to establish a youthful, good reputation, thanks to its sales both to the trade and to a small group of faithful private customers which grows of its own accord every year.

Millaud-Montlabert (Château)

Grand Cru

Commune: Saint-Emilion. **Proprietors:** M. and Madame Claude Brieux. Consultant oenologist: M. Pauquet. **Size of vineyard:** 3.98 hectares. **Average age of vines:** 25 years. **Varieties:** 20% cabernet-sauvignon. 70% merlot. 10% cabernet-franc. **Production:** 24,000 bottles CB. **Visits:** tel. 57 24 71 85. **Direct sales and by mail order:** in France and abroad. *This estate has been in the hands of the Brieux family since the beginning of the century. The major part of the vineyard lies at Montlabert not far from Pomerol.*

Milon (Château)

Grand Cru

Commune: Saint-Christophe-des-Bardes. **Proprietor:** Christian Bouyer. **Size of vineyard:** 18 hectares. **Average age of vines:** 35 years. **Varieties:** 13% cabernet-sauvignon. 75% merlot. 12% cabernet-franc. **Production:** 100,000 bottles CB. **Visits:** Monday to Friday from 9 to 11 a.m. and 2 to 5 p.m. Tel. 57 24 77 18. **Direct sales and by mail order:** in France and abroad. *Eighteen hectares at the bottom of the hill for the vineyard of Château Milon and six hectares on a plateau of clayey limestone for the Clos de la Cure. Their origin goes back to the Middle Ages.*

Moines (Clos des)

Commune: Saint-Christophe-des-Bardes. **Proprietor:** Jean Ménager (father). **Director:** Jean Ménager (son). Consultant oenologist: C.B.C. Libourne. **Size of vineyard:** 9.5 hectares. **Average age of vines:** 15 years. **Varieties:** 15% cabernet-sauvignon. 65% merlot. 20% cabernet-franc. **Production:** 40 tonneaux. 15,000 bottles CB. **Visits:** tel. 57 24 77 02. **Direct sales and by mail order. Retail sales:** despatched in plastic containers. *This good* cru, *with tannic, well-structured wines, has increased its size in 1988, from a little over three hectares to nine and a half without loosing any of its quality. A label to watch.*

Monbousquet (Château)

Grand Cru

Commune: Saint-Sulpice-de-Faleyrens. **Proprietors:** Daniel Querre heirs. Directed by: S.C. du Château Monbousquet. Vineyard manager: Guy Thoilliez. Cellar master: Alain Querre. Consultant oenologist: M. Chaine. **Size of vineyard:** 30 hectares. **Average age of vines:** 25 years. **Varieties:** 10% cabernet-sauvignon. 50% merlot. 40% cabernet-franc. **Production:** 150 tonneaux. 100,000 bottles CB. **Visits:** tel. 57 51 56 18. **Direct sales and by mail order:** Alain Querre, B.P. 140, 33500 Libourne. **Retail sales:** Daniel Querre.

It is impossible to say a few words about this *cru* without mentioning old Daniel Querre. He was one of the most striking figures of his generation in Saint-Emilion. Love of the land, enthusiasm and competence, joviality and cordiality made up his personality, enhanced by an understanding of the soil almost unparalleled in the area – except perhaps by Georges Chailleau, his old friend from La Clotte. Today it is mainly his son Alain who presides over the estate. He has inherited from his father that incisive character which shocks because of its unshakeable conviction but which is mitigated by the freshness and delicacy of his good humour.

Monbousquet: a country manor-house in a romantic park.

For all that, Monbousquet is a fine, large estate whose vineyard is in perfect condition. Without wanting to put my oar in once again, I will take the liberty of saying that this *cru* merits being classified. Alain Querre replies: "I prefer to be the first of the non-classifieds rather than the last of the classifieds." Classified or not, Monbousquet holds its place well and its sonorous and powerful voice can be heard in the choir of the Saint-Emilions, like Chaliapin intoning Gregorian chant. If by chance you have a few hours to devote to the voluble but sincere Querre brothers, you will not regret your stop at Monbousquet, or tasting the recent vintages which will fill your mouth and open your taste-buds. The wine of Monbousquet is not one for the flippant.

Mondotte-Bellisle (Château)

Ⴂ Ⴂ Ⴂ Ⴂ Ⴂ

Grand Cru

Commune: Saint-Laurent-des-Combes. **Proprietor:** Marie-Antoinette Chaput. Tenant: M. Hibert. **Size of vineyard:** 5.8 hectares. **Average age of vines:** 30 years. **Varieties:** 75% merlot. 25% cabernet-franc. **Production:** 30 tonneaux. **Direct sales:** tel. 57 24 72 84. **Retail sales.** *A wine which will not break any records, but it would be a shame simply to rinse the glass round with it. That is to say that it is mild to the point of weakness.*

236

Mondou Mérignan (Château)

→ *Union de Producteurs*

Monlot Capet (Château)

Grand Cru

Commune: Saint-Hippolyte. **Proprietor:** G.F.A. Château Monlot Capet. Tenant: Palatin-Micheau-Maillou. Consultant oenologist: C.B.C. Libourne. **Size of vineyard:** 8.04 hectares. **Average age of vines:** 22 years. **Varieties:** 5% cabernet-sauvignon. 65% merlot. 30% cabernet-franc. **Production:** 45,000 bottles CB. **Direct sales and by mail order:** in France and abroad. Tel. 57 24 77 48. **Retail sales:** Savour Club, Sichel. *A name which resounds well even to the extent of creating an illusion, and an unpretentious wine which can give the customer pleasure.*

Montagu (Château de) → *Merlin*

Monte-Christo (Château)

Commune: Libourne. **Proprietor:** Philibert Rousselot. Consultant oenologist: Michel Rolland. **Size of vineyard:** 2.81 hectares. **Average age of vines:** 20 years. **Varieties:** 25% cabernet-sauvignon. 60% merlot. 15% cabernet-franc. **Production:** 16 tonneaux. 5,000 bottles CB. **Direct sales and by mail order:** Château Monte-Christo, 185 avenue de l'Epinette, 33500 Libourne. Tel. 57 74 06 71. **Retail sales:** Borie-Manoux. *It could well be called "Château d'If" but, even in the famous Dumas novel, Father Faria has never said mass with this wine.*

Montlabert (Château)

Grand Cru

Commune: Saint-Emilion. **Proprietor:** Socité Civile du Château Montlabert. Tenant: René Barrière. Vineyard manager: Jean-Michel Lalande. Cellar master and consultant oenologist: M. Le Menn. **Size of vineyard:** 13 hectares in one unbroken strech. **Average age of vines:** 20 years. **Varieties:** 10% cabernet-sauvignon. 50% merlot. 40% cabernet-franc. **Production:** 72,000 bottles CB. **Visits:** by appointment. Tel. 56 39 59 86 (in Bordeaux) or 57 24 70 75. **Direct sales and by mail order:** in France and abroad. **Retail sales.**

Linked by the love of wine, a group of international friends came together in 1967 and formed a limited company. The sponsors were the two Barrière brothers, Armand and René on the French side, the Canadian Donald Webster and the Englishman Montague Curzon. Thanks to their remarkable contacts, they created a group of great wine-lovers in order to buy Château Montlabert. This fine property of seventeen hectares is made up of thirteen hectares of vines in one unbroken stretch graced by a splendid park with different varieties of trees. Its origin goes back to the eighteenth century. A deed dated September 15, 1791 indicates that it then belonged to the Decazes family. Its surface area was larger. In the middle of the last century, it was split up several times, only the heart of the vineyard round the château being preserved. The partners of today's business have formed a sort of elitist club which is a private brotherhood: the Knights of Château Montlabert. Their greatest satisfaction is to be able to drink their dividends. The first thing they did was to have a brochure published in 1969 by Etienne Braillard of Geneva, which is a little masterpiece of typography. In superb condition today, the *cru* of Montlabert could justifiably claim a classification. The quality of the wines is constant and very satisfactory.

Morillon (Château)

Commune: Saint-Christophe-des-Bardes. **Proprietor:** Clotaire Sarrazin. Consultant oenologist: C.B.C. Libourne. **Size of vineyard:** 6.75 hectares. **Average age of vines:** 25 years. **Varieties:** 15% cabernet-sauvignon. 70% merlot. 15% cabernet-franc. **Production:** 28 tonneaux. 5,000 bottles CB. **Direct sales and by mail order:** Clotaire Sarrazin, Badette, 33330 Saint-Christophe-des-Bardes. Tel. 57 24 76 18. **Retail sales:** Maison Lebègue. *When soubriquets were in vogue, the Sarrazins were called "Morillons", a variety of black grape, doubtless because of their dark complexion. This Morillon however is sometimes too light in colour to deserve its name.*

Moulin Bellegrave (Château)

Grand Cru

Commune: Vignonet. **Proprietors:** Max and Florian Périer. Consultant oenologist: Grézillac Laboratory. **Size of vineyard:** 13 hectares. **Average age of vines:** 25 years. **Varieties:** 15% cabernet-sauvignon. 70% merlot. 15% cabernet-franc. **Production:** 60,000 bottles CB. **Direct sales and by mail order:** in France. Tel. 57 84 53 28 or 57 74 97 08. **Retail sales:** to the wholesale trade and private clients. *Well structured and tannic, making a wine suitable for long keeping. All proposals for special rates for commercial agents will be considered.*

Moulin de Cantelaube (Château) 🍷
→ Gros Caillou

Moulin de la Chapelle (Château du)
→ Union de Producteurs

Moulin de Lagnet (Château)

Commune: Saint-Christophe-des-Bardes. **Proprietor:** GFA Olivet Heirs. Tenants: Anne-Lise Goujon and Pierre Chatenet. Consultant oenologist: C.B.C. Libourne. **Size of vineyard:** 6 hectares. **Average age of vines:** 25 years. **Varieties:** 30% cabernet-sauvignon. 70% merlot. **Production:** 20,000 bottles CB. **Visits:** tel. 57 74 40 06. **Direct sales and by mail order:** Château Moulin de Lagnet, Larguet, 33330 Saint-Christophe-des-Bardes. **Retail sales:** through the Bordeaux trade. *This cru has just been taken in hand. The size of the vineyard has been increased to six hectares and is planned to go up to eight. Increase in quality should follow.*

Moulin de Pierrefitte (Château)

Grand Cru

Commune: Saint-Sulpice-de-Faleyrens. **Proprietor:** Jean-Louis Fayard. Consultant oenologist: M. Hébrard. **Size of vineyard:** 6.5 hectares. **Average age of vines:** 30 years. **Varieties:** 5% cabernet-sauvignon. 70% merlot. 25% cabernet-franc. **Production:** 30 tonneaux. 18,000 bottles CB. **Direct sales and by mail order:** J.-L. Fayard, Le Bourg, 33330 Saint-Sulpice-de-Faleyrens. Tel. 57 24 75 18. **Retail sales:** through Libourne.

In the locality known as Pierrefitte, there is a mill whose name J.-L. Fayard inherited in 1978 and he lavishes his most loving care on some six hectares of sandy gravel, split up into six different parcels. Although his second vineyard, Grand Bigaroux, is better known, I prefer the wines of Moulin de Pierrefitte as being better structured and conforming more to the idea one has of a Saint-Emilion *Grand Cru*.

Moulin du Cadet (Château)

Grand Cru classé

Commune: Saint-Emilion. **Proprietors:** Mouliérac Heirs and Ets Jean-Pierre Moueix. Estate manager and vineyard manager: Michel Gillet. Cellar master: Jean Veyssière. Oenologist: Jean-Claude Berrouet. **Size of vineyard:** 5 hectares. **Average age of vines:** 25 years. **Varieties:** 75% merlot. 25% cabernet-franc. **Production:** 25,000 bottles CB. **Retail sales:** Ets. Jean-Pierre Moueix.

Like Château La Clotte, Moulin du Cadet is in partnership with the Mouliérac heirs and the firm of Jean-Pierre Moueix. Its 75% merlot guarantee that the wine is round and velvety – the delight of gourmets. The wine bears the hallmark of Jean-Claude Berrouet, the brilliant oenologist of the large firm of Moueix, who has always had an inspired nose, a delicate palate, the gift of tongues and is an old hand. All his *crus* have a distinctive style marked by fine concentration.

Moulin Saint-Georges (Château)

ŢŢŢŢŢ

Grand Cru

Commune: Saint-Emilion. **Proprietor:** Vauthier family. Director: Alain Vauthier. Consultant oenologists: Mademoiselle Cazenave-Mahé and M. Chaine. **Size of vineyard:** 6.5 hectares. **Average age of vines:** 25 years. **Varieties:** 60% merlot. 40% cabernet-franc. **Production:** 30,000 bottles CB. **Direct sales and by mail order:** Alain Vauthier, Château Ausone, 33330 Saint-Emilion. Tel. 57 24 70 26. **Retail sales:** through the Bordeaux trade. *A good ancient label, the Moulin Saint-Georges is a younger brother of the great Ausone.*

Naude (Château)

ŢŢŢŢŢ

Grand Cru

Commune: Saint-Etienne-de-Lisse. **Proprietor:** Alain Bonneau. Vineyard manager: Jean-Christian Lacoste. Cellar master and consultant oenologist: Daniel Gaston. **Size of vineyard:** 6.25 hectares. **Average age of vines:** 15 years. **Varieties:** 30% cabernet-sauvignon. 70% merlot. **Production:** 45,000 bottles CB. **Visits:** by appointment. Tel. 57 84 50 01. **Direct sales and by mail order:** Alain Bonneau, 33420 Branne.

Alain Bonneau, the mayor of Branne and the proprietor of this *cru*, although turning grey, is a brisk, jovial person in his forties. Apart from his merlot and cabernet-sauvignon, this qualified oenologist cultivates a discreet but delightful regional accent which bears witness (if need were) to his complete sincerity. With his heart on his sleeve to welcome visitors and his hand on his heart to declare that his wine is the best, he has reigned paternally over his vineyard, Naude, since he inherited it from his father in 1975.

The vines are still rather young and they are called on to give abundant yields which are in the order of about 60 hectolitres per hectare. But the science of oenology is present to ensure a very "commercial" quality, in the best sense of the term.

Orme Brun (Château)

→ Belle Assise Coureau

Page Les Terres Rouges (Château) ♚♚♚♚♚

Commune: Saint-Laurent-des-Combes. **Proprietors:** Georgette, Gaston and Jean Page. **Size of vineyard:** 1.35 hectares. **Average age of vines:** 12 to 40 years. **Production:** 7 tonneaux. **Direct sales and by mail order:** tel. 57 24 62 65.

Pagnac (Château)

→ Union de Producteurs

Pailhas (Château) ♚♚♚♚♚

Commune: Saint-Hippolyte. **Proprietor:** Michel Robin-Lafugie. **Size of vineyard:** 15 hectares. **Average age of vines:** 25 years. **Varieties:** 10% cabernet-sauvignon. 60% merlot. 30% cabernet-franc. **Production:** 50 tonneaux. **Direct sales and by mail order:** in France and abroad. Michel Robin-Lafugie, 33350 Saint-Genès-de-Castillon. Tel. 57 40 10 01. **Sales through brokers** in all distribution networks. *This modest label adorns well made wines which are very agreeable to drink, young or old.*

Palais-Cardinal-La-Fuie (Château) ♚♚♚♚♚

Grand Cru

Commune: Saint-Sulpice-de-Faleyrens. **Proprietors:** Gérard Frétier & Fils. Consultant oenologist: M. Hébrard. **Size of vineyard:** 16 hectares. **Average age of vines:** 30 years. **Varieties:** 15% cabernet-sauvignon. 50% merlot. 35% cabernet-franc. **Production:** 84,000 bottles CB. **Visits:** by appointment. Tel. 57 24 75 91. **Direct sales and by mail order:** in France. **Retail sales.**

Gérard Frétier is a local man who can as well make a cask as fill it. Or rather... that is merely a way of speaking, for the wines of Palais-Cardinal-La-Fuie never age in wood. Vinification and storing are carried out in cement vats, which favours the development of a good fresh fruitness.

Panet (Château)

Grand Cru

Commune: Saint-Christophe-des-Bardes. **Proprietor:** Jean-Claude Carles. Consultant oenologist: Michel Rolland. **Size of vineyard:** 8 hectares. **Average age of vines:** 20 years. **Varieties:** 10% cabernet-sauvignon. 70% merlot. 20% cabernet-franc. **Production:** 54,000 bottles CB. **Visits:** by appointment. Tel. 57 24 78 92. **Direct sales and by mail order:** in France and abroad. Jean-Claude Carles, Château Coudert, 33330 Saint-Christophe-des-Bardes. **Retail sales:** through Libourne. *The vineyard is on a hillside to the west of the village. It is an estate which has been in the family for more than a century.*

Paradis (Château du)

Grand Cru

Commune: Vignonet. **Proprietor:** Vignobles Raby-Saugeon. Director: Janine Raby-Saugeon. Cellar master: Honoré Nadaud. Consultant oenologist: M. J.-F. Chaine. **Size of vineyard:** 35 hectares. **Average age of vines:** 20 years. **Varieties:** 5% cabernet-sauvignon. 70% merlot. 25% cabernet-franc. **Production:** 240,000 bottles CB. **Visits:** by appointment. Tel. 57 84 53 27. **Direct sales and by mail order:** in France and abroad. Château du Paradis, B.P. 1, 33330 Saint-Emilion. **Retail sales:** for export. (Notably Reidemeister & Ulrichs in Bremen in whose catalogue it has been a "must" for a long time).

Paradis Sicard ♟ → Tourans

Paran Justice (Château) ⌂
→ Union de Producteurs

Grand Cru

Parc (Château du)

Commune: Saint-Sulpice-de-Faleyrens. **Proprietor:** Marcel Tabarlet. Consultant oenologist: M. Rolland. **Size of vineyard:** 2 hectares. **Average age of vines:** 40 years. **Varieties:** 10% cabernet-sauvignon. 50% merlot. 40% cabernet-franc. **Production:** 9 tonneaux. 4,000 bottles CB. **Direct sales and by mail order:** tel. 57 24 74 82. **Retail sales.** *This retired schoolteacher cultivates his Château du Parc like any garden, with painstaking care .*

Pasquette (Domaine de)

Commune: Saint-Sulpice-de-Faleyrens. **Proprietor:** G.F.A. Jabiol. **Size of vineyard:** 3 hectares. **Average age of vines:** 30 years. **Varieties:** 15% cabernet-sauvignon. 70% merlot. 15% cabernet-franc. **Production:** 12,000 bottles CB. **Direct sales and by mail order:** in France. Alain Jabiol, B.P. 24, 33330 Saint-Emilion. Tel. 57 74 47 69. **Retail sales:** Belgium, Holland, Denmark, England. *Riper grapes and more care taken with removing the stalks would help to improve the quality.*

Patarabet (Château)

Commune: Saint-Emilion. **Proprietor:** G.F.A. du Château Patarabet. Tenant: S.C.E. du Château Patarabet. **Size of vineyard:** 6.97 hectares. **Average age of vines:** 25 years. **Varieties:** 20% cabernet-sauvignon. 60% merlot. 20% cabernet franc. **Production:** 60,000 bottles CB. **Visits:** daily. Eric Bordas. Tel. 57 24 74 73. **Direct sales and by mail order:** in France and abroad. *Having bought out the other interested parties, Eric Bordas and his wife are now the sole owners of this* cru, *which they have made into a little gem.*

Patris (Château)

Commune: Saint-Emilion. **Proprietor:** Michel Querre. Vineyard manager and consultant oenologist: Christian Durand. **Size of vineyard:** 9.5 hectares. **Average age of vines:** 25 years. **Varieties:** 15% cabernet-sauvignon. 70% merlot. 15% cabernet-franc. **Production:** 60,000 bottles CB. **Visits:** tel. 57 51 00 40. **Retail sales:** Maison Michel Querre S.A.

The name of Querre is inextricably linked to the vineyards of Libourne. Michel Querre is also the proprietor of Château Mazeyres, a good *cru* in Pomerol. Patris is at the foot of the southwest slope of the hill of Saint-Emilion, on overwhelmingly sandy land. The wine is wonderfully round and has a very supple tannic structure. It approaches certain Pomerols in type.

Pavie (Château)

1er Grand Cru classé

Commune: Saint-Emilion. **Proprietor:** Consorts Valette S.C.A. Director: Antoinette Valette. Estate manager: Patrick Valette. Cellar master: Pierre Rabeau. Consultant oenologist: Pascal Ribéreau-Gayon. **Size of vineyard:** 37 hectares. **Average age of vines:** 40 years. **Varieties:** 20% cabernet-sauvignon. 55% merlot. 25% cabernet-franc. **Production:** 150,000 bottles CB. **Visits:** by appointment. Tel. 57 24 72 02. **Retail sales:** through the Bordeaux trade.

No illustration could better suit the label of this *cru* than the panoramic view of Pavie's hillside. Indeed, it serves as a geographical reference for the majority of vineyards situated on the southern hill of Saint-Emilion and everybody agrees that it is also a reference for quality. And yet the name of Pavie appeared late in the records of the region. It was cited for the first time in the 1868 *Bordeaux et ses Vins*. In

From Pavie's hillside, a superb panoramic view of the vineyards.

the preceding year, a group of thirty-six proprietors from Saint-Emilion had jointly taken part in the Universal Exhibition in Paris and had obtained the gold medal for great wines. It should be mentioned that at the time the wines of Saint-Emilion were not called "wines of Bordeaux". It was the Médocs, the Graves and the Sauternes which held absolute sway twelve years after the famous classification. If the thirty-six proprietors had had their list ratified, Saint-Emilion would have a long-standing classification dating from the time of that of the Médoc (and all for the sake of a formality?). Pavie is clearly mentioned. It then belonged to Adolphe Pigasse, a doctor. It was he who created the *cru* by buying as much good land under vines as he could pay for. The current owners suppose that the name Pavie comes from the word *pavière*, or a "quarry producing paving-stones". I should point out here that, firstly, as far as I know the word *pavière* does not exist in the French language, and secondly, stones taken from Saint-Emilion's subsoil are highly unsuitable for making paving-stones. They are good for dressing, and for building. I am not saying this to be contrary, but because I have another explanation to put forward, which is more plausible. Not just relating to several precise *crus* (Pavie, Pavie-Decesse, Pavie-Macquin...), the name of Pavie designates, as we have already seen, all the southern slope of Saint-Emilion. Formerly, the vines planted on the plains or the rocky hillsides were dotted with peach trees. These little wild trees, called gave a fruit

whose flesh was firmly attached to the stone. It was with these that the vignerons used to prepare peaches in wine, after their wives had already gathered a few flowers for infusions with laxative and vermifugal qualities. In my book on the Côtes de Bourg, I mentioned that François Mauriac adored these *pêches de vigne.* I remember eating some of these delicious fruit at his house in Malagar one intensely hot afternoon when I was in my teens. Forgive my recalling this memory. It still remains with me very strongly; as strongly as the flavour of these *pavies,* for that is what they were called. At one time, at the end of April and the beginning of May, the vineyard of Pavie's hillside presented a pretty panorama of peach blossom. The rationalization into one single crop, the vine, during the second half of the last century put an end to this subsidiary product. All over the Bordeaux area, tractors eradicated any surviving wild peach trees.

CHATEAU PAVIE
S⸖ ÉMILION

1ᴱᴿ GRAND CRU CLASSÉ

After the death of Doctor Pigasse, his wife survived by selling off, parcel by parcel, the various plots which had been patiently reunited by the practitioner. The Fayard-Talleman family took the major part of these, but it seems that the family name was never entered in the Who's Who of Saint-Emilion. After the height of the phylloxera crisis in 1885, the Bordeaux wine merchant Ferdinand Bouffard came on the scene with his patent leather dancing shoes. He had inherited the Domaine de la Sable, at the very foot of Pavie's hillside and, his ambitions being backed by his financial resources, he set about climbing it. After acquiring the lands of the Fayard-Tallemans, he bought one after the other the parcels of Pimpinelle, Dussaut, Larcis-Bergey, and to set the seal upon his efforts, he acquired the last plot of the late Pigasse. From that time, Pavie contained more than fifty hectares and its production was of the order of 150 *tonneaux* (fortunately there was no I.N.A.O. commission to sanction this excessive "consistency". See Beau-Séjour Bécot!). None the less, Château Pavie climbed to the summit of the distinguished *crus* of Saint-Emilion and sold its wines at higher prices even than the second *crus* of the Médoc. Between the two world wars, Albert Porte took over from Bouffard. Without changing the site but by reducing the size, the estate went down a notch in the esteem of wine connoisseurs. At Pavie, the buildings are on three levels of the hill. At the bottom: the vat-house and offices; half way up: the château in the form of a large farm; at the top but underground: the cellars. These latter are old building-stone quarries. The earliest excavations go back to the eleventh century. Their relatively shallow depth (less than 25 feet) caused a certain amount of caving in brought about by the infiltration of rain water. In 1974, 53 *tonneaux* of wine were crushed while the staff were having lunch.

Since 1943 Château Pavie has been in the hands of the Valettes. It is Jean-Paul, Alexander's grandson, who runs the estate today. In the seventies, Emile Peynaud gave new life to the wines and lifted the reputation of the *cru.* Pascal Ribéreau-Gayon has followed him as consultant oenologist. For a wine from the hillsides, Pavie maintains a good level with a slender, filigree structure akin to flamboyant gothic. It is certainly architecturally fine but it rather lacks body and solidity. One day somebody asked Tristan Bernard if the coffee he had been served was good. "It is so good you might call it a weakness", he replied. Yes, but weakness goes together with delicacy and finesse. The wines of Pavie are distinguished by these two qualities, and they are for lovers of flavours of liquorice who have a very sensitive palate.

Pavie Decesse (Château)

Grand Cru classé

Commune: Saint-Emilion. **Proprietor:** S.C.A. du Château Pavie Decesse. Director: Madame Antoine Valette. Estate manager: Patrick Valette. Manager: Jean-Paul Valette. Cellar master: Pierre Rabeau. Consultant oenologist: Pascal Ribéreau-Gayon. **Size of vineyard:** 9.5 hectares. **Average age of vines:** 40 years. **Varieties:** 15% cabernet-sauvignon. 60% merlot. 25% cabernet-franc. **Production:** 48,000 bottles CB. **Visits:** by appointment. Tel. 57 24 72 02. **Sales by mail order:** in France and abroad. **Retail sales:** through the Bordeaux trade and foreign merchants: Switzerland, Belgium, U.S.A., Japan, Australia.

"Pavie's hillside" is a guarantee of quality for all the *crus,* great or small, which lie on its slope... and even for those who merely contemplate it. It is the south face of Saint-Emilion's hill, which has a relatively steep slope down to the plain of the Dordogne. At the end of the last century, Ferdinand Bouffard, the Bordeaux wine merchant, bought all the land under vines that he could find on Pavie's hillside. In this empire of more than fifty hectares, it was the *cru* of Pigasse which was run separately and was to become Pavie Décesse. After World War I, the estate was bought by Marcel Larget, who was also the proprietor of Clos Villemaurine and Château des Bardes. Then we saw Robert Marzelle and a limited company which contributed little to the fame of the label. Since 1970, Pavie Decesse has joined the Valette vineyards. The estate is administered by Jean-Paul Valette, who lavishes the same care on it as at Château Pavie. But they are two distinct *crus* and not one organization in which Pavie Decesse is simply Pavie's second label. This physical separation of two *crus* which are in the same hands and the same appellation bears witness to the professionalism and conscientiousness of the Valette family.

Pavie Macquin (Château)

Grand Cru classé

Commune: Saint-Emilion. **Proprietor:** G.F.A. du Château Pavie Macquin. Director: Marie-Jacques Charpentier. Vineyard manager and cellar master: Marc Joudinaud. Consultant oenologist: M. Rolland. **Size of vineyard:** 10 hectares. **Average age of vines:** 20 years. **Varieties:** 5% cabernet-sauvignon. 80% merlot. 15% cabernet-franc. **Production:** 48,000 bottles CB. **Visits:** Marie-Louise Barre. Tel. 57 51 26 44. **Direct sales and by mail order. Retail sales:** S.D.V.F. (sole rights).

"I was a farmer in the department of Seine-et-Marne, where I come from, when I was drawn to the department of Gironde in 1885, partly by the degeneration of properties due to the ravages of phylloxera and partly by the certainty I had at that time that the vine would come back into its own and its former prosperity." This visionary was Albert Macquin. During the last quarter of the last century, he was the genius who restored the Libourne vineyards. Buying up as much land as he could, planted with vines which had been devastated, and this for a song, he regenerated viticulture with his selected graft stock. Between 1885 and 1895, he had 4,879,000 sets grafted, of which more than three million were successful. The profit he made from selling to local growers enabled him to restore his own estates. He was the owner of 70 hectares in Saint-Georges-de-Montagne and in Saint-Emilion, a considerable amount at that time. In 1887, he bought 24 hectares in the neighbourhood of Pavie. Amassing practical observations, scientific facts and statistics resulting from experiments, he stood out in his time by his indomitable confidence in the future of Libourne's terrain. He was one of the very first to correlate the analysis of the soil to that of the wine. He rationalized the organization of his employees' working hours and went so far as to study how best his oxen worked according to their food. A great forerunner of modern viticulture, Albert Macquin deserves to have his statue erected somewhere at the top of a hill of vines in the area. Château Pavie Macquin has all the recognized qualities of Pavie's hillside. Its wines are fine, light, fruity and strong in alcohol. Perhaps they need just a little more tannin to be a very great *cru*. I think this idea is in the process of being put into practice. With a slower and better controlled vinification, a longer period for maturing in new wood, Pavie Macquin will be capable of raising itself to the highest level of the wines from the hillsides in other words of the most authentic and typical wines of Saint-Emilion. The most recent vintages display a highly remarkable growth in quality. The day is approaching when Pavie Macquin will be able to match Pavie simple.

Pavillon-Figeac (Château)

Commune: Saint-Emilion. **Proprietor:** Madame Boisseau. Tenant: René de Coninck. Consultant oenologist: M. Rolland. **Size of vineyard:** 3.5 hectares. **Average age of vines:** 25 years. **Varieties:** 45% merlot. 55% cabernet-franc. **Production:** 21,600 bottles CB. **Direct sales and by mail order:** René de Coninck, B.P. 125, 33501 Libourne. Tel. 57 51 06 07. **Retail sales:** through Libourne, via the honourable firm of Horeau-Beylot.

Pavillon-Lavallade (Château) ⚲ → Robin

Pendary (Château)

Commune: Saint-Sulpice-de-Faleyrens. **Proprietor:** Société de fait Cubilier (Serge and Jean-Luc). Consultant oenologist: M. Rolland. **Size of vineyard:** 8 hectares. **Average age of vines:** 15 years. **Varieties:** 10% cabernet-sauvignon. 80% merlot. 10% cabernet-franc. **Production:** 40 tonneaux. 3,000 bottles CB. **Visits:** by appointment. Tel. 57 24 75 29. **Direct sales and by mail order:** in France and abroad. **Retail sales:** Jean-Pierre Moueix.

Serge and Jean-Luc Cubilier began the estate of Château Pendary in January 1985. The property is an inheritance which has come down from their grandfather Robert-Louis Pendary. He was a tenant-farmer. In his lifetime, there were no vines there. The land was given over to growing maize, potatoes, beetroot..., as well as rear-ing a dozen cattle. Gradually, vines gained ground. "It is difficult to be a young proprietor." says Serge, who is almost thirty and rather timid. But already the two brothers are planning the development of their property. They bottled their first wines in 1987. I wish them all the success they deserve because both of them are already accomplished growers.

Perey (Château)

Ｐ Ｐ Ｐ Ｐ Ｐ

Commune: Saint-Sulpice-de-Faleyrens. **Proprietor:** Denis Martegoutes. Consultant oenologist: M. Pauquet. **Size of vineyard:** 2.25 hectares. **Average age of vines:** 12 years. **Varieties:** 30% cabernet-sauvignon. 62% merlot. 8% cabernet-franc. **Production:** 12 tonneaux. **Retail sales:** in bulk to wine merchants. *This cru is undoubtedly worth being château bottled.*

sold in bulk

Perey-Grouley (Château)

Ｐ Ｐ Ｐ Ｐ Ｐ

Commune: Saint-Sulpice-de-Faleyrens. **Proprietor:** Remi Xans. Vineyard manager: Alain Xans. Cellar masters: Remi and Alain Xans. Consultant oenologist: C.B.C. Libourne. **Size of vineyard:** 10.84 hectares. **Average age of vines:** 36 years. **Varieties:** 10% cabernet-sauvignon. 70% merlot. 20% cabernet-franc. **Production:** 65 tonneaux. 3,000 bottles CB. **Visits:** daily from 8 a.m. to noon and 2 to 7 p.m. Sundays by appointment. Tel. 57 24 73 17. **Direct sales and by mail order:** in France. **Retail sales:** Ets. Hilhade de Galgon.

In Saint-Sulpice-de-Faleyrens for more than four hundred years, the Xans family is one of the oldest in the area. The large elegant family home is on the east side of the commune, very close to Château Monbousquet. The vineyard is made up of different types of land which, along with a happy proportion of different grape varieties, produces a rather complete and well-balanced wine. Remi Xans's two sons, Bernard and Alain, are there to ensure continuity. It is to be wished that they would do more château bottling. The quality of the wines justifies its being bottled on site. Visitors will always find a warm welcome from this very friendly family, who are ever ready to uncork a bottle of their best wine.

Perey-Grouley (Clos)

Ｐ Ｐ Ｐ Ｐ Ｐ

Commune: Saint-Sulpice-de-Faleyrens. **Proprietor:** Francis Campaner. **Size of vineyard:** 1.54 hectares. **Average age of vines:** 30 years. **Varieties:** 10% cabernet-sauvignon. 90% merlot. **Production:** 7 tonneaux. **Direct sales and by mail order:** in France. *This modest vineyard offers wines worthy of a real wine-lover's cellar.*

Petit Bigaroux (Château)

Commune: Saint-Sulpice-de-Faleyrens. **Proprietor:** Jacques Brisson. Consultant oenologist: C.B.C. Libourne. **Size of vineyard:** 9 hectares. **Average age of vines:** 20 years. **Varieties:** 20% cabernet-sauvignon. 60% merlot. 20% cabernet-franc. **Production:** 40 tonneaux. 25,000 bottles CB. **Direct sales and by mail order:** in France and abroad. Tel. 57 24 72 57. **Retail sales.** *Modern cultivation and vinification for supple, light wines...capable of offering great pleasure to the lovers of authentic Beaujolais.*

Petit Bois La Garelle (Château)

Commune: Saint-Emilion. **Proprietor:** Jean Chatonnet. **Size of vineyard:** 4.82 hectares. **Production:** 25 to 30 tonneaux. **Visits:** tel. 57 24 74 17. **Direct sales. Retail sales.**

Petit Clos Figeac (Château)

Grand Cru

Commune: Saint-Emilion. **Proprietor:** S.C.E. des Vignobles A. Janoueix. Director and vineyard manager: Michel Janoueix. Cellar master: Guy Janoueix. Consultant oenologist: C.B.C. Libourne. **Size of vineyard:** 3.87 hectares. **Average age of vines:** 20 years. **Varieties:** 15% cabernet-sauvignon. 70% merlot. 15% cabernet-franc. **Production:** 18 tonneaux. 2,500 bottles CB. **Retail sales:** through the Bordeaux trade.

Petit-Faurie-de-Soutard (Château)

Grand Cru classé

Commune: Saint-Emilion. **Proprietor:** Françoise Capdemourlin. Director: Jacques Capdemourlin. Vineyard manager: Paul Jenck. Cellar master: Bernard Oiseau. Consultant oenologist: Michel Rolland. **Size of vineyard:** 8 hectares. **Average age of vines:** 34 years. **Varieties:** 10% cabernet-sauvignon. 60% merlot. 30% cabernet-franc. **Production:** 42,000 bottles CB. **Direct sales and by mail order:** in France. Tel. 57 74 62 06. **Retail sales:** through the Bordeaux trade.

Petit Faurie de Soutard and Petit Faurie de Souchard were separated from Château Soutard in 1850. Since 1977, the first mentioned has belonged to Madame Jacques

Capdemourlin who received it from the private company formed by the Aberlen family, which manages the *cru*, Jacques Capdemourlin being the director. Monsieur Aberlen, the grandfather, was estate manager at Vieux Château Certan and Troplong Mondot. Harvesting is done at Petit-Faurie-de-Soutard before Capdemourlin and Balestard la Tonnelle. Vinification is not backward. It is carried out in cement vats. Half the wine spends several months in casks. Bottling is done relatively soon. The wine is agreeable, light and easy. It can even be drunk slightly chilled.

Petit-Figeac (Château)

Grand Cru

Commune: Saint-Emilion. **Proprietor:** Domaines Prats. Director: Bruno Prats. Vineyard manager and cellar master: Gilbert Xans. Consultant oenologist: Pascal Ribéreau-Gayon. **Size of vineyard:** 1.5 hectares. **Average age of vines:** 30 years. **Varieties:** 50% cabernet-sauvignon. 50% merlot. **Production:** 7,500 bottles CB. **Sales by mail order:** Domaines Prats, 84 rue Turenne, 33000 Bordeaux. **Retail sales:** Domaines Prats. *This very small vineyard is the immediate neighbour of Château Figeac. Vinification is carried out at La Fleur Pourret, another property of the Domaines Prats.*

Petit-Garderose (Château)

Commune: Libourne. **Proprietor:** Jacques Henocque. Consultant oenologist: M. Rolland. **Size of vineyard:** 4.5 hectares. **Average age of vines:** 25 years. **Varieties:** 10% cabernet-sauvignon. 55% merlot. 35% cabernet-franc. **Production:** 16 tonneaux. 10,000 bottles CB. **Visits:** daily except from August 25 to September 10. Tel. 57 51 58 84. **Direct sales and by mail order:** in France and abroad. Jacques Henocque, 94 boulevard Garderose, 33500 Libourne. **Retail sales:** through the Bordeaux trade.

Having arrived from the cold regions of the beetroot, Jacques Henocque settled in Libourne in 1963. When he arrived, of the lands he bought half were used for market gardening and half were vineyards. His integration into the area was not achieved overnight. Today, recognized for his qualities as a grower and his personal qualities too, Jacques Henocque has forgotten this difficult past. He is extremely grateful for the help given to him by M. Robert Delol (the father of Yves Delol, the proprietor of Château Gueyrosse) who taught him the rudiments of the profession. Jacques Henocque is at the service of his client, who will always be warmly received at any hour of the day and a bedroom will be put at his disposal if he wishes to benefit to the full from the château's hospitality. If Jacques Henocque had the wherewithal, his house would be transformed into a Spanish inn, whose warmth would conjure up the essence of his native region. Situated in the heart of a busy suburb near the road to Bergerac, Petit-Garderose is an agreeable stopping point. For his vines, Jacques Henocque uses old rootstock which has a slender yield but which consistently produces full, powerful wines.

Petit-Gravet (Château)

Grand Cru

Commune: Saint-Emilion. **Proprietor:** Marie-Louise Nouvel. Manager: Jean-Jacques Nouvel. Consultant oenologists: Mademoiselle Cazenave and M. Chaine. **Size of vineyard:** 6 hectares. **Average age of vines:** 30 years. **Varieties:** 20% cabernet-sauvignon. 50% merlot. 30% cabernet-franc. **Production:** 20,000 bottles CB. **Sales by mail order:** Ch. Petit-Gravet, Porte-Bouqueyre, Saint-Emilion. *A pleasant wine for customers in search of a "good little wine".*

Petit Gueyrot (Château) ⚱ → Latte de Sirey

Petit-Mangot (Château)

Grand Cru

Commune: Saint-Etienne-de-Lisse. **Proprietor:** G.A.E.C. Décamps Père & Fils. Director and cellar master: Jean-Yves Décamps. **Size of vineyard:** 12 hectares. **Average age of vines:** 30 years. **Varieties:** 65% merlot. 35% cabernet-franc. **Production:** 80,000 bottles CB. **Visits:** by appointment. Tel. 57 40 25 44. **Direct sales. Retail sales.** *A relatively large production which seems to sell with ease.*

Petit Pindefleurs (Château)

Commune: Saint-Emilion. **Proprietor:** Henri Bonnemaison. **Size of vineyard:** 0.45 hectares. **Average age of vines:** 70 years. **Varieties:** 30% cabernet-sauvignon. 50% merlot. 20% cabernet-franc. **Production:** 3 tonneaux. 1,200 bottles CB. **Direct sales and by mail order:** in France. Tel. 57 24 70 10. *Henri Bonnemaison is a retired post-office worker who is sprucing up his (almost) half-hectare to make a "super" wine.*

Petit Val (Château)

Grand Cru

Commune: Saint-Emilion. **Proprietor:** Michel Boutet. Vineyard manager and cellar master: Jean-Claude Micoine. Consultant oenologist: Rémy Cassignard. **Size of vineyard:** 9.2 hectares. **Average age of vines:** 35 years. **Varieties:** 10% cabernet-sauvignon. 60% merlot. 30% cabernet-franc. **Production:** 42,000 bottles CB. **Visits:** by appointment. Tel. 57 24 70 86. **Direct sales and by mail order:** in France. **Retail sales:** Belgium. *Finesse and elegance in this wine made with great care.*

Peymouton (Château)

Commune: Saint-Christophe-des-Bardes. **Proprietor:** M. and Mme Paul-Joseph Dussol. Consultant oenologist: M. Rolland. **Size of vineyard:** 54.8 hectares. **Average age of vines:** 28 years. **Varieties:** 10% cabernet-sauvignon. 60% merlot. 30% cabernet-franc. **Production:** 5 tonneaux. 2,500 bottles CB. **Direct sales and by mail order:** in France. Tel. 57 24 77 53. *This good little vineyard producing sincere wines has been in existence for more than a hundred years. More commercial drive would make it better known.*

Peyreau (Château)

Grand Cru

Commune: Saint-Emilion. **Proprietor:** S.C. du Château Peyreau. Director: Michel Boutet. Consultant oenologist: Rémy Cassignard. **Size of vineyard:** 13.68 hectares. **Average age of vines:** 32 years. **Varieties:** 25% cabernet-sauvignon. 50% merlot. 25% cabernet-franc. **Production:** 84,000 bottles CB. **Visits:** by appointment. Tel. 57 24 70 86. **Direct sales and by mail order:** in France. **Retail sales:** through the Bordeaux trade. *A large and good production of regular quality can be expected from this* cru, *well run by Michel Boutet.*

Peyrelongue (Château)

Grand Cru

Commune: Saint-Emilion. **Proprietor:** Jean-Jacques Bouquey. Consultant oenologists: M. and Madame Rolland. **Size of vineyard:** 10 hectares. **Average age of vines:** 20 years. **Varieties:** 15% cabernet-sauvignon. 70% merlot. 10% cabernet-franc. 5% malbec. **Production:** 65,000 bottles CB. **Visits:** by appointment. Tel. 57 24 71 17. **Direct sales and by mail order:** in France and abroad. **Retail sales.** *"The fame of the wines of Châteaux Peyrelongue and Badon La Garelle exempt them from all modesty". And Jean-Jacques Bouquey's modesty makes up part of his fame.*

Peyrelongue (Domaine de)

Grand Cru

Commune: Saint-Emilion. **Proprietor:** GFA Cassat & Fils. Director and cellar master: Pierre Cassat. Consultant oenologist: Libourne. **Size of vineyard:** 13 hectares. **Average age of vines:** 30 years. **Varieties:** 15% cabernet-sauvignon. 55% merlot. 30% cabernet-franc. **Production:** 90,000 bottles CB. **Visits:** tel. 57 24 72 36 or 57 24 62 57. **Direct sales and by mail order:** in France and abroad. G.F.A. Cassat & Fils, B.P. 44, 33330 Saint-Emilion. **Retail sales.** *Situated at the foot of the hills of Pavie and Arcis on land of clayey limestone, this* Grand Cru *produces elegant wines not lacking in seductive powers.*

Peyrouquet (Château)

→ *Union de Producteurs*

Peyroutas (Château)

Commune: Vignonet. **Proprietor:** Robert Chaineaud. Tenant, vineyard manager and cellar master: Jean-Bernard Gagnerot. Consultant oenologist: M. Hébrard. **Size of vineyard:** 6.5 hectares. **Average age of vines:** 25 to 30 years. **Varieties:** 10% cabernet-sauvignon. 80% merlot. 10% cabernet-franc. **Production:** 33 tonneaux. 3,500 bottles CB. **Direct sales and by mail order:** in France. Tel. 57 84 55 73. Robert Chaineaud, Les-4- Chemins, 33330 Vignonet. **Retail sales:** Lichine. *This is an old name much respected by the wine merchants of the Chartrons. Its wines are in conventional style and of average quality, with welcome surprises from time to time.*

Peyroutas (Château)

Commune: Vignonet; **Proprietor:** Baye-Dupin de Beyssat. **Size of vineyard:** 4 hectares. **Average age of vines:** 25 years. **Varieties:** 60% merlot. 40% cabernet-franc. **Production:** 25 tonneaux. 10,000 bottles CB. **Direct sales and by mail order:** in France and abroad. Baye-Dupin de Beyssat, 73 rue Michel Montaigne, 33500 Libourne. Tel. 57 51 00 49 or 57 74 61 55. **Retail sales.** *This estate is a twin of the preceding château which has been in the same family for several generations.*

Picau Pena (Château) → *Sicard*

Piganeau (Château) ♟ → Cantenac

Pimpineuilh (Clos)

Commune: Libourne. **Proprietor:** Domaine Wery. Vineyard manager and cellar master: Denis Wery. Consultant oenologist: M. Rolland. **Size of vineyard:** 0.34 hectares. **Average age of vines:** 13 years. **Varieties:** 30% cabernet-sauvignon. 47% merlot. 23% cabernet-franc. **Production:** 1,500 bottles CB. **Direct sales and by mail order:** tel. 57 51 06 91. *It was in 1972 that the Werys, from the department of the Nord, restored this attractive little estate.*

Pindefleurs (Château)

Grand Cru

Commune: Saint-Emilion. **Proprietor:** Madame Dior. Vineyard manager: Roger Toulon. **Size of vineyard:** 8.38 hectares. **Varieties:** 53% merlot. 47% cabernet-franc. **Production:** 30,000 bottles CB. **Visits:** by appointment. Tel. 57 24 71 78. **Direct sales and by mail order:** in France. Madame Dior, 142 rue de la Tour, 75116 Paris.

Philippe Larcher was an eminent wine merchant from the Chartrons who, for several years, ran the firm founded by my grandfather. He was a close friend of all the old Bordeaux brokers. He used to buy Saint-Emilion wines at the offices of Brun and Leperche. I can still see Gaston Leperche bringing him samples in tiny nine centilitre bottles with their labels written in an elegant sloping hand. "Ah! You've brought me Pindefleurs, Gaston. Come on then, we'll taste it straight away." When Philippe Larcher used to pronounce "Pindefleurs" clearly something clicked in his mind. The poetry of this name was reawakened, just as when a breath of wind rekindles the embers of a fire. "Ah! Pindefleurs, Pindefleurs... what a pretty name!" he used to say with a discriminating air. "My dear Gaston, I think we're going to do business!" Since then, I have never read or heard the name of Pindefleurs without recalling these genial scenes.

The origin of the estate appears to go back to the time of Louis XIV, to judge by the syle of the panelling in the house. It belonged to a distinguished Saint-Emilion family, the Sèze de Mondots. Anthoine de Sèze had been the mayor of the town between 1625 and 1632. His son Pierre had four sons. One of the boys became the priest of Saint-Sulpice-de-Faleyrens, a parish which had no presbytery. In all probability, he lived at Pindefleurs, which his father had bequeathed to him. After him, it was the property of his nephew Paul Romain de Sèze who, with Malesherbes, defended Louis XVI against the National Convention. Towards 1780, he wrote to his brother who was still in Saint-Emilion: "Next Saturday, send me a basket of bouchet and a basket of sauvignon. I have promised my wife to let her taste these two types of grapes." This is interesting evidence clearly confirming that there were these different varieties of vines in the eighteenth century. In 1811, in his old age, he recalled his memories of childhood and youth: "I frequently think of that very privileged climate in which I had the good fortune to be born." Today, Pindefleurs belongs to Madame Dior, a cousin by marriage of the famous fashion designer. 255

Pindefleurs is a pretty holiday residence where good wine is made.

Her husband is a *conseiller honoraire* in the Paris Court of Appeal. She succeeds her grandfather Adolphe Charoulet who was a brilliant *député* representing of the Gironde in the *Parlement* in the first part of this century. For her, Pindefleurs is in some measure a magic, sacred place to which she feels strongly attached by invisible bonds. Every year, from August 25 to Hallowe'en, the Diors come back to their holiday residence in Saint-Emilion and preside over the harvest which is carried out under the masterly hand of Roger Toulon.

The wine of Pindefleurs deserves its name for the powerful bouquet it offers the connoisseur. It happily blends body with delicacy. So, is it a *cru classé*? Better still: it is a *Grand Cru* which has class.

Pineuilh (Château)

Y Y Y Y Y

Commune: Saint-Christophe-des-Bardes. **Proprietors:** M. and Madame Claude Cubillier. Consultant oenologist: M. Pauquet. Size of vineyard: 0.15 hectares. **Average age of vines:** 50 years. **Varieties:** 90% merlot. 10% cabernet-franc. **Production:** 1 tonneau. **Retail sales:** Jean-Pierre Moueix.

sold in bulk

Château Pineuilh is a minute property a little over 0.15 hectares of heavy land, between the roads to Saint-Christophe-des-Bardes and Saint-Emilion. It has been handed down from mother to daughter. Madame Claverie, Madame Cubillier's grandmother, was its first proprietor. At the time, the vineyard did not exist. It was Monsieur Claverie, the road-mender of Saint-Christophe-des-Bardes, who planted it. "I can remember", says Madame Cubillier, "coming back from confirmation class seeing my grandfather planting vines with a spade." Monsieur Cubillier, cellar master at Château Tour Saint-Christophe, takes care of this micro-vineyard.

Piney (Château)

→ Union de Producteurs

Grand Cru

Pipeau (Château)

Grand Cru

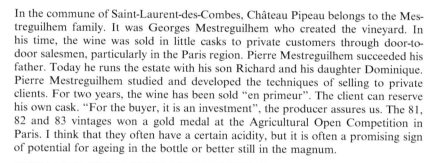

Commune: Saint-Laurent-des-Combes. **Proprietor:** GAEC Mestreguilhem. Consultant oenologist: M. Chaine. **Size of vineyard:** 30 hectares. **Average age of vines:** 25 to 30 years. **Varieties:** 5% cabernet-sauvignon. 75% merlot. 20% cabernet-franc. **Production:** 160,000 bottles CB. **Visits:** by appointment. Tel. 57 24 72 95. **Direct sales and by mail order:** in France.

In the commune of Saint-Laurent-des-Combes, Château Pipeau belongs to the Mestreguilhem family. It was Georges Mestreguilhem who created the vineyard. In his time, the wine was sold in little casks to private customers through door-to-door salesmen, particularly in the Paris region. Pierre Mestreguilhem succeeded his father. Today he runs the estate with his son Richard and his daughter Dominique. Pierre Mestreguilhem studied and developed the techniques of selling to private clients. For two years, the wine has been sold "en primeur". The client can reserve his own cask. "For the buyer, it is an investment", the producer assures us. The 81, 82 and 83 vintages won a gold medal at the Agricultural Open Competition in Paris. I think that they often have a certain acidity, but it is often a promising sign of potential for ageing in the bottle or better still in the magnum.

Plaisance (Château)

Commune: Saint-Sulpice-de-Faleyrens. **Proprietors:** Pierre and Didier Dubois. **Size of vineyard:** 8 hectares. **Average age of vines:** 20 to 50 years. **Varieties:** 70% merlot. 30% cabernet-franc. **Production:** 40 tonneaux. 30,000 bottles CB. **Visits:** by appointment. Tel. 57 24 78 85. **Direct sales and by mail order:** in France and abroad.

The family home of the Dubois dates from 1886. It was also the time the vineyard was created. So it is right and proper first of all to acknowledge Plaisance's hundred years of existence and its descent in direct line over four generations which have, one after the other, worked to achieve perfection. Didier Dubois, Pierre's son, is the proprietor in his own right of part of the estate, which he runs under the name of Vieux Château des Moines.

Pomone (Château) → Vieux Rivallon

Pontet-Clauzure (Château)

Commune: Saint-Emilion. **Size of vineyard:** approximately 10 hectares. **Average age of vines:** 32 years. **Varieties:** 6% cabernet-sauvignon. 46% merlot. 48% cabernet-franc. **Direct sales:** in France and abroad. **Retail sales.** See Château Le Couvent.

Pontet-Fumet (Château) ♟ → Val d'Or

Pressac (Château de)

Grand Cru

Commune: Saint-Etienne-de-Lisse. **Proprietor:** Jacques Pouey. Consultant oenologist: M. Chenard. **Size of vineyard:** 35.69 hectares. **Average age of vines:** 25 to 30 years. **Varieties:** 58% merlot. 40% cabernet-franc. 2% malbec. **Production:** 190,000 bottles CB. **Visits:** by appointment. Tel. 56 81 45 00. **Direct sales and by mail order:** in France and abroad. Jacques Pouey, 59 rue Minvielle, 33000 Bordeaux. **Retail sales:** through the trade.

"An old château, partly in ruins, with moats, workers' living-quarters, cellars, vathouses, dovecot, forecourt, completely surrounded by walls." This was how the notary of the time described Château de Pressac when it was sold in 1775 by the *sieur*

Château Pressac is a huge manor whose origins go back to the Middle Ages.

d'Anglade, to Jean-Marc Constantin, a captain of the Marmande regiment. These details are interesting in the sense that they prove positively that there was a vineyard in existence round the château in the eighteenth century. On the other hand, we know that this fortified manor was remodelled several times and that its foundation dates back to the Middle Ages. Towards the beginning of the Renaissance, it was an imposing building which had no less than twenty-seven towers, traces of some of them remaining today.

As far as its vine-growing history is concerned, Professor Henri Enjalbert tells us that Vassal de Montviel, the proprietor at that time, planted in his vineyard the variety known as "Auxerrois". That was between 1737 and 1747. This variety gave deep coloured grapes which in turn gave the wine a dark colour. Auxerrois, which probably came from Quercy, was rechristened "Noir de Pressac" and is better known today under the names of malbec or cot de Bordeaux. The estate is situated on a vein of clayey limestone with red soils, which stretches in a narrow strip from Saint-Emilion to Saint-Etienne-de-Lisse. The suitability of these soils for viticulture is undeniable. Pressac is at the extreme eastern point of the formation.

The predominance of merlot today brings a supple character which makes the wine agreeable to drink when young. I can recall several tastings in the time of André Pouey, the father of the current owner. He had in particular a 1943 which was quite staggering by its body and richness in tannin. Even if the style of Château de Pressac has evolved along with modern oenology, it is none the less an excellent product, capable of competing in certain years with the greatest *crus* of Saint-Emilion.

Prieuré-Lescours (Château)

Grand Cru

Commune: Saint-Sulpice-de-Faleyrens. **Proprietors:** M. and Madame Sinsout. Cellar master: M. Oiseau. Consultant oenologist: M. Rolland. **Size of vineyard:** 4 hectares. **Average age of vines:** 30 years. **Varieties:** 75% merlot. 20% cabernet-franc. 5% malbec. **Production:** 20,000 bottles CB. **Visits:** tel. 57 24 61 12. **Direct sales and by mail order:** in France. *A nice, well-coloured wine, produced since 1980 by a 150 year old dynasty of vignerons. Of its type, it is of dependable value insured by experience.*

Prince Noir (Château du) 🏚 → Barbeyron

Puy-Blanquet (Château)

Grand Cru

Commune: Saint-Etienne-de-Lisse. **Proprietor:** Roger Jacquet. Cellar master: H. Lambert. Consultant oenologist: J.F. Chaine. **Size of vineyard:** 23 hectares. **Average age of vines:** 4 to 55 years. **Varieties:** 20% cabernet-sauvignon. 75% merlot. 5% cabernet-franc. **Production:** 130,000 bottles CB. **Direct sales and by mail order:** tel. 57 40 18 18. **Retail sales:** Ets. Jean-Pierre Moueix. *A former property of Count de Malet Roquefort, bought in 1958 by Roger Jacquet, who comes from a family of growers in Algeria.*

Puyblanquet Carrille (Château)

Grand Cru

Commune: Saint-Christophe-des-Bardes. **Proprietor:** Jean-François Carrille. Cellar master: J.-P. Regrenil. Consultant oenologist: M. Rolland. **Size of vineyard:** 10 hectares. **Average age of vines:** 20 years. **Varieties:** 10% cabernet-sauvignon. 70% merlot. 20% cabernet-franc. **Production:** 60,000 bottles CB. **Visits:** by appointment. Tel. 57 24 74 46. **Direct sales and by mail order:** in France and abroad. Maison d'Aliénor, place du Marcadien, 33330 Saint-Emilion. **Retail sales:** S.D.V.F., Chemin Lissandre, 33310 Lormont. *This vineyard, which separated from Puyblanquet in 1971, is today in the hands of Jean-François Carrille (see Château Boutisse).*

Puy-Razac (Château)

Grand Cru

Commune: Saint-Emilion. **Proprietor:** Guy Thoilliez. Consultant oenologist: C.B.C. Libourne. **Size of vineyard:** 6 hectares. **Average age of vines:** 15 years. **Varieties:** 30% cabernet-sauvignon. 40% merlot. 30% cabernet-franc. **Production:** 30,000 bottles CB. **Visits:** by appointment. Tel. 57 24 73 32. **Retail sales:** Maison Daniel Querre.

It was the downfall of the government in 1940 which drove M. Paul Thoilliez and his family to leave the north of France and come and settle in Saint-Emilion. At the time, the few vines which existed were hybrids. From 1940 to 1945, the property remained dormant because M. Guy Thoilliez, the son, had been deported. On his return, he replanted the vineyard. Although he had begun his studies at the school of Bréguet, Guy Thoilliez did not want to leave his parents. "I have always loved the land. My grandparents were farmers in the department of the Nord." Today, Guy Thoilliez is vineyard manager at Château Monbousquet. "I learned my work on site." he says. As a small proprietor, he is anxious to champion a wine of quality. "I don't want to disappoint my customers. That is why the 63, 65 and 68 vintages were not bottled." Ageing of the wine takes place in the vat. "Wood plays no part in making wine." declares Guy Thoilliez confidently.

Quatre Vents (Clos des)

Commune: Libourne. **Proprietor:** Marcel Beaufils. Consultant oenologist: Michel Rolland. **Size of vineyard:** 0.33 hectares. **Average age of vines:** 13 years. **Varieties:** 100% merlot. **Production:** 1,500 bottles CB. **Direct sales:** Marcel Beaufils, 49 rue des Réaux, 33500 Libourne. Tel. 57 51 46 19. *Marcel Beaufils's six children are enough to do the harvesting, each having an area of 660 square yards to work.*

Quentin (Château)

Grand Cru

Commune: Saint-Christophe-des-Bardes. **Proprietor:** Société Civile du Château Quentin. Managers: Jacques de Coninck and M. Laffort. **Size of vineyard:** 29.58 hectares. **Average age of vines:** 15 to 40 years. **Varieties:** 30% cabernet sauvignon. 70% merlot. **Production:** 150 to 180 tonneaux. **Visits:** by appointment. Tel. 57 51 31 05. **Sales by mail order. Retail sales:** for clients abroad. *A beautiful vineyard with a few old vines, and, since very recently, new casks.*

Queyron (Château)

Commune: Saint-Emilion. **Proprietor:** Christian Goujou. Consultant oenologist: C.B.C. Libourne. **Size of vineyard:** 9.4 hectares. **Average age of vines:** 50 years. **Varieties:** 10% cabernet-sauvignon. 25% merlot. 65% cabernet-franc. **Production:** 29 tonneaux. 15,000 bottles CB. **Direct sales and by mail order:** tel. 57 24 74 62. **Retail sales:** either in bulk or château bottled.

Stiff letters of protest, insulting telephone calls: Christian Goujou had soon had enough. What was being levelled against him? Delivering "sparkling vinegar" in his bottles. That three generations of honest, conscientious growers should come to this! He decided to report the matter to the police with a view to taking legal action.

And the truth came out: an unscrupulous competitor, living in the Fronsac region, was delivering ignominious wines under the name of "Château du Queyron", and actually mentioning the name of the proprietor as Goujou. After the lengthy proceedings characteristic of French justice, the miscreant was fined a mere 20,000 francs. But at least the source of the fraudulent wines had been stopped. None the less, for Christian Goujou, this unfortunate episode was a sort of bad storm accompanied by huge hail-stones in the form of court summonses. The storm has passed and the wine of this likeable grower is still as good at Haut-Ferrandat as at Queyron. But do not get the address wrong. The right one is his.

Queyron Patarabet (Château)
→ Union de Producteurs

Quinault (Château)

ΥΥΥΥΥ

Grand Cru

Commune: Libourne. **Proprietor:** Henri Maleret-Mons.
Consultant oenologist: M. Chaine. **Size of vineyard:**
11 hectares. **Average age of vines:** 25 years. **Varieties:**
5% cabernet-sauvignon. 70% merlot. 25% cabernet-franc.
Production: 60,000 bottles CB. **Visits:** by appointment.
Tel. 57 51 13 39. **Direct sales and by mail order:** in France
and abroad. Château Quinault, avenue du Parc des sports,
33500 Libourne. **Retail sales:** for export.

In the Maleret-Mons family for sixty years, the vineyard was restored after the
1956 frosts. It is in one unbroken stretch. Formerly, the wines had the advantage of
bearing the Sables Saint-Emilion appellation until they were attached to the Saint-
Emilion appellation by the law of December 24, 1973, the proprietor, Quinault,
being then the President of the Federation of the Sables Saint-Emilion. The vineyard
is an integral part of the town of Libourne, entirely surrounded by main roads. Its
land is made up of siliceous sand on a sub-stratum of ferruginous gravel. The wine,
an AOC *Grand Cru,* has a very agreeable finesse and bouquet which make one
think of a "little Pomerol". It is a style of wine to which one can easily become
accustomed, even to the point of remaining faithful.

Raby-Jean Voisin (Château) 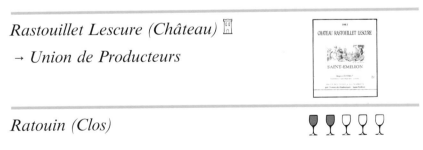 → Paradis

Rastouillet Lescure (Château)
→ Union de Producteurs

Ratouin (Clos)

ΥΥΥΥΥ

Commune: Saint-Emilion. **Proprietor:** Pierre Ratouin. Consultant oenologist: C.B.C. Libourne. **Size of vineyard:**
2.04 hectares. **Average age of vines:** 15 years. **Varieties:**
20% cabernet-sauvignon. 60% merlot. 20% cabernet-franc.
Production: 7,200 bottles CB. **Direct sales and by mail order:** Pierre Ratouin, 91 avenue de l'Epinette, 33500 Libourne. Tel. 57 51 15 43. *This professional market-gardener
is an able small "Sunday" grower.*

Régent (Château)

Commune: Saint-Emilion. **Proprietor:** Florette Labatut.
Manager: Christian Pascaud. Consultant oenologist: CBC
Libourne. **Size of vineyard:** 4.2 hectares. **Average age of
vines:** 30 years. **Varieties:** 50% merlot. 50% cabernet-franc.
Direct sales: Florette Labatut, 38 rue Jean-Mermoz, 33500
Libourne. Tel. 57 24 74 34. **Retail sales:** Ets. Jean-Pierre
Moueix. *That sales should be handled by J.-P. Moueix is in
itself a recommendation.*

Reillon (Clos du)

Commune: Saint-Etienne-de-Lisse. **Proprietor:** Anne-Marie
Ollivier. **Size of vineyard:** 0.46 hectares. **Average age of
vines:** 25 years. **Varieties:** 30% merlot. 70% cabernet-franc.
Production: 2 to 2.5 tonneaux. **Retail sales.** *In the good
years, bottling is done for clients (friends); otherwise everything goes to the trade.*

*label
not
communicated*

Religieuses (Château des)

Commune: Saint-Christophe-des-Bardes. **Proprietor:** Pierre
Coiffard. Consultant oenologist: M. Rolland. **Size of vineyard:** 4.2 hectares. **Average age of vines:** 30 years. **Varieties:**
65% merlot. 35% cabernet-franc. **Production:** 20 tonneaux.
2,500 bottles CB. **Direct sales and by mail order:** Pierre
Coiffard, La Pierre du Maréchal, 33330 Saint-Christophe-
des-Bardes. Tel. 57 24 77 04. **Retail sales:** through the cave
coopérative. *The château-bottled wine of this estate is highly
recommended.*

Rimbaud (Château) ♙ → Bigaroux

Ripeau (Château)

Grand Cru classé

Commune: Saint-Emilion. **Proprietor:** G.F.A. du Château
Ripeau. Directors: M. and Madame Michel Janoueix de
Wilde. Consultant oenologist: Gilles Pauquet. **Size of vineyard:** 15 hectares. **Average age of vines:** 20 years. **Varieties:**
40% cabernet-sauvignon. 40% merlot. 20% cabernet-franc.
Production: 78,000 bottles CB. **Visits:** tel. 57 51 41 24.
Sales by mail order: M. and Madame Janoueix, 169 avenue Foch, B.P. 17, 33502 Libourne Cedex. **Retail sales:**
through the trade.

At Ripeau, an attractive reception room has been created.

The name of Ripeau appeared about the middle of the last century. I have found it mentioned for the first time in the 1868 edition of Cocks and Féret's *Bordeaux et ses Vins*. It was then in the "second crus" of Saint-Emilion although at the time, the wines from the "graves" were much more clearly distinguished from the wines from the hillsides than they are today: each category had its own list. It is on the boundary of Pomerol, which provides its clayey land on a foundation of iron-pan. Spring frosts are not rare and the production has its ups and downs. In accordance with the Janoueix family's tradition, friends and clients are invited to come and harvest. Did the previous owner Raoul Gunsbourg, a Rumanian composer and director of the Monte Carlo Opera for more than fifty years, enlist his team of dancers for harvesting before the 1914 war? What we do know is that he brought himself down in ruin and at crisis point, he sold Ripeau, and the house fully furnished, to the great-grandfather of Madame Michel Janoueix de Wilde.

Robin (Château)

Commune: Saint-Christophe-des-Bardes. **Proprietor:** Jean Buzet. **Size of vineyard:** 8.75 hectares. **Average age of vines:** 20 years. **Varieties:** 11.50% cabernet-sauvignon. 70% merlot. 18.50% cabernet-franc. **Production:** 20,000 bottles CB. **Direct sales and by mail order:** in France and abroad. Tel. 57 24 77 64. **Retail sales.**

Rochebelle (Château)

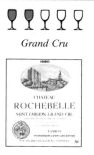

Grand Cru

Commune: Saint-Laurent-des-Combes. **Proprietor:** Philippe and Georges Faniest. **Size of vineyard:** 2.5 hectares. **Average age of vines:** 40 years. **Varieties:** 70% merlot. 30% cabernet-franc. **Production:** 13,000 bottles CB. **Sales by mail order:** in France. Philippe Faniest, 75 rue Trocard, 33500 Libourne. Georges Faniest, rue Gaucher Piola, 33500 Libourne. *Family traditions and a firm list of faithful customers, most of them friends. Reserve your wine well in advance.*

Rochebrune (Château de) ♟ → Grand Faurie

Rocher (Château du)

Grand Cru

Commune: Saint-Etienne-de-Lisse. **Proprietor:** G.F.A. du Château du Rocher. Director: Baron Stanislas de Montfort. Consultant oenologist: M. Chaine. **Size of vineyard:** 14 hectares. **Average age of vines:** 25 years. **Varieties:** 30% cabernet-sauvignon. 50% merlot. 20% cabernet-franc. **Production:** 84,000 bottles CB. **Visits:** by appointment. Tel. 57 40 18 20. **Direct sales and by mail order:** in France. **Retail sales:** agents abroad.

Château du Rocher is one of the oldest dwellings in Saint-Etienne-de-Lisse. In the fifteenth century, the du Rocher family (at the time Rochet was written with a "t") already owned the château bordering the road leading to the village. In 1731, by the marriage of the only daughter of this same du Rocher family, the property came

into the ownership of the Graillys. After the Revolution, the estate passed, by direct marriage, from the Graillys to the Monteils then the Grateloups, and finally to the Montforts. Baron Stanislas de Montfort has run the property since 1969, but came to settle permanently on the estate only in 1975. When he arrived, the establishment was in decay. Before living in Saint-Etienne-de-Lisse, Stanislas de Montfort was in public administration in Paris. Today, his competence is at the service of the property, but also at the service of the commune, of which he is mayor. At the foot of the slope facing southeast, the vineyard rolls gently down behind the old dwelling. The wine is aged in metal vats in order to preserve its first perfumes of fruit. It is a wine which has as exquisite manners as its owner, the baron.

Rocher-Figeac (Château)

Commune: Saint-Emilion. **Proprietors:** M. Tournier & Fils. **Size of vineyard:** 4 hectares. **Average age of vines:** 30 years. **Varieties:** 85% merlot. 15% cabernet-franc. **Production:** 24,000 bottles CB. **Visits:** by appointment. Tel. 57 51 36 49. **Direct sales and by mail order:** in France. Max Tournier & Fils, Tailhas, 194 route de Saint-Emilion, 33500 Libourne. **Retail sales:** Maison A. De Luze & Fils. *The area of Figeac is well situated on a gravelly plateau, but one of Max Tournier's ancestors was called Rocher. The same is true moreover for his Pomerol property called Rocher Beauregard. Geology therefore has nothing to do with the name of this cru, contrary to what one might imagine.*

Rocher-Parent (Château)

Commune: Saint-Etienne-de-Lisse. **Proprietor:** Franck Barthome. Vineyard managers and cellar masters: Franck Barthome and Fernand Contreras. Consultant oenologist: M. Tabouy. **Size of vineyard:** 4.5 hectares. **Average age of vines:** 15 years. **Varieties:** 80% merlot. 20% cabernet-franc. **Production:** 20 tonneaux. 6,000 bottles CB. **Direct sales and by mail order:** Franck Barthome, Bourg, 33350 Saint-Magne-de-Castillon. Tel. 57 40 08 75. **Retail sales:** Bordeaux Tradition. *Modern cultivation and vinification methods, making economic sense for a wine which is commercial in the modern sense of the term.*

Roc Saint-Michel (Château)

Grand Cru

Commune: Saint-Etienne-de-Lisse. **Proprietor:** Jean-Pierre Rollet. Vineyard manager: Marcel Zamparo. Cellarmaster: Luca Zamparo. Consultant oenologist: François Maurin. **Size of vineyard:** 4 hectares. **Varieties:** 67% merlot. 33% cabernet-franc. **Production:** 27,000 bottles CB. **Direct sales and by mail order:** in France and abroad. Vignobles Rollet, B.P. 23, 33330 Saint-Emilion. Tel. 57 47 15 13. *This château represents a very honest standard of quality offered by one of the oldest families of growers in the Saint-Emilion region.*

Rol (Château de)

Grand Cru

Commune: Saint-Emilion. **Proprietor:** Jean Sautereau. **Consultant oenologist:** M. Rolland. **Size of vineyard:** 7 hectares. **Average age of vines:** 25 years. **Varieties:** 10% cabernet-sauvignon. 80% merlot. 10% cabernet-franc. **Production:** 40,000 bottles CB. **Visits:** "From Monday to Sunday at any hour of the day." Tel. 57 24 70 38. **Direct sales and by mail order:** in France.

Jean Sautereau is like his wine. Closed up within himself at first, he opens up warmly as soon as you start to talk with him. Installed here on his estate since 1951, he has rationalized the work both on the vineyard and in the vat-house. He is a partisan of mechanical harvesting, because the machine completely eliminates the stalks. His personal cellar still contains wines of the 1924, 1934 and 1945 vintages, which proves the suitability of the *cru* for ageing.

Roland (Château) → Pressac

Rol de Fombrauge (Château)

Grand Cru

Commune: Saint-Christophe-des-Bardes. **Proprietor:** Marie Madeleine Bonnet. **Consultant oenologist:** Mademoiselle Cazenave. **Size of vineyard:** 5.5 hectares. **Average age of vines:** 25 years. **Varieties:** 20% cabernet-sauvignon. 70% merlot. 10% cabernet-franc. **Production:** 30 tonneaux. 6,000 bottles CB. **Retail sales:** Marie Madeleine Bonnet, Tel. 57 24 77 67. *This is an old label of good reputation with very reasonable wines. The place name of Fombrauge on a label being in itself a guarantee of quality.*

Rol de Fombrauge (Clos)

Commune: Saint-Christophe-des-Bardes. **Proprietor:** Roland Gaury. **Directors:** Micheline and Roland Gaury. **Consultant oenologist:** C.B.C. Libourne. **Size of vineyard:** 4 hectares. **Average age of vines:** 35 years. **Varieties:** 75% merlot. 25% cabernet-franc. **Production:** 12,000 bottles CB. **Direct sales and by mail order:** tel. 57 24 77 75. **Retail sales:** through the Bordeaux trade. *Before 1924, the land of this estate belonged to Château Fombrauge. It produces a very correct wine which is rather difficult to find in the trade owing to its small production.*

Roquefort (Château de) → Tertre Daugay

Roquemont (Château de)

Grand Cru

Commune: Saint-Sulpice-de-Faleyrens. **Proprietor:** Jean-André Robineau. Consultant oenologist: M. Hébrard. **Size of vineyard:** 4.50 hectares. **Average age of vines:** 25 years. **Varieties:** 10% cabernet-sauvignon. 60% merlot. 30% cabernet-franc. **Production** 20,000 bottles CB. **Visits:** tel. 57 84 52 26. **Direct sales and by mail order:** in France. Jean-André Robineau, "Bouchet" Grézillac, 33420 Branne. **Retail sales:** Maison Mau (Gironde-sur-Dropt).

On the border between Saint-Sulpice-de-Faleyrens and Vignonet, the vineyard of Roquemont is in one single stretch on deep filtering gravel. Merlot and cabernet can thrive happily in agrological comfort to attain the best possible maturity. Château Roquemont has belonged to the Robineau family for more than a century. It is a *cru* which offers excellent value for money. I can recommend it both as a young *primeur* wine and as a nature wine after about five years of ageing.

Roy (Château du)

Grand Cru

Commune: Saint-Emilion. **Proprietor:** Charles Bouquey. **Size of vineyard:** 3 hectares. **Average age of vines:** 35 years. **Varieties:** 50% merlot. 45% cabernet-franc. 5% malbec. **Production:** 14,400 bottles CB. **Visits:** by appointment. Tel. 57 51 35 27. **Sales by mail order:** in France and abroad. Charles Bouquey, Le Rivallon, 33330 Saint-Emilion. **Retail sales.** *Part of the vineyard is by the side of the King's Tower in Saint-Emilion. A confidential clientele for an attractive wine.*

Rozier (Château)

Grand Cru

Commune: Saint-Laurent-des-Combes. **Proprietor:** G.F.A. du Château Rozier. Tenant and vineyard manager: Jean-Bernard Saby. Consultant oenologist: M. Rolland. **Size of vineyard:** 18 hectares. **Average age of vines:** 40 years. **Varieties:** 10% cabernet-sauvignon. 75% merlot. 15% cabernet-franc. **Production:** 100,000 bottles CB. **Visits:** tel. 57 24 73 03. **Direct sales and by mail order:** in France. **Retail sales:** 75% for export, 5% through the Bordeaux trade.

Jean-Bernard Saby is a qualified oenologist. He places all his knowledge at the service of a supple, gentle easy to drink wine. The style of this *cru* is to Saint-Emilion what the "nouvelle cuisine" is to French gastronomy. You can like it...

Sable (Domaine du)

Commune: Saint-Christophe-des-Bardes. **Proprietor:** François Tourriol. Consultant oenologist: C.B.C. Libourne. **Size of vineyard:** 1.1 hectares. **Average age of vines:** 30 years. **Varieties:** 10% cabernet-sauvignon. 80% merlot. 10% cabernet-franc. **Production:** 6,000 bottles CB. **Direct sales and by mail order:** François Tourriol, Troquart-Montagne, 33570 Lussac. Tel. 57 74 61 62. *On March 11, 1840, Marie-Bernard Arnaudet bought the vineyard for the sum of 4.000 francs. She was the great-great-grandmother of the present owner.*

Saint-Christophe (Château)

Grand Cru

Commune: Saint-Christophe-des-Bardes. **Proprietor:** Gilbert Richard. Vineyard manager and cellar-master: Benoît Richard. Consultant oenologist: M. Gendrot. **Size of vineyard:** 10 hectares. **Average age of vines:** 25 years. **Varieties:** 10% cabernet-sauvignon. 70% merlot. 20% cabernet-franc. **Production:** 60,000 bottles CB. **Visits:** by appointment. Tel. 57 24 77 17. **Direct sales and by mail order:** in France and abroad. *Harvesting is done by hand because it is the tradition but the wine is not put into wood because "it gives them a heavy character". That's a flighty observation.*

"Saint-Emilion"

Commune: Saint-Emilion. **Proprietor:** Pierre Musset. Consultant oenologist: M. Rolland. **Size of vineyard:** 0.48 hectares. **Average age of vines:** more than 60 years. **Varieties:** 70% merlot. 30% cabernet-franc. **Production:** 1 tonneau. *A wine reserved for the large Musset family.*

Saint-Emilion

Commune: Saint-Emilion. **Proprietor:** Raymond Visage. Consultant oenologist: Mademoiselle Cazenave. **Size of vineyard:** 0.3 hectares. **Average age of vines:** 12 years. **Varieties:** 25% cabernet-sauvignon. 50% merlot. 25% cabernet-franc. **Production:** 2 tonneaux. 1,500 bottles CB. **Direct sales and by mail order:** in France. Raymond Visage, Carret, 33500 Pomerol. Tel. 57 51 44 87. *Did I say "Saint-Emilion"? I thought I was drinking a Pomerol. A good wine, in any case.*

Saint-Georges Côte Pavie (Château)

Grand Cru classé

Commune: Saint-Emilion. **Proprietor:** Jacques Masson. Vineyard manager: Roger Toulon. Cellar master: Philippe Lauret. **Size of vineyard:** 5.42 hectares. **Average age of vines:** 30 years. **Varieties:** 40% cabernet-sauvignon. 60% merlot. **Production:** 240,000 bottles. **Visits:** by appointment. From April until the end of October. M. Masson, tel. 57 74 44 23. **Direct sales and by mail order:** in France and abroad. **Retail sales.**

The words in brackets on the label are indispensible to enable this *cru* to be situated precisely and not to be confused with Château Saint-Georges in Montagne Saint-Emilion. Once more, I realize to what extent a thorough knowledge of the Libourne vineyards is a subtle and erudite matter. Professor Henri Enjalbert mentions the hypothesis, without quite endorsing it, of the possible existence of Ausonius' villa in Saint-Georges, which in older times might have been the parish of Saint-Georges de Lucaniac. Towards the end of the eighteenth century, Vidal, the priest, mentioned that the lands in this spot were a "little living" in the control of the Benedictine monks of La Sauve. Traces of mediaeval foundations are buried in the land in the northwest corner of the estate. Similarly, behind the principal house, whose foundation-stones cannot be dated, Gallo-Roman mosaics were discovered at the time of replanting. They may have belonged to the "residential complex" discovered at the mill of Le Palat, nearly. But the "little living" being what counts most, the discovery was immediately covered over again and vigorous merlots stand guard over the secrets of the god Bacchus and his disciple Ausonius Decimus Magnus. Without giving my opinion on the authenticity of Ausonius' presence in the place, I am inclined to believe that there was a religious institution here during the decline of the Roman Empire. Examples of this are frequent in the southwest of France and in the Gironde in particular. It should not be forgotten that Christianity readily grafted itself onto the Bacchic stock of Gallo-Roman second residences because *de facto* it found the divine and mystic liquor, "the fruit of the land and the work of men", indispensable to the cult. "O tempora, o mores!" No, I have not got the gift of the great Cicero's rhetoric. By Saint George! This *cru* is an excellent wine!

Saint-Hubert (Château)

Grand Cru

Commune: Saint-Pey-d'Armens. **Proprietor:** M. E. Aubert. Director and consultant oenologist: Daniel Aubert. **Size of vineyard:** 3 hectares. **Average age of vines:** 18 years. **Varieties:** 30% cabernet-sauvignon. 50% merlot. 20% cabernet-franc. **Production:** 19,000 bottles CB. **Sales by mail order:** in France and abroad. M. Aubert, B.P. 40, 33330 Saint-Emilion.

With an average annual production of barely 20,000 bottles at the most, Château Saint-Hubert represents about five per cent of the total capacity of the output of the three Aubert brothers who buy nearly one million bottles from the glassworks every year. Their eight vineyards have proliferated all over the regions of Libourne and

Entre-deux-Mers. But in a way Saint-Hubert is the cradle of this family of growers, which has been on this land since 1750. The gem of the collection of the Auberts' labels is Château La Couspaude, a Saint-Emilion Grand Cru classé. As to quality, Saint-Hubert is a happy medium with even and regular productions. It goes without saying that a wine of Saint-Hubert (the patron saint of hunters) is predestined to accompany a good meal of game. For the record, I mention a sparkling wine, *blanc de blanc*, champagne method, in the panoply of the Aubert brothers. So they have whatever is needed for important family occasions.

Saint-Jean (Château)

Commune: Saint-Emilion. **Proprietor:** Danielle Torelli. Director, vineyard manager and cellar master: Paul Torelli. Consultant oenologist: M. Rolland. **Size of vineyard:** 2 hectares. **Average age of vines:** 20 years. **Varieties:** 65% merlot. 35% cabernet-franc. **Production:** 12,000 bottles CB. **Visits:** tel. 57 51 19 49. **Direct sales:** Danielle Torelli, 109 route de Saint-Emilion, 33500 Libourne. *A friendly welcome and agreable wines.*

Saint Jean de Béard (Château)
→ *Béard la Chapelle*

Saint-Julien (Clos)

Grand Cru

Commune: Saint-Emilion. **Proprietor:** Jean-Jacques Nouvel. Consultant oenologists: Mademoiselle Cazenave and M. Chaine. **Size of vineyard:** 2 hectares. **Average age of vines:** 30 years. **Varieties:** 50% cabernet-sauvignon. 30% merlot. 20% cabernet-franc. **Production:** 10,000 bottles CB. **Direct sales and by mail order:** in France. Jean-Jacques Nouvel, Fontfleurie, 33330 Saint-Emilion. Tel. 57 24 72 05. *Saint-Julien and Saint-Emilion have joined hands to bless Monsieur Nouvel's product. The label looks quite mediaeval so stick to the most recent vintages.*

Saint-Martial (Château)

Grand Cru

Commune: Saint-Sulpice-de-Faleyrens. **Proprietor:** Guy Dupeyrat. Tenant: M. Palatin Micheau-Maillou. Consultant oenologist: C.B.C. Libourne. **Size of vineyard:** 3.46 hectares. **Varieties:** 60% merlot. 40% cabernet-franc. **Production:** 20,000 bottles CB. **Direct sales and by mail order:** in France. Palatin Micheau-Maillou. *Three parcels of flat ground come together in an honest Saint-Emilion which has nothing in common with rhe first bishop of Lyon.*

Saint Martin (Clos)

Grand Cru classé

Commune: Saint-Emilion. **Proprietor:** S.C.E. des Grandes Murailles. Tenants: M. and Madame Reiffers. Vineyard manager: Jean Brun. Consultant oenologist: Michel Rolland. **Size of vineyard:** 1.9 hectares. **Average age of vines:** 30 years. **Varieties:** 10% cabernet-sauvignon. 70% merlot. 20% cabernet-franc. **Production:** 9,600 bottles CB. **Direct sales and by mail order:** S.C.E. des Grandes Murailles, Château Côte Baleau, 33330 Saint-Emilion. Tel. 57 24 71 09. **Retail sales.** *This is the one* cru *of the Reiffers productions not to have suffered the outrage of being declassified. Such discrimination is quite incomprehensible in view of the high level of quality of all the Reiffers' wines. (See Côtes Baleau and Grandes Murailles.)*

Saint-Pey (Château de)

Grand Cru

Communes: Saint-Pey-d'Armens, Saint-Hippolyte. **Proprietors:** Maurice and Pierre Musset. Consultant oenologist: Grézillac Laboratory. **Size of vineyard:** 16 hectares. **Average age of vines:** 25 years. **Varieties:** 10% cabernet-sauvignon. 70% merlot. 20% cabernet-franc. **Production:** 75 tonneaux. 60,000 bottles CB. **Visits:** tel. 57 47 15 25. **Direct sales and by mail order.** *Where merlot predominates, you may find the wines a little too easy going.*

Saint-Pey "Branche aînée" (Château de)

Grand Cru

Commune: Saint-Pey-d'Armens. **Proprietors:** L. & J.-P. Musset. Consultant oenologist: C.B.C. Libourne. **Size of vineyard:** 20 hectares. **Average age of vines:** 30 years. **Varieties:** 10% cabernet-sauvignon. 60% merlot. 30% cabernet-franc. **Production:** 120,000 bottles CB. **Visits:** tel. 57 51 40 07 or 57 47 15 01. **Direct sales and by mail order:** in France and abroad. Bel-Air, 33500 Lalande de Pomerol. **Retail sales:** in the traditional way.

The total area of this estate covers nearly 40 hectares, but it has been split up between the two branches of the Musset family, which can count six generations of growers. Positive traces of their presence can be found on this land in 1711, without being able to go further back in time for want of records. The two châteaux with the name Saint-Pey are run jointly by Jean-Pierre and Maurice Musset. The first claims its birthright with the mention of "Branche aînée" (elder branch) printed on the label. Recent tastings of this *cru* have greatly disappointed me but here one should tread cautiously, for however often you taste a wine, your judgement remains subject to different influences. Every taster has his moments of doubt.

Saint-Pierre (Château) 🛡 → Saint-Pey

Saint-Valéry (Clos)

ᵧ ᵧ ᵧ ᵧ ᵧ

Grand Cru

Commune: Saint-Emilion. **Proprietors:** Hélène and Pierre Berjal. Consultant oenologist: M. Chaine. **Size of vineyard:** 4 hectares. **Average age of vines:** 30 years. **Varieties:** 30% cabernet-sauvignon. 40% merlot. 30% cabernet-franc. **Production:** 22,000 bottles CB. **Visits:** by appointment. Tel. 57 24 70 97. **Direct sales and by mail order:** in France and abroad. Hélène and Pierre Berjal, Châtelet, 33330 Saint-Emilion. *In the place name known as Le Châtelet, at the foot of the hillside of Pavie, this estate is characterized by aeolian sand and harvesting by machine. Ageing takes place in vats.*

Saint Vincent (Clos)

ᵧ ᵧ ᵧ ᵧ ᵧ

Commune: Saint-Sulpice-de-Faleyrens. **Proprietor:** Pierre Ripes. **Size of vineyard:** 4.14 hectares. **Average age of vines:** 40 years. **Varieties:** 20% cabernet-sauvignon. 50% merlot. 30% cabernet-franc. **Production:** 20 tonneaux. 7,500 bottles CB. **Visits:** tel. 57 24 74 21. **Direct sales and by mail order:** in France. **Retail sales.** *At the bottom of the label, we read: "A wine produced from vines not treated with chemical weed-killer, grapes not harvested by machine. Made according to tradition. Aged in oak casks". Take note; and may Saint Vincent, the patron saint of vignerons, bless us!*

Sansonnet (Château)

ᵧ ᵧ ᵧ ᵧ ᵧ

Grand Cru classé

Commune: Saint-Emilion. **Proprietor:** Francis Robin. Estate manager: Jean-Loup Robin. Vineyard manager and cellar master: Dominique Robin. Consultant oenologist: Michel Rolland. **Size of vineyard:** 7 hectares. **Average age of vines:** 25 years. **Varieties:** 20% cabernet-sauvignon. 60% merlot. 20% cabernet-franc. **Production:** 48,000 bottles CB. **Visits:** by appointment. Tel. 57 51 03 65. **Direct sales and by mail order:** in France and abroad. Francis Robin, Château Doumayne, 142 route de Saint-Emilion. 33500 Libourne. **Retail sales:** for export.

Sansonnet sits on the top of the hillside on the east of the town of Saint-Emilion. The vineyard's seven hectares surround the château in one unbroken stretch on a layer of chalky rocks leaving little room for friable land. It was the property of the Duke Decazes who sold it in 1846 to General Coutard who gave it to his daughter, the Viscountess de Montaudon, as her dowry. Prosper Robin bought it in 1892 and since that time it has not left the family. The Robin productions represent the know-how of six generations. They well illustrate the variety of the different Libourne terrains. Apart from Saint-Emilion, they can be found in the appellations of Pomerol, Puisseguin and Lussac. All is very conscientious. Tradition sometimes takes the place of inspiration, especially when it is founded on such sincerity.

Sarenceau (Château de)

Commune: Saint-Emilion. **Proprietor:** Simone Horse. Vineyard manager and cellar master: Ludovic Delage-Horse. Consultant oenologist: C.B.C. Libourne. **Size of vineyard:** 7.6 hectares. **Average age of vines:** 30 years. **Varieties:** 90% merlot. 10% cabernet-franc. **Production:** 35 tonneaux. 12,000 bottles CB. **Direct sales and by mail order:** tel. 57 24 60 15. **Retail sales.**

Sauvenelle (Château)

Commune: Libourne. **Proprietor:** Danielle Torelli. Director, vineyard manager and cellar master: Paul Torelli. Consultant oenologist: Michel Rolland. **Size of vineyard:** 1 hectare. **Average age of vines:** 15 years. **Varieties:** 65% merlot. 35% cabernet-franc. **Production:** 7,000 bottles CB. **Direct sales:** Danielle Torelli, 109 route de Saint-Emilion, 33500 Libourne. Tel. 57 51 16 18. *Agreeable bottles can be bought on the spot, but you will find more or less the same wine as at Château Saint-Jean (which may taste better).*

Sicard (Château)

Commune: Saint-Pey-d'Armens. **Proprietor:** G. Duboudin. Consultant oenologist: Grézillac Laboratory. **Size of vineyard:** 6 hectares. **Average age of vines:** 20 years. **Varieties:** 33% cabernet-sauvignon. 33% merlot. 33% cabernet-franc. **Production:** 32 tonneaux. 10,000 bottles CB. **Direct sales and by mail order:** tel. 57 47 14 43. **Retail sales.** *A cru which makes you regret that not at all of it is château-bottled.*

Simard (Château)

Commune: Saint-Emilion. **Proprietor:** Claude Mazière. **Size of vineyard:** 20 hectares. **Average age of vines:** 20 to 30 years. **Varieties:** 70% merlot. 30% cabernet-franc. **Production:** 120,000 bottles CB. **Visits:** by appointment. Tel. 57 24 70 42. **Retail sales:** for export through Barton & Guestier.

A bourgeois family of Saint-Emilion called Simard was to be found in the seventeenth century. Were they conferred with a title later? Under Napoleon I, we find Count Pierre de Simard as the proprietor of Château Simard. His two children died without issue. The property changed hands and the Delormes, Navailles and Charoulets follow one after the other. It is from these latter that Claude Mazière bought the property in 1954. Among his clients, he counts some Canadians by the name of Simard. For him, Haut-Simard and Simard have exactly the same virtues. "They have the same father," he says. I will go one better: they are Siamese twins.

Soutard (Château)

Grand Cru classé

Commune: Saint-Emilion. **Proprietor:** The des Ligneris family. Director: Jacques des Ligneris. Estate manager, vineyard manager and cellar master: François des Ligneris. Consultant oenologist: C.B.C. Libourne. **Size of vineyard:** 22 hectares. **Average age of vines:** 30 years. **Varieties:** 60% merlot. 40% cabernet-franc. **Production:** 120,000 bottles CB. **Visits:** by appointment. Tel. 57 24 72 23. **Direct sales and by mail order:** in France. **Retail sales:** distributors abroad: Belgium, Germany, Switzerland, Holland, England, United States, Australia, New Zealand, Denmark.

"We try to live our lives according to our own ideas," declares the heir to this château, François des Ligneris, almost as if he were apologizing. Beside, Soutard has been in the family for more than two hundred years. Obviously, that creates an outlook which others call tradition. The estate can be self-sufficient in an autarchy which starts at the laundry (still in use) extending to the bread oven and the kitchen garden, not forgetting the lime-tree, whose copious blossom guarantees infusions at bed-time. The self-sufficiency becomes ecological when the ladybirds of the *cru* are relied on to eat up the aphids, chemical treatment being excluded. In the time of their forebears, there were no pesticides nor fungicides... yet they made good wine. Why then should one change methods? But this self-sufficiency can also be called anachronism when it enshrines attitudes which some might call backward-looking. However, this form of independence compels respect if only because of the proud manner in which all the protagonists play their part. Each number of the family gulfills his own rôle. It falls to the grandmother to teach all the youngest offspring about mushrooms. Each of them personally has to look after his or her own flower-bed. And so, each person has his or her own cleerly defined function whithin the family unit, lending coherence to the whole entreprise. And those who do not work in the garden play a part in the farm-yard. The hundred and one different activities of daily life then take on their real human dimension. The Ligneris family forms a highly organized society of long standing.

Over the generations, Château Soutard was more often than not handed down by dowry. Going back to the earliest records, we find Jean Laveau, the son of Laveau l'Aîné, whom we have already met, whose daughter Marie married Gérôme de

Château Soutard: you would almost expect to see the mistress of the house...

Chaussade de Chandos, an equerry, and lord of Beauregard. What is to be admired with these families is that their genealogy does not get lost. The Ligneris know the smallest little branches and have the details at their finger-tips. Right up to the day when Jeanne du Foussat de Bogeron, the daughter of a *conseiller général* for the Gironde, married a distant cousin, Michel des Ligneris. Soutard was in her trousseau and the husband was kitted out with diplomas in agronomy. They had a son, Jacques who, in his turn, has three children: François, Isabelle and Hélène. Today they know all about mushrooms, carrots and peas, and the problems posed by chicken farming when there are Bresse chickens and Leghorns side by side. Soutard is an elegant property and forms one single entity, with a genuine château, constructed in the middle of the eighteenth century, and an attractive park and outbuildings which also respect tradition: the cow has its meadow and the donkey its own field. The vineyard is large: 22 hectares in one unbroken stretch, and that is not common in Saint-Emilion. In point of fact, Soutard is the largest production unit among the Grands Crus classés. Its average harvest works out at about 100 tonneaux. Despite Soutard's reverence for its ancestors, vinification can be called modern. The wines are classical in the best sense of the term. They have recently moved away from their former austere nature and now fortunately develop more rapidly. For the last ten years, Soutard has been building a new reputation. That is in no way to

appearing in a crinoline dress with her angelic little daughters.

say that the old one was bad... but today this *Grand Cru classé,* which is widely distributed moreover, is in keeping with current tastes. Without altering the charm of its chiselled ageing features, Soutard has had a face-lift on the quiet. It should not be mentioned. But one is allowed to notice.

Soutard-Cadet (Château) ♟ ♟ ♟ ♟ ♟

Commune: Saint-Emilion. **Proprietor:** Jacques Darribé-haude. Consultant oenologist: M. Pauquet. **Size of vineyard:** 2 hectares. **Average age of vines:** 40 years. **Varieties:** 60% merlot. 40% cabernet-franc. **Production:** 12,000 bottles CB. **Direct sales and by mail order:** tel. 57 24 73 64. **Retail sales.** *The vineyard is in one unbroken stretch but part comes from Château Soutard and the other from Cadet. Hence the name which was registered in the last century.*

Tauzinat l'Hermitage (Château)

Commune: Saint-Christophe-des-Bardes. **Proprietor:** Marcel Moueix heirs. Director and vineyard manager: Armand Moueix. Consultant oenologist: M. Crébassa. **Size of vineyard:** 8.84 hectares. **Average age of vines:** 25 years. **Varieties:** 70% merlot. 30% cabernet-franc. **Production:** 48,000 bottles CB. **Sales by mail order:** in France. S.A.A. Moueix & Fils, Château Taillefer, 33500 Libourne. Tel. 57 51 50 63. **Retail sales:** S.A.A. Moueix & Fils. *Marcel Moueix's heirs have been the proprietors since 1953. The dwelling dates from the seventeenth century. The* cru *thankfully has been enjoying a new lease of life over recent years.*

Templiers (Château des)

Grand Cru

Commune: Saint-Emilion. **Proprietor:** Jean-Fernand Mèneret Capdemourlin. Estate manager: Philippe Mèneret Capdemourlin. Cellar master: Roland Dudilot. Consultant oenologists: Emile Peynaud and Guy Guiberteau. **Size of vineyard:** 2.6 hectares. **Average age of vines:** 30 years. **Varieties:** 10% cabernet-sauvignon. 65% merlot. 25% cabernet-franc. **Production:** 12,000 bottles CB. **Retail sales:** Jean-Fernand Mèneret Capdemourlin, rue Guadet, 33330 Saint-Emilion. Tel. 57 24 71 41. *The name comes from "the house of the Templars" where Jean-Fernand Mèneret lives. The vineyard comes from a great-aunt who used to call her wine: "my velvet". Her nephews think she could have been a great poet.*

Tertre Daugay (Château)

Grand Cru classé

Commune: Saint-Emilion. **Proprietor:** Count de Malet Roquefort. Vineyard manager: Edouard Garin. Cellar master: Jean-Louis Faure. Consultant oenologist: Guy Guimberteau. **Size of vineyard:** 16 hectares. **Average age of vines:** 25 years. **Varieties:** 10% cabernet-sauvignon. 60% merlot. 30% cabernet-franc. **Production:** 60,000 bottles CB. **Visiting hours:** Monday to Friday from 8 a.m. to noon and 2 to 6 p.m. Tel. 57 24 72 15. **Direct sales and by mail order:** Château la Gaffelière, 33330 Saint-Emilion. **Retail sales:** through the Bordeaux trade.

From his earliest childhood, Léo de Malet listened to his father speaking to him of Tertre Daugay with great affection – an affection he poured out on two objects: first and foremost, the family. There was "poor old Clairette" a cousin (distant certainly, but a cousin none the less) who had made such a bad deal when she had sold the estate in very bad conditions. And secondly, business: "Poor old Tertre Daugay",

Tertre Daugay is an important site at Saint-Emilion.

excellent, well-situated land which had fallen into careless hands who had run it down into a pitiful state. "Is it not a great shame to see that?" When the son of a titled grower hears such a lament at a tender age, his soul becomes the sounding brass of family piety, here chanted like a *Miserere* in G minor. The years passed by and the brass hardened, tempered by the realities of life. The boy Léo kept in his soul his secret garden called Tertre Daugay. For him it was promised land; he swore to have it back and breathed not a word to a living soul.

In 1978, Tertre Daugay was up for sale. Léo de Malet and his notary Jacques Guillon, from Targon, began negotiations with the agent in charge of the affair. But the price was too high and the situation too complicated. They decided to wait until the estate was put up for public auction. So there he was: Léo Malet, in the auction room amongst a handful of inquisitive folk. The judge called on the bidders to make themselves known and he lit the first candle. Léo de Malet announced his offer. Silence all round. The candle went out. The second was lit. Léo Malet waited for a counter-bid, which was not forthcoming. He had been told that wealthy buyers, notably Swiss or Belgians, had the intention of pushing the price up, but still there was silence. The second candle went out. It was time for the last one. There was an 279 atmosphere of intense drama. Each candle lasts only a minute, but the third would have lit up all eternity. It went out. Léo de Malet could not believe his eyes. Was he really the proprietor of Tertre Daugay? Unfortunately, he had to agonize for yet another month. Day after day, he waited for the announcement that the higher bid of 10% had been made, but nothing materialized. The fateful Monday to close the deal finally dawned. The countdown marked off the hours, then the minutes. A quarter of an hour before the official knocking down, the increased offer of 10% came into the hands of the judge. Apparently, it was from a Belgian. Léo de Malet was bowled over. The following Thursday was the day for the final settlement. The buyer did not appear. Léo de Malet covered the higher bid with 10,000 francs. Château Tertre Daugay finally belonged to him.

The estate has now been completely renovated. To the 3,530,000 francs which he paid, he has added more than one million francs for the improvement of the land and complete restoration of the cellars and vat-house. All the profits of La Gaffelière have been ploughed back here. Today, Tertre Daugay has a new face. Léo de Malet feels that the shades of his ancestors are appeased. Beware, Tertre Daugay has become a redoubtable challenger to the *Grands Crus classés!*

Tertre de Sarpe (Château) ♟

→ *Vieux Château Pelletan*

Tonneret (Château) ♟♟♟♟♟

Commune: Saint-Christophe-des-Bardes. **Proprietor:** Albino Gresta. Vineyard managers and cellar masters: Albino and Jacky Gresta. Consultant oenologist: C.B.C. Libourne. **Size of vineyard:** 3.2 hectares. **Average age of vines:** 35 years. **Varieties:** 75% merlot. 25% cabernet-franc. **Production:** 18 tonneaux. 7,000 bottles CB. **Visits:** tel. 57 24 60 01. **Direct sales and by mail order. Retail sales.** *Albino Gresta has been at Le Tonneret for twenty years. He runs the estate himself and looks after marketing by direct sales, hoping that his son will follow in his footsteps. But he has not yet made up his mind.*

Tourans (Château) ♟♟♟♟♟

Grand Cru

Commune: Saint-Etienne-de-Lisse. **Proprietor:** S.A. Vignobles Rocher Cap de Rive. Director: Jean Lafaye. Vineyard manager and cellar master: Gabriel Audebert. Consultant oenologist: M. Chaine. **Size of vineyard:** 11.5 hectares. **Average age of vines:** 25 years. **Varieties:** 20% cabernet-sauvignon. 60% merlot. 20% cabernet-franc. **Production:** 60,000 bottles CB. **Visits:** by appointment. Tel. 57 40 08 88. **Retail sales:** for export: Benelux countries. *Harvesting by machine. Stainless steel vats. New barriques. Fining with egg-whites. There has been progress in the methods of this estate which have always had an eye to economy.*

Tour Baladoz (Château)

Grand Cru

Commune: Saint-Laurent-des-Combes. **Proprietors:** Messieurs de Schepper. Director: Firmin de Schepper. Estate manager, vineyard manager and cellar master: Jean-Marie Faux. Consultant oenologist: M. Nauzin (Laffort Laboratory). **Size of vineyard:** 8 hectares. **Average age of vines:** 30 years. **Varieties:** 10% cabernet-sauvignon. 70% merlot. 20% cabernet-franc. **Production:** 36,000 bottles CB. **Visits:** by appointment. Tel. 57 40 61 57. **Retail sales:** Société Rabotvins (Belgium).

Tour Berthonneau (Château)

Commune: Saint-Emilion. **Proprietor:** Gilberte Grolière & Fils. Consultant oenologist: Mademoiselle Cazenave-Mahé. **Size of vineyard:** 3.34 hectares. **Average age of vines:** 30 years. **Varieties:** 65% merlot. 35% cabernet-franc. **Production:** 10 tonneaux. 6,000 bottles CB. **Direct sales and by mail order:** in France. Tel. 57 51 06 46. **Retail sales:** in bulk. *A "Grand Cru" up to 1981, this property contents itself with very feeble yields, which are not served by a real marketing policy. It is to be regretted that justice is not done to excellent* terroirs *such as this one.*

Tour Blanche (Château) 🏺

→ Côte de la Mouleyre

Tour de Bardes (Château) 🏺 → Labarde

Tour de Beauregard (Château)

Commune: Saint-Emilion. **Proprietor:** Ilario Fritegotto. Consultant oenologist: M. Chaine. **Size of vineyard:** 15 hectares. **Average age of vines:** 20 years. **Varieties:** 75% merlot. 20% cabernet-franc. 5% malbec. **Production:** 80,000 bottles CB. **Visits:** by appointment. Tel. 57 24 73 15. **Direct sales and by mail order:** in France. **Retail sales:** through the Bordeaux trade. *The vineyard is in two pieces on sandy land, one in Saint-Emilion and the other in Vignonet. Harvesting by machine. Maturing in wood and a wine that could be mistaken for an honest Bordeaux Supérieur.*

Tour de Capet (Château) 🏺 → Capet-Guillier

Tour de Corbin Despagne (Château)

Commune: Saint-Emilion. **Proprietor:** G.F.A. Despagne-Rapin. Directors: Gérard and Françoise Despagne. Vineyard manager: Yves Richard. Cellar master: François Gil. Consultant oenologist: C.B.C. Libourne. **Size of vineyard:** approximately 5 hectares. **Average age of vines:** 30 to 40 years. **Varieties:** 20% cabernet-sauvignon. 60% merlot. 20% cabernet-franc. **Production:** 15 to 20 tonneaux. **Visits:** tel. 57 74 62 18. **Direct sales and by mail order:** in France. G.F.A. Despagne-Rapin, Maison Blanche, 33570 Montagne. **Retail sales:** through wine merchants outside Bordeaux (local merchants and importers abroad).

Two parcels of vines to represent all the vineyard. But not any old parcels in any old situation. Each is surrounded by *Grands Crus classés*. So what is the ostracism which prevents Tour de Corbin Despagne from having its letters of nobility? The reply is easy: the grapes are "exported" to Montagne Saint-Emilion instead of being vinified on the spot. Unlike stars and champions, it is on home soil that the harvest should display its talents.

Dura lex sed lex. It does not prevent this wine from blending the delicacy of the land of Figeac with the keen aromatic savour of the Corbins. It does not prevent the grapes from preserving their natural qualities despite the journey of a few miles. It does not prevent Gérard Despagne from being an attentive wine-maker and his wines are superb. I place them on a par with many of the *crus classés*.

Tour de Pressac (Château)

Grand Cru

Commune: Saint-Etienne-de-Lisse. **Proprietor:** Jacques Pouey. **Size of vineyard:** 7 hectares. **Varieties:** 58% merlot. 40% cabernet-franc. 2% malbec. **Production:** 18,000 bottles CB. **Visiting hours:** Monday to Friday from 9 a.m. to noon and 2 to 5 p.m. Tel. 56 81 45 00. **Direct sales and by mail order:** in France and abroad. Jacques Pouey, 59 rue Minvielle, 33000 Bordeaux (offices). **Retail sales.** *Château La Tour de Pressac is the younger brother of Château de Pressac (see this name) a few of whose virtues it occasionally recaptures.*

282

Tour des Combes (Château)

Grand Cru

Commune: Saint-Laurent-des-Combes. **Proprietor:** Jean Darribéhaude. Director: Brigitte Darribéhaude. **Size of vineyard:** 13 hectares. **Average age of vines:** 35 years. **Varieties:** 15% cabernet-sauvignon. 70% merlot. 15% cabernet-franc. **Production:** 78,000 bottles CB. **Direct sales and by mail order:** in France and abroad. Château Tour des Combes, Au Sable, Saint-Laurent-des-Combes, 33330 Saint-Emilion. Tel. 57 24 70 04. **Retail sales:** through Bordeaux and Libourne.

The tower really existed in the last century. Its stones served to construct the oldest part of the buildings of today. The vineyard was created starting with a few parcels bought in 1849 from the Meynards and Marie-Françoise de Malet Roquefort, whose descendants are the owners of the famous Château La Gaffelière. It spreads out over the communes of Saint-Emilion, Saint-Laurent-des-Combes, Saint-Hippolyte, Vignonet and Saint-Sulpice-de-Faleyrens. (I know that is a large area but that is how it is). You take spontaneously to this wine which is rather rich in style and well structured. My according to this estate only two glasses may seem a little over-severe, but I am convinced that this *cru* has the potential to do much better.

Tour Fortin (Château) ♟ → Haut-Segottes

Tour Grand Faurie (Château)

Grand Cru

Commune: Saint-Emilion. **Proprietor:** Jean Feytit. Consultant oenologist: M. Chaine. **Size of vineyard:** 11.45 hectares. **Average age of vines:** 30 years. **Varieties:** 5% cabernet-sauvignon. 85% merlot. 10% cabernet-franc. **Production:** 60,000 bottles CB. **Visits:** daily. Tel. 57 24 73 75. **Direct sales and by mail order:** in France and abroad: Belgium, Germany, United States, England.

Jean Feytit's grandfather was factotum on the estate which at that time comprised three hectares. In those days, such a job was split between work on the vines and in the cellars, and the pleasure of smoking one's packet of tobacco while carefully putting money on one side for the future. Tour Grand Faurie is made up of three parcels, of which one is situated in the centre of Saint-Emilion. All through the last war, this parcel was looked after by the daughter-in-law who pruned the vines and sold the wine as well. Like his father, Jean Feytit was born on the estate where he has always worked. In 1969 he increased the vineyard. In 1973 his wife inherited the parcel in Saint-Christophe-des-Bardes. And in 1974, Jean Feytit bought his daughter's share to become the sole owner. The wine has an attractive bouquet. Its first rather austere style disappears over the years, although recent vintages have gained in suppleness. The off-years can be remarkable. To the connoisseur it is an unmistakable sign that denotes a good *terroir's* potential.

Tour Monrepos (Château)

Commune: Libourne. **Proprietor:** Christian Manaud. Consultant oenologist: M. Legendre. **Size of vineyard:** 0.82 hectares. **Average age of vines:** 40 years. **Varieties:** 5% cabernet sauvignon. 75% merlot. 20% cabernet-franc. **Production:** 3,000 bottles CB. **Direct sales and by mail order:** in France. Christian Manaud, 37 rue des Réaux, 33500 Libourne. Tel. 57 51 49 53. *For Christian Manaud, the vines, which he has inherited from his father, are a hobby.*

Tour Musset (Château) 🛉
→ Tour Saint-Christophe

Tour Peyronneau (Château) 🛉 → Côtes Bernateau

Tour Puyblanquet (Château)

Commune: Saint-Etienne-de-Lisse. **Proprietor:** Daniel Lapoterie. Consultant oenologist: M. Hébrard. **Size of vineyard:** 10 hectares. **Average age of vines:** 30 years. **Varieties:** 20% cabernet-sauvignon. 60% merlot. 20% cabernet-franc. **Production:** 40 tonneaux. 18,000 bottles CB. **Direct sales and by mail order:** in France. Tel. 57 40 17 11. **Retail sales:** through the Bordeaux trade. *Good quality: the list of private customers has grown by itself, without any publicity other than word of mouth. This* cru *probably needs more energetic marketing.*

Tour Saint-Christophe (Château)

Grand Cru

Commune: Saint-Christophe-des-Bardes. **Proprietors:** Monsieur and Madame Henri Guiter. Vineyard manager: Max Itei. Cellar-master: Claude Cubillier. Consultant oenologist: M. Pauquet. **Size of vineyard:** 19 hectares. **Average age of vines:** 30 years. **Varieties:** 50% merlot. 50% cabernet-franc. **Production:** 100,000 bottles CB. **Visiting hours:** Monday to Friday from 8 a.m. to noon and 2 to 6 p.m. Saturdays and Sundays by appointment. Tel. 57 24 77 15. **Direct sales and by mail order:** in France.

Over ninety years of age, Henri Guiter had been the owner of Tour Saint-Christophe since July 1940. The former owner of a château in Pacy-sur-Eure, he had settled in the Saint-Emilion region to escape from the Germans. "I have always been in charge," he used to say with a firm voice despite his age. "I am not a manual worker. I am not even capable of driving a nail home." Until his death in December 1989, M. Henri Guiter used to divide his time between Paris and Saint-Emilion. Behind his desk, a suitcase was always ready. The 85 and 86 vintages won a silver medal at the *Concours général agricole* in Paris, respectively in 1987 and 1988.

Tour Saint-Pierre (Château)

Grand Cru

Commune: Saint-Emilion. **Proprietor:** Jacques Goudineau. **Size of vineyard:** 10 hectares. **Average age of vines:** 25 years. **Varieties:** 5% cabernet-sauvignon. 90% merlot. 5% cabernet-franc. **Production:** 57,000 bottles CB. **Direct sales and by mail order:** in France and abroad. Tel. 57 24 70 23.

Tour Vachon (Château)

Grand Cru

Commune: Saint-Emilion. **Proprietor:** René Rebinguet. Tenant, vineyard manager and cellar master: Jean-Paul Soucaze. Consultant oenologist: M. Hébrard. **Size of vineyard:** 3.53 hectares. **Average age of vines:** 20 years. **Varieties:** 10% cabernet-sauvignon. 70% merlot. 20% cabernet-franc. **Production:** 20,000 bottles CB. **Visits:** by appointment. Tel. 57 24 70 27. **Direct sales and by mail order:** in France and abroad.

Tour Vachon belongs to M. René Rebinguet, the deputy mayor of Saint-Emilion. But it is Jean-Paul Soucaze, his son-in-law, who runs the estate. The vineyard is planted on heavy clinging soil, rich in clay. It faces due north. The 1985 frosts have left their mark. Harvesting is traditional. Vinified in concrete vats, the wine matures in wood. This is all classic stuff, without any trumpery which gives rise to a well-deserved reputation which can only increase.

Touzinat (Château)

Grand Cru

Commune: Saint-Pey-d'Armens. **Proprietors:** Messieurs Seguinel. Consultant oenologists: M. Tabouy and M. Plomby. **Size of vineyard:** 8 hectares. **Varieties:** 75% merlot. 25% cabernet-franc. **Production:** 40 tonneaux. 28,000 bottles CB. **Visits:** tel. 57 47 15 32. **Direct sales and by mail order. Retail sales.**

It's a promise. They will roll out the red carpet to welcome you. Moreover, it is already there in case you should pass by tomorrow. The carpet will lead you to an altar supported by two threaded shafts from grape-presses and housing a famous tabernacle in the shape of a cask, the *chef-d'œuvre* of a master-cooper. Then you will be taken into the cellars where order, calm and tidiness reign supreme and you will be told: "Here, wine is a religion... it is not simply grape-juice but a personality to be recognized, acknowledged and encouraged." The perfectionism resulting from this approach is to be found in the bottle. How I adore tradition when it takes on this aspect! Away with badly scoured *barriques* and dusty phials! Is the stage production pretentious? No sir! It is genuine. And the music that of a superb operetta. As for the wine of Touzinat, it holds its quality over the years.

Trapaud (Château)

Grand Cru

Commune: Saint-Etienne-de-Lisse. **Proprietor:** André Larribière. Consultant oenologist: C.B.C. Libourne. **Size of vineyard:** 12 hectares. **Average age of vines:** 40 years. **Varieties:** 30% cabernet-sauvignon. 60% merlot. 10% cabernet-franc. **Production:** 50,000 bottles CB. **Visits:** by appointment. Tel. 57 40 18 08. **Direct sales and by mail order:** in France and abroad. **Retail sales:** Descas & Fils.

From 1400 to 1807, the Trapaud de Colombes were rich landowners. They lived in the manor of Le Bois, a vine-growing estate belonging to the "Côtes de Castillon" AOC. The religious wars separated the Trapaud de Colombe brothers. That was how it came about that after the battle of Castillon, one set off for England, the other for Denmark, and the third for Germany. In 1967, M. André Larribière, the owner of Château Liamet, was the tenant farmer of four hectares of the Trapaud vineyard. His father, Gaston Larribière, was its owner, but he was too extravagant. That is why André Larribière took it in hand in 1977. But even today, Gaston Larribière, who is more than seventy years old, still retains one hectare which he works with his own tractor. Château Trapaud is situated to the west of Saint-Etienne-de-Lisse. The vines are ploughed in the old-fashioned way and the land is banked up again before harvest.

In 1910, Château Trapaud was listed as a Saint-Emilion second *cru*. At the time, declared yields per hectare were staggering. Now they appear rather feeble, doubtless because of the average age of the vines.

Trianon (Château)

Commune: Saint-Emilion. **Proprietor:** Madame Hubert Lecointre. Consultant oenologist: M. Chaine. **Size of vineyard:** 6.5 hectares. **Average age of vines:** 25 years. **Varieties:** 65% merlot. 35% cabernet-franc. **Production:** 25 tonneaux. **Visits:** tel. 57 51 42 63. **Retail sales:** through the Bordeaux trade.

Trimoulet (Château)

♀ ♀ ♀ ♀ ♀

Grand Cru classé

Commune: Saint-Emilion. **Proprietor:** Michel Jean. **Size of vineyard:** 20 hectares. **Average age of vines:** 40 years. **Varieties:** 10% cabernet-sauvignon. 60% merlot. 25% cabernet-franc. 5% malbec. **Production:** 120,000 bottles CB. **Visits:** by appointment. Tel. 57 24 77 54. **Sales by mail order:** in France and abroad. **Retail sales:** Ets. Pierre Jean S.A.

"Blessed be the Name of God. I, Jean Trimoulet, one-time jurat of Saint-Emilion, recognizing the certainty of death but the uncertainty of its hour, having care for the salvation of my soul and wishing to provide for the disposal of my goods, have duly made my last will and testament..." The will of Jean Trimoulet, dated July 15 1713, contains eight closely written pages. This document has come down over the centuries into our hands in a perfect state of preservation. I would particularly point out the patriarchal mentality which motivated the testator, dividing out all his goods as equitably as possible among his six surviving children (he had had eight by his marriage to Catherine Jourdan). We note that he counts the area of the land in "journals" and "spans". If the measure known as a journal was common (a journal is approximately equivalent to 0.32 hectares) the "span" seems to be a regional measurement in the Libourne area. (In the Médoc, for example, the smallest unit of farm land was the "sadon" – 957 square yards). The "span" represented approximately 59.5 square yards, that is to say that 24 spans made up one journal. In my opinion, this small measurement clearly illustrates the parcelling out of the vineyards in Saint-Emilion, principally on the slopes. By adding up the different parcels of land which he bequeathed to his children, we see that the landed estate of Jean Trimoulet represented about 37 journals, that is approximately twelve hectares. Jean Trimoulet appears to distinguish clearly between "vines" and "arable land". The use of the different lands was mentioned quite specifically in the will. The vineyard of Trimoulet at the beginning of the eighteenth century must have covered 4 to 5 hectares: moreover, the property contained woodlands and coppices which the testator designated by the vague term of "plots".

It is interesting to note that if Jean Trimoulet was anxious to bequeath real estate to each of his children so that each should possess his own land, he was also anxious to preserve the family community. He details linen chests, furniture and utensils, naming the legatees, but he expressly declares that "the house shall be for everybody, so that my children can all live there together in happy peace and union, just as the press and vessels for wine-making shall also be for the use of everybody, and if any repairs are necessary, the expenses shall be shared out equally...". He also mentions precisely the joint ownership of the fountain and the bread oven: "Without quarrelling amongst themselves, they will be able to make their bread in the said oven, one by one, keeping the fire going together with their sisters." The head of the family also thought of the youngest member of the family, who was in the army: "If my children behave correctly and live intelligently in peace and union, I wish that they should enjoy their brother Janot's share during the time he is in the service of the King, without rendering account to him, it being understood that they do not act separately and that they share out their revenues jointly amongst themselves as they do for me." History does not tell us what happened, but each of the heirs was warned: "Wishing that everything should be observed under penalty of being disinherited if they oppose my will."

It was towards 1800 that the Jean family appeared as proprietors of Château Trimoulet. The descendants of today can clearly retrace their family tree right back to the beginning of the eighteenth century, but they cannot establish with any certainty a marriage between themselves and the Trimoulets round about the time of the Revolution. None the less, it is a clear descent in direct line which today leads Michel Jean and his wife to the foot of the slope of Le Cadet, on the north part of the commune of Saint-Emilion. The continuation of the family name is assured but it should also be said that the wines of Trimoulet are at the head of their class: rather rich and tannic with elegant fruit, they are very often wines for long keeping and should be allowed to age. Progress appears to be being made in recent years.

Trimoulet (Clos)

Grand Cru

Commune: Saint-Emilion. **Proprietor:** Guy Appolot. **Size of vineyard:** 7 hectares. **Average age of vines:** 30 years. **Varieties:** 10% cabernet-sauvignon. 80% merlot. 10% cabernet-franc. **Production:** 35 tonneaux. **Visits:** weekdays. Tel. 57 24 71 96. **Direct sales and by mail order:** in France and abroad. *Clean, tidy and spick and span, this château will always offer a delightful welcome to the visitor and agreeable wines.*

Troplong Mondot (Château)

Grand Cru classé

Commune: Saint-Emilion. **Proprietor:** Claude Valette. Manager: Christine Fabre. Cellar master: Jean-Pierre Taleyson. Consultant oenologist: Michel Rolland. **Size of vineyard:** 30 hectares. **Average age of vines:** 40 years. **Varieties:** 15% cabernet-sauvignon. 65% merlot. 10% cabernet-franc. 10% malbec. **Production:** 120,000 bottles. **Visits:** daily except Sunday, preferably by appointment. Tel. 57 24 70 72. **Direct sales and by mail order:** in France. **Retail sales.**

"It is easy to understand that a man at a banquet who has eaten copiously of every course should no longer be hungry and that he should try to revive his satiated palate with the thousand darts of spices and titillating wines; but when a man who has only just sat down at table and has hardly tasted the first dishes is already overcome with extreme repugnance, cannot touch dishes with a delicate flavour without retching

Christine Fabre in the library of Troplong Mondot.

and who likes only gamey meats, cheese marbled with blue, truffles and wines which smell of flint, this is a phenomenon which can result in only one particular outcome; it is like a child of six months who finds his mother's milk insipid and wants to drink *eau-de-vie*."

Was it at Troplong Mondot that Théophile Gautier partly found inspiration for his work? This extract from *Mademoiselle de Maupin* does not lead us directly to think so, but from the literary point of view, it is very much in line with the unsatisfied author's quest for an ideal balance approaching perfection. From a historical standpoint, Théophile did not yet know Senator Raymond Troplong when he wrote his first novel. They became friends during the fifties of the last century and the Father of the Parnassians often found refuge on the President of the Senate's estate. He appreciated good living and his poetic inspiration was awakened when he came into contact with good wine. After dinner, there were interminable conversations. More than once at Mondot, Théophile Gautier and Raymond Théodore Troplong recreated the world. Then they would blow out the candles on the desk and the poet would yawn before droning his favourite pun: "The speeches at Trop-long ("too long") are the shortest of all."

In the eighteenth century, the estate of Pavie-Mondot belonged wholly to the Abbé de Sèze, the brother of one of the defenders of Louis XVI. The *cru* was already well known at court and it held its place in the business world amongst the vineyards of high quality. But it was the jurist Raymond Troplong who created its present unity by bringing several parcels together around a central nucleus, to 289 create an estate of 30 hectares of vines opposite the château. Edouard Troplong, his nephew, succeeded him. He was an administrator who was economical to the point of being avaricious. At the beginning of this century, outraged harvesters burst into the proprietor's dining-room and emptied their plates of inedible lentils over his Aubusson carpet. Milord Troplong, who had not digested the communist leader Waldeck-Rousseau's reading very well, although diatetic, heaved so violently that he disgorged his estate, selling it for a song to the first comer. He came from Belgium. It was Thienpont, the old and famous wine merchant in Etikhove and the future proprietor of Vieux Château Certan in Pomerol: "Look, I bought Troplong Mondot for pleasure. But Vieux Certan is for business, don't you see?"

CHAU TROPLONG·MONDOT
St ÉMILION
GRAND CRU CLASSÉ

Today it is Claude Valette who reigns over the "butte of Mondot" whose highest point is 320 feet, like a dromedary's hump. The soil of clay mixed with decalcified rubble makes the wine extremely concentrated in very hot years. Recently, vinification has made perceptible progress. A fine monument to the past, it seems that Troplong Mondot represents a positive value for the future. Starting from the 82s, which I hope will wait for several years yet before shedding their impatient and dazzling youth.

Trotte Vieille (Château)   ♉ ♉ ♉ ♉ ♉

1er Grand Cru classé

Commune: Saint-Emilion. **Proprietor:** Emile Castéja. Director: Philippe Castéja. Estate manager, vineyard manager and cellar master: Jean Brun. **Size of vineyard:** 10 hectares. **Average age of vines:** 40 years. **Varieties:** 10% cabernet-sauvignon. 50% merlot. 40% cabernet-franc. **Production:** 30,000 bottles CB. **Sales by mail order:** tel. 57 24 71 34 or 56 48 57 57. **Retail sales:** Borie-Manoux, 86 cours Balguerie-Stuttenberg, 33300 Bordeaux.

One fine autumn day in the year of grace 1948, Marcel Borie and his son-in-law Emile Castéja decided to take a trip to Saint-Emilion. Accompanied by Déjean, the broker, an immensely rich man from Bordeaux dressed in the style of Beau Brummel, with the finest waxed moustache in the department, they had an appointment at Troplong Mondot to conclude a purchase of wine. On the way, they passed in front of Trotte Vieille, a more or less abandoned estate, three-quarters of whose vineyard represented an intestate succession lacking inheritors. In front of the cellar, someone was busy cleaning old casks. The visitors started up conversation, and out of curiosity bought two bottles of the new wine, the 1947 vintage. After having finished their dealings at Troplong Mondot, they went off to lunch at the village inn which, at the time, offered hardly any wines of reasonable quality. They gave one of the bottles of Trotte Vieille to the owner and drank the other. A superb wine. Magnificent. Sumptuous. "Tell me, Monsieur Déjean, would this property be on the market?" That was how Borie bought Trotte Vieille, an ancient staging-post, whose reputation as an excellent *cru* had already been established in the nineteenth century. Since then, the vineyard has been restored and maintained at an average age of

Trotte Vieille: a cru *with a poetic name and an enchanting wine.*

40 years, the optimum age to obtain high quality. The cellars have been completely re-styled and their square colonnades have a striking effect. The charming mansion which once used to serve as the principal dwelling has not yet been restored after being completely ransacked in 1964. This is a shame. Emile Castéja has announced his intention of looking into this in the very near future. It would also be possible to arrange the many underground galleries as cellars for ageing, but the lie of the land makes access difficult. Without any troglodytic ageing, the wines of Trotte Vieille are perfectly typical of the clayey-chalky terrain of the best *crus* of Saint-Emilion and entirely deserve their classification among the Firsts.

Truquet (Château)

Commune: Saint-Emilion. **Proprietor:** Jean Maison. Consultant oenologist: Mademoiselle Cazenave. **Size of vineyard:** 6 hectares. **Average age of vines:** 16 years. **Varieties:** 65% merlot. 35% cabernet-franc. **Production:** 30 tonneaux. 20,000 bottles CB. **Direct sales:** tel. 57 51 04 81. **Retail sales.**

Union de Producteurs
de Saint-Emilion (Cave Coopérative)

ᵧ ᵧ ᵧ ᵧ ᵧ

Communes: All the communes of the appellation. **President:** M. Claude Tribaudeau. Vice-Presidents: Messieurs Jean Catusseau and Alain Robin. Manager: M. Jacques-Antoine Baugier. Superintendent: M. Pierre Chaumet. Vineyard specialist: M. Claude Pérès. **Size of vineyard:** 1,000 hectares. **Varieties:** 70% merlot. 20% cabernet-franc. 10% cabernet-sauvignon. **Storage capacity:** 217,000 hectolitres. **Average quantity in hand:** 400 tonneaux and 7,000,000 bottles. **Average annual quantity in bottle:** 3,500,000. **Direct sales:** approximately 500,000 bottles. **Retail sales:** in bulk and in the bottle. **Shop for direct sales:** in Saint-Emilion, Pl. Général de Gaulle, Tel. 57 24 71 80. Open from 9.30 a.m. to 12.30 p.m. and 2 to 7 p.m. every day except Wednesdays. **Offices and cellars:** Haut-Gravet, 33330 Saint-Emilion. Tel. 57 24 70 71. Visits from 8 a.m. to noon and 2 to 6 p.m. every day except Sundays and Public Holidays.

"Saint-Emilion will make a richly inventive poet of you!" The Saint-Emilion Union de Producteurs overlooks no detail in an endeavour to preserve its up-to-date image. The attractive dynamism of this institution can be seen by its commercial approach which is, to use the modern term, very "with it": newspaper articles, receptions for customers and salesmen, public relations, attractive formulae, aesthetic labels, etc., make up part of the co-operative work, as well as vinification, ageing, packing and marketing, and all this assisted by a computer system in the very forefront of technology. Conceived in 1930 and born in 1932, this old lady has become one of the most important in the department. Today she reigns over one thousand hectares within the ancient borough of Saint-Emilion, and her large family counts 386 growers/co-operative members. This dimension alone bears witness to the extent of the affair's importance. At the beginning, it was Robert Villepigue who enrolled a handful of

The Union des Producteurs complex stands out boldly against the vines.

members and communicated to them his confidence in a future to be assured by their solidarity. Despite all the risks inherent in this type of undertaking, it continued to increase steadily, and if we are able to applaud its economic success, we should particularly recognize that the guiding spirit of the *cave* has always engendered a policy of striving after high quality. Right from the start, those responsible had marked out three viticultural areas corresponding to three categories of wine. Naturally, the people bringing their harvest were paid according to the land the grapes came from, and the marketing of the wines rigorously reflected this grading system. Today, the differences in quality are even more clearly established by having been tried and tested over a long time. The different labels of the Saint-Emilion *Grand Cru* represent five levels, and the consumer can easily find the one which best suits his pocket. For the "château" wines, the authenticity of their various origins is respected. Indeed, the vat capacity and the way it is apportioned out enables some fifty *crus* to be vinified separately. The list is as follows:

Château and proprietor	Size (hectares)	Average production (tonneaux)
Saint-Emilion Grand Cru		
Arcie (Ch. d') Baugier, Jacques	4.71	28
Basque (Ch. du) Lafaye, Elie	10.13	65
Bel-air Ouÿ (Ch.) G.F.A. Bel Air Ouÿ	5.5	33
Destieux Berger (Ch.) Cazenave, Alain	10.15	60
Franc Lartigue (Ch.) C. and M. Lafourcade	7.86	48
Grangey (Ch.) Araoz, Félix	6.2	36
Haute-Nauve (Ch.) S.C.E. Haute-Nauve	8.51	35
Haut-Montil (Ch.) Vimeney, André	4.3	23
La Boisserie (Ch.) Boisserie, Louis	7.84	37
La Bonnelle (Ch.) Sulzer, François	6.5	36
Lamartre (Ch.) Vialard, C.	10.55	65
Le Loup (Ch.) Garrigue, Patrick	6.27	40
Mauvinon (Ch.) G.F.A. Mauvinon	14.18	70
Paran Justice (Ch.) Barbier, Odette	10.25	60
Peyrouquet (Ch.) Cheminade, Maurice	16.28	104
Piney (Ch.) S.C.E. Piney	8.58	54
Viramière Dumon, Pierrette	9.85	57
Saint-Emilion		
Barail du Blanc (Ch.) Ellies, Jean-Jacques	5.55	32
Benitey (Ch.) Simon, Guy	5.67	35
Billerond (Ch.) Robin, Alain	10.15	60
Capet-Pailhas (Ch.) Duverger, Michel	6.77	41
Cazenave (Ch.) Champagne, Maxime	7.81	48
Côte de Tauzinat (Ch.) Bernard, Alain	5.89	36
Despagnet (Ch.) Faure, Paule	6.02	33
Franc Jaugue Blanc (Ch.) Borde, Michel	7.48	32
Franc Le Maine S.C.E. Franc Le Maine	11.13	66
Francs Bories (Ch.) Roux, Jean	8.15	53
Gombaud Ménichot (Ch.) Piccolo, Bernard	10.33	65
Grand Bouquey (Ch.) Robles, Joseph José	8.73	53

Haut-Bruly (Ch.)			
Cante heirs	6.83	40	
Hautes Versannes (Ch.)			
Lacoste Père & Fils	10.98	67	
Haut-Lavergne (Ch.)			
Macaud, Yves	4.93	27	
Haut-Moureaux			
G.A.E.C. Courrèche	9.02	55	
Jauma (Ch.)			
G.F.A. Larcis Jauma	8.92	49	
Juguet (Ch.)			
Landrodie, Maurice	8.77	55	
Labrie (Ch.)			
Baylan, Michel	10.09	61	
Larguet (Ch.)			
S.C.E. Larguet	8.12	49	
La Rouchonne (Ch.)			
Lapelletrie, Claude	9.21	52	
La Tonnelle (Ch.)			
Arnaud Père & Fils	12.01	75	
Lavignère (Ch.)			
Vallier, Dominique	11.87	70	

Les Graves d'Armens (Ch.)			
Dubuc Père & Fils	4.55	40	
Lisse (Ch. de)			
Nebout, Germaine	4.5	28	
Mazouet (Ch.)			
Pouillet, Jean-Claude	6.59	36	
Mondou Mérignan (Ch.)			
Danglade, Georges	6.44	26	
Moulin de la Chapelle (Ch.)			
Magontier Succession	4.78	29	
Pagnac (Ch.)			
Pagnac, Jean	6.21	40	
Queyron Patarabet (Ch.)			
Itey, François	9.48	47	
Rastouillet Lescure (Ch.)			
Duvergt, Régina	8.24	50	
Vieux Garrouilh (Ch.)			
Servant Père & Fils	8.05	40	
Vieux Labarthe (Ch.)			
G.A.E.C. de Labarthe	7.38	45	
Yon (Ch.)			
Quenouille, Jean	4.10	25	

When the director, Jacques-Antoine Baugier, says that his wines are a clear and perfect example of Saint-Emilion wine, we have the right to let ourselves be convinced. In this *cave coopérative*, quantity and quality are judiciously determined. It would have been easy to practise a certain levelling out of more or less standardized products. This concept is practised now only at the level of the basic appellation, improperly called "generic", but, on this foundation, an easily identifiable pyramid has been constructed. At one and the same time, the Union de Producteurs is able to provide wine merchants with sizeable quantities of wines coming from clearly differentiated vats and it can offer the widest choice of individual wines that could

A traffic jam: the procession of harvesters at the co-opérative.

The members of the Executive Board.

hope to be found in the co-operative movement of the Gironde. In addition, note should be made of the happy balance of this production within the framework of the whole of the appellation, a balance expressed by an important rôle in regulating the market, for if the same volumes were under the control of several *caves*, there would be inevitable marketing hiatuses. It is said that a nation gets the government it deserves. We can also say that Saint-Emilion deserves such a *cave coopérative*.

The Executive Board of the Cave Coopérative "Union de Producteurs de Saint-Emilion"

		Members
President	Claude Tribaudeau	
Vice-Presidents	Jean Catusseau	Guy Arnaud
	Alain Robin	Alain Bernard
		Michel Borde
Secretary	François Sulzer	Maurice Cheminade
		Jean Dumon
Treasurer	Maurice Landrodie	Michel Duverger
		Charles Lafourcade
		Patrick de Lesquen
		Dominique Vallier
		Claude Vialard

Val d'Or (Château du)

Grand Cru

Commune: Vignonet. **Proprietor:** Anne-Marie Bardet. Vineyard manager and cellar master: Philippe Bardet. Consultant oenologist: M. Hébrard. **Size of vineyard:** 23 hectares. **Average age of vines:** 25 years. **Varieties:** 5% cabernet-sauvignon. 80% merlot. 15% cabernet-franc. **Production:** 138,000 bottles CB. **Visits:** by appointment. Tel. 57 84 53 16. **Direct sales and by mail order. Retail sales:** through the Bordeaux trade.

Orval, a little commune in the department of Dordogne where M. Henri-Gabriel Bardet came from, became Val d'Or. Roger Bardet, his son, made every effort to construct a cellar. On either side of the vat-house, three imposing stainless steel vats rear up to the roofing-timbers. The wine is aged in underground glass-lined tanks.

Vallon de Fongaban (Clos)

Commune: Saint-Emilion. **Proprietor:** Roger Roberti. Consultant oenologist: M. Pauquet. **Size of vineyard:** 0.075 hectares. **Average age of vines:** 30 years. **Varieties:** 60% merlot. 40% cabernet-franc. **Production:** 250 bottles CB. Roger Roberti, 12 avenue de l'Epinette, 33500 Libourne. Tel. 57 74 01 22. *Without any doubt, Saint-Emilion's rarest wine, crushed in a hand-press and aged in its one and only cask.*

Veyrac (Château)

Commune: Saint-Etienne-de-Lisse. **Proprietor:** Jean-Robert Bellanger. Consultant oenologist: M. Chaine. **Size of vineyard:** 13.5 hectares. **Average age of vines:** 30 years. **Varieties:** 10% cabernet-sauvignon. 80% merlot. 10% cabernet-franc. **Production:** 72,000 bottles CB. **Direct sales and by mail order:** in France and abroad: Switzerland, England. Tel. 57 40 18 37. **Retail sales:** C.V.C.B. Joanne. *"The one thing that counts is the land", he says, "and it is better to live independently – but that creates problems when you are old."*

Vieille Tour la Rose (Château)

Commune: Saint-Emilion. **Proprietors:** Messieurs Jean Ybert & Fils. Consultant oenologist: Grézillac Laboratory. **Size of vineyard:** 5 hectares. **Average age of vines:** 20 years. **Varieties:** 5% cabernet-sauvignon. 80% merlot. 15% cabernet-franc. **Production:** 25 tonneaux. 20,000 bottles CB. **Visits:** Daniel Ybert. Tel. 57 24 73 41. **Direct sales and by mail order:** in France. **Retail sales.** *Daniel Ybert likes you to wait a few years before tasting his wine. He is right.*

Vieux Cantenac (Château)

Grand Cru

Commune: Saint-Emilion. **Proprietor:** Marcel Rebeyrol. Cellar master: Alain Rebeyrol. Consultant oenologist: C.B.C. Libourne. **Size of vineyard:** 5.22 hectares. **Average age of vines:** 30 years. **Varieties:** 10% cabernet-sauvignon. 70% merlot. 20% cabernet-franc. **Production:** 35 tonneaux. 20,000 bottles CB. **Direct sales and by mail order:** in France and abroad. Tel. 57 51 35 21. **Retail sales.** *Vieux Cantenac is characterized by very high yields and a very low fixed level of acidity. This wine is modern in style, and is at its best when drunk young and chilled.*

Vieux Château Bois Grouley 🍾

→ *Perey-Grouley*

Vieux Château Carré

Grand Cru

Commune: Libourne. **Proprietor:** Yvon Dubost. Consultant oenologist: M. Callède. **Size of vineyard:** 3 hectares. **Average age of vines:** 15 to 20 years. **Varieties:** 25% cabernet sauvignon. 50% merlot. 25% cabernet-franc. **Production:** 24,000 bottles CB. **Visits:** tel. 57 51 74 57. **Direct sales and by mail order:** M. Dubost, Catusseau, 33500 Pomerol. **Retail sales.**

"Vieux Château Carré is situated at the very gates of Libourne. Close to Châteaux Tailhas and Taillefer in Pomerol, it benefits from the extension of the substrata of that appellation. The land is of very warm ferruginous sand, allowing early harvesting. The substratum is a bed of iron-pan giving the wine a rich bouquet." That is how Yvon Dubost, the mayor of Pomerol, describes his Saint-Emilion estate. He welcomes the visitor very warmly at his house in Catusseau, and everybody will appreciate both the quality of his wine and the warmth of his hospitality.

Vieux Château Croix de Figeac

Grand Cru

Commune: Saint-Emilion. **Proprietor:** Georges Meunier. Consultant oenologist: M. Pauquet. **Size of vineyard:** 3.5 hectares. **Average age of vines:** 35 years. **Varieties:** 10% cabernet-sauvignon. 60% merlot. 30% cabernet-franc. **Production:** 18,000 bottles CB. **Retail sales:** Villars & Salin (Bordeaux).

Vieux Château des Moines ♟ → Plaisance

Vieux Château Haut-Béard

Commune: Saint-Laurent-des-Combes. **Proprietor:** Jean Riboulet. **Size of vineyard:** 4.24 hectares. **Varieties:** 5% cabernet-sauvignon. 95% merlot. **Direct sales and by mail order:** in France. Jean Riboulet, 23 route de Saint-Emilion, 33500 Libourne or Les Grandes Plantes, 33330 Saint-Laurent-des-Combes. Tel. 57 24 62 71 or 57 51 36 40. *Monsieur Jean Riboulet is also the owner of Vieux Château Hautes Graves Beaulieu in Pomerol.*

Vieux Château l'Abbaye

Grand Cru

label
not
communicated

Commune: Saint-Christophe-des-Bardes. **Proprietor:** Françoise Lladères. Consultant oenologist: M. Chaine. **Size of vineyard:** 0.75 hectares. **Average age of vines:** 25 years. **Varieties:** 70% merlot. 30% cabernet-franc. **Production:** 4,800 bottles CB. **Direct sales and by mail order:** Françoise Lladères, Le Cauze, 33330 Saint-Christophe-des-Bardes. Tel. 57 24 77 01. *A pocket handkerchief newly taken in hand to make a luxury fancy kerchief of it. This is simply a way of saying that there will never be enough for everybody.*

Vieux Château la Demoiselle

Commune: Saint-Christophe-des-Bardes. **Proprietor:** Jean-Roland Macaud. Consultant oenologist: Gilles Pauquet. **Size of vineyard:** 2 hectares. **Average age of vines:** 20 years. **Varieties:** 5% cabernet-sauvignon. 90% merlot. 5% cabernet-franc. **Production:** 8 tonneaux. 1,900 bottles CB. **Direct sales and by mail order:** tel. 57 24 77 24. **Retail sales.** *The mayor of Saint-Christophe-des-Bardes is in love with his old Demoiselle, which has belonged to his family for more than a century.*

Vieux Château Mazerat ♟ → Haut-Mazerat

Vieux Château Montlabert

Commune: Saint-Emilion. **Proprietor:** M. and Madame Moulinet. Tel. 57 24 74 27. Consultant oenologist: M. Rolland. **Size of vineyard:** 0.76 hectares. **Average age of vines:** 12 years. **Varieties:** 65% merlot. 35% cabernet-franc. **Production:** 4 tonneaux. **Retail sales:** to Belgium in bulk.

Vieux Château Pelletan

Grand Cru

Commune: Saint-Christophe-des-Bardes. **Proprietor:** Marc Magnaudeix. Consultant oenologist: M. Chaine. **Size of vineyard:** 8 hectares. **Average age of vines:** 30 years. **Varieties:** 5% cabernet-sauvignon. 60% merlot. 35% cabernet-franc. **Production:** 45,000 bottles CB. **Visits:** all the year round. Tel. 57 24 77 55. **Direct sales and by mail order:** in France and abroad. *The parcelling out of the vineyard brings about a variety of different soils, producing a wine with its own individual character.*

Vieux Château Peymouton

Commune: Saint-Christophe-des-Bardes. **Proprietor:** Joseph Hecquet-Milon. Consultant oenologist: C.I.V.R.B. Bergerac. **Size of vineyard:** 8.5 hectares. **Average age of vines:** 15 years. **Varieties:** 20% cabernet-sauvignon. 60% merlot. 20% cabernet-franc. **Production:** 43 tonneaux. 20,000 bottles CB. **Direct sales and by mail order:** Joseph Hecquet-Milon, Les Petities, Saint-André-et-Appelles, 33220 Sainte-Foy-la-Grande. Tel. 57 46 00 52. **Retail sales:** A. Quancard; Johnston. *Modern methods for an old château.*

Vieux Château Vachon

Commune: Saint-Emilion. **Proprietor:** Michel Lavandier. Vineyard managers and cellar masters: Thierry and Michel Lavandier. Consultant oenologist: Grézillac Laboratory. **Size of vineyard:** 5 hectares. **Average age of vines:** 25 years. **Varieties:** 85% merlot. 15% cabernet-franc. **Production:** 30,000 bottles CB. **Visits:** tel. 57 24 71 14. **Direct sales and by mail order. Retail sales:** Maison Sichel & Cie. *Constant and carefully controlled quality at reasonable price.*

Vieux Clos Saint-Emilion (Château)

Grand Cru

Commune: Saint-Emilion. **Proprietor:** G.F.A. Le Hénanff-Terras. Director: Michel Terras. Consultant oenologist: C.B.C. Libourne. **Size of vineyard:** 6 hectares. **Average age of vines:** 30 years. **Varieties:** 20% cabernet-sauvignon. 50% merlot. 25% cabernet-franc. 5% malbec. **Production:** 36,000 bottles CB. **Visits:** tel. 57 24 60 91. **Direct sales and by mail order. Retail sales:** through the Bordeaux trade. *Modern cultivation and vinification with 30% of the harvest aged in new wood. This* cru *lackes that little something which might turn it into a great wine.*

Vieux Faurie (Château)

Commune: Saint-Emilion. **Proprietor:** Daniel Giraud. Vineyard managers: Daniel and Sandrine Giraud. Consultant oenologist: C.B.C. Libourne. **Size of vineyard:** 6 hectares. **Average age of vines:** 25 years. **Varieties:** 10% cabernet-sauvignon. 80% merlot. 10% cabernet-franc. **Production:** 36,000 bottles CB. **Visits:** tel. 57 24 75 45. **Direct sales and by mail order. Retail sales:** Jean-Pierre Moueix. *When his father died in 1967, Daniel Giraud was only nineteen. Since then, he has run the family estate entirely alone, although he is now helped by his daughter Sandrine.*

Vieux Fortin (Château)

Grand Cru

Commune: Saint-Emilion. **Proprietor:** Marie-Thérèse Tomasina. Tenant: S.C.I. Georges Bigaud and Matignon. Vineyard manager and cellar master: Georges Bigaud. Consultant oenologist: Gilles Pauquet. **Size of vineyard:** 5.4 hectares. **Average age of vines:** 40 years. **Varieties:** 60% merlot. 20% cabernet-franc. 20% pressac. **Production:** 22,000 bottles CB. **Direct sales and by mail order:** in France. Georges Bigaud, 150 av. du Général de Gaulle, 33500 Libourne. Madame Tomasina, 31 rue Manin, 75019 Paris. **Retail sales:** through the Bordeaux trade. *A little enclave between Châteaux Figeac and Cheval Blanc, this land has the basic requirements for giving good quality.*

Vieux-Garrouilh (Château)
→ Union de Producteurs

Vieux Grand Faurie (Château)

→ Champion

Vieux-Guadet (Château)

Grand Cru

Commune: Saint-Emilion. **Proprietor:** Jean-François Carrille. Cellar master: J.-P. Regrenil. Consultant oenologist: M. Rolland. **Size of vineyard:** 2.5 hectares. **Average age of vines:** 30 years. **Varieties:** 10% cabernetsauvignon. 70% merlot. 20% cabernet-franc. **Production:** 14,000 bottles. **Visits:** by appointment. Tel. 57 24 74 46. **Direct sales and by mail order:** in France and abroad. Maison d'Aliénor, place du Marcadien, 33330 Saint-Emilion. **Retail sales:** Société Producta, 24130 La Monzie Saint-Martin. *In an old building belonging to this* cru *the will and testament of the father of the* député *Guadet – guillotined during the Reign of Terror – was found.*

Vieux Guillou (Château)

Commune: Saint-Emilion. **Proprietor:** Paul Menguy. Consultant oenologist: C.B.C. Libourne. **Size of vineyard:** 0.7 hectares. **Average age of vines:** 50 years. **Varieties:** 30% cabernet-sauvignon. 40% merlot. 30% cabernet-franc. **Production:** 4,500 bottles CB. **Direct sales and by mail order:** Paul Menguy, Saint-Georges, 33570 Lussac. Tel. 57 74 62 09.

Vieux-Guinot (Château du)

Grand Cru

Commune: Saint-Etienne-de-Lisse. **Proprietor:** Jean-Pierre Rollet. Vineyard manager: Marcel Zamparo. Cellar master: Luca Zamparo. Consultant oenologist: François Maurin. **Size of vineyard:** 10 hectares. **Varieties:** 20% cabernetsauvignon. 55% merlot. 25% cabernet-franc. **Production:** 59,000 bottles CB. **Direct sales and by mail order:** in France and abroad. Vignobles Rollet, B.P. 23, 33330 Saint-Emilion. Tel. 57 47 15 13.

"A wine as seductive in its aromatic dashing youth as in the bouquet of its fully-blown maturity." The Rollets have been growers/poets from father to son since Louis XV came into his majority. As for the wine, its colour is of heavy velvet and its bouquet has a subtle femininity. But according to its creators, its body is firm and virile. When very young, the wines of Vieux-Guinot have cherry aromas in which, time, develop into something rather resembling dried fig and crystallized fruit.

Vieux Jean-Marie (Château)

Commune: Saint-Emilion. **Proprietor:** Georges Fauchier.
Size of vineyard: 1.37 hectares. **Average age of vines:**
25 years. **Varieties:** 10% cabernet-sauvignon. 80% merlot.
10% cabernet-franc. **Production:** 7,000 bottles CB. **Visits:**
tel 57 51 46 07. **Direct sales and by mail order:** in France.
Vieux Jean-Marie can be trusted to make honest wines.
Georges Fauchier is a serious and conscientious grower in
whom one can safely have complete confidence.

Vieux Labarthe

→ Union de Producteurs

Vieux Larmande (Château)

Grand Cru

Commune: Saint-Emilion. **Proprietor:** Marc Magnaudeix.
Consultant oenologist: M. Chaine. **Size of vineyard:** 4 hectares. **Average age of vines:** 30 years. **Varieties:** 70% merlot.
30% cabernet-franc. **Production:** 20,000 bottles CB. **Visits:**
all the year round. Tel. 57 24 77 55. **Direct sales and by**
mail order: in France and abroad. *I am not entirely sure*
that fermentation taking place with grape stalks still present
is in the best of traditions. Rather I would say it is bad prac-
tice.

Vieux Lartigue (Château)

Commune: Saint-Sulpice-de-Faleyrens. **Proprietor:** S.C.I.
Vieux Lartigue. Director: Claude Mazière. **Size of vine-**
yard: 6 hectares. **Average age of vines:** 20 to 30 years.
Varieties: 30% merlot. 70% cabernet-franc. **Production:**
36,000 bottles CB. **Retail sales:** S.A.R.L. Mazière & Cie.
Tel. 57 24 70 42.

"I know quite well what I am like," says Claude Mazière with a grin. "The French-
man is a curious individual who knows how to make the best wine, but wine which
is less good, too. He is not lazy when it comes to manipulating the corkscrew. You
don't collect wine; you drink it. Before us, there were the Romans, then the Spanish.
We competed with them. Tomorrow there will be the Americans then the Russians.
We are resting on our laurels. Wine: you make it, you sell it, you drink it and you
piss it out!" After these discharging remarks, I award him two glasses, with honours
in History and a special mention in the Order of Bacchus.

Vieux Lescours (Château) ♟

→ Carteau Côtes Daugay

Vieux-Maurins (Château)

Commune: Saint-Sulpice-de-Faleyrens. **Proprietors:** M. and Madame Michel Goudal. **Size of vineyard:** 8 hectares. **Average age of vines:** 25 years. **Varieties:** 22% cabernet-sauvignon. 55% merlot. 20% cabernet-franc. 3% malbec. **Production:** 55 tonneaux. **Visits:** tel. 57 24 62 96. **Direct sales and by mail order:** in France and abroad. **Retail sales:** 75% sold to wine merchants.

Created thirty years ago by Michel Goudal's parents, this property lies on the plain of Saint-Emilion, between the hillside and the river Dordogne. Formerly it was entirely given over to the cultivation of cereals but they realized that wine nourished better than bread. Michel Goudal and his wife took this estate over in January 1984, and every year they hope to improve the conditions of cultivation, vinification and ageing. Their recent vintages appear highly successful. I think that this château ought to make a commercial breakthrough and that the wine merchants should offer encouragement to make it the general rule to bottle at the château in order to make it a Saint-Emilion *Grand Cru*. If this *cru* is not very well known, it is the gault of these who sell it and not of those who make it.

Vieux Moulin du Cadet (Château)

Grand Cru

Commune: Saint-Emilion. **Proprietor:** Gilbert Gombeau. Consultant oenologist: M. Chaine. **Size of vineyard:** 4 hectares. **Average age of vines:** 28 years. **Varieties:** 22% cabernet-sauvignon. 70% merlot. 8% cabernet-franc. **Production:** 24,000 bottles CB. **Direct sales and by mail order:** in France and abroad. Tel. 57 74 47 16. *The same team of gipsies has been coming to harvest every year for twenty-two years. The origin of the vineyard goes back as far as 1870.*

Vieux Pineuilh (Clos)

Commune: Saint-Christophe-des-Bardes. **Proprietors:** Madame Moreau & her son François. Consultant oenologist: Alain Routurier. **Size of vineyard:** 0.78 hectares. **Average age of vines:** 20 years. **Varieties:** 30% cabernet-sauvignon. 35% merlot. 35% cabernet-franc. **Production:** 2 tonneaux. **Direct sales:** tel. 57 24 77 61. **Retail sales.**

Vieux Pourret (Château)

Grand Cru

Commune: Saint-Emilion. **Proprietor:** S.C. du Château Vieux Pourret. Director: Michel Boutet. Consultant oenologist: Rémy Cassignard. **Size of vineyard:** 4 hectares. **Average age of vines:** 35 years. **Varieties:** 80% merlot. 20% cabernet-franc. **Production:** 24,000 bottles CB. **Visits:** by appointment. Tel. 57 24 70 86. **Direct sales and by mail order:** in France. *One of the many vineyards of Michel Boutet, which produces a wine of a good average quality.*

Vieux Rivallon (Château)

Grand Cru

Commune: Saint-Emilion. **Proprietor:** Charles Bouquey. **Size of vineyard:** 12 hectares. **Average age of vines:** 35 years. **Varieties:** 10% cabernet-sauvignon. 50% merlot. 35% cabernet-franc. 5% malbec. **Production:** 60,000 bottles CB. **Visits:** by appointment. Tel. 57 51 35 27. **Direct sales and by mail order:** in France and abroad: Belgium, Switzerland, England. **Retail sales.**

At the foot of the hillside, Vieux Rivallon lies to the west on the plain of Saint-Emilion. It is next to the vines of Châteaux Le Grand Mayne and Couvent des Jacobins. Charles Bouquey, its proprietor, is a man of the soil who knows what he is about. "My roots are in growing," he says proudly. Coming from a long line of vignerons, Charles Bouquey also runs Château Le Grand Faurie and Château du Roy. He and his wine deserve to be known.

Vieux Sarpe (Château)

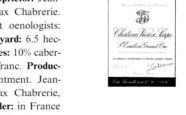

Grand Cru

Commune: Saint-Christophe-des-Bardes. **Proprietor:** Jean-François Janoueix. Vineyard manager: Max Chabrerie. Cellar master: Paul Cazenave. Consultant oenologists: M. Legendre and M. Pauquet. **Size of vineyard:** 6.5 hectares. **Average age of vines:** 20 years. **Varieties:** 10% cabernet sauvignon. 70% merlot. 20% cabernet-franc. **Production:** 48,000 bottles CB. **Visits:** by appointment. Jean-François Janoueix, tel. 57 51 41 86 or Max Chabrerie, tel. 57 24 70 98. **Direct sales and by mail order:** in France and abroad. Jean-François Janoueix, 37 rue Pline Parmentier, 33500 Libourne.

The mill of Sarpe dates from 1732. It has been carefully restored. The vines are sandwiched in between Haut-Sarpe and Trotte Vieille. Recently, furrows dug out by the Romans have been discovered. This was how they prepared their plantations. During the last twenty years, the wines of Château Vieux Sarpe have collected many

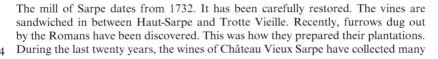

distinctions. Every year, customers of the château are invited to help with the harvest. The *cru* has made inroads into the world of restaurants of standing and vaunts its now traditional position as supplier to the President of the Republic. Presidents may come and go, but Vieux Sarpe goes on for ever. For the true connoisseurs, this wine may justifiably claim to represent the deepest heartland of Saint-Emilion.

Ville des Maures (Château) 🗓

→ *Cardinal-Villemaurine*

Villemaurine (Château)

🍷 🍷 🍷 🍷 🍷

Grand Cru classé

Commune: Saint-Emilion. **Proprietor:** Robert Giraud. Consultant oenologist: M. Guimberteau. **Size of vineyard:** 8 hectares. **Average age of vines:** 40 years. **Varieties:** 30% cabernet-sauvignon. 70% merlot. **Production:** 45,000 bottles CB. **Visiting hours:** Tuesday to Saturday from 8 a.m. to noon and 2 to 6 p.m. Madame Ramos, tel. 57 74 46 44. **Direct sales:** Robert Giraud, Château Timberlay, 33240 Saint-André-de-Cubzac. Tel. 57 43 01 44. **Retail sales:** Robert Giraud S.A., B.P. 31, Domaine de Loiseau, 33240 Saint-André-de-Cubzac.

"Among the seventy-two *Grands Crus*, there are two excellent ones which warrant being upgraded in the near future: Château Villemaurine and Château Balestard-la-Tonnelle... During the period of the 1977 harvest, while I was wandering through the spectacular cellars of Villemaurine, I spotted a recess where the former proprietors had stacked old bottles. M. Giraud was behind me. I gently lifted one up. It was covered with mould and spiders' webs. It was a Villemaurine 1899. I suggested to M. Giraud that I invite him to lunch on condition that we open this bottle. We went straight away to the restaurant called *Chez Germaine* to eat some Bayonne ham and cheese. After drawing the cork, which crumbled into powder, Giraud and I drank an unforgettable wine. A month later, already knowing this hiding-place, we took a bottle of the same vintage to the *Hôtel de Plaisance*, near Villemaurine. Our lunch consisted of lamprey *à la bordelaise*, that is, cooked in a sauce of red wine. This second bottle of 1899 was good, even excellent, but less memorable than the one we had drunk the preceding month. So we then understood how identical wines of the same *cru* and the same vintage can be different after a long period of ageing."

That was the High Pontiff of wine, the late Alexis Lichine, relating one of his pilgrimages into the Holy Land of Saint-Emilion. I must acknowledge that he had good business sense for I would willingly exchange two meals at more than one thousand francs each for two glasses of Villemaurine 1899! In my opinion, the amiable Robert Giraud was rooked. I would at least have demanded the nationally famous chef Michel Guérard in person to be in the kitchen! In any case, this anecdote enables you to judge the exquisite simplicity of the master of the place and the occasionally excessive demands of the master of ceremonies. The place is called Villemaurine – that is well known – since the occupation of the Moors who made a fortified area of it.

The château itself was constructed in the middle of the last century. The architect was fortunately sober. Apart from the venerable vines planted on the high limestone plateau to the east of the town, the most remarkable site is that of the underground

Villemaurine is the one Moorish town where wine features in local religion.

cellars, certainly the largest in the region. It is incredible, but true: they extend under almost the whole of the vineyard and, in particular, house the most distinguished collection of vintages you could dream of, from 1865 up to today. Just imagine that recent harvests can age perfectly in comfort without any need for the tonneaux to be piled one on top of the other and that one thousand five hundred visitors can sample the wine (what a severe racking off!), and all conforming to the rules of classical theatre, in a perfect unity of time, place and action. Yes, Villemaurine is a great Saint-Emilion classic. Today Robert Giraud exports directly to more than forty countries. But it is particularly Philippe who is the globe-trotter. The proof: he brought back an excellent article on Villemaurine from Venezuela. You would say it was a translation from Féret: *"Entre los excelentes vinos disponibles en el mercado*

con buena relacion de callidad-precio, el Château Villemaurine aporta la distincion de su clase que ha merecido los elogios de los catadores mas exigentes." Next time, I shall try to procure the eighth century literal Arabic version for you. La noblesse Villemaurine oblige. But, had he been acquainted with it, Mahomet would not have forbidden drinking wine. Prophets are sometimes lacking in perspicacity.

Viramière (Château)

→ *Union de Producteurs*

Grand Cru

Viramon (Château)

🍷🍷🍷🍷🍷

Commune: Saint-Etienne-de-Lisse. **Proprietor:** G.A.E.C. Vignobles Lafaye Père & Fils. Director: Joël Lafaye. Estate manager: Michel Lafaye. Consultant oenologist: Ets. Chaine & Cazenave. **Size of vineyard:** 6 hectares. **Average age of vines:** 25 years. **Varieties:** 30% cabernet-sauvignon. 70% merlot. **Production:** 42,000 bottles CB. **Visits:** by appointment. Tel. 57 40 18 28. **Direct sales and by mail order:** in France. **Retail sales:** through Bordeaux and Libourne. *Joël Lafaye is an erudite man who never refuses you a taste of his wine.*

Vray Petit Figeac (Château)

🍷🍷🍷🍷🍷

Commune: Saint-Emilion. **Proprietors:** Messieurs Raymond and Jean-Claude Pateau. **Size of vineyard:** 1.73 hectares. **Average age of vines:** 12 years. **Varieties:** 10% cabernet sauvignon. 75% merlot. 15% cabernet-franc. **Production:** 8 tonneaux. **Direct sales:** M. Pateau, tel. 57 24 76 56. **Retail sales.**

The large parcel of Petit Figeac on the Land Register covers an area of almost eight hectares. It is split up between several proprietors, of whom Thierry Manoncourt of Château Figeac is the principal one. The others are: Dumon, Pateau, the domaines Prats, Signiska, and Viaud-Gimberteau. Any use of the name of Petit Figeac other than by the above-named growers is unauthorized. Raymond and Jean-Claude Pateau's vines are on the east side of the locality. They are protected from the northwest winds by the forest land of Château Figeac. Since 1974, bottling has been done at the château. The merlot is currently giving maximum yields.

Yon (Château)

→ *Union de Producteurs*

Yon-Figeac (Château)

Grand Cru classé

Commune: Saint-Emilion. **Proprietor:** G.F.A. du Château Yon-Figeac. Director: Bernard Germain. Vineyard manager and cellar master: Pierre Meunier. Consultant oenologist: Jean-François Gadeau. **Size of vineyard:** 22.8 hectares. **Average age of vines:** 25 years. **Varieties:** 80% merlot. 20% cabernet-franc. **Production:** 120,000 bottles CB. **Visits:** daily. Tel. 57 74 47 58. **Retail sales:** through the Bordeaux trade.

"The wine of Château Yon-Figeac, is known for its qualities of finesse and mellowness, which make it much sought after by gourmets. In addition to its bouquet, which is very much appreciated by connoisseurs, derived from the geological composition of the subsoil, there is the attractiveness of its clear, bright colour, a sure testimony to the assiduous and expert care lavished on this property to ensure its perfect purity." *(Bordeaux and its wines.*Ed. Féret, 1986).

Yon-La-Fleur (Château)

Commune: Saint-Christophe-des-Bardes. **Proprietor:** Jean Menozzi. Consultant oenologist: C.B.C. Libourne. **Size of vineyard:** 3 hectares. **Average age of vines:** 30 years. **Varieties:** 70% merlot. 30% cabernet-franc. **Production:** 14,000 bottles CB. **Retail sales:** Maison Vins de France. *In 1965, Jean Menozzi succeeded his father-in-law at this little vineyard.*

Yon Lavallade (Château) ⚲ → Lavallade

Yon Tour-Figeac (Château)

Commune: Saint-Emilion. **Proprietor:** Raymond Dusseaut. Consultant oenologist: C.B.C. Libourne. **Size of vineyard:** 5 hectares. **Average age of vines:** 23 years. **Varieties:** 65% merlot. 35% cabernet-franc. **Production:** 25 tonneaux. 14,000 bottles CB. **Visits:** tel. 57 24 73 92. **Direct sales and by mail order. Retail sales:** Maison Lebègue.

The Dusseauts' genealogical tree is deeply rooted in the soil of Libourne, both at Saint-Emilion and at Fronsac. For this family of growers, simplicity makes up their *joie de vivre* and sincerity can also be called love of their work. For the visitor, the reception room is the kitchen. No hint of contrived rusticity for the tourist, but great and genuine nobility, what Mauriac called honest simplicity.

The Universal Exhibition Awards List of 1867 (in which 37 Saint-Emilion crus obtained the jury's Great Gold Medal)

Twelve years after the famous classification of the *crus* of the Médoc, the best Saint-Emilion *crus* were recompensed. But the awards list was not officially recognized. However, the list is a historical document, a formal reference which can serve to indicate the best terrains, according to objective criteria.

Name of the cru	Proprietor
MONDOT	His Excellency, President Troplong
L'ARROSÉE	Requier, mortgages' register
AUSONE	Cantenat
BALESTARD LA TONNELLE	Du Courrech
BEAUSÉJOUR	Ducarpe junior
BÉLAIR (FORMERLY CRU DE CANOLLE)	Baron de Marignan
BELLEVUE	Gaston Lacaze
CADET	Albert Piola
CADET	Duperrieu
CADET	Justin Bon
CANON	Count de Bonneval, medical practitioner
LA CARTE	Martineau
CHAPELLE-MADELEINE	Bon Barat
CLOS FOURTET	Emile Leperche
LA CLUSIÈRE	Amédée Thibeaud
CÔTE BALEAU	Commander Coste-Cotty
LA COUSPAUDE	Commander Lolliot
DAUGAY	Alezais
FONPLEGADE	Countess de Galard
GAUBERT	Corre
LES GRANDES MURAILLES	Malen, station-master
LARCIS	Ducasse
LA MADELEINE	Domecq-Cazaux
PAVIE	Adolphe Pigasse, medical practitioner
PEYGENESTOU	Count Léo de Malet-Roquefort
PIMPINELLE	Fayard
PIMPINELLE	Chapus
SARPES	Ducarpe senior
SARPES	Count de Carles
SOUTARD	Madame Barry-Berthomieux d'Allard
SAINT-GEORGES	Henri Gourssies
SAINT-JULIEN	Lacombe-Guadet
LES TROIS MOULINS	Duplessis-Fourcaud
TROTTEVIEILLE	Georges Isambert
LAROQUE	Marquis Maurice de Rochefort-Lavie
FOMBRAUGE	Ferdinand de Taffard Saint-Germain
FERRAND	Fornerod de Mons

Saint-Emilion: the last thirty-four vintages

Year	Points	Comments
1956	8	Year of the terrible frosts. Cheval Blanc harvested a single *tonneau*.
1957	12	Hard acidic wines which will never open up, except those from sheltered slopes.
1958	11	Light and delicate. To be drunk now if there are any left in the cellar.
1959	16	Not up to their reputation although the *grands crus* are still very good.
1960	10	A rainy year. Soutard was particularly successful.
1961	19	An all-round success for the finest vintage of the half-century.
1962	16	Wines closed up at the outset which have now absorbed their acidity. Excellent today.
1963	0	No harvest declared as Saint-Emilion AOC.
1964	15	Harvesting before the Médoc saved the crop from the rain.
1965	0	No harvest declared as Saint-Emilion AOC.
1966	14	A good year. Wines which developed rapidly but are beginning to decline elegantly.
1967	15	Well-structured, tannic wines. Magdelaine and Figeac remarkable.
1968	3	Less than a quarter of the harvest was declared as Saint-Emilion AOC.
1969	12	A year which did not live up to its promise. A few agreeable bottles.
1970	17	Good overall quality. Wines for the future and which should be kept.
1971	16	An underestimated year. Wines which are perfect today, especially from the hillsides.
1972	10	Will improve no further. Without any great character.
1973	13	Irregular successes in Saint-Emilion. The "graves" are the best.
1974	12	An average year, with neither vice nor virtue.
1975	17	Superb and generous. Slow to mature. To be left to your grandchildren.
1976	16	A year of excessive maturity. All the *premiers crus* from the hillsides are magnificent.
1977	8	As in the Médoc, a very disappointing year. Hard, acidic wines.
1978	15	Supple and well-balanced. Floral, charming wines ready to drink now.
1979	16	Some people prefer them to the '78s. They are more full-bodied but rather less fine.
1980	11	Uneven. Some *crus* declassified all or part of their production. A few successes.
1981	14	A rapid and favourable development. Consistent in quality, by and large.
1982	18	Good harvest. Quality and quantity. Very ripe wines showing no acidity.
1983	16	Good vintage. Already "drinkable" but requires a selection.
1984	10	Inconsistent. The "graves" are relatively more successful than the hillsides.
1985	17	A well-balanced vintage that should still develop.
1986	16	Concentrated wines, sometimes vitiated by too high a yield.
1987	13	Delightful primary aromas thanks to the merlot, but an undeniably acid base.
1988	17	A great, classic year, combining structure and suppleness.
1989	19 ?	To be tasted regularly over a 100 years to check if really the vintage of the century.

Other growers in the Saint-Emilion AOC

The following is a list of growers whose characteristics can be resumed thus: the majority are small growers, not depending exclusively on the produce of their vineyard for a living. They do very little, if any, bottling, and sell their wine in bulk to wine merchants. Their wine may have a name, which is generally taken from the Land Register, but it may be that they have not created a label. In this case, the merchant who buys the wine has the right to have labels printed, bearing the name of origin and his own trade name without specifying "bottled at the château". But he must be able to present to any official tax authority the supplier's invoice (or possibly the broker's memorandum) bearing the name of the *cru*.

Size in hectares

Barail du Maréchal 0.66
Pierre Barre. Barraud, 33330 Vignonet

Belle Nauve (Ch.) 4.75
Carmen Castan. La Nauve, 33330 St-Laurent-des-Combes

Bois de l'Or (Ch.) 1.50
M. and Mme R. Lenne. Ch. du Bois, 33350 St Magne-de-Castillon

Cantemerle (Dom. de) 1
André Chatonnet, 33570 Montagne

Castel (Château) 0.85
Marcelle Castel-Sarton. 5 rue Dumas, 33500 Libourne

Côtes Bagnol 0.15
Louis Fontaniol. Franc-Patarabet, 33330 Saint-Emilion

Ferrandat (Ch.) 1.40
Pierre Martin. 33330 Saint-Laurent-des-Combes

Fine Grave (Château) 3
Patrick Picaud. La Grave, 33330 Vignonet

Fleurus (Château) 1.56
Raymond Barraud. Fleurus, 33330 Saint-Sulpice-de-Faleyrens

Font-Froide (Château) 4
Achille Chagneau. Gueyrosse, 33500 Libourne

Franc-Rozier 2.25
(Château)
M. André Joussamme. 33330 Saint-Laurent-des-Combes

Fumet Peyroutas 2
(Château)
Jean Valadier. Fumet, 33330 Vignonet

Gerbaud (Château) 5.5
Ginette Chabrol. 33330 Saint-Pey-d'Armens

Grand-Nauve (Château) 5
Joseph Castan. La Nauve, 33330 St-Laurent-des-Combes

Grave d'Artus (Ch.) 1.9
Jean Corbière. Dartus, 33330 Vignonet

Guerin Bellevue (Ch.) 2
Marie-Christine Rambaud. La Croix, 33330 St-Pey-d'Armens

Haute-Rouchonne 6.15
(Château)
Jean Couder. La Rouchonne, 33330 Vignonet

Haut-Guillot (Château) 0.5
Claude Castan. Jean Guillot, 33330 St-Christophe-des-Bardes

Jean-Marie (Château) 4
Michel Nicoulaud. 33330 Saint-Emilion

Jehan du Mayne 1.03
(Château)
Gérard Mie. Jehan du Maynes, 33330 Saint-Emilion

Joly (Château) 3
Marc Vergniol. Le Canton, 33570 Lussac

La Croix d'Artus
(Château) 3.71
Gilles Roux. Fumet, 33330 Vignonet

La Croix du Merle 2
(Château)
Alain Coustillas. 33330 Saint-Hippolyte

La Mouleyre (Château) 6
Beaucousin. 30 rue des Cordiers, 59400 Cambrai

La Nauve (Château) 3.37
Courriere-Simard. St-Aignan, 33126 Fronsac

L'Ancien Manège 0.67
(Domaine de)
Denis Dubois. Chemin de Verdet, 33500 Libourne

La Rose d'Artus (Ch.) 6
Jean-Claude Arnaud. Brisson, 33330 Vignonet

Le Roudey 4.45
(Château)
Raymond Arnaud. Lara, 33240 Saint-André-de-Cubzac

Lerville (Château) 0.9
Dominique Nicoletti. Le Bourg, 33570 Montagne

Le Sable (Clos) 1.5
Michel Batard. Le Sable, 33330 Saint-Christophe-des-Bardes

Les Trois Ormeaux 2.9
(Château)
Max Degal. Le Bert, 33330 Saint-Sulpice-de-Faleyrens

Ligadey (Clos du) 0.44
M. and Mme. Paul Pallaro. Ch. Rouzerol, 33350 Sainte-Colombe

Perey (Château) 6
Jean-Claude Faure. Perey, 33330 St-Sulpice-de-Faleyrens

Petit-Bert (Château) 10
S.C. Ch. Le Couvent 33330 Saint-Emilion

Peymouton (Château) 0.6
Pierre Dussol. Peymouton, 33330 St-Christophe-des-Bardes

Pont (Domaine de) 0.5
Jean-Paul Feyzeau. Condat, 33500 Libourne

Rol (Domaine de) 1.5
Françoise Vivien. Petit-Gontey,
33330 Saint-Emilion

Roucheyron (Château) 4
M. and Mme Pierre Cazenave.
Roucheyron, 33330
Saint-Christophe-des-Bardes

Rouey (Clos du) 0.5
Hector Chenard. Le Bourg,
33330 Vignonet

Saint-André (Château) 1.5
P. Arpin. 33570 Montagne

Saint-André (Clos) 0.6
André Desmarty. Grand
Mouliney, 33500 Pomerol

Sommeliers (Domaine des) 0.75
Lilaine Blanchet. 28 chemin de
Barreau. 33500 Libourne

Tertre de la Mouleyre
(Château) 4.8
J. Guilhon. Moulin du Villet,
33330 Saint-Etienne-de-Lisse

Treilles de Fonzerade 0.65
(Château)
Achille Chagneau. Gueyrosse,
33500 Libourne

Vachon (Château) 1.5
Félicien Barfige. Vachon,
33330 Saint-Emilion

Vieilles Versannes
(Château) 1.15
Michel Huck. Les Grandes
Versannes, 33330 St-Emilion

Vieille Tour Lescours 0.2
(Château)
Justin Arnaud. La-Chapelle-
Les-Cours, 33330 Saint-Sulpice-
de-Faleyrens

Vieux Chantecaille 1.20
(Domaine du)
Jean-Marie Estager.
55 rue des 4 Frères Robert,
33500 Libourne

Vieux Peyrouquet 2.33
(Château)
J.-J. Cruchet. Boulezon,
33350 Castillon-La-Bataille

Vieux Pin Figeac 0.8
(Château)
La Fleur des Prés,
33500 Pomerol

Dattas, Roger 0.38
126 avenue de l'Epinette, 33500
Libourne

Fonteneau, Armande 0.15
Rue Masson, 33000 Caudéran

Fredont, Rolland 0.32
Les Vergnes, Carré, 33500 Libourne

Gagnaire, Joël 1.50
Le Garrouil, 33330 St-Sulpice-
de-Faleyrens

Guimberteau, Claude 0.5
Arrialh, 33570 Lussac

Hervé, Jean-Claude 4.5
Daugay, 33330 Saint-Sulpice-
de-Faleyrens

Laudu, Pierre 0.8
Binet, Montagne, 33570 Lussac

Paris, Francis 0.75
Résidence le Verdet,
5 allée du Grand Chêne,
33500 Libourne

Paulin, Moïsette 0.56
Cantenac,
33330 Saint-Emilion

Privat, Robert 0.63
12 chemin des Réaux,
33500 Libourne

Ricco, Francis 0.3
81 avenue Louis Didier,
33500 Libourne

Roux, Jean-André 0.6
Le Pontet, 33330 Vignonet

Sarlat, Henri 0.5
Rue Porte Ste Marie,
33330 Saint-Emilion

List of the 268 members of the Union de Producteurs

AMBLARD Marcel
15 rue Georges Guyemer,
33500 Libourne
AMBLEVERT Guy
33350 Sainte-Florence
ARAOZ Félix
Grangey, 33330 Saint-
Christophe-des-Bardes
ARBOUET Henri
33350 St-Magne-de-Castillon
ARNAUD Bernard
Pont Neuf, Sainte-Terre,
33350 Castillon-la-Bataille
ARNAUD Jean Pierre
Merlande, Sainte-Terre,
33350 Castillon-la-Bataille
ARTEAU Roger
Rue de Mme Bouquey,
33330 Saint-Emilion
AUDIGAY Michel
Bellerive, 33330 Saint-
Sulpice-de-Faleyrens
BABEAU Georges
Rés. Parc Saint Amand,
3 allée Ronsard
33200 Bx Caudéran
BALLUE Robert
La Grave, 33330 Vignonet
BARBIER Odette
Malus, 33270 Bouliac
BARTCHIES Bruno
Lagrange, 33330 Vignonet

BAUGIER Jacques Antoine
Chantegrive, 33330 St-Emilion
BAYLAN Françoise
Labrie, 33330 Vignonet
BEL AIR OUY (G.F.A.)
33330 Saint-Etienne-de-Lisse
BELY Robert
32 rue du Pradas,
33700 Mérignac
BENEYTOUT Josette
Darthus, 33330 Vignonet
BENTHENAT Thérèse
(Family Trust)
Le Bourg,
33330 Saint-Pey-d'Armens
BERGADIEU Jeanne
La Coste de Papey,
Ste-Terre,
33350 Castillon-la-Bataille
BERGERIE Yvon
Le Bidon, 33330
Saint-Sulpice-de-Faleyrens
BERNARD Alain
Port de Branne,
33330 St-Sulpice-de-Faleyrens
BERTHOUMEYROUX
Christian,
33350 Ste-Colombe
BERTIN Pierrette
Darthus, 33330 Vignonet
BION Claude
Carteau, 33330 Saint-Emilion

BIRET Jean
La Coste de Papey,
33350 Sainte-Terre,
BOISSERIE Louis
Guérin,
33330 Saint-Pey-d'Armens
BONNEFON Abel
33330 St-Sulpice-de-Faleyrens
BONNEFON Georges
33330 St-Sulpice-de-Faleyrens
BONNEMAISON M.-Cl.
Mondu,
33330 St-Sulpice-de-Faleyrens
BONNET Jean-Marc
Lartigue Ouest,
33330 St-Sulpice-de-Faleyrens
BONNIN Jean-Claude
Pichon, 33570 Lussac
BORDAS Roland
33330 Saint-Hippolyte
BORDE Denise
Le Bourg, Sainte-Terre,
33350 Castillon-la-Bataille
BORDE Michel
Le Bourg, Sainte-Terre,
33350 Castillon-la-Bataille
BORDIER Alain
route de Branne, 33330 Saint-
Sulpice-de-Faleyrens
BORDIER Jean-Pierre
route de Branne, 33330 Saint-
Sulpice-de-Faleyrens

313

BORDRON Eric
Petit-Bouquey,
33330 Saint-Hippolyte
BORDRON Pierre
Petit-Bouquey,
33330 Saint-Hippolyte
BORTOLUSSI Jeanne
Au Panet, 33330 St-Emilion
BOST Henri
Monturon, 33330 Saint-
Laurent-des-Combes
BOULADOU Guy
La Grange, 33330 Vignonet
BOULADOU Michel
33330 Vignonet
BOUQUEY Guy
rue de la Petite Fontaine, 33330
Saint-Emilion
BOUTHE Marc
Mède, 33330 Saint-Emilion
BOUYER Irène
Haut-Piney,
33330 Saint-Hippolyte
BRUGEILLE André
33330 St-Sulpice-de-Faleyrens
CANTE Catherine
33420 Saint-Jean-de-Blaignac
CANTE Roger
Fampeyre, 33350 Saint-Magne-
de-Castillon
CANTIN Yvan
Lavergne,
33330 Saint-Pey-d'Armens
CARREAU Jean
Pey du Prat, 33420 Grézillac
CARRIERE Annie
37 rue Charles Doumercq
33000 Bordeaux
CASTAING Charles
33350 Sainte-Terre
CASTAING Pierre
Lavagnac, Sainte-Terre,
33350 Castillon-la-Bataille
CASTANET Jean
Le Bourg,
33330 Saint-Pey-d'Armens
CASTANET Michel
Le Bourg,
33330 Saint-Pey-d'Armens
CASTEL Jean
Biquet, 33330 St-Hippolyte
CASTEL Gilbert
Biquet, 33330 St-Hippolyte
CAZENAVE Alain
Destieux, 33330 Saint-
Sulpice-de-Faleyrens
CHAMPAGNE Maxime
Clos Cazenave,
33330 Vignonet
CHAMPEAU Moïse-Georges
Le Garrouilh, 33330 Saint-
Sulpice-de-Faleyrens
CHANTUREAU Arlette
Pey de Prat, 33420 Grézillac
CHARRIER Albert-Arnaud
Bicot, 33330 Saint-
Sulpice-de-Faleyrens
CHARRIER Patrick
33330 Saint-Pey-d'Armens
CHARRON Andrée
Résidence Pierre Ier,
20 Av.
Victor Hugo, 33110 Bouscat
CHAUMET Guy
19 route des Castors,
Le Barp,
33830 Belin

CHAUMET Pierre
Bord, 33330 Saint-Emilion
CHEMINADE Maurice
Peyrouquet,
33330 Saint-Pey-d'Armens
CHEVAL Christiane
Monturon,
33330 St-Laurent-des-Combes
CLAMENS Raymond
33330 Vignonet
COCETTA Terzo
Micouleau, 33330 Vignonet
COIFFARD Pierre
La Pierre du Maréchal, 33330
Saint-Christophe-des-Bardes
CORBIERE Christian
Merlande, 33330 Vignonet
CORBIERE Jean
Darthus, 33330 Vignonet
COURCELAS René
Pinson, 33330 Saint-Sulpice-de-
Faleyrens
COURRECHE Père & Fils
(G.A.E.C.)
Les Moureaux,
33330 Saint-Etienne-de-Lisse
CROIZET Jean
Les Billaux, 33500 Libourne
CRAMAIL Pierre
Sainte-Terre,
33350 Castillon-la-Bataille
DANGLADE Georges
Clos Lardit, 33940 Barsac
D'ANTHOUARD
198 bis, av. Charles de
Gaulle,
92200 Neuilly-sur-Seine
DATAS
35 chemin de Roudet,
33500 Libourne
DELAHAUT Pierre
La Grave,
33330 Vignonet
DELPECH Charles
Les 4 Chemins,
33330 Vignonet
DELPECH Simon
Les 4 Chemins,
33330 Vignonet
DESCUBES Pierre
Ferrandat, 33330 St-Emilion
DUBUC Père & Fils (GAEC)
Le Bourg,
33330 Saint-Pey-d'Armens
DUCAS Yves
141 ter av. Georges-
Clemenceau, 33500 Libourne
DUCHAMP Jacques
La Glaye,
33330 Saint-Pey-d'Armens
DUMIGRON Pierre
La Roseraie, 33500 Libourne
DUMIGRON Yvette
33330 St-Laurent-des-Combes
DUMON Pierrette
Le Bourg,
33330 Saint-Etienne-de-Lisse
DUTASTA Gérard
33330 Vignonet
DUVERGE Raymonde
33330 St-Sulpice-de-Faleyrens
DUVERGER Michel
Pailhas, 33330 St-Hippolyte
DUVERGT Régina
Pailhas, 33330 St-Hippolyte
DUVIGNAUD Serge
33350 Mérignas

ELLIES Jean-Jacques
Sainte-Terre,
33350 Castillon-la-Bataille
ESCAICHE Claude
Sainte-Terre,
33350 Castillon-la-Bataille
EYMAUZIE Michel
Gombeau,
33330 Saint-Pey-d'Armens
FABERES Jeanne
La Glaye,
33330 Saint-Pey-d'Armens
FAURE Chantal
Le Cloux, 33330 Saint-Emilion
FAURE Henri-Arnaud
Bicot, 33330 Saint-Sulpice-de-
Faleyrens
FAURE Jean-Michel
33330 Vignonet
FAURE Paule
6 rue Berthelot, 33130 Bègles
FAURE Robert
La Croix, Sainte-Terre,
33350 Castillon-la-Bataille
FAURIE Christian
Les Cabannes, 33330 Saint-
Sulpice-de-Faleyrens
FAURIE Jacques
33330 Saint-Pey-d'Armens
FAURIE Pierre
Moulon, 33420 Branne
FENOUILLAT Louis
Les 4 Chemins,
33330 Vignonet
FORT Pierre
Le Sourd, 33330 Saint-
Sulpice-de-Faleyrens
FORTIN Maurice
Labrie, 33330 Vignonet
FOURCADE Serge
Pailhas, 33330 St-Hippolyte
FRANC LE MAINE
(SCE Château)
Place du Marché,
33330 Saint-Emilion
FRETTIER Jean André
Les Bigaroux, 33330 Saint-
Sulpice-de-Faleyrens
FRITEGOTTO Mario
Cazenave, 33330 Vignonet
FUGIER Dominique
Billerond, 33330 St-Hippolyte
GADRAT Eugénie
Le Bourg, 33330 St-Sulpice-de-
Faleyrens
GARDRAT Jean
Les Pintey, 33500 Libourne
GARRIGUE Georges
Le Thibeaud, 33330 Saint-
Etienne-de-Lisse
GARRIGUE Henriette
Thillet, 33330 Saint-
Christophe-des-Bardes
GARRIGUE Patrick
Le Loup, 33330 Saint-
Christophe-des-Bardes
GAURY Pierre
Lavallade, 33330 Saint-
Christophe-des-Bardes
GEMON Jean-Georges
La Nauve, 33330 Saint-
Laurent-des-Combes
GILLOD Juliette
Darthus, 33330 Vignonet
GINTRAC Gilberte
Micouleau,
33330 Vignonet

GIPALOUX Jean
Le Bourg, 33330 Saint-
Christophe-des-Bardes
GOINEAU (succ.)
Le Bourg, 33330 Saint-
Christophe-des-Bardes
GOUIDON Micheline
Bigaroux,
33330 St-Sulpice-de-Faleyrens
GOUREAU René
33480 Castelnau-du-Médoc
GRANDET Henri
Peyrouquet,
33330 Saint-Pey-d'Armens
GUERIN Daniel
Mézieres, 33350 Saint-
Magne-de-Castillon
HAAG André
33330 St-Sulpice-de-Faleyrens
HAUTE NAUVE (SCE Ch.)
33330 St-Laurent-des-Combes
HERNANDEZ Martine
Guérin,
33330 Saint-Pey-d'Armens
ITEY François
33420 Lugaignac
JACQUIER Séraphine
Labrie, 33330 Vignonet
JAMET Lucien
Rabion,
33330 Saint-Pey-d'Armens
JARJANETTE Paul
Pierrefitte,
33330 St-Sulpice-de-Faleyrens
JOLLE Jeanne
Les Maurins,
33330 St-Sulpice-de-Faleyrens
JOLLE Yvan
Les Maurins,
33330 St-Sulpice-de-Faleyrens
JOURDAIN Marthe
12 rue Amanieu, 33130 Bègles
LA BARTHE (GAEC de)
La Grave, 33330 Vignonet
LABONNE Henri
La Croix,
33330 Saint-Pey-d'Armens
LABRUGERE René
33330 Saint-Pey-d'Armens
LACOSTE Jean-Paul
Pierrefitte,
33330 St-Sulpice-de-Faleyrens
LACOSTE Jean-Pierre
Pierrefitte,
33330 St-Sulpice-de-Faleyrens
LACOSTE Pierre
Pierrefitte,
33330 St-Sulpice-de-Faleyrens
LACROIX Arlette
9 rue Marteau, 33420 Branne
LAFAGE Simone
Matras, 33330 Saint-Emilion
LAFAYE Elie
Le Basque,
33330 Saint-Pey-d'Armens
LAFAYE Jean-Pierre
Picot, 33330 St-Pey-d'Armens
LAFOURCADE Charles
Lartigue,
33330 St-Sulpice-de-Faleyrens
LANAU Jean-Claude
Lartigue, 33330 St-Emilion
LANDRODIE Maurice
Juguet,
33330 St-Pey-d'Armens
LAPELLETRIE Claude
La Rouchonne,
33330 Vignonet

LARCIS JAUMA (G.F.A.)
Larcis, 33330 Saint-
Christophe-des-Bardes
LARGUILLON Robert
Le Bourg,
33330 Saint-Pey-d'Armens
LASTOUILLAT Huguette
33330 Saint-Pey-d'Armens
LAUTRETTE Arsène
Villemaurine,
33330 Saint-Emilion
LAVIGNAC Michel
33330 St-Sulpice-de-Faleyrens
LEDOUX Gisèle
Pierrefitte,
33330 St-Sulpice-de-Faleyrens
LE MENN Raymond
33330 St-Laurent-des-Combes
LESPINE (S.C.E.)
Place du Marché,
33420 Branne
LESQUEN Marie de
159 bld Bineau,
92200 Neuilly-sur-Seine
LOISEAU Renée
13 rue F. Dalat,
33500 Libourne
MACAUD Frédéric
Lavergne,
33330 Saint-Pey-d'Armens
MACAUD Yves
Merlande, Sainte-Terre,
33350 Castillon-la-Bataille
MADILLAC Yannick
Maison Neuve, 33330 Saint-
Etienne-de-Lisse
MAGADOR Jean
Darthus, 33330 Vignonet
MAGADOR Jérome
Darthus, 33330 Vignonet
MAGARDEAU Monique
rue Vienne Y. Vienne,
33350 Castillon-la-Bataille
MAGONTIER Jean (Family
Trust)
Pierrelongue,
33330 St-Laurent-des-Combes
MALLO Christian
33330 Saint-Hippolyte
MARTIN Jacky
Labrie, 33330 Vignonet
MARTY Elie
Pierrefitte,
33330 St-Sulpice-de-Faleyrens
MARTY Irène
33330 Saint-Christophe-
des-Bardes
MARTY Martin
Ferrachat,
33330 Saint-Pey-d'Armens
MAUVINON (GFA du Ch.)
33330 St-Sulpice-de-Faleyrens
MAYE Raymond (Sté)
Mérignas,
33350 Castillon-la-Bataille
MAZOLENNI Noël
33330 Saint-Pey-d'Armens
MEYNIER Henri
Doulezon,
33350 Castillon-la-Bataille
MICHELET Simone
Lescure, 33330 St-Hippolyte
MIE André
Merlande, Sainte-Terre,
33350 Castillon-la-Bataille
MINARD Didier
Laubier,
33420 St-Jean-de-Blaignac

MODET Huguette
rue Guadet, 33330 St-Emilion
MONSALUT Elisée
La Garelle, 33330 St-Emilion
MOULIN Georges
La Glaye,
33330 Saint-Pey-d'Armens
MOULINIE Antoinette
33570 Saint-Georges
MOURGUET Jean
Micouleau,
33330 Vignonet
MOYRAND Jean Yves
Lamothe, Montravel,
24230 Velines
NAULET Gisèle
105 avenue Louis Didier,
33500 Libourne
NEBOUT Germaine
Le Bourg,
33330 St-Etienne-de-Lisse
NICOT René
Le Bourg,
33350 St-Genès-de-Castillon
NIOTEAU Maurice
Gontey,
33330 Saint-Emilion
NOUVEL Jean-Jacques
Fontfleuri,
33330 Saint-Emilion
NOUVEL Josette
Porte Bouqueyre,
33330 Saint-Emilion
NOUVEL-GROS Françoise
Porte Bouqueyre, 33330 Saint-
Emilion
OUVRET Jean
Chemin de la Bordette,
33500 Libourne
PAGE Michel
Rotebœuf,
33330 St-Laurent-des-Combes
PAGES Robert
La Chapelle-Lescours,
33330 St-Sulpice-de-Faleyrens
PAGNAC Jean
La Glaye,
33330 Saint-Pey-d'Armens
PAGNAC Léopold
Le Fraiche,
33330 Saint-Pey-d'Armens
PALLARO Denis
Justice,
33330 St-Etienne-de-Lisse
PALLARO Jean
Parsac, 33570 Lussac
PALMERI Charles
33330 St-Sulpice-de-Faleyrens
PALMERI Gérard-J.-M.
33330 St-Sulpice-de-Faleyrens
PAPILLAUD René
Saint Quentin de Chalais,
16210 Chalais
PAVAGEAU Loïc
Thillet, 33330 Saint-
Christophe-des-Bardes
PENARD Suzanne
Rue de la Fontaine,
33330 Saint-Emilion
PENCHAUD Guy
Bigaroux,
33330 St-Sulpice-de-Faleyrens
PERRIER Joëlle
33330 Saint-Christophe-
des-Bardes
PETIT-GRAVET (SCE Ch.)
Porte Bouqueyre,
33330 Saint-Emilion

PEYRAT Michel
Lartigue, 33330 St-Emilion
PICCOLO Bernard
33330 Saint-Hippolyte
PIERRE Jean
203 rue de Lossegrand,
75014 Paris
PINAUD Michel
Brisson, 33330 Vignonet
PINEY (SCE Ch.)
33330 Saint-Hippolyte
POUILLET Jean-Claude
33330 St-Magne-de-Castillon
QUENOUILLE Jean
Yon, 33330 Saint-
Christophe-des-Bardes
QUINSAC Jean
Brisson, 33330 Vignonet
QUINTANA
Micouleau, 33330 Vignonet
REDON Denis
Cuzor, 33330 Vignonet
RIBOULET Jean
Haut-Béard,
33330 St-Laurent-des-Combes
RIPES René
Le Garrouilh,
33330 St-Sulpice-de-Faleyrens
RIVIERE René
Résidence de
la Croix Rouge n° 7,
33230 Coutras
ROBIN Alain
Billerond, 33330 St-Hippolyte
ROBIN Joëlle
Darthus, 33330 Vignonet
ROBISSOUT Andrée
130 rue du Président Doumer,
33500 Libourne
ROBLES Joseph
Petit-Bouquey,
33330 Saint-Hippolyte
ROCHE Jean
Le Grand Sable,
33330 Saint-Hippolyte
ROCHEREAU Roger
Le Cros, 33330 Saint-Emilion
RODHAIN François
Les Bigaroux,
33330 St-Sulpice-de-Faleyrens

ROLAIT Serge
Courpiac, 33119 Frontenac
ROUSSELOT Daniel
Micouleau, 33330 Vignonet
ROUX Gilles
Darthus, 33330 Vignonet
ROUX Jean-André
Darthus, 33330 Vignonet
ROY Jean
Sainte-Terre,
33350 Castillon-la-Bataille
SABY Marie-Françoise
Rue Pline Parmentier,
33500 Libourne
SABY Roger
Rue Pline Parmentier,
33500 Libourne
SAHUNET Jean Claude
Grande Rue, 33420 Branne
SAUJON Jeanne
Le Bourg,
33330 St-Sulpice-de-Faleyrens
SEGONZAC Michel
6 Impasse François Mauriac,
33500 Libourne
SERRE Jean
Caperot,
33330 St-Sulpice-de-Faleyrens
SERRE Pierre
33330 St-Sulpice-de-Faleyrens
SERVANT Elisée
Pierrefitte,
33330 St-Sulpice-de-Faleyrens
SERVANT Patrick
Le Garrouilh,
33330 St-Sulpice-de-Faleyrens
SIMON Guy
Le Gueyrot,
33330 St-Laurent-des-Combes
SINSOU André
Lavallade, 33330 Saint-
Christophe-des-Bardes
SOULAS Jean-Pierre
Les Dagueys, 33500 Libourne
SOULET Henri
Le Bourg,
33330 St-Sulpice-de-Faleyrens
SOUPRE Pierre
La Glaye,
33330 Saint-Pey-d'Armens

SOUPRE Roger
33330 Saint-Pey-d'Armens
SULZER François
La Bonnelle,
33330 Saint-Pey-d'Armens
SUSZKA Conrad
Le Bourg,
33330 St-Sulpice-de-Faleyrens
TABBACCHIERA (SDF)
Bourret, 33330 Saint-
Pey-d'Armens
TARIS-LOIRY Michel
Les Alizées,
33560 Carbon Blanc
THILLET Gabriel
Sainte-Terre,
33350 Castillon-la-Bataille
TRIBAUDEAU Marc
Mauvinon,
33330 St-Sulpice-de-Faleyrens
VALADE Francis
Charlot, 33330 Saint-Emilion
VALADE Philippe
Le Bourg,
33330 St-Sulpice-de-Faleyrens
VALADIER Michel
33330 Saint-Hippolyte
VALADIER P. et Mr. et Mrs.
DUFAGET (SDF)
Fonrazade,
33330 Saint-Pey-d'Armens
VALLADE Albert
Petit-Bigaroux,
33330 St-Sulpice-de-Faleyrens
VALLIER Dominique
La Michelette,
33330 St-Laurent-des-Combes
VERGNE Michel
19800 Rouffiat-de-Sarran
VIALARD Claude et Colette
(SDF)
25 rue Brochand, 75017 Paris
VIMENEY André
Le Bourg,
33330 St-Sulpice-de-Faleyrens
VIROL Simone
Cazenave, 33330 Vignonet
XANS Roger
Le Jonc,
33330 St-Sulpice-de-Faleyrens

Index of owners

318

Picture acknowledgements:
All the photographs in this book are by
Luc Joubert, Bordeaux
with the exception of those by
Claude Hervé, Libourne (61)
and Douglas Metzler, Paris (jacket, 16, 72, 134, 155)